THE RIVER WHY

Bantam Windstone Books
Ask your bookseller for the books you have missed

THE RIVER WHY

David James Duncan

BANTAM BOOKS
TORONTO · NEW YORK · LONDON · SYDNEY

This low-priced Bantam Book
has been completely reset in a type face
designed for easy reading, and was printed
from new plates. It contains the complete
text of the original hard-cover edition.
NOT ONE WORD HAS BEEN OMITTED.

THE RIVER WHY

A Bantam Book / published by arrangement with
Sierra Club Books

PRINTING HISTORY

Sierra Club edition published February 1983

A selection of Book-of-the-Month Club, April 1983
and Quality Paperback Book Club, March 1983.
Serialized in *United Mainliner*, April 1983.

Bantam Windstone edition / March 1984

Windstone and accompanying logo of a stylized W
are trademarks of Bantam Books, Inc.

The Sierra Club, founded in 1892 by John Muir, has devoted itself to the study and protection of the earth's scenic and ecological resources—mountains, wetlands, woodlands, wild shore and rivers, deserts and plains. The publishing program of the Sierra Club offers books to the public as a nonprofit educational service in the hope that they may enlarge the public's understanding of the Club's basic concerns. The point of view expressed in each book, however, does not necessarily represent that of the Club. The Sierra Club has some fifty chapters coast to coast, in Canada, Hawaii, and Alaska. For information about how you may participate in its programs to preserve wilderness and the quality of life, please address inquiries to Sierra Club, 530 Bush Street, San Francisco, Ca. 94108.

Bantam Books are published by Bantam Books, Inc. Its trademark, consisting of the words "Bantam Books" and the portrayal of a rooster, is Registered in U.S. Patent and Trademark Office and in other countries. Marca Registrada. Bantam Books, Inc., 666 Fifth Avenue, New York, New York 10103.

PRINTED IN THE UNITED STATES OF AMERICA

CW   12   11   10   9   8   7   6   5   4   3

Contents

Book Three
Characters in Nature

Book Four
The Line of Light

Book Five
At the End of the Line

THE RIVER WHY

Book One

The Compleat Angler

My birthday began with the water.

—*Dylan Thomas*

What house is this? here's neither coal nor candle,
Where I no thing but guts of fishes handle . . .

—*Zachary Boyd, "Jonah"*

1

"Gus the Fish"

"It is a doubt if my body is flesh or fish," he sang in his grief; "hapless the woman who loves me. . . ."

—*Charles Williams,*
Taliessin Through Logres

HAVING HARBORED TWO SONS in the waters of her womb, my mother considers herself something of an authority on human foetuses. The normal foetus, she says, is no swimmer; it is not fish-, seal-, eel-, or even turtlelike: it is an awkward alien in the liquid environment—a groping land creature confused by its immersion and anxious to escape. My brother, she says, was such a foetus. I was not. My swimming style was no humanoid butterfly-, crawl-, back- or breaststroking: mine were the sure, swift dartings of a deformed but hefty trout at home with the water, finning and hovering in its warm black pool.

Having harbored no one anywhere in his body and lacking a womb, my father knows almost nothing about human foetuses. This did not stop him from penning and publishing a grotesque article about a human birth. My father is a writer secondarily and a famous flyfisherman primarily, and his stories, books and lectures on the latter art—not to mention his ruddy face and dumpy, wader-swathed figure—are renowned throughout the flyfishing world. One of his favorite articles was published in a 1954 *Field and Stream* under the title "Gus the Fish." Written in a painfully contrived and uncharacteristic Doc-And-Me-Went-Fishin' style, "Gus the Fish" treats of the angling adventure of a certain obstetrician who finally succeeded in hooking and landing "a chubby eight-pounder" who had "eluded all anglers for over nine months" despite being trapped in "a small pool in a river only five feet, five inches long"; then in the concluding paragraph my father spills the beans all over his little allegory with the forgettable intimation that "Ol' Gus is not some wily brown trout lurking in the waters of a Letort, Beaverkill or Firehole. Oh no. Ol' Gus is nothing less than my new little lunker son, my first-born fish and flyfisherman to be!"

That's the kind of mind my father has. . . . The fisherman's is an inexplicably privileged place in this hard world: there are people wearing straitjackets and living under lock and key for innocuous crimes such as dressing or speaking like Sherlock Holmes, Caesar, or Armstrong Custer, yet there goes my dad—famed and respected in his twenty-five-pound vest, hat full of phony insects, rubber trousertops flapping about his nipples—trudging scot free along the world's trout streams armed with dangerous hooks and fish knives, whipping the flesh of innocent bodies of water while amusing himself with such mental marvels as his wife the dwarfish river, and his son, Gus the Fish.

Yet his condition should surprise no one. Consider: when even a small quantity of water is inserted in a human posterior, a dramatic purgation results. Mightn't it follow that the constant proximity of vast quantities of the same fluid to a man's *anterior* could effect an analogous purgation? Perhaps the physiological truth of the matter is that my father's head—so long and relentlessly bombarded by trout waters—has been the unintentional victim of a cranial enema: his brains have been voided of everything unrelated to fish and fishing, with weird, watery artifacts such as "Gus the Fish" the result.

My father's name is Henning Hale-Orviston. His parents were English aristocrats, and his speech and manners derive from them. He carefully maintains his distinguished accent; he drinks Glenfiddich Single Malt Scotch; he smokes Rattray's Highland Targe and Balkan Sobranie in meerschaums and briar perfects; he drives a Rover in the city and a Winnebago on the road; he lectures in white shirt and tie, fishes in tweeds and sleeps in silk pajamas; his flies are constructed with a scrupulousness rivalling the Creator's; his handwriting is like calligraphy, and when he autographs a book he writes the entire name. He is, to my chagrin, the one person in the world who calls me by my legal name, Augustine,

so to his chagrin I call him H2O.

To his greater chagrin, Ma calls him "Hen." To her way of thinking, *Hen* is a rough-and-ready handle on her man. To H2O's way of thinking, *Hen* is a ludicrous and unwarranted insult. To my way of thinking, *Hen* is a nickname with several features of interest: among Northwest fishermen, a *hen* is a female steelhead; according to H2O, Ma is a river; if these designations are accurate, it is obvious which of my parents would contain, sustain and determine the fate of the other—and through observation of our family the truth of the symbology is apparent. Under the Orviston roof it's Ma who calls the shots.

That's not all she does. If ever a man's wife was his nemesis, his antagonist, his antithesis, Ma is H2O's. In those rarefied circles of purist anglers among whom Henning Hale-Orviston is considered the last word, Ma Orviston is considered the last laugh—for though she has never published a word on fishing, and though H2O has struggled to keep her existence under wraps, Ma has, through the medium of fish-gossip, attained to an infamy rivalling H2O's fame. The reason? O Heresy! Lower than Low Church, lower than pariah, lower than poacher, predator or polluter, Ma is the Flyfisherman's Antipode: she is a bait fisherman. A fundamentalist. A plunker of worms.

One of my father's least favorite stories was diluted, distorted and published in a 1954 *Sports Afield* under the unlikely title "Nijinsky"—an artifact not worth a glance apart from the color glossies. The story's uncut version lacks color glossies; it has never seen print; it is hard to believe despite its historicity; it is *never* told when H2O is around. But once a year it is recited at the Carper Clan Gathering (the Carpers being Ma's kin) by my bardic uncle, Zeke, who calls it "The Deschutes River Episode." Zeke tells it in two installments, pausing to chug a beer between: the first part is a pretty fair imitation of my father's accent and Literary Sportsman writing style—but after the beer the story transmogrifies into a Zeke-yarn delivered in his most exaggerated, overcooked Eastern Oregon drawl. It goes like this:

'Twas early in the autumn of nineteen hundred and fifty-three that the then-unmarried Henning Hale-Orviston endured the most extraordinary adventure of his already illustrious angling career. Beneath a brilliant brass sky and enclosed by canyon walls rendered ovenlike by the relentless desert sun, Orviston had spent an entire day plying the glistening green waters of Oregon's famed Deschutes River for summer-run steelhead, but despite his unflagging efforts and unrivalled skill, he had nothing to show for his labours but the memory of a few small trout caught and, of course, carefully released. Worn to exhaustion by heat, glare and the constant drag of waist-deep current, Orviston elected to make the proverbial "one last cast" before undertaking the toilsome return to his car and small mobile home. His day of frustration was complete when, near the tail of that last drift, his masterfully tied bucktail streamer ceased its oceanward journey with that inexorable dull pull that can only signify a snag. Hoping for nothing but an end to his day of thwarted efforts, Orviston reefed disgustedly at his line, attempting to snap the 2x tippet. To his great good fortune, he failed even in this—for the instant he raised the rod the once-serene river exploded with the heart-stopping leap of the mightiest steelhead he had ever seen! No sooner did the magnificent fish shatter the water into glassy splinters than it was airborne again, and so again, continuing with literally scores of impossible, soaring, twisting leaps till its mortal enemy was inspired to dub it "Nijinsky," after the famed supernatural hero of the ballet. Thus commenced a battle between wily fisherman and godlike fish worthy of comparison to some savage encounter of knight and dragon in the Legends of Yore. . . .

Seeming to realize that this was no mere worm-dangler with which he was dealing, Nijinsky soon ceased his mad leaping. Applying his wiles—and his brutish strength—the monster turned toward the long rapids downstream and set off at a calculated, untiring pace that the 2x tippet could not possibly thwart. Running, plunging, clambering through brush and water, Orviston followed, holding his rod high, increasing his pace when the line-backing grew dangerously thin, easing the pace and taking up slack when Nijinsky would allow it. Relentlessly, craftily, he pursued his silver leviathan with the determination of Ahab.

Two miles downstream and an hour and a half into the battle, Nijinsky retreated to the depths of an eerie, ink black pool. Here he remained as the daylight first reddened, then fled; here he entrenched himself as the sinking sun's shafts ascended the tortured rimrock, suffusing juniper, sage and canyon wall with a last liquid light. Exhausted himself, Orviston could only hope the mighty fish was also tiring. With stout heart and reptilian patience, he applied all the pressure the feeble but faithful tippet could sustain. Inch by painstaking inch, he worked Nijinsky toward him through the seething depths of the ebony pool. . . .

Here's where Zeke chugs his beer—a fact especially worth noting because it's a *thirty-two*-ouncer! And if you could see the look in Zeke's carbonated eyes afterward, if you knew how vast the gap between H2O's published climax and the true tale he was about to tell, then you would know that the story of Nijinsky's End is offered here at the risk of my being disowned—if not drowned.

Zeke quiets his listeners with a six-second belch. Then—

High over the rimrock the Milky Way come poppin' out like God's false teeth—but ol' Hen Orviston never seen it. He never seen neither that it weren't him that had no fish on, but a fish that had on him: while he was thinkin' he was workin' his lunker in, the lunker was eyeballin' Hen's submerged shins, sniffin' the blood in the water from the fresh dings in 'em, thinkin' how he'd swallered crawdads big as what they was, fightin' off a nasty pair o' pinchers into the bargain. So it was lucky fer Hen a rockslide come rattlin' down the canyonside just then, spookin' Nijersey back to the deeps.

Hen turned one bloodshot eye to the hill t'see what was comin', his brains thinkin' somethin' mercenary an' Englishy, like, "By Jorj! Behaps the Very Gods residing in Heavenabove are sending some soul to witness my artful captuation of this noteable bloody fishe here by means of naught more than an artificial fly and frailest of 2x whippets. Jolly Ho! Now I'll have positivistic veracification of my performance, thereby enabling me to enhance the thickness of my wallet with scads of bloody endorsements from the makers of my rod and reel and line and boots and hat and creel and undershorts!"

An' sure nuff, through the dollar signs in his eyes Hen made out a handsome young cowpoke scramblin' down the scree, fitted out in Levis, Pen'lt'n shirt, sheepskin vest, ratty Stetson, J. C. Penney cowboy boots an' red bandana. He was slim, whiskerless, smokin' a Hump,* an' he packed a saddlebag an' a Sears Roebuck castin' rod'n'reel with ropy thick line, baseball-size sinker, an' three squirmin' nightcrawlers on a treblehook wishin' they was somewheres else. When H. H. made out this fishin' perfernailey, he thought somethin' more along these lines: "Zounds, Drat and Bother the Bleeding Fates! This is no gentleman! This young brute is a Neanderthal, come here to practise the illegeale bloody art of bait fishing after dark!"

He wasn't far off. But witnesses is witnesses an' money's money, so Hen held his peace an' his pole, played Stravinski, an' calmed his nerves with dreams 'bout the sweet shitload o' fat endorsement checks sure to stuff his mailbox, once he nailed his whale. But what was this? With his gizzard in his gorge, Hen saw the cowpoke fixin' t'cast dead into the pool where Nijin-skivoffnev was hidin'! In a unEnglishmanly vocabulary reserved fer emergencies, H. H. Orviston Esquire hollered, "Hey! Gitcher young ass outta there! Can't you see I got a huge fish on!?"

The plunker held up'n took a gander at Hen's rod, but Niggerovskopf was layin' low sinch the averlanch so the flyrod was just bent, not throbbin' or twitchin' at all. Never havin' laid eyes on a fly outfit, the cowpoke didn't know 'bout 2x tipplers made o' catgut an' all that class of equipment. He only seen Hen's fly-line, which he judged heavy enough t'horse in a wild bull, an' the Fancy Dan fishin' duds, camera purse, silly hat an' all. That made his mind up. In a boyish, friendly voice he hollered, "Hells bells, Cityslick, yer hung on the bottom! How long you been standin' there that way you rascal? Just bust that thang off'n come on over here—I got worms enough fer both of us."

At the thought of hisself usin' worms (he'd ruther been offered leprosy), H. H. Orviston was struck dumb. It was a piss-poor time to be struck so: he only smarted up enough t'howl out one terrible word 'fore the cowpuncher let fly with his lead baseball. . . . The splash o' the lead spurred Bozinski back into action. The sinker plummeted down, the steelhead plummeted up, the two lines crossed, and Henning Hale-Orviston's 2x nipplet snapped like a cobweb: Nijerkov leaped one last time an' was seen no more. . . .

H. H. took his three-piece nine-foot eighty-dollar flyrod an' busted it over his knee four times. He threw the splinters as far as he could, which was maybe six, eight feet. Then he picked up a waterlogged tree branch an' advanced on the young cowpoke in a manner that was s'posed t'look

*filterless Camel cigarette

menacin' but which really looked sorta surly an' pitiful, considerin' the size o' his white-meaty little English-man muscles. At least his voice sounded good: "You had best refrain from that pole and defend yourself!" he boomed, "because one of the bloody twain of us is going to journey perforce into that river to search for my fish, *by jorj!*"

"So be it, Slicker," said the cowpoke coolly. "An' I'll guaran-goddamn-tee ya it ain't gonna be me!" Settin' down the castin' pole an ' steppin' away from the water, he took off his vest and ratty Stetson . . .

an' a long braid o' pretty blond hair fell from under the hat an' down acrosst a chest that even ol' Hen could see was far from flat. By Bleedin' Jorj! The cowpoke was a girl!

Henning Hale-Orviston hunkered down on a rock an' started to laugh. So he says. The cowgirl says he was cryin'. "Well, come on," says she. "Come on an' fight me!" (Bein' used to her brothers and unused to British Chival-rousness, she waited fer action, holdin' up a small but damned efficient pair o' dukes.) Hen just kept on laughin'—the high, hysterical squeals of a man whose brains rode on down the trail an' left him all alone on the nightwide prairie.

Then, forgotten among the rocks, the Sears Roebuck started screamin' like it was alive. "Wellp," says the girl. "If you're only gonna set there, I'm gonna man my pole, 'cause it's plain as pee there's a fish on it." She pulled a bowie knife an' stuck it in a handy log, addin' "Try an' jump me an' I'll gut ya!"

Hen's weird caterwaulin' got berserker an' berserker while he watched the girl pick up the Roebuck, set the hook into somethin' damn heavy, an'—in a unsightly tug-a-war that didn' last five minutes—haul a thirty-pound ballet-dancin' steelhead onto the bank . . . an H. H. Orviston bucktail streamer still stickin' in the corner of its jaw!

Poor Hen's lunatic laughter floated out over the swirlin' eddy an' up the black rimrock walls; it ricocheted an' spilled undimmed outta that čanyon an' onto the scrub plains where a pack o' maraudin' coyotes took it up in glass-smashin' unison dissonance—with cadenzas. From coyote to coyote it carried out over the desert an' jackpine country, givin' cowboys an' ranchwives an' loggers the willies an' their kids creamed jeans from Mosier clear east to Ukiah, an' north on up the Columbia River Basin to the Seven Devils Mountains, where it belonged. The followin' Sunday there was a rash o' new faces in the region's Houses of Worship, an' every hymn was sung fortissimoso in hopes a drowndin' out all recollection o' that godawful laugh still boundin' from bone to bone inside the troubled skulls o' the faithful. . . .

The cowgirl found a driftwood club an' whacked ol' Burrzinsky till one eyeball popped out. This she took as a sign that he was dead. She'd have liked to've sat an' admired her fish awhile—but things weren't so pictur-esque somehow with the one eye hangin' down the cheek on a nerve string an' the blue-devil din pourin' nonstop outta the Slicker. So she turned to the rubble of a man on the rocks . . .

an' that strange, universal compassion women have fer any creature too wounded, sick or crazy to care fer its ownself suddenly flooded her heart. Seein' H. H. soaked to the gills, scraped an' bloodied, rubbin' his eyes', huggin' his knees, suckin' his thumbs, howlin' an' howlin', she gathered deadwood an' scraps o' nine-foot flyrod fer a fire. From the saddlebag she produced a flask o' Redeye, took a stiff swig, poured a drop into ol' Nijer-key's toothy mouth, an' passed it on to Hen—who left off his warwhoopin' an' downed half the bottle at a chug: a damned nice piece o' drinkin'. As campfire an' firewater dried his clothes an' brains respectively, he finally seen the cowgirl was a pretty little thing an' a differnt fire lit up an' dried him out quicker'n what wood or whiskey could o' done. Meanwhile she was hittin' the Redeye pretty good herself, an' feelin' pretty bad 'bout bustin' the Slicker's 2x pippit an' catchin' the fish he'd pooped out an' who'd pooped out him; an' it was mighty dark an' lonely; an' the coyotes sounded *weird* tonight; an' the fire was cozy an' the whiskey good, an' the Slicker awful pitiful lookin'; an' she'd've liked to've cheered him up, an' she'd growed up watchin' horses an' bulls an' chickens an' her brothers; an' the blind red passion was siftin' through the air; an' she judged Hen was quite a feller, even if she hadn't figgered which kind he was quite a feller of. . . .

So as the flyrod blazed an' the juniper brands smoked off the evil spirits, as the river grumbled an' the crickets sang loud, Henning Hale-Orviston an' the cowgirl cuddled up an' giggled—an' damn if they didn't fall in love. Or leastways into what folks in those situations fall in. When the night grew cold the two grew warm by beddin' down in the sand, an'—

—just their luck: a child was conceived.

One day the cowgirl would name that child *Gus*. But high-falutin' Hen'd stick'm with *Augusteen*.

That's how Zeke tells it. That's how it was. The cowgirl was Zeke's little sister, Carolina Carper, my very own Ma.

2

The Rogue River
Fishing War

I'm a-goin' fishin', Mama's goin' fishin'
An' de baby's goin' fishin' too.
Bet yo' life
Yo' sweet wife's
Gonna catch mo' fish dan you.

—*Taj Mahal*

I AM ASHAMED TO REPORT that back in '53 my parents were not as scrupulous (nor as affluent) as they are now. Upon learning that their riverside romance had ignited an inexorable series of metabolic transformations in Ma's belly, they drew up a secret pact: due to the incompatibility of Sears Roebuck fishing gear to endorsement money, they would proceed as if Nijinsky had been the conquest of H2O with his cremated cane rod, 2x tippet, and name-brand equipage, and Ma would forever hold her peace. Thus the steelhead's gaping treble-hook wounds were described as evidence of an earlier run-in with a less-skilled angler, and the repeatedly fractured skull and popped eye were attributed to an overdose of adrenalin coursing through the veins of the conquering (conking?) hero. Official photographs and measurements were taken, the corpse was mummified and hung over the fireplace, and H2O unabashedly cranked out one of his patented How-To-Land-A-Lunker stories full of useless tips for flyfishing rookies and ill-disguised hints that Nijinsky would never have met his demise were it not for SuchandSuch-brand rods and reels and lines and boots and hat and creels and undershorts. Within three months of the Deschutes River Episode they collected enough endorsement money to finance a hasty wedding and two-week winter steelheading honeymoon on the Rogue River—H2O's idea being that the Rogue trip would soften Ma's Desert-Ranch to Portland-Suburb culture shock, but might still wean her of her homespun ways; he could take some photos and dredge up a few articles if the fishing were any good—maybe something like "Flyfishing Bride" or "Love and Lunkers on the Rogue"—thereby allowing the trip to pay for itself; the only unforeseeable problem was the weather, and if it should sleet ceaselessly, so much the better for consummating the marriage ad infinitum beside a cozy fire in their suite at the lodge. Such was the plan. So much for plans.

The "Rogue River Fishing War" at least served the traditional purpose of the honeymoon, for honeymoons are intended to seal the union of bride and groom till death does them part. But whereas we imagine the usual chemistry of such excursions to be a uniting through corporeal and spiritual familiarity—a sharing of meals, scenic wonders, wines and bathrooms, of kisses, caresses and inane little foofoo names—my parents enjoyed no such chemistry. Their honeymoon was more fusion than union—the resulting bond not that of lovebirds, but of a tough metal alloy. The effete angler and the raucous cowgirl were the *materia prima*, the Rogue River the crucible, worms and flies the catalysts, angling the white-hot fire, and a marriage that has stood the tests of time, backbiting, frontbiting, hells, highwaters and haymakers the resulting compound.

Because of the extreme bias of the War's two survivors, I can only list those events which they agree took place:

1. H2O's efforts to instruct Ma in the hallowed art of fly-angling met with the most invisible species of success, achieving a kind of catharsis when the instructee's reluctant attempts at false-casting left a #4 Humptulips Hellion dangling from the lobe of the instructor's ear.

2. To atone for the ear, Ma chucked her flyfishing equipment (a costly wedding gift from H2O) far out into the roily waters of the Rogue and returned to the Sears Crane-and-Cable.

3. Entrenched like European War troopers in their respective styles, my parents proceeded to grimly ply the waters while the honeymoon degenerated into a two-man Fishing Derby. H2O denies there having occurred a contest, but pictures of him in his 1954 *Outdoor Life* article, "Roguish Steelies Love Brightly Colored Flies," reveal the face of a man strapped to a bullet-pocked wall—hollow eye sockets, stubbled beard, strained grin at the Kodak he adored. It was a contest all right. And H2O's appearance was inspired by

4. The Fishing Derby Results: Ma—thirteen fish landed; thirteen fish killed; four fish lost once hooked; largest fish seventeen pounds. H2O—three fish landed; zero fish killed; eight fish lost once hooked; largest fish nine pounds.

5. H2O's policy of releasing his catch after a quick photograph resulted in the ugliest altercation of all. It seems that two of his three prizes were identical seven-pound bucks that, though caught on successive days, were taken from the same hole. Pondering this, Ma waited till they sat sipping whiskies in the crowded lodge bar, then suddenly loudly accused him of catching a single seven-pounder, snapping its picture, burying it in the sand, digging it up and photographing it again the next day, throwing it away, and then shamelessly claiming to have released it unharmed! (I must point out here that apart from the Nijinsky fabrication—for which he paid in blood—I have never known my father to lie about his angling accomplishments, not even such typical fibs as the adding of inches and ounces to fish taken in the Long Ago.) H2O heard her out, threw his Scotch in her face and walked away; just as he reached the door, Ma's chair splintered against the wall over his head.

6. At the lodge, anglers and employees viewed the fledgling marriage with rabid interest: bets were made and small fortunes won and lost as wagerers gambled on what date or hour the divorce would commence, who would murder whom, or what article of tackle, furniture or anatomy would be destroyed next. H2O was considered the villain of the drama—unjustly I think, but Ma stacked the deck by giving steelhead steaks to everyone she saw. Soon a cavalcade of rumors marched in their wake, among them these: *a*) the famous Henning Hale-Orviston couldn't catch his ass in a fish hatchery. *b*) the only fly of Orviston's that had ever hooked anything worth keeping was the one manufactured by Levi Strauss and Company. *c*) the increasingly wasted appearance of the groom as the war dragged on could signify but one thing: he was spawned out.

7. The barroom outburst proved the first of a series of eruptions wherein the cultural, genetic, mental and metaphysical makeup of bride and groom received simultaneous (and therefore, luckily, incomprehensible) slander. Being the less skilled rhetorician, Ma ended one argument by punctuating H2O in the nose. Whether he didn't punch back because he's a gentleman (as he maintains) or because he'd have been used as a floor mop (as Uncle Zeke maintains) is open to debate.

8. Strangest of all were sudden truces called at unexpected hours of day or night wherein Derby contestants would schizophrenically and unconditionally disarm, disrobe and engage in fiery embraces.

Among the perceptible outcomes of the Rogue River Fishing War were these: never again would my parents employ anything resembling Reason in their discussions of the Art of Angling; never again would they go a-fishing together; never would their marriage vows waver or weaken—

for Angling had formed for them a bond far stronger than the fickle ties of Romantics. Theirs was a bond of enemies at war, of mongoose and cobra, Robin Hood and the Sheriff of Nottingham, Heresiarch and Inquisitor. But the Rogue Fishing War had *im*perceptible outcomes as well. After all, I was there in the thick of it, finning in the River Ma, and insofar as foetuses can intuit the meaning of adult speech, I intuited a realm outside where nothing mattered half so much as the manner in which one engaged in a mysterious activity called "Fishing." Thus it can be said that I was interested in this art not just from an early age, but from literally before any age at all: I felt the adrenalin rush as Ma set the hook to those steelhead, experienced her excitement as she played them, heard her satisfied grunts as she clubbed them, grew strong as she ate them. Before I ever saw the light of day, my fate was inextricably entwined in the fates of my fellow aquatic creatures, fish.

It should surprise no one, then, that as a small child I became a "fishing prodigy" and am to this day not unjustly known as a "fishing genius." It has been given to me to understand the way in which fish think; it is therefore as easy for me to catch fish as it is for a skilled huckster to swindle honest and innocent men. And anyone who thinks I brag in stating that I understand fish-thought is obviously ignorant of the way in which fish think. Believe me, it's nothing to brag about.

3a

Concerning Statistics

(The skate) was 6 ft. 8 in. from point of nose to end of tail, and 5 ft. 4 in. across. . . . Ten dogfish (12 lb. down) were caught on another handline. We also caught, on rods, one large crawfish, 14 pollack (4 lb. down), 30 pouting, 40 small breams, seven mackerel, two John Dorys, 4 gurnards, one whiting, and six scad.

Yours faithfully,
Stewart Thompson

—*London Fishing Gazette*

There have been caught in Walden pickerel, one weighing seven pounds . . . perch and pouts, some of each weighing over two pounds, shiners, chivins or roach (*Leuciscus pulchellus*), a very few breams, and a couple of eels, one weighing four pounds—I am thus particular because the weight of a fish is commonly its only title to fame. . . .

—*Henry David Thoreau*

LIKE GAMBLERS, BASEBALL FANS and television networks, fishermen are enamored of statistics. The adoration of statistics is a trait so deeply embedded in their nature that even those rarefied anglers the disciples of Jesus couldn't resist backing their yarns with arithmetic: when the resurrected Christ appears on the morning shore of the Sea of Galilee and directs his forlorn and skunked disciples to the famous catch of *John* 21, we learn that the net contained not "a boatload" of fish, nor "about a hundred and a half," nor "over a gross," but precisely "an hundred and fifty and three." This is, it seems to me, one of the most remarkable statistics ever computed. Consider the circumstances: this is *after* the Crucifixion and the Resurrection; Jesus is standing on the beach newly risen from the dead, and it is only the third time the disciples have seen him since the nightmare of Calvary. And yet we learn that in the net there were "great fishes" numbering precisely "an hundred and fifty and three." How was this digit discovered? Mustn't it have happened thus: upon hauling the net to shore, the disciples squatted down by that immense, writhing fish pile and started tossing them into a second pile, painstakingly counting "one, two, three, four, five, six, seven . . ." all the way up to an hundred and fifty and three, while the newly risen Lord of Creation, the Sustainer of their beings, He who died for them and for Whom they would gladly die, stood waiting, ignored, till the heap of fish was quantified. Such is the fisherman's compulsion toward rudimentary mathematics!

Statistics are a tool upon which anglers rely so heavily that a fish story lacking numbers is just that: a Fish Story. A fish without an exact weight and length is a nonentity, whereas the sixteen-incher or the twelve-pounder leaps out of the imagination, splashing the brain with cold spray. The strange implication is that numbers are more tangible than flesh; fish without vital statistics are fish without being. And this digital fisherman-consciousness has seeped into most facets of life. One of the most telling examples is this: a human child at birth undergoes a ritual almost identical to that inflicted upon trophy trout at death, to wit 1) the fish is whacked on the head, thus putting it out of its misery; the infant is whacked on the behind, thus initiating it *into* its misery. 2) the fish is placed on a scale, weighed to the quarter ounce and mea- sured to the quarter inch; the infant endures identical treatment. 3) the fish is stripped of the coating of slime that protected it in the water; the infant is purposelessly relieved of its equivalent coating. 4) the fish is placed in a cold rectangular receptacle to await the taxidermist who will stuff it, creating an illusion of healthy flesh on its lifeless body; the infant is placed in a *warm* rectangular receptacle to await the par- ents who will stuff it, hopefully creating genuine healthy flesh upon its living body.

Further examples of fishlike human predicaments are too numerous to explore at length, but the disquieting analogies between students in public schools and smolts in rearing ponds, dancers in nightclubs and salmon on their spawning beds, suburbanites in housing tracts and hatchery trout in reservoirs, and industrialists who pollute and trash fish who like pollution, should be obvious to any angler.

I was afflicted with as pernicious a case of the numerical lease on life as any I've encountered, but I had the good fortune to discover that the essential pleasures of fishing are as independent of statistics as are the joys of childbirth independent of little Bosco's length in quarter inches. Most of us appear to be plagued by the notion that digits describe a thing (for instance an infant) more accurately than do the qualities the thing possesses (for instance the infant's drooling smiles, watery eyes, redundant dimples, pathetic coiffure, tiered chins and helpless unignorable outcries). Accuracy is a useful thing, certainly. A skyscraper designed by an architect with a head for nothing but drooly smiles and tiered chins is likely never to scrape the sky. But there are times and places to employ statistics and times and places not to—and the times-and-places-not-to comprised one of many lessons I was doomed to learn "the hard way."

Concerning those disciples huddled over the pile of fish, another possibility occurs to me: perhaps they paid the fish no heed. Perhaps they stood in a circle adoring their Lord while He, the All-Curious Son of His All-Knowing Dad, counted them all Himself!

3b
Some Biographical Statistics

He sought with dry and lifeless hands . . . unmindful of what he was
doing or not doing he felt his way . . . allured like an animal by water,
hankering for what was still earthly, still living, still moving; with
hanging head he crept. . . .

—*Hermann Broch*,
The Death of Virgil

A FISHING PRODIGY, like a musical prodigy, is perforce a solitary. Because of
fishing I started school a year late; because of fishing I failed the fifth
grade; because of fishing I was considered a kind of mild-mannered freak
by my schoolmates; because of fishing I grew up osprey-silent and trout-
shy and developed early on an ability to slide through the Public School
System as riverwater slides by the logjams, rockslides and dams that bar
its seaward journey. It wasn't that I was antisocial; I simply suffered from
that lopsidedness of character typical in prodigies. As young Mozart
cared for nothing but keyboards, strings and woodwinds, so I cared for
nothing but lakes, rivers, streams and their denizens. Years before I could
have put it into words, I realized that my fate would lead me beside still
waters, beside rough waters, beside blue, green, muddy, clear, and salt
waters. From the beginning my mind and heart were so taken up with the
liquid element that nearly every other thing on the earth's bulbous face
struck me as irrelevant, distracting, a waste of my time.

A statistic: literally every weekend and school vacation of my boyhood was spent fishing in the company of H2O or Ma. If the weather
were foul we'd spend the day tying flies, building rods, studying manuals
or reading books related to angling.

Statistics: I caught my first steelhead, a ten-pounder, when I was
four, on a worm. I caught my first steelhead on a fly at six. I caught my

hundredth steelhead when I was eight, and roughly my nine-thousandth trout. (My parents' fishing logs confirm these precocious figures. I began to keep my own log when I was nine.) Ma considered me an expert bait-fisherman at age six. H2O pronounced me an unsurpassed fly-angler, fly-tier and rod-builder at fourteen, and still favors a nine-foot graphite I designed, despite its inability to earn him endorsement money. When I stopped keeping track I had completely worn out twelve pairs of chest-waders, seventeen landing nets, and five wicker creels.

A quasi-statistical attribute that should be mentioned is my memory. My entire memory is not photographic, but my fishing memory is. I recall the number of trout caught during a week-long trip with H2O to the Rockies when I was five, and the name of every hole in the three famous rivers plied. I know how to tie esoteric wet-flies designed for Argentine brown trout, not because I've been to Argentina, or tied them, but because I happened to read about them. If it has to do with fishing, it sticks. But like my ability to understand fish-thought, this fishing-memory is no great blessing; it's not so much an ability to remember as an inability to forget.

If there is any statistic from childhood in which I take pride, it is not an angling but a diplomatic one: I managed, up to the day I left home, to avoid serious conflict with either Ma or H2O over my own use of bait and fly. Carrying both kinds of gear everywhere I went, I fished simply to catch fish, outfished them both, and stayed out of the fray.

Due, then, to prodigyhood, my general knowledge of the world is inordinately full of gaps and lapses. In school I often amazed cohorts and teachers by displaying a degree of ignorance seldom attained by students whose minds were unscathed by amnesia or retardation. Certainly I'd heard of Mickey Mouse, Vietnam, Richard Nixon and the New York Yankees. But the differences between slightly subtler names, things and places such as Hoss Cartwright and Wilbur Wright, the political right and the New Left, Park Place and Peyton Place, or Wall Street, the Waldorf and the Great Wall of China were all Sanskrit to me. Having nothing to do with my obsession, they flowed off my brain like water off a merganser. Were it not for my brother's sporadic attempts to fill me in on these objects of popular knowledge, my ignorance might have gotten me into all sorts of unsavory psycho- or sociological research experiments. As it was, I was voted Mr. Most-Out-Of-It by my senior class in high school.

Certainly every man's ignorance is a darkness of infinite dimensions. But suburban and urban Americans who read the same papers, see the same ads and billboards, and suck in the same radio and TV waves have a right to expect a certain commonality of knowings among themselves.

Growing up in such a suburb, I should have shared these knowings; thanks to fanatical fishermanliness I did not. And my parents never questioned this lopsidedness—not even when I failed fifth grade: I passed the one intelligence test recognized in our house; I fished as skillfully as they.

4

Statistical Improbabilities

The Compleat Angler is, taken by and large . . . a jolly book, a
book with which . . . we can feel at home.

—*Henry Williamson*

DESPITE THEIR DIVERGENT fishing techniques and cultural backgrounds,
my parents have many similar traits. Both are hot-tempered, hyperactive,
ambitious, loquacious and extremely loyal. Their loyalty, particularly to
each other, can be violent—an odd paradox considering that not a day
goes by without them vilifying each other. Though Ma might guffaw over
H2O's Britannic ways when the Carper uncles are around, the instant she
imagines genuine scorn (unless it's hers) she lets them have it—not just
with words, and not always above the belt. And when a High Church
friend gets too snide about Ma's cowgirl crudity, H2O explodes—he
hasn't punched anybody yet but he did once utter an icy Anglo-Saxon
challenge to a duel, and was only dissuaded when his second pointed out
that flyrods and beer openers were the only available weapons. Even then
H2O had to give it some thought: he finally reasoned that to kill his
adversary by whipping him to death with his beloved flywand was too like
Launcelot using Guinevere as a lance in a joust, and to perforate him to
death with a beer opener was just too laborious and absurd.

My brother and I, in contrast, are slow-moving, dispassionate, pacifistic, close-lipped, and not at all defensive of the family honor. My
"calm" was never a genuine tranquility; I endeavored at an early age to
master the "poker face," and had some success—but often as not I'd be
wearing it while my innards were churning like a creek at June run-off. As
for my brother, I believe his tranquility is genuine; I doubt if his peace
passeth understanding, but sometimes it comes close.

When I was christened, Ma wanted my name to be "Gus" pure and
simple, but Henning Hale-Orviston insisted that, whatever Ma might call
me, legal documents at least would sport a "proud, manly name." Hence

Augustine. . . . But by the time my brother was born the family balance of power had tipped so far to the matriarchal side that H2O was helpless when Ma pointed out that it was her turn: now they would have a son with a no-frills Eastern Oregon name. Now, by the powers she had vested in herself, Ma decreed that their second son would be known both officially and familially not as William Robert, nor Willis Robin, nor Wilberforce Robersly, but just as plain old *Bill Bob*. Bill Bob Orviston by God and that's it. When H2O eyes welled and he begged for some infinitesimally less cornpone alternative, Ma's demeanor grew surprisingly soft. "OK Hen," she said. "Let's call the little rugbug Buck Gilly-Bob."

Henning Hale-Orviston blanched.

"Jim-Ed Donny-Bob?"

H2O shuddered, approved the original Bill Bob plan, and departed on a long, solitary angling excursion, lugging his long name like a sullen kid who takes his ball and goes home. "How many poets," he asked himself as he Winnebagoed down the lonesome highway, "How many statesmen, heroes, senators and sea captains strolling down the dim corridors of Time have been named Bill Bob?" The answer needed no statistician. Yet, as Bill Bob points out, Ma could have done worse. She swears that had he been a girl she'd have named him after her grandma, Celestial Darling Carper! Next to that brain-boogering malapropism "Bill Bob" exudes a certain charm.

My brother Bill Bob is a living refutation of those behavioral and genetic theories claiming that men are largely determined by their blood kin and home environment, for not only is Bill Bob tranquil, he neither likes nor dislikes that most Orvistonian of passions, Fishing. From his genesis not a day has passed wherein H2O, Ma or I was not preparing for, returning from or engaged in a fishing trip, yet Bill Bob isn't merely disinterested in fishing: he knows nothing about it. He is not mentally debilitated, idiotic or otherwise damaged; he is no troglodyte, troll, hodag, dwarf, dingbat, ditzel or bideep. He was simply born with a prodigious ability to ignore things aquatic, which to a massive extent implies an ability to ignore his entire family. He has no water in his astrological chart; he bathes as seldom as possible; he employs galoshes, full-length slicker, wide-brimmed rain-hat and umbrella when it even threatens to precipitate; he'll drink any liquid but water. And he is as clean, healthy and happy a person as I've ever had the good fortune to meet. I remember a winter's night from boyhood: I sat at a desk with H2O at my side instructing me in the art of fly-tying. Ma sat on the couch with tiny Bill Bob in her lap, reading a book called *Angling With Bait*.

From the TV blared a special documentary on "The Freshwater Fishes." But when I looked over at Bill Bob from my # 14 Blue Upright I was startled by his intensity and fixedness of gaze: his little bald head was wobbling the way babies' heads do—like an earth gone off its axis—but his look was ageless, rapt in its one-pointed stare. Following his eyes to find what transfixed him, I discovered—on a shelf beneath a lamp made of a landing net, wedged between fly-manuals, dismantled reels, spools of line, casting trophies and stuffed fish—a single, empty 7-Up bottle. That 7-Up bottle is a good example of what I mean by Bill Bob's air of profundity: of course there's nothing mystical about an empty 7-Up bottle unless you're familiar with the symbology of 7's, have a Buddhist conception of emptiness, or a Taoist conception of Up, which Bill Bob didn't. But that bottle may have been the sole object in that room not directly related to angling, and he located it, zeroed in on it, and contemplated it till he entered that infantine samadhi known as sleep. Even if it was just a pop bottle, there is profundity in such behavior.

Despite ten years' physical proximity to Bill Bob, an intangible barrier separated us: I was a water creature, he a land creature, and though we silently wished each other well, we scarcely knew each other. But then he always was an inscrutable little fart. Perhaps not to know him is to know him well. He has a height and weight, face, voice, hair, the usual number of limbs—all the accoutrements of a brother. Yet there is an impregnability about him that thwarts easy intimacy. Perhaps to know a person's attributes is to know the person. I have perceived in my brother these attributes: he likes baseball, likes to eat, likes to talk himself to sleep and to sleep ten hours nightly, likes TV, rockets, radios, fire trucks, and basketball when baseball season is over; he likes movies, erector sets, bow ties, M&M's, Bibles, True cigarettes, citrus fruit, and reading the want ads when he doesn't want anything—which is every day. He's never excited, surprised or ebullient, nor is he ever bored, disappointed or depressed. I once heard him say in perfect seriousness that McDonald's is his kind of place.

There. Now everyone knows Bill Bob as well as I do.

Since my general knowledge has begun to improve I have learned that no book ever published has generated so much tension, division and strife in the American Family as that conglomeration of myths, laws, genealogies, songs, visions, poems, histories, letters and tall tales known as the Holy Bible. Not only is the Bible the most explosive book in existence, it is also the most common. Houseflies and tires are two species of black-colored objects numerous beyond count, but those black-backed tomes the Holy Bibles need kowtow to no fly or tire on that account, for they too constitute a quasi-infinite army—the most widespread and imperialistic that any black horde can claim. So, it should be apparent that it's going to be damned tough to explain how all but one of the countless book-caused arguments had by Ma and H2O were *not* over the Bible, but over that docile classic *The Compleat Angler.* To warm up, I'll recount first that solitary ruckus stemming from the volume so ironically dubbed "The Good Book."

From somewhere—no one knew where—when Bill Bob was three he got hold of this pocket-sized Holy Bible. He carried it around all the time and he called it his "Good Book," but he couldn't talk too straight yet so it came out "Bood Gooky." Perhaps I should point out that the main difference between Bill Bob at three and Bill Bob at seventeen is he's three feet taller and can talk. Otherwise he's the same—baseball, want ads, McDonald's and all.

So here's little three-year-old Bill Bob chugging around the neighborhood—baggy little trousers, crewcut, white shirt and bowtie. Between the outfit and the Bible he had Ma worried he was getting religious on us. I wasn't worried; I saw the healthy way he carried the Bood Gooky about: in his back trouser pocket. Like a wallet. Anyhow, he couldn't read a lick.

One day H2O gave Bill Bob a multiple-color ball-point pen. When he clipped it in his shirt pocket it really added something. Made him look like Eisenhower or Khrushchev or somebody. The following day I happened to come home from the grocery with a pack of candy cigarettes. Ol' Bill Bob Nikita Eisenhower spotted me and wanted some, but I told him to forget it unless he forked out some money. So what did he do? Like a dwarf executive he hauled out the wallet-Bible, snatched the multicolor pen from his shirt, switched it on red, straightened his bowtie, opened the Bible sideways, scribbled across a page of *Deuteronomy*, tore out the page and handed it to me. I understood exactly what had transpired: he'd just written me a check! I was so impressed I gave him two candy cigarettes, and only one was broken.

He put the broken butt in his pocket along with the pen. He stuck the whole one in his face, letting it dangle from his lip, Bogart-style. Then he pulled a rubber eraser from one of the fathomless trouser pockets, gave it a flick with his thumb, held it carefully to the end of his fag.

"Hey," I said. "Where'd you get the solid-gold lighter?"

"Eh's duss goad pwated," said he. "Eh's a Zippo." He squinted to keep the smoke out of his eyes.

"Looks like the genuine article," I said.

He nodded, gave me a thumbs-up sign and trudged off toward the sand-box, a dapper little man of few words.

I looked over my check. Under Bill Bob's scribbles it said,

The Lord will smite thee with the botch of Egypt,
and with the emerods, and with the scab,
and with the itch . . .
The Lord shall smite thee with madness,
and blindness, and astonishment of heart . . .
The Lord shall smite thee in the knees,
and in the legs,
with a sore botch that cannot be healed. . . .

Well, that gave me something to think about! I decided to beat cheeks in to H2O, get him to cash the scribbled part for me, and he could hoard the Biblical part all to himself if he wanted.

He was in his study, but he was working on an article; interrupting articles is taboo, so I went looking for Ma.

She was in the kitchen, starting dinner. I handed her the page. She looked at it blankly, scratched under her nose, said, "What's thissy here?"

I said, "I sold Bill Bob some of my candy. He wrote me out this check. What's it worth?" (She'd got biscuit makings on her nose by accident. It looked pretty stupid, but I figured I'd wait and see what became of my check before I said anything.)

"Well well well well," she said. "A check. Yes. Well . . . yes." She started to smile. "So much for Reverend Bill Bob's e-van-jelly-sizin'." (This was a non sequitur to me, but a kid at thirteen has an enormous tolerance of adult non sequiturs and lets most run him through like prune juice—which is what I did with this one.)

"What's it worth?" I repeated.

"Oh!" She jumped, as if I'd woke her. "Yes, worth, well, uh . . . let me figger the writin' here—um . . . Five cents. Yup. Five cents. Let me gitcha a nickel."

I kept my poker face, but inside I was leaping like a trout in a mayfly hatch: FIVE CENTS! Why the whole pack of cigarettes only cost me five cents! This checkbook thing could turn out to be a goldmine! I felt a little worried about the words under the scribbling, but nobody came down with any exotic diseases, which only made sense in the end since a check is just paper till you cash it and you cash it at a bank where what you cash it for is stashed, and where would anybody find an Egyptian Botch, Itch and Emerod Bank?

Ma got me a nickel from the cookie jar. I said, "You got a mushtash on your nose," ran off and stashed the loot in my tacklebox—the safest place for valuables since Bill Bob was the only thief in the family, and he'd never open anything that had to do with fishing.

Two days later I took my nickel to the grocery and bought a pack of M&M's, knowing they were Bill Bob's favorite candy. When I got home I found him by the garage, sitting in a cardboard box with an old dead radio in it. This was his "SkaySkopSkool," which translated "space capsule." I knew better than to interrupt while he was traversing the vacancies of space; I'd tried it before and he ignored me completely, refusing to return to earth till I left him alone. So this time I just strolled by like I didn't even see him, whistling and tossing around the M&M's . . . . In seconds I heard the sounds a kid might make when travelling at the speed of light, followed by a "Sploorsh!," which signified a splash-down (this contact with imaginary ocean being about as close as Bill Bob was willing to come to water). Then an instantaneous transformation occurred—astronaut to businessman—and here came Dwight D. Khrushchev armed with pen, Bood Gooky and determination.

Faking annoyance, I said, "I s'pose ya wanna buy my M&M's."

"Yeth," said Bill Bob, and before I could even begin to dicker he ripped out a good twenty-five pages of *II Chronicles* and started scribbling across them in multifarious colors like a madman! He had them made out in seconds. I was so happy I gave him the whole pack of candy without even tasting a single M. The way I figured it, he'd just made me a rich man. I sprinted for the Cookie Jar Bank, careful this time not to read between Bill Bob's lines.

Ma was in the bathtub. I had a premonition that I should wait for her but was too excited for caution. I went to find H2O. He was in the study tying flies. There is a rigid code of conduct with regard to the interruption of fly-tiers in the Orviston family: streamers, nymphs and bucktails, being relatively easy to execute, may be interrupted in lowered tones at any time; but any hackled fly—particularly any dry fly smaller than a 16—requires the interrupter's patience until the fly is completed, dressed and removed from the vise. Spying the burly body and bright throat of a Montana nymph I strode forward and threw my wad of *II Chronicles* loot triumphantly on the table. Expecting H2O to reach deep in his pocket and shell out a few bucks like any reputable banker, I was surprised to see his face grow dark.

"*Who*," he rumbled in his King Henryest voice, "has done this thing to the Holy Bible?"

Without hesitation or qualm I blurted, "Bill Bob."

He turned his Spanish Inquisition Gaze upon me in an attempt to discern whether I was lying. Well accustomed to this torment, I made myself look ignorant and trivial and small, like a little dog that turns belly-up to keep a big dog from chewing on it. Appeased by this display, H2O snatched up the checks and stalked out in search of Bill Bob. I was so immersed in doghood I half expected him to pause in the doorway and lift his leg on the wall. I followed at a safe distance.

Outside Bill Bob had resumed his explorations in the SkaySkop-Skool, and, contrary to the M&M's slogan, there was chocolate mess everywhere. Usually a cleanly fellow, Bill Bob had obviously been chewing up the candies, spitting them into his hands and wiping them all over his face and arms. The situation did not look good.

Applying his limited powers of ratiocination to the conundrum of why the chocolate lay upon the exterior, rather than the traditional interior, of his son's person, H2O concluded that Bill Bob was in the grip of one of those inexplicable fits of infantile madness endemic in habitually naughty children (which he believed both his sons to be). Applying my own more astute powers of speculation, I quickly and correctly conjectured that the chewed-up M&M's were stage makeup applied for the purpose of simulating some horrid intergalactic skin disease—and with this advantage over conventional makeup: it could be licked off once the infection had run its course. But I said nothing.

The fuming H2O, with a low-budget science-fiction movie's disregard for natural laws, reached far into the wastes of space and plucked Bill Bob from his vehicle by the belt of his trousers, stood him upright on the lawn, confronted him with the mutilated fragment of *II Chronicles* and demanded, "Was this your doing Willia–er, Bill Bob?" (He'd never stopped trying to convince himself his son's name wasn't what it was.)

"Yeth!" snapped Bill Bob, surly at this astronomical intrusion upon his epidermal anguish.

Mistaking the annoyance for a show of guilt, H2O thundered, "WHY?"

"Bood Gooky Boobob's jeb gook," said Bill Bob, offering what I thought a concise explanation of his activities with the Bible.

But H2O didn't understand a syllable. Believing Bill Bob to have lapsed into baby talk to protect himself, he commenced the frequently delivered "This-is-going-to-hurt-me-more-than-you" address. Meanwhile, believing he'd explained himself succinctly and was now being innocuously garbled at in adult talk, Bill Bob busied himself with licking the tasty space disease off his arms. Knowing what was about to happen, seeing Bill Bob's poor chocolate face all calm and unsuspecting, being too afraid to speak up, knowing H2O hadn't understood anything that transpired and that I'd started it by not waiting for Ma and by telling on Bill

Bob when all he'd done was single-handedly figure out a way to glean sweet gifts from a book that was *supposed* to be a source of sweetness when his fishy old agnostic father could never have squeezed a drop from it himself, and then having to stand there listening to H2O appease his conscience before inflicting senseless pain upon a three-foot human being by inanely stating that what he was about to do would hurt his blunted old psyche and calloused meathook more than Bill Bob's tender little butt . . . hells bells. It all saddened me so much I started to cry. And then, though he wasn't concerned for himself or even aware of the danger he was in, Bill Bob started crying too, out of sympathy for me.

But behold! Fresh from the bath and garbed in a brown robe, Ma came rushing toward us like a vision of Diana. "Sweet Jesus! What's all this caterwaulin' an' blubberin' about?" (Her speech was not Diana's.)

Sensing his patriarchal power about to be shot full of arrows, H2O's brow furrowed like a bloodhound's. Snatching the ratty residue-of-a-Bible from Bill Bob's pocket and holding it and the checks up to the Eye in the Sky, he thundered, "Our son here has destroyed a Bible, for what reason, God knows! (His tone of voice implied that this meant *he* knew.)

Bill Bob's Bood Gooky had grown mighty thin; he must have been drawing pretty heavily on his checking account lately. Ma snatched the Bible from Hen, scrutinized it, understood the situation, handed it back to Bill Bob, cackled, "Looks like you been on a spendin' spree, boy!" and brayed like a donkey at her own wit.

The sound of that bray reduced our Grand Inquisitor to the peevish paternal limey we knew so well. The situation lost its religious overtones, leaving H2O looking rather deflated and pitiable. (Ma knew perfectly well how frequently he read his own Bible.) Sensing our troubles were over, Bill Bob grinned at me with gucky brown teeth, scraped the chocolate from his face, sucked his fingernails like Havana cigars, looked up at H2O, snorted good-humoredly and said, "Jeb gook!" holding up the shredded—and now chocolate-smeared—Bible.

"That's right honeybunch," said Ma. Then she glared at H2O. "Well Hen, so he ripped hell out of it. So what? What else did he do?"

H2O's frown transcended the bloodhound stage and entered the realm of apple dolls. "*Isn't that enough?*"

"Enough for what?" Ma snapped.

"Enough to warrant a sound spanking and a stern admonition not to destroy . . . books." This was his last-ditch defense of Propriety.

"Why hell no it ain't enough!" screeched Ma. "You were gonna whup lil' Bill Bob fer playin' sech a cute game and him findin' the damned ol' thing and thinkin' up what to do with it all his ownself? Hell no it ain't enough! Who the hell stuck the bee in *your* bonnet, Hen Orviston!"

At this point H2O's fuse burnt entirely away and they exploded into one of the usual messy vociferations from which the wiry Ma would sooner or later emerge victorious. Bill Bob and I wandered off to play.

5a

The Great Izaak Walton Controversy:
The Parental Version

H2O's thesis:

> O sir, doubt not angling is an art. Is it not an art to deceive a trout with an artificial fly?
>
> —*Izaak Walton*, The Compleat Angler

> There is no activity so conducive to the health and happiness of a civilized man as angling with an artificial fly. As for the uncivilized, who would care to contemplate what writhing creatures their inchoate consciences allow them to skewer upon a hook?
>
> —*Henning Hale-Orviston*, Summa Piscatoria

Ma's antithesis:

> The pleasant'st angling is to see the fish
> Cut with her golden oars the silver stream,
> And greedily devour the treacherous bait. . . .
>
> —*Shakespeare*, As You Like It

> A fisherman stands on a projecting rock with a long rod, throws in ground bait to attract little fishes, drops in hook and line . . . and at last gets a bite and whips him out gasping. . . .
>
> —*Homer*, The Odyssey

FOLLOWING THE ROGUE RIVER Fishing War my father was at his wit's end as to how to convince his bride to take up the flyrod, but then the end of his wit was a place only inches away wherever Ma was concerned. Flyfishing is an art he takes so seriously that one may say it constitutes his religion—and religious men on the make for converts are notoriously witless. Perhaps H2O's evangelic approach to flyfishing was fueled by genuine religious sentiment; perhaps he felt that in flyfishing he had discovered an unsullied form of worship, and so wanted to share his discovery with everyone he met—whether they wanted to share it or not. In any case, there is something admirable about such one-pointed devotion, and Henning Hale-Orviston is without question a much-admired man: few would argue with the angling publications that characterize him as "The King of the Troutists" and "The Bishop of Brooks"—and many's the time that hardened old bait-slingers have been so moved by the sight of him working the riffles of some flickering river that they straightaway repented of their heretical ways and seated themselves at the "Bishop"'s feet in hope of his sagacious instruction. Such conversions are H2O's greatest joy in life.

Among the purists themselves my father is a legend. His *Summa Piscatoria* is said to be the most detailed, Attic-prosed manual of the flyfisher's art in the world today (even Ma said of it, "Cripes, Hen! What a fat sucker! You write that all yer ownself?"), and men have journeyed literally thousands of miles to consult his illustrious mentations on nuances of dogma and lore. But woe is he: if there is a creature on this planet less appreciative of his prowess than is my mother, I have not yet met it. And he never stops mulling stratagems that might spark her conversion.

One day just before I was born he visited the Portland chapter of the Izaak Walton League—an angler's organization whose various groups gather once or twice monthly to discuss matters of fishing, water politics, tackle technology, and conservation. After delivering a well-received lecture entitled "The Supremacy of the Sinking-tip in Nymph Fishing," it suddenly occurred to him that the namesake of this excellent club might be the solution to the problem of his unsporting wife. Wasn't Ma unaccountably fond of antiques? And wasn't Izaak the dusty old father of flyfishermen everywhere? And wasn't his famous book, *The Compleat Angler*, an antiquated yet alluring exposition of the fly-angler's art as it was practiced of old? Upon returning home from the League meeting, H2O went straight to his library, extracted his first-edition heirloom copy, smiled fondly at its quaint appearance, pocket size, and price (1s. 6d.), then took it directly to Ma. He forgot one thing: *he had never read it. . . .*

Ma accepted the book on the basis of its being "old-fashionedy," began to read it aloud in a flat, uncomprehending monotone, and in seconds the first of thousands of Izaak Walton Controversies commenced: it will be known to most readers that very old English publications employed a script that fashioned its small "s" like our present-day "f"; somehow it didn't bother Ma to take such s's to *be* f's, despite the hash it made of the words. H2O has always been a stickler about language, and Ma's regional dialect has been a torment equalling her bait fishing at times. So when she commenced her lobotomized droning, he was soon gnawing at his lips. She began—

"'The Com-pleee-at Angler . . . ' heh heh. Ol' Izaak Walton don't spell no better'n me, Hen. What's this now? . . . 'or the contemplative man'f recreation' hmmmm. *Man'f*. That's a new one on me."

H2O said, "I believe it's 'man's,' dear."

"Nope. It's *man'f*. Plain as pie. An' listen what comes next! 'Being a Discourfe of,' um, 'Riverf,' uh, 'Fifhpondf Fifh and Fifhing . . .' Haha! Lordy, Hen! I can't read French!"

"It isn't *French*, dear. It's perfectly proper English, but you're mistaking the s's for f's!"

"The hell I am! Bunchabloody Frog-talk's what we got here! What's next? Ha! Listen: 'Simon Peter faid, "I go a -fifhing": and they faid, "We *alfo* will go with thee."' ALFO! Hahahahaha! Some kinda Frog dogfood, I reckon! I'm likin' this book, Hen. I'm likin' it a lot!"

At thif point my father wifely left Ma to her own devicef. Fortunately only the introductory pages employed the f-type s's, so Ma was soon cruising along relatively smoothly. But to this day she speaks of what she calls the book's "French subtitles," and fondly refers to it as a "Difcourfe 'bout Fifh an' Fifhin'."

She finished the book in two days, slammed it shut and stormed into H2O's study as he hunched over a #22 Midge, arousing a violent start and unraveling of hackle that was the ruin of the fly. He whirled savagely—but spying *The Compleat Angler* clutched in her hands, managed a smile. This smile turned out to be one of a curious species indigenous to H2O's face—a species Bill Bob would one day dub "The Overparked Winnebago." Now the orthodox conception of smiles is not stringent or dogmatic; it allows for a wide array of permutations—smiles that signify joy, or hate; bewildered smiles; cynical smiles; knowing smiles; idiot smiles; condescending smiles; phony camera smiles. But all these types have a fundamental attribute: they visit the face for a moment or two and then depart, their purpose served. But the Overparked Winnebago is no orthodox smile; it is the Methuselah of smiles. H2O climbs into it, drives it onto his face, parks it, climbs out and abandons it there; its purpose forgotten, it lingers on—a gigantic anachronism rusting and mildewing at the curb of his mouth. As Ma came closer, H2O perceived coffee stains on his heirloom volume; closer yet a broken binding came into view; then, as she pawed enthusiastically through the pages, he heard rending sounds, glimpsed underlinings, saw stars, "Whoopie"s, "Wow"s and other spectacular marginalia applied by brightly inked felt pens; his eyes grew watery, his knees grew weak, his stomach waxed acidic and cried out for Pepto-Bismol . . . but the abandoned Winnebago clung to his lips. Bubbling with dangerous excitement, Ma proposed an impromptu out-loud reading, commencing with—

1. The Otter Hunt, wherein Piscator (Walton's genius) accompanies Venator (the straight man) and an entire army of armed and mounted hunters and sharp-fanged hounds in relentless pursuit of a single care-worn female otter upon which they all converge, gleefully watching as she is torn to pieces by a vicious brute of a dog dubbed "Sweetlips"! One of the conquering storm troop then perceives by her swollen teats, or what's left of them, that the otter was the mother of a family—so away to her den they thunder, and there join hands in bludgeoning her helpless whelps to death. . . . "Come, let's kill them all. . . . Now let's go to an honest alehouse, where we may have a cup of good barley wine, and sing 'Old Rose,' and all of us rejoice together." (H2O's smile paid his clammy skin and queasy gut no heed; he muttered something about protecting trout from predators. Ma didn't hear as she moved on to—)

2. Fishing for Chubs (a species the mere thought of which causes my father's gorge to rise. He'd only recently spied one floating like a corpse on the Willamette, happily munching at some buoyant, orange-colored thing that looked very like a human turd), wherein the knowledgeable Piscator enthralls his disciple Venator by catching several corpulent chubs—not on a fly, but on live grasshoppers skewered on a bait-hook. To celebrate this feat they retire together to the inevitable alehouse, hand the squalid fish over to the proprietress with a curt order to cook them up pronto, seat themselves before frothy pints to await supper, and when the chubs are cooked and the inebriated pair are happily munching at the buoyant orange-colored flesh, Venator exclaims, "'Tis as good meat as ever I tasted!" (H2O said nothing, but poured himself a tall brandy the bulk of which he deftly threaded straight through the halves of his undying smile. Ma proceeded to the next Waltonian wonder—)

3. Fishing for Pike, a humorous chapter featuring Piscator's penchant for anecdote, particularly anecdotes of bizarre atrocities in the

English aquatic world. Take, for instance, the thirsty mule who wet its parched throat in a pike pond: no sooner had it gulped an innocent gulp than a huge pike shot from the water and fastened its fangs to the poor beast's lips where it clung like a bulldog (or like H2O's smile), affording all ale-swigging spectators paroxysms of laughter, and the mule a mandible mutilated for life. Also interesting are the pike who commit suicide by devouring venomous frogs, and, amazing to tell, the pike who get themselves straddled like saddle-broncs by a sinister species of cowboy-frog who ride 'em till they tire and die (whether of insanity or embarrassment Walton fails to say). Elsewhere Izaak happily assures us that a hungry pike will "bite at and devour a dog that swims in a pond" (Hawhawhaw!). But Ma's favorite bit just had to be Piscator's prankish instruction to bait hooks with live fish and frogs, tie these in turn to the "bodies or wings of a goose or a duck," toss the helpless fowl into a pike-infested lake, then sit back with your tankard and take care not to split your sportsmanly belly as the blood and feathers fly! (H2O's smile remained, but the teeth in the middle of it began to gnash against his brandy glass; Ma moved on to—)

4. Fishing for Trout (that species described in the *Summa Piscatoria* as "designed by the Universal Powers to render—via the flyrod—the most aesthetically perfect experience available to mortal man"), wherein the sagacious Piscator catches and kills a number of trout—employing the crudest, barley-buttedest kind of plunking available to mortal man, using grasshoppers, grubs, maggots, minnows and worms. (H2O bit his glass, smashed it in the wastebasket, and commenced smashing himself, pouring brandy through the crack in his smile straight out of the receptacle the Christian Brothers shipped it in. The Brothers' brandy, by the way, was Ma's loathed brand, but H2O would gratefully have chugged cologne as Ma raced on to—)

5. Fishing for *Trophy* Trout, wherein Piscator reveals that the Highway to Hefty Trout is traversed through no matching of hatch, nor lengthening nor lightening of leader, nor perfection of presentation or imitation, nor naturalness of drift, but through fishing in the *dead of night* "with a strong line, and not a little hook; and let him have time to gorge your hook"; for a fish with bloody wounds in its vital organs will scarcely quarrel with you at all (as Ma illustrated when she set the treble-hooks to poor Nijinsky). Recommended for nighttime fishbait are such cunning materials as "a piece of cloth" and, even more interestingly, "a dead mouse"!

At the words "dead mouse" H2O garrotted the Christian Brothers and staggered out the door. Ma was not concerned: the sudden inexplicable craving men get for alcohol was nothing new to her; she rather approved of her over-cultivated husband behaving in down-home ranch-hand fashion for a change. Meanwhile, down at the neighborhood tavern, H2O was still grinning as he wished botches, itches and emerods that can't be healed upon the gentle father of modern angling.

But zealots are disgustingly indefatigable. After the evening with the Christian Brothers and subsequent night spent offering fluid gifts to the Porcelain Buddha (among these gifts the Winnebago smile), H2O happened to glance through *The Compleat Angler* before burning it, and was surprised to find the case far less hopeless than he'd feared. Ma's selections had been highly colored; indeed, it seemed she'd ferreted out every gruesome and uncharacteristic passage in a subversive attempt to delude him into believing Izaak Walton a traitor to the fly-angler's great cause. With increasing fervor and decreasing rationality he read and reread, taking copious notes, marking salient passages, and emerging after several days in his study with a lengthy thesis in which he claimed to account once and for all for Walton's "apparent indiscrimination toward what species he fished for and what methods he employed." In the article, "Izaak Walton: The Veiled Purist" (*Angler's Quarterly*; Spring 1955, p. 154ff.), Henning Hale-Orviston wrote,

. . . yet surely the discerning reader intuits, in these more poetic and impassioned passages, Walton's unfaltering commitment to the artificial fly and preference for trout and salmon. His unwillingness to express these priorities more openly is not the result of some Hindoo-like inability to perceive the superiority of the finer techniques and species over the coarse and crude; Walton is merely employing a literary convention characteristic of the Encyclopedists, and indeed of most late-Renaissance writers. To openly defend the fly and the salmonoids, however much he longed to do so, would have opened his admirable study to unfounded accusations of bias and subjectivity. (Walton was writing, after all, in an England where residues of the Dark Ages still lingered in the lesser minds of the intelligentsia.) Piscator thus conceals somewhat his one-pointed devotion to flyfishing, Walton trusting that Venator's good judgment and sensitivity (and the reader's as well!) will pierce the flux of superficial and cavalier discoursings upon bait, chumming, night fishing, inferior species of fish, didactic Christian philosophy, irrelevant songs and poetry, meetings with Milkmaids, Gypsies and Country Rustics, absurd fish-tales, and all such extrania. *The Compleat Angler* was intended to be taken as a "Microcosm" (if you will) of the Angling World, wherein the reader and Venator must—just as we modern anglers must—fight their way through all distractions, superfluities and inferior modes of fishing to discover the joys which only the committed fly-angler may know!

This is, undeniably, remarkable rhetoric; in fact the article created a small sensation among literary fishermen and was called "the first real advance in Walton criticism in fifty years or more." But it is also, undeniably, compleat bilgewater, asking us in effect to ignore all but two or three pages of a two-hundred-twenty-page book, and to forget the fact that when Walton wished to include a section on fly angling he considered himself ignorant of the subject and hired a friend, Charles Cotton, to write an addendum. But the really pathetic thing about H2O's piece was that by the time he'd finished penning it, he'd actually come to *believe* it. After its publication he invited Ma to read the article (thinking it would have more authority in magazine print); Ma complied, then offered this succinct critical evaluation: "Shit, Hen! This is nuthin' but commie hogwash an' you know it!" But Hen now insisted that he didn't know it—so Ma took off on an extemporaneous counter-argument wherein she asserted that "Ike Walton was nuthin' but a limeyfied cattle-puncher an' a boozer an' a rowdy good ol' boy, an' I'd like t'shake his hand fer tossin' in that token bit o' snot-nosed crap about flyfishin', 'cause it's plain as pee he only done it so rich snobs'd buy the book, which'd give him plenty o' pocket money fer fishin' gear an' ale an' nightcrawlers. . . ." And, strange to say, by the time Ma finished she had somehow bamboozled herself into thinking that *her* rendition of *The Compleat Angler* was the one godly interpretation.

Thus began that marathon debate, The Great Izaak Walton Controversy; thus my childhood home became a fishy little Belfast, strife-torn by an interdenominational "dialogue" that consisted of little more than name calling, jibes, scoffing, bragging and weird wrestling matches that eventually resulted in the advent of my little brother. The one interesting addition Izaak Walton brought to the fray was the Quotation. Like Southern Bible-belters backing harebrained theology with Dale Carnegie Translations of Scripture, H2O and Ma grew adept at trotting out lines wrenched from *The Compleat Angler*. The book became our family bible, and from the time I could toddle I heard it quoted, and misquoted, daily. So, naturally, as soon as I could read I set out to solve the Great Izaak Walton Controversy for myself.

5b

The Great Izaak Walton Controversy: My Own Rendition

... most men forget to pay their praises ... to Him that made that sun and us, and still protects us, and gives us flowers and showers, and stomachs and meat, and content and leisure to go a-fishing in.

—*Izaak Walton*, The Compleat Angler

... when I would beget content, and increase confidence in the power, and wisdom, and providence of Almighty God, I will walk the meadows by some gliding stream.

—*Izaak Walton*

I labour to possess my own soul.

—*Walton again*

BY THE TIME I WAS fifteen I had read *The Compleat Angler* perhaps as many times as Moses read the Commandments, and (like Moses?) the more I read the more confused and disillusioned I grew. The more I read the more I doubted whether Izaak Walton gave a coot's hoot whether one fished with a flyrod, plunking poles, trot-lines, harpoons or gill-nets. The more I read the more obvious it became that there was only one thing he cared for deeply—a thing completely alien to my experience, a thing that made me most uncomfortable, a thing too vague to grasp but too frequently alluded to to ignore. The more I read, the more it seemed that *The Compleat Angler* was almost casually and incidentally a fishing book. Its deepest *raison d'être* was not love for Angling, but love for that nebulous Personage men call *God*.

Walton credits God with providing all the savor a person gleans from any form of angling whatsoever; thus even the pleasures achieved by employment of bait or fly are, for Walton, references to the omnirecurrent gifts bestowed by our Spendthrift Creator. Izaak further credits his busy Deity with the manufacture and maintenance of the Universe, and though little evidence is forwarded as to how this extravagant hobby is practiced, Piscator calmly assures us that every "various little living creature is not only created but fed (man knows not how) by the goodness of the God of nature. . . ."

> Sherlock Holmes shook his head like a man who is far from being satisfied. "These are very deep waters," said he; "pray go on with your narrative."*

Who was this "God of nature"? Why hadn't I met Him, or at least learned something substantial about Him, or at the very least heard His Name consistently taken in some way other than in vain? Why—when I had fished the fresh and saline waters of Montana, Idaho, Nevada, Oregon, Washington, Wyoming, Colorado, Canada and Alaska for five kinds of salmon, four kinds of bass, three kinds of catfish, two kinds of steelhead, ling cod, flounder, halibut, bluegill, carp, crappie, sole, shad, smelt, snappers, shark, sturgeon, perch, pogies, mullet, whitefish, squawfish, dogfish, crawfish, trash fish, frogs, turtles, chub, nine kinds of trout, and so many more species that to name them might mesmerize me—had I failed to even hear of this Illimitable King who created, fed and ruled them all? Why—when I had laughed, leapt, shouted, sung, gloated, grinned, sighed, wept, cackled, cursed, capered, crowed and careened every which way in the fishing for and catching of every which fish—had the Magician behind these million moods not put in an Appearance, or even a Word? Why did Old Izaak so insistently insist that my myriad jubilations, desolations and preoccupations did not come from the sensible domain of water-whisper, fish-leap, rod-arc, rises at dusk, heart-jolt at savage strike or night wind on mountain lake, but from imperceptible wee bliss-bolts shot from the bow of his hyperactive Deity? And if somehow I forced myself to rant and ballyhoo about God's goodness and learned to turn ever and anon to the Invisible Zero of His Face, might I, like Piscator, come to be "so transported and amazed, and so admire the glory of it, that I would not willingly turn my eyes from that

*from *The Complete Sherlock Holmes*

first ravishing object, to behold all the various beauties this world could present"?. . .

> "We are bound to take every possibility into account. But the poor devil has certainly got himself into very deep water," said Holmes, "and it is a question whether we shall ever be able to get him ashore."*

Holmes's was my conclusion also. After all, I'd fished as intently as perhaps any boy had ever done, and I not only failed to encounter Walton's God, I failed to see the least evidence of His existence. Perhaps He resided only above England. Or perhaps He had retired since Walton's day and now lived quietly in some remote Condominium Galaxy where He enjoyed a game of intergalactic golf now and again, deftly driving, pitching and putting stars into eighteen black holes in space, loosing devils on us whenever He scored a bogey. Or perhaps He hid behind every tree, rock and bush, or was closer than my very breath so that just as I had never laid eyes on my lungs, so I'd never seen Him. . . . Whatever He did, however He did it, Whoever and Whatever He wasn't or was, if He wanted *my* attention He'd have to leave off making Himself so scarce.

As for Izaak Walton, it seemed to me he forced Piscator into wasting a lot of fishing time yammering on about his divine Will-o'-the-Wisp; this would have been legitimate had the book been called *The Compleat Vicar*, but a truly "compleat angler" ought to angle more compleatly. So despite having been led since foetushood to believe *The Compleat Angler* the most important book and the Bait-versus-Fly controversy the most profound question I would ever encounter, I came in my fifteenth year to some new conclusions based on my own observations: *1)* my parents' debate was an absurd mare's nest stemming not from any paradox inherent in *The Compleat Angler*, but from their own invincible stubbornness. *2)* unless it was somehow proven to me that this soundless and unseen Sky-Pie of Izaak Walton's was crucial to the art of angling, I would be forced to conclude that Walton's classic was a misnamed antique of no use to any pure incarnation of fishermanliness—such as I believed myself to be. *3)* unless and until such proof were provided, to hell with the bloody book and the whole dumb business.

Being of a fiery constitution, Moses did not hesitate to smash the Commandments the moment he suspected them of failing him in leading the people of Israel. Being of watery constitution, I simply took *The Compleat Angler* from its prestigious place among the autographed

---

*from *The Complete Sherlock Holmes*

fishing books of Joe Brooks, Sparse Grey-Hackle, Vincent Marinaro, Charles Ritz, Roderick Haig-Brown, Lee Wulff and company, and let it gather cobwebs in H2O's library among his countrymen, Herbert, Spenser, Milton, Shakespeare and Smart. I could think of no more ultimate symbol of rejection.

I did pay Walton one last consideration: I had for years kept notebooks—many volumes of mathematically precise accounts of where, when and how I caught every fish I caught; it now occurred to me that, on the off-chance there was something to this God character, I might employ the same system of note-taking with regard to Him. I titled these records "the God-notebook."

6

Excerpts from the God-notebook

I have been in the buttery
In the land of the Trinity . . .
It is not known what is the nature
Of its meat and its fish. . . .

—*Hanes Taliesin*

SCANNING THE "God-notebook" I find my most frequent entries tell of certain door-to-door-salesman–like persons purportedly devoted to a variety of invisible beings with names like "Great-Gawd-Amighty," "Fathern Heaven," "Parsonal Lord N. Savior," Jehovah, and "R. Lord." Judging by the fact that these people seem never to fish and, so far as I know, are found nowhere but on the denatured streets of America's urbs and burbs, it seems unlikely that their gods are in any way similar to the "God of nature" of Izaak Walton. Neither does their behavior evince harmonious comparisons to Piscator's, for they are found to be nervous, twitchy, often belligerent people—terrified of ale, ignorant of poetry, oblivious to the possibility of error in their views, and not about to say anything so interesting as "There is also a fish called a sticklebag" or "I have been much pleased to walk quietly by a brook with a little stick in my hand" or even "the primitive Christians were, as most Anglers are, quiet men, and followers of peace." It even seems likely that the tranquil Piscator would have been hard pressed to maintain his customary good nature in the company of a typical door-to-door urb-and-burb god's devotee—for these inexplicable people make it their business to bombard unsuspecting citizens in the privacy of their homes with little comic books full of the most grandiose and depressing threats, prophecies and admonitions imaginable; and they paste all kinds of weird epigrams and doom prophecies on their cars, causing many an innocent motorist to drive to his death trying to read the blasted things; and a common edition of these bumper legends promises worse havoc, flatly warning that the drivers of these stickered cars could at any moment evaporate away to Heaven in a process called "Rapture," showing no concern for the holocaust of traffic fatalities they would unavoidably leave behind!

The door-to-door comic-book distribution is part of an activity these folk call "Witnessing"—"Witlessing," as my mother renders it. The divergent courses of action my family members took when these threat-peddlers came knocking are worth noting: H2O classified the "Witless" according to gender—the men he called "the Christian Brothers" after Ma's brandy, the women "the Weird Sisters" after the witches in *Macbeth*. When they offered him the comics they called "littercher"—"a term," said H2O, "the first two syllables of which approach the truth"—he would coolly misinform them that he and his family were passionately attached to the Church of England and had no use for their propaganda. (This confused the hell out of the Avon lady.) Of course, none of us but H2O had ever been to church except for weddings, but the Witless—tongue-tied by the frigid eloquence of one of God's Frozen People (H2O's nickname for himself and all Anglicans)—would either take silent leave or find themselves conversing with an abruptly closed door.

Ma's technique was less articulate, more woodsy, and such a delight to Bill Bob and me that a dull rainy day would sometimes sink us to our knees to beseech Fathern Heaven or R. Lord to send along a Witless. When the knocker sounded, Ma would size up the visitor through a fisheye peephole she'd installed for such occasions. If she spotted comic books she would repair to the closet, return to the door, let it swing slowly open, and stand there—wordless, immobile and menacing—while the unfortunate caller grew cognizant of the fact that a wild, unreliable-looking woman had a double-barreled shotgun aimed at his or her knees. (Ma figured if you shot their knees you shot their ability to pray.) Her invitations to "clear the hell offa my property" were never refused or even discussed.

My technique was to wait for someone else to go to the door so I could record whatever transpired in my notebook.

Bill Bob seldom responded to door knocks, but one time when H2O was away and Ma was momentarily occupied he went to the door and admitted a Witless—a surly looking, obese, red-faced Christian Brother who made no attempt to return Bill Bob's friendly greeting and eyed my notebook and me with extreme suspicion. Grinning hideously, he presented Bill Bob (who was six at the time) with one of the unhappy comics and growled "Where's your muthah, Sonny?," not realizing that Ma and a wounded water buffalo were two of the last creatures on earth he'd like to see. Always grateful for a gift, Bill Bob thanked him courteously and trotted off. Our guest naturally assumed he'd gone to fetch "muthah," but Bill Bob was back in a jiffy with a Bugs Bunny and Elmer Fudd funnybook—one of his personal favorites—which he presented to the stranger in gentlemanly fashion. Realizing the exchange to have been highly advantageous to the Witless since his comic was bereft of jokes and color pictures, I was startled when he glowered and started hollering about what he called "baiting a servant of Thlord." He threw Bugs and Elmer on the floor and looked like he might grab Bill Bob and shake him or something . . . when Ma slipped up behind him, jammed the shotgun in his back and hissed, "Gitch yer commie ass outta my house 'fore I blow yer lungs out." Hearing this, Bill Bob stepped quickly aside lest he be spattered with debris.

The Witless leaned over and picked up Bugs and Elmer with such reverence you'd have thought Thlord were the cartoonist, then reeled toward the door making little "hrgch-hrnk" noises in his throat like he was trying to be polite and not blow lunch all over Ma's carpet. Once down the front steps he tried to run a little, but his chest seemed to be bothering him because he stopped at the curb and sort of half sat, half collapsed onto the sidewalk, clutching at his shirt front in a seizure of some kind. When he finally went away he still carried Bugs and Elmer tucked carefully under his arm. I think we changed his life. And I never forgot that phrase, "baiting a servant of Thlord": my only understanding of the word *baiting* forced me to conclude that the poor Witless considered himself some sort of fish hook, and Bill Bob's comic a kind of worm. This conundrum constituted the single connection I ever made between door-to-door doomsayers and my beloved art of angling.

I also find in my notebook numerous references to the god of my great-grandmother, Celestial Darling Carper. I noted that her Deity was "apparently a Christian" and that his son Jesus was, according to her, the author of the Bible. But GG's choicest discoursings (we called her "GG" because both "Greatgrandmother" and "Celestial" were somewhat un-wieldy) emerged during what we called her "pretoddy tirade": whenever she came to visit she would scarcely sit down (and she could barely stand up) before she started scolding Ma for letting me fish on Sundays. "Ca-rolina, you always done it, you still do it, and if'n your boy ends up shanghaied t'hell in the divil's fishnet, *on your head be it!*" etc. etc. And Ma would listen with incredible patience (explaining to Bill Bob and me that she "always made it a rule o' thumb never t'mouth off at a soul in its nineties") until GG started to run down a bit; then she'd say, "I'm sorry I'm so bad, GG. Would you like a nice toddy now?," to which GG invariably replied, "I shorely wouldn't mind a spot, being's it ain't the Sabbath." So Ma would whip up a nasty concoction of lemon, hot water and good Kentucky bourbon which they'd pour from a teapot into china cups and saucers and ruin with heaped spoons of sugar. Then presto! sermons and chastisings would give way to girlish giggling and shrieks of laughter, the pair of them talking family and old times like two tough fingers living on the same old hand. I recall an afternoon when, especially looped and happy, GG leaned over, squeezed Ma's knee and said, "My my my my Carolina, if Jesus could see me here sipping with you this way, He'd roll right over in His grave!"

Eavesdropping on this ritual, I gleaned many pages of amazingly unreliable information; the most relevant are these references to angling:

1. GG's devil is a fisherman whose favorite fishing day is Sunday.
2. GG's devil doesn't use bait or flies. He catches people in a net you can't see and drags them off to Hell, which is like a fish cannery where GG worked, except people are the fish Down There.
3. God doesn't let the devil net folks who go to church on Sunday.
4. God *does* let the devil net folks who fish on Sunday.
5. God doesn't care who nets what or who fishes when, once GG has some toddy.
6. GG says Jesus was a fisherman who fished for men, like the devil.
7. GG says he showed his disciples how to do it, too. I think she says they used tongues.
8. GG says Jesus and the disciples are bait-fishermen with invisible hooks, and heaven and the Golden Mansions and nice music Up There are the bait.
9. GG isn't sure whether the devil or Jesus catches more people, but she expects the devil does.

I concluded the God-notebook experiment by skimming the entire Bible, afterward summarizing its relevance to me thus:

The Bible is good in some places, dull as a seed catalogue in others, and bloody and horrible in others besides that. I liked the fishermen disciples, and Jonah (who H2O calls "the Human Fly") and Jesus and Noah best. Balaam's ass was neat too. I also like how four of the disciples were just plain old commercial fishermen till they started to follow Jesus around on dry land, and how they didn't start to do that until he kept asking them to, and after he died they went right back out fishing again, and probably would have kept fishing if Resurrected Jesus hadn't come for them, and when he came the first thing he did was show them where to catch the hundred and fifty and three fish they caught. And until all that happened those disciples were pretty much like me, except technique-wise. They just fished. And even after they quit fishing for fish they still fished, for men—whatever that means. That's why I like them. They just minded their business, which was fishing, and only started praying and preaching when they were lured into it—and it took *God's son* to lure them! And maybe God told Izaak Walton about Himself, how do I know? But He never told me nothing. And until He or some new son of His comes along and tells me straight out that they want me to be different than how I am, I'm going to be like the disciples, and how me and them are is we're fishermen, plain and simple. I'm going to fish as long as I can as hard as I can, and wherever that takes me is where I'm going, be it Good Place or Bad. Because if God is everything the Bible and the Compleat Angler crack Him up to be, it's Him that's making me want to fish anyhow, and Him who will turn me into a fish or worm or fly or angel or star or saint or sun or frog or taco whenever He decides and what could I do about it? Nothing. Just keep fishing. That's all.

And this was precisely what I proceeded to do.

7

Being "Educated" & "Gittin' Brung Up"

The Common Dragonet . . . indulges in elaborate nuptial displays, yet afterwards abandons the eggs to float about in the sea, showing no concern for the fate of the offspring.

—*J. R. Norman and P. H. Greenwood,*
A History of Fishes

WHEN PEOPLE ARE KIDS their parents teach them all sorts of stuff, some of it true and useful, some of it absurd hogwash (example of former: *don't crap your pants*; example of latter: *Columbus discovered America*). This is why puberty happens. The purpose of puberty is to shoot an innocent and gullible child full of nasty glandular secretions that manifest in the mind as confusion, in the innards as horniness, upon the skin as pimples, and on the tongue as cocksure venomous disbelief in every piece of information, true or false, gleaned from one's parents since infancy. The net result is a few years of familial hell culminating in the child's exodus from the parental nest, sooner or later followed by a peace treaty and the emergence of the postpubescent as an autonomous, free-thinking human being who knows that Columbus only trespassed on an island inhabited by our lost and distant Indian relatives, but who also knows not to crap his pants.

H_2O was of the opinion that a parent's most sacred duty was the education of his children. Ma adhered to a more primitive philosophy, holding that a child will educate itself and that a parent's job is to simply "git 'em brung up." But "Education" as provided by H_2O proved to consist of no end of fine words and no beginning of practical instruction (except in flyfishing), while "Gittin' Brung Up" as overseen by Ma proved to consist of no fine words at all, yet nearly everything Bill Bob and I can do with our bodies and hands is a result of something Ma taught us. While H2O stole a few moments from his illustrious career to address us on such abstractions as Humanitarianism, Progress, Good Manners, The Scientific Method, Evolution, Liberality, and that finest virtue, Ambition, Ma just showed us how to walk, talk, read, write and cuss, taught us basic carpentry, plumbing, gardening, marksmanship, auto repair, meat butchering and curing, canning, cooking, wrestling, boxing, how to fight dirty, and (in my case) bait fishing. When I first perceived this contradiction I got very angry at H2O. I managed to maintain my poker face; what I couldn't maintain was control of my glands. Too much rain in a river makes a flood. Too many secretions in a teenager makes a vandal.

Vandalism, among American teens, is a flourishing low-brow art form: the sleepy teacher, late for school, hurries to his car—it's full of wet shredded newspaper; the hemorrhoidal vice-principal rushes to the WC, squats, screams and bursts from the stall trouserless as a race horse—there's a live possum hissing in the toilet bowl; the truant officer home after a hard day—to an unordered truckload of manure in the middle of his driveway; the toilet-papered trees; the prank calls; the strategic placement of snake or slug in purse or pocket; and around the corner or behind the bush, the inevitable pimply faces, sniggering. . . .

As a fisherman, the popular permutations of vandalism bored me. But I too had glands and zits. Who knows that young Mozart didn't loose an occasional rat in his tutor's clavichord? As for me, I put fish in strange places. Live fish. Trash fish. The trunk of my car—a '55 Buick Special—contained a metal tank. From this tank there poured a prodigious array of squawfish, suckers, chubs, carp, and other pariah species destined to flavor some of the most staid and respectable fountains, swimming pools, bathtubs, punchbowls and other domesticated bodies of water in the greater Portland area. When I found myself wondering what a four-pound buck channel-cat might do to the residents of the Hawaiian-style aquarium owned by the debutante cheerleader who called me "Fishface" when I bumped into her in the hall, or how a colony of live crawdads might spice up that big, bland tossed salad at my Uncle Zeke's wedding reception, or what reaction a school of squawfish might get from a convocation of derelicts waking from a night of DT's beside the Skidmore Fountain, I loaded my trunk, drove off into the night, and found out. I found out other things too:

One day as I was stuffing down a burger at the Dairy Queen near my high school a chicano kid the jocks called "Barf-breath" came in. Barf-breath looked hungry. He also looked dirty, tired, sickly, and soaked with rain. He had fifteen cents. He ordered a lidded styrofoam cup of coffee, poured most of it in the trash, filled it with cream and sugar, and drank it.

Then he loitered near the garnish counter till he thought nobody was watching, filled the cup with hotdog relish, onion and ketchup, popped on the lid and slipped outside. I trailed him down to the football field where he crawled back under the bleachers and, with his dark, dirty, emaciated hands, devoured the contents of the cup.

I couldn't get that kid out of my mind—the belly-flop pushups he did in PE, the naps he took at study hall, his breath and hands. I found out where he lived: the house looked like a shoebox, rotting in the rain. The yard was stomped to hard bare dirt by the bevy of kids who played in it, kids with two names—Spanish American names, and the names they went by at school. Names like Barf-breath. I noticed a huge mud puddle at the head of their driveway, so from time to time through the school-year they found catfish, perch, bluegill and crappie swimming in that puddle; if they cleaned the fish, they found dimes in the gullets. It was stupid, I know. It couldn't really help, I know. I'm not God. I'm just a fisherman.

Our high school was named Hoover, after Herbert, but we called it "J. Edgar" to capture the spirit of the place. Whoever designed the J. Edgar parking lot didn't know much about Oregon: every fall the lot became a lake. One spring I stocked the lake with an eight-pound carp that lived in there for three weeks before someone spotted it feeding by a stalled-out Studebaker. Word got around; kids chased it and fished for it, but it was a strong, smart old fish; somebody called the Portland newspaper—they ran an AP photo of the lot and a write-up in the sports section by one of the senile but tenured editors that paper was renowned for. This editor calls his column "The Fishing Dutchman." In the column he accounted for the carp's presence by noting the existence of a three-season sewer ditch a quarter mile away; he theorized that the fish, one flooded night, half swam, half crawled its way overland to the J. Edgar parking lot. He then, for the tenth time in the history of his column, went on to say that to cook a carp you broil it on a cedar shingle till it turns golden brown, then throw away the carp and eat the shingle.

When the carp was finally caught, I stocked the lot with two more. "The Fishing Dutchman" responded with another column, citing the presence of this pair not only as proof of his overland migration theory, but as an example of

> the unwarranted skepticism of our ecologists and oversensitive nature-wor-
> shippers concerning the ability of fish and game to survive.... There would
> be less hysteria and a healthier economy if some of these people would ...
> get out and fish or hunt and see for themselves just how tough and smart all
> of these "poor threatened creatures" really are in the face of "pollution"
> and "encroachment" by man....

—a strange conclusion, given the photo at the head of his column: both carp dead as dodo birds, skewered on the arrow of a happy teen bow-hunter. The Dutchman then went on to fume about the kind of match-books that have the sandpaper striker on the wrong side.

From then on the J. Edgar parking lot was known as the Karping Lot, and I thought I was pretty clever—till a couple of things happened: first, the publicity inspired the school board to repair the drainage, so the Karping Lot was destroyed; then three third-graders—two girls and a boy—were hospitalized with an almost-fatal fever contracted the night after fishing the worthless ditch mentioned in the Dutchman's column. I felt awful. I could just see the little farts ogling the picture in the paper, then scampering down to the sewer all excited, no idea how to fish, their dads too busy at the office to teach them, so they sat all day by the inches-deep water waiting for some gold-plated buffalo-backed monster to come bulldozing up out of nowhere. And when no carp came they got bored and thirsty. And when they'd waited so long that they forgot the roughage reek of the water, they drank. . . . So one morning during their recovery they awoke to the news that a foot-long catfish had been found alive and well in the hospital's indoor fountain. This catfish had been wearing a collar. Taped to the collar was a pill container. In the container was a note that said all the fishes hoped they'd get well soon. Sure, it was silly; sure it didn't help at all. But when you grow up in those suburbs—when you've seen the streams, woods, farms, and ponds dying all around you but have been lucky enough to escape every weekend or vacation to a wild river full of beautiful game fish, only to return home to the sight of hopeful little kids with impossibly crappy poles plying poisoned creeks where even the crawdads have died—it does something: something way inside me would start to die. I'd want to load up every kid into H2O's Winnebago and take them away to some Angler's Val-halla forever. Or I'd want to shout at H2O and his purist pals to stop bitch-ing and bribing and begging for Flyfishing Only streams, and start screaming for fish-filled drinkable waters for kids whose creeks had been murdered. . . .

But I didn't take those kids anywhere. I didn't tell H2O and his pals anything. I just moped, and fished, and stewed in my glands. So now and then I'd try and ease the pain by putting live fish, trash fish, in strange places.

H2O and I had both been in the room when nine-month-old Bill Bob uttered his first sentence. I happened to be writing in my Fishing Log; H2O was tying flies. Bill Bob had been a close-lipped little scrapper, rarely crying, never babbling, occasionally given to a terse "Cooo," "Glooo," or "Glarglar." But on this particular evening, as he lay on his back fingering the toes of both feet with both hands, he suddenly uttered seven distinct syllables. Though the sentence was swift, I heard it closely and transcribed it in my journal, thus: "Law-wall-law-haw-ill-all-aw."

H2O's response was more dramatic. Hearing the strange syllables he leapt up and cried, "Augustine! Augustine, did you hear? Bill Bob is trying to say 'Dada'!" He picked Bill Bob up and held him to his face. "Come come, little man! You can do it! Say *Dada*. Come on, *Dada, Dada, Dada, Dada*!"

Bill Bob hung in the air like a lump of wet Wonderbread, his mouth as inexorably closed as a bank vault on weekends.

A month later Bill Bob and I were watching TV. H2O slouched in a nearby armchair, reading a letter from Arnold Gingrich. I happened to be eating potato chips, much to the interest of Bill Bob, who waited for a commercial then crawled in my lap, extended a hand and said, "Pay-chup." I said, "Yeah, Bill Bob. Potato chip. That's good." And I handed him one which he proceeded to gum till it turned to a yellow paste which he smeared across his eyes and forehead. At the next commercial he again reached out and said, "Paychup." But this time H2O heard. He jumped out of his chair: "Did you catch that, G—Augustine? That's closer, Bill Bob! Try again! It's *Da-da*. Dadadadadadadada. . . ." Bill Bob looked up just as a blob of spud-goo slithered down his chin. H2O watched it plop onto the carpet, glanced at the paste on Bill Bob's face, said "Be sure and wipe that," and retired to his study to watch the aquarium, whose residents washed themselves unendingly. Bill Bob stared at the door he'd gone through, turned to me and said "Dadadadadadada!" Then he grinned, held out his hand and added, "Paychup." I gave him another.

A few days later Bill Bob crawled into H2O's lap, looked him square in the eye and said, "Mama." H2O's face caved in. Though Bill Bob's vocabulary was already substantial, he didn't know it; he believed "Mama" to be the first English word his son ever said. When I was small I was certain that H2O was the world's greatest father—but I loved to flyfish, and my first word (according to him, anyway) was "Dada." Bill Bob never fished; Bill Bob said "Mama"; even the name "Bill Bob" was a pain in H2O's cerebral ass. So, sad and dumb as it sounds, he let Bill Bob grow up on an unwatched channel. When I saw this going on I began to question what sort of father my father really was to me. I wondered what he'd think of me if I didn't flyfish. I wondered what would happen if I fell in his presence, as I often fell in his absence, into the Carper drawl and dialect. I wondered if, apart from his art and himself, he really loved anything or anyone. Then I wondered the same about myself. And all these wonders made me miserable. I tried to stop wondering. I tried just to fish.

I remember an adventure which shows a lot about the way Ma "got me brung up." Bill Bob wasn't born yet, but he had her stomach bulging. I was ten. It was December. And because Ma forced me to it I was engaged in the despicable business of selling Christmas cards door to door—her equivalent to teaching a coyote pup to forage for rodents. . . . I felt like a damned Witless. But if I sold 48 boxes I could get a little fiberglass canoe, so I dutifully beat the streets. I ended up selling twelve boxes, the last four of them to Ma. The reason Ma bought the last four was what happened on the last day of my sales career.

We lived in a posh Portland suburb, which was H2O's doing; for him, flyfishing was a business, and like most businesses it depended upon a city for its health. But though he picked the home-place, Ma ruled it, and as long as Ma lives, there will be a tinge of juniper, sage, dust and fresh blood in the air of the Orviston home. A few houses down and across the street from us was a space-age domicile, painted black, with lots of skylights and remote-control doors and gadgets, owned by a surgeon. The surgeon also owned a black speedboat, a black Oldsmobile and a black Doberman pinscher. This Doberman was a notorious mauler of children. It lived in the surgeon's backyard, which was surrounded by a cyclone fence, painted black. The creature was usually satisfied to roar and slaver at people passing on the street, but now and again it would get unusually excited by a solitary passing child, hop the five-foot fence as easily as a hurdler might a milkbox, perforate the unfortunate's arms, legs or face, hop back into its backyard, and wag its repulsive little circumsized tail at the surgeon when an irate parent came with a complaint and a medical bill. Of course these wounds were petty compared to the great slashes and slits the surgeon inflicted upon humanity daily, so he would calmly point to the five-foot fence, tell the parent how much it cost him and how unjumpable it was, refer to the great numbers of black Doberman pinschers roaming our suburbs, and send them home smiling and promising to come to him next time they needed a vital organ pruned or transplanted. Meanwhile the Doberman continued to ape its master with its own surgical methods, protected by the surgeon's suavity, the worthless fence, the timidity of suburbanites, and the fact that it had done one thing right throughout its life: it had never crossed paths with Ma Orviston's boy—

until the day I sold my last box of Christmas cards.

I was pedalling home fast, trying to make it in time to watch a "Gadabout Gaddis Show" about steelheading in British Columbia, and it wasn't until I was right in front of the surgeon's black lair that I remembered why I'd never bicycled down that side of the street before .... I peeked toward the backyard: the Doberman hung high above the fence, its insane eyes rivetted to my ten-year-old flesh. When its feet struck earth it let out a Baskerville howl that turned my brains to cottage cheese. Blind and sick with panic, I set my crummy bike pedals whirring like an egg beater, hoping like any terrified young coyote to make it home to the protection of my ferocious mother. I swerved into the street and wove between two cars, hoping they'd mash my pursuer, but at the sight of me they slammed on their brakes and the monster shot between them unscathed. I plowed straight into the curb, caving in my front rim, but clung somehow to the lurching bike, crossing our yard now and screaming "MAAA! MAAA!" Then the Doberman sprang, hit my shoulder and sent me sprawling like a gunned jackrabbit. I curled instinctively into a ball, waiting for the beast to gut me, so drunk with horror I thought I only imagined the explosion in my ears. But when the attack never came I uncurled just enough to see what delayed it. The Doberman lay quivering and jerking on the lawn a few feet away, its eyes rolled back, its tongue lolling out and turning gray, a hole in its chest the size of a cantaloupe. I squinted toward the house. There stood Ma, twelve-gauge still smoking and the wildest green-eyed grin I'd ever seen on her face. She said,

"Got'm."

Anyone would have tended to agree. She sauntered over and warned, "Plug yer ears." I plugged. She discharged the second barrel into the dog's head.

I started to bawl, then threw up.

Ma stood me up, cleaned me off, hugged me, then—seeing my knees were mush—slung me over her shoulder like a big bag of dog chow and headed for the house. Jouncing along in the air I looked back at the scene of the showdown: in the street the cars I'd slipped between had been joined by a dozen others, and twenty or more wall-eyed Burbites stood gaping across H2O's manicured lawn where the Doberman still twitched amid spattered brain, four strewn boxes of gore-flecked Christmas cards twittered jolly Xmases to the wind, and Ma strode easily away, a hundred pounds of guns and sons on her shoulders and in her belly.

While I watched Gadabout catch Canadian steelhead Ma threw the dead Doberman in her pickup, covered it with leaves, drove to the landfill and dumped it, picked up a bike rim at the repair shop, started for home, but was interrupted by a brainstorm: she turned around, drove to the dogpound, searched the kennels and came out with a ratlike mongrel of the Mexican hairless/Chihuahua clan—eight inches tall, colored black. She took this snivelling creature to the poodle parlour, had its tail circumsized and its ears clipped Doberman style. Then she deposited it in the surgeon's backyard.

When the black Oldsmobile hove into sight that night some neighbors who'd witnessed the afternoon's gunplay concealed themselves in upstairs windows overlooking the infamous backyard. According to their reports, the surgeon entered his house bearing two brown bags of groceries, turned on the kitchen light and began to put the groceries away; in one of the bags were two smaller bags, each containing a fifth of Bombay gin; in the other bag was an old newspaper wrapped around what proved to be an enormous bone covered with shreds of raw, bloody meat. The surgeon threw the bone onto the flood-lit back patio but didn't wait to see his dog snatch it, knowing he might be out munching children. The neighbors peered hard at this bone, hoping it came from the butcher's, not from the surgeon's place of employment.

After pouring himself a cocktail which he downed at two gulps, the surgeon poured himself a second which he downed at three gulps, followed closely by a third which he downed at four gulps. One of the neighbors computed that at this rate the surgeon would require seventeen gulps to down his sixteenth cocktail; we needn't argue with her mathematics, but must point out that one-seventeenth of a cocktail is scarcely a sip, let alone a gulp. Another neighbor conjectured that what the poor surgeon needed instead of a slough of cocktails was somebody to keep him company; this neighbor was a single woman in her late thirties who didn't yet realize that Ma had provided for this lack.

During his fourth cocktail the surgeon glanced at the patio to see what his black Doberman thought of the dubious bone. When he perceived the bone wandering across the shadowy lawn toward the shrubs—apparently of its own accord—he threw a suspicious look at the cocktail, took a careful sip, shook his head and stepped outside to investigate. Closer examination revealed the bone's deviant migration to be effected by a Doberman rat—a fantastic yet unmistakable little creature he had not known to exist. Full of wonder (and gin), he dropped to his hands and knees and began crawling toward it. The Doberman rat let him get within arm's length, then began to emit a soft, whirring sound something like a dentist's drill. This was its growl. This was also a signal. It meant that the rat had staked claim to the bone. It meant, "Back off, Jack." But being accustomed to his late Doberman's vastly more blatant

signals, the surgeon extended a foolhardy finger, intending to validate the dear little thing's existence with a few gentle strokes. That finger promptly received four perforations that looked like this: •   •
                                                                          • •

Hearing the surgeon cry out, the neighbors felt uniform fear for the little rat's safety—but the neighbors had forgotten two things: one was the four cocktails, the other was the surgeon's profession. Instead of growing angry he examined the wounds with expertise, awed by their perfect symmetry and the precision with which they'd been inflicted; his full-sized Doberman had certainly been incapable of any such performance. He finished his cocktail, sucked his finger, watched the Doberman rat chew, listened to it whir, and a lasting friendship was formed. He never inquired after the whereabouts of his child-mauler, and when he was forced by a malpractice scandal to change cities some years later, he took the Doberman rat with him.

Ma's account of how she happened to be in the yard with her shotgun at the very moment the Doberman attacked was quite simple: she reasoned that since Gadabout Gaddis's show had started I'd be hurrying, that in my hurry I might forget the Doberman, that hurrying children were its favorite prey, and that the world would be a better place without the Doberman; so she jumped up from the TV, grabbed the shotgun (it's always loaded), heard the tires and me shrieking as she rounded the house, took aim and squeezed the trigger. Given her martial skills, the rest was a foregone conclusion. Yet the fact that she could instantaneously assimilate and act upon these details implies a high degree of intelligence—an intelligence utterly belied by such deeds as her flunking out of high school, her inane piscatorial wrangling with H2O, and her inability to perceive that the wholesale slaughter of fish in the present must have some effect on the angling of the future. I think "native intelligence" is the best name for the type Ma possesses.

A native is a man or creature or plant indigenous to a limited geographical area—a space boundaried and defined by mountains, rivers or coastline (not by latitudes, longitudes or state and county lines), with its own peculiar mixture of weeds, trees, bugs, birds, flowers, streams, hills, rocks and critters (including people), its own nuances of rain, wind and seasonal change. Native intelligence develops through an unspoken or soft-spoken relationship with these interwoven things: it evolves as the native *in*volves himself in his region. A non-native awakes in the morning in a body in a bed in a room in a building on a street in a county in a state in a nation. A native awakes in the center of a little cosmos—or a big one, if his intelligence is vast—and he wears this cosmos like a robe, senses the barely perceptible shiftings, migrations, moods and machinations of its creatures, its growing green things, its earth and sky. Native intelligence is what Huck Finn had rafting the Mississippi, what Thoreau had by his pond, what Kerouac had in Desolation Lookout and lost entirely the instant he caught a whiff of any city. But some have it in cities—like the Artful Dodger, picking his way through a crowd of London pockets; like Mother Teresa in the Calcutta slums. Sissy Hankshaw had it on freeways, Woody Guthrie in crowds of fruit pickers, Gandhi in jails. Almost everybody has a dab of it wherever he or she feels most at home—like H2O in his tweeds at a hall full of fly-dabbling purists. But the high-grade stuff is, I think, found most often where the earth, air, fire and water have been least bamboozled by men and machines. In the scrub desert of Eastern Oregon, or along any river, Ma's got it. She may have it in coyote-raw form, but she's got it for sure: I've seen her stand and watch for an approaching flight of geese long minutes before it came within range of ear or eye; I've seen her sneak up and goose muskrats with the toe of her hipboot; she predicts storms, deaths in the family, weddings, hard winters; she guesses who'll get the next fish when the riverbank is choked with plunkers; she always spots the culprit when somebody farts in a crowd; she's saved me twice from drowning; she once dawdled into the yard just as Bill Bob toddled into a car with some old Sicky who'd offered him candy and a fun ride, and before you could say "Henning-Hale-Orviston" she had Bill Bob in her arms and the candy-man taking a chunk of brick and a smashed back window for a ride instead. And she shucks these feats off, calling them "dumb luck." I think "educated luck" is closer to the mark: I think by the time her native intelligence gets through with it, Ma's luck has a PhD.

I don't think you get native intelligence just by wanting it. But maybe through long intimacy with an intelligent native, or with your native world, you begin to catch it kind of like you catch a cold. It's a cold worth catching.

To complete the picture of Ma the Parent I must point out one flagrant limitation. Ma exhibits two emotions; she calls them "orneriness" and "happiness." She says that H2O exhibits the same two and no more, and she credits Bill Bob with no emotions at all—which is one reason he's the apple of her eye. But me she credits with three: "happiness," "orneriness" and "glumness," and she claims that for every hour I spend in the grip of the first two, I spend ten in the throes of the last. "Glum Gus" she calls me. I might be feeling pensive, preoccupied, mystified, fatigued, introspective, or any of a hundred ways resulting in what seems to me merely an expressionless expression—but to Ma these moods are all one: "Glum *AGIN*? Cheer up, boy! Always limpin' around with a burr in yer ass! *Smile*, dammit!" I don't think this is quite what Thoreau meant when he said, "Simplify." When it comes to noting differences between two elk on a distant ridge, two vultures half a mile overhead, two trout, two fawns, two foals, two fools or any two physical objects, Ma is capable of incredible subtlety. But when it comes to any sort of intellectual or emotional distinction—like recognizing differences between Hindus and Moslems, abject misery and petty sulking, *Hamlet* and *A Comedy of Errors*, philosophical verities and verbal quibblings, Rilke and Rod McKuen, and so on—you may as well talk to a rock as Ma. During puberty this didn't just bother me: it tortured me. I even convinced myself I hated her for it. But eventually I came to see that what I really hated was Ma's shoot-from-the-hip thinking style in *me*. In me it was an ugly, acquired thing. In Ma it was just an old habit. She didn't mind if you told her she was full of beans; she knew she was full of beans; she enjoyed it. When it came to "gittin' us brung up" full of know-how, good food, spunk and savvy, there was never a better ma than Ma. As for matters such as What-Is-The-Meaning-Of-Life?, or how to seek it, or where, or why, she farted out such cornpone, cantankerous opinions that we were forced to plug our noses, bail out of the nest, and start looking for answers ourselves.

8

The "Ideal Schedule"

I believe that as long ago as 1930 a movement was started to make a standard list of gut sizes. . . . One word of caution if you wish to calibrate your own gut. Gut bruises easily and when it is bruised is really worse than broken because it is deceptive, not noticeable and yet weak.

—*Ray Bergman,*
"Dry Fly Fundamentals," Trout

IN THE COMPLEAT ANGLER Izaak Walton writes,

O the gallant fisher's life,
It is the best of any!
'Tis full of pleasure, void of strife,
And 'tis beloved by many.

But the fact is, Walton is only guessing. He was an iron-monger by trade, and spent most of his spare time at church or in scholarly pursuits; little wonder that an infrequent fishing trip would inspire ecstatic doggerel in a book-worming, pew-perching hardware peddler. The once-monthly fisherman adores his rare day on the river, imagining that ten times the trips would yield ten times the pleasure. But I *have* lived the gallant fisher's life, and I learned that *not* fishing is crucial to the enjoyment of fishing: fishing is a good thing, but too much of a good thing is a bad thing. I don't know why the chronic candy-lover so quickly becomes the toothless hypoglycemic, the athletic champ the has-been chump, the dashing Don Juan the diseased lecher, but I know they do. And so does the constant angler become a water-brained, jibbering jerk-worshipper. But at nineteen I believed that Not-Fishing was the Bad, Fishing was the Good, everything else under sun and moon was the Indifferent, and "too much of the Good" was inconceivable. My one nonfisherman friend in the world was Bill Bob, who was only nine, and who moved through a dehydrated universe that only rarely overlapped mine. So even had I desired to explore other modes of existence, who could have showed them to me? H2O? Ma? No, my life was confused enough limited to its single interest with my rasslefrassing folks and the Great Izaak Walton Controversy around. As the G.I.W.C. raved on, all sorts of psychological -isms and -oids were undoubtedly wrought upon me; lacking psychiatric scratch, I resorted to homegrown remedies. The crucial one consisted of this:

Exposed since tadpolehood to my parents' noisy irrationality, I embraced a compensatingly extreme rationality to prevent my soggy cosmos from lapsing into chaos. There was, I came to believe, no limit to what a Scientific Angler might accomplish through the relentless application of his Reason—no fish that couldn't be caught, no fly that couldn't be tied, no secret left undiscovered, no problem however unarithmetical and abstruse that could not, step by logical step, be solved. So it was that I applied my powers of ratiocination to the invention of a device called a "Life-Quality Balancing System," or "L.Q.B.S."

The L.Q.B.S. consisted of a scale (two pans of equal weight hanging in balance), 1,400 #8 medium-shank fishhooks (one for each minute of the day), and a meticulous list dividing my Standard Day into Neutral Minutes (N.M.'s), Unsatisfactory Minutes (U.M.'s), and Satisfactory Minutes (S.M.'s). For every U.M. I put a hook on the left scale-pan, for every S.M. I put one on the right, N.M. hooks I put in a neutral box. I then constructed a series of charts and graphs dealing with ways to turn U.M.'s and N.M.'s into S.M.'s, fully convinced that this simple scientific process would eventually allow me to attain a state called "Unending Satisfaction Actualization," or "U.S.A." I was thrilled with this program, and baffled that I hadn't come up with it sooner. Nothing but unadulterated fishing went into the plus pan; I put Bill Bob–hooks in the neutral box—not because he wasn't satisfactory, but because neutral is the way he prefers to be. Of course Ma- and H2O-hooks were piled high in the junk pan, along with school, yard work, Flyfishing Clubs, pimple-popping, constipation and other nasty imbalances. The historian-type reader with his high tolerance for dull but factual material may be disappointed to learn that, though I still use the hooks, the lists and graphs were reduced to fluffy gray ash when "U.S.A." failed to pan out. One fragment survived, however, and since it exemplifies the quasi-logical gymnastics my polarized brain was wont to perform, I include it:

THE IDEAL 24-HOUR SCHEDULE

1. sleep: 6 hrs.
2. food consumption: 30 min. (between casts or while plunking, if possible)

3. school: 0 hours!
4. bath, stool, etc: 15 min. (unavoidable)
5. housework and miscellaneous chores: 30 min. (yards unnecessary; dust not unhealthy; utilitarian neatness easily accomplished)
6. nonangling conversation: 0 hrs.
7. transportation: 45 min. (live on good fishing river)
8. gear maintenance/fly tying/rod building/log keeping, etc: 1 hr. 30 min.
9. fishing time: 14½ *hrs. per day!*

WAYS TO ACTUALIZE IDEAL SCHEDULE

1. finish school; *no college!*
2. move *alone* to year-round stream (preferably coastal)
3. avoid friendships, anglers not excepted (wastes time with gabbing)
4. experiment with caffeine, nicotine, to eliminate excess sleep
5. do all driving, shopping, gear preparation, research, etc. after dark, saving daylight for fishing only.

Result (allowing for unforeseeable interruptions):
4,000 *actual fishing hrs. per year!!!*

The strangest thing about this lunatic schedule is that it proved prophetic: having started school a year late and flunking away another year, I graduated from J. Edgar High in the spring of 1974 just after my twentieth birthday, my 2.3 G.P.A. earning me the distinction of finishing 205th in a class of 290. Through harrowing experimentation I arrived at a carefully staggered schedule of stimulant injections in the form of teas, coffee, and pipe tobacco, resulting in the desired six hours sleep per night. In the spring, just weeks before graduation, I obtained (unbeknownst to my parents, and by lying about my age) a year's lease on a fisherman's cabin overlooking a beautiful coastal stream; I junked my Buick, bought a '65 Chevy pickup and started smuggling my possessions to the coast whenever Ma and H2O were fishing. Through earnings from my custom-built rods and flies tied to order I had a sizeable savings account and means of support, so when H2O added a couple of G's on graduation day (for college, he presumed, forgetting that the only institution my grades would get me into was the Oregon State Pen), I figured I was set for life. The only problem left was how to spring the news on Ma and H2O.

9

Voiding My Rheum

I am not very fond of living with fellows like that. There's nothing to eat there but stinking fish and watery ale.

—*Piers Plowman*

ON THE DAY AFTER graduation I went bass fishing in the suburbs of Portland. I returned home to find H2O just back from a disastrous expedition to the Madison in Montana: trying for rainbows and browns during the salmon-fly hatch, he was washed out by a freak monsoon after a single morning's fishing. Already home and fixing dinner was a jubilant Ma, who in a three-hour jaunt to Sauvie Island had landed and killed 55 pounds of prime meat in the form of two June hogs; the salmon steak she plopped on H2O's plate weighed three pounds easy—more than every trout caught on his Montana excursion put together. He eyed it like it was a turd.

His mood didn't help my nerves; I was sweating, shaking, couldn't swallow, and the bold parting speech I'd rehearsed a thousand times had vanished, leaving pig Latin in its place. But no one seemed to notice: H2O was too miffed, and though Ma's eyes miss nothing, she had only the single meaningless category to place my wretched appearance in—Glum. Glumness on my face was, to her, about as rare as crumbs on toast. Bill Bob might have noticed if he'd looked across the table, but since the evening meal is invariably a soapbox for Ma and H2O, he comes massively prepared to ignore it. These preparations are worth noting: they consist basically of a ravenous appetite and two transistor radios plugged into both sides of his head not for stereo effect but for listening to two stations at once—usually classical music on top of some athletic extravaganza, preferably baseball; for good measure he leaves the TV on in the next room and sneak-reads a comic book stashed beneath the napkin on his lap. As he enjoys the music, eyeballs the tube, follows the game and scans the comic, he devours his food like a greedy dog. And his taste for bubbling stews of activity carries over into the culinary dimension, for the courses of his meal are never left autonomous, but are enthusiastically swizzled into an indistinguishable swill. This evening he inhaled a mish-mash of cabbage, butter, honey, sour cream, biscuit, pepper, tartar sauce, blackberry preserves, peas, potato, salmon, lemon, and ketchup.

This multi-media-multi-flavor-multi-everything attribute is the one thing that can spur my brother to some semblance of passion. Serene and slow moving as he appears, the older he gets the more he likes doing more things at once. A classic example is bicycling. Bill-Bobbian Bicycling can only be done on Bill Bob's bike: other models are too sparingly equipped to satisfy him. His handlebar alone is studded with a basket carryall, two horns, two bells, a buzzer and a red weather-vane rooster that leans with him into every curve. His spokes are painted different colors and flap playing cards attached with clothespins. A strongbox is mounted on his back fender. Behind his seat is a metal tank with a tube running out the bottom, along the frame to the handlebars, and thence to his mouth; it is kept filled with orange juice, which fuel he sips at a rate commensurate with his acceleration, and he frequently burns two tanks a day, necessitating frequent pit stops in roadside shrubberies. The strongbox might contain any number of things, but you can depend on plenty of spare playing cards, M&M's, comics, tools, and the inevitable transistor radios. Thus when Bill Bob Orviston goes bicycling he performs, as at mealtime, a variety of incongruent actions and emits a conflagration of diseuphonious noise: he becomes a kind of Yankee Concentrate. . . . On a windless day, long before you see him, you discern a rhythmic honking, buzzing and jingling in the air, as at the approach of a flock of mechanical geese; then, still blocks away, the anemic motorcycle card-flap becomes audible; finally you make out a small crew-cut towhead atop a whirring blaring circus vehicle—a tube in his mouth, wires running from each ear, the benign hint of a smile playing upon his lips. And if you turn your head sideways before it passes out of legibility you can read the bumper sticker Ma gave him: SAVE GAS. FART IN A JAR.

The first half of an Orviston meal is wordless—full of gulps, smacks and chewing. But by second-helping time Ma and H2O start getting stoned on a pancreatic high, start talking, talk nothing but fishing, and the talk is never reasonable for long. On the evening I was to void my room, Ma made the opening speech:

"By the way Gus, speakin' of fishin' . . ." (no one had been speaking, let alone of fishing) "tell Hen 'bout that record bass ya pulled outta Blue Lake this morny, how big an' how ya fooled it an' what on an' all. You're gonna love this, Hen, listen up now!"

The tale of this bass was one I wanted to forget, but I reasoned that if I delivered the vital statistics Ma would move on to her own heroics with the June hogs, so I said, "All right. Dad, the fish was seven pounds, eleven ounces—the biggest bass taken from Blue Lake in a decade according to a local authority named Gnat Buckley . . ."

"HA!" Ma blurted. "Ol' bass-brained bean-farmin' Gnat! Hope ya give him a Howdy-do fer me, Gus. Gock-eyed Gnat. Knows more 'bout the seven B's than any man alive."

Right on cue, H2O asked, "And *what* are the *seven B's?*" . . . tip-toeing over the last three syllables like he was barefoot and they were a clovered lawn full of honeybees.

In an obviously rehearsed recital, Ma rattled out, "Beans, Bait, Bass, Beer, Blue Lake, Jim Beam, an' Bullshit!" And right on cue H2O made his face all crooked and revolted-looking—as if Ma's funkicity were some-thing new.

". . . and I caught it on bait," I said, doggedly finishing my ampu-tated sentence.

Ma paid no heed. "Ol' Gnat Buckley! Ain't seen'm in years. Used t'play git-fiddle the way it made ya wanna cry, an' not fer happiness neither. But now tell Hen what kind o' bait, Gussy. That's the best part o' yer story, boy. Yer gettin' just like yer father—always leavin' off the best chunk o' things—leavin' the beer in the icebox, the fish in the river, the pie crust on yer plate, swallerin' yer best hockers, holdin' in yer farts, prob'ly ain't shat fer three weeks neither. . . ."

"ALTHOUGH ADMIRED IN THE DEEP SOUTH," H2O boomed, "where the fetid, yellow-brown lukewarm waters make it im-possible for the noble salmonoids to eke out an existence, the largemouth bass is an outlander, a devouring pestilence, a freakish invader to the salubrious waters of the North and Northwest. . . ." (Ma stopped her yammering and hung on H2O's every word, craving some flagrant slur or insult so they could get down to blasting each other.) "Of indelicate appetite, sluggish disposition, negligible intelligence, paltry stamina, and possessing a head, mouth and stomach of ludicrous bulk in comparison with its stultified body, the largemouth bass is easily America's most overrated, overstocked fish. If it possesses any exceptional quality what-soever, it is its suicidal viciousness: these demented creatures have been known to attack alligators, outboard-motor propellors, and even small yachts; they frequently inhale live ducks, muskrats, water moccasins and swimming house pets, only to die of the effects. Largemouth bass have even attacked children, some of whom have been terribly mu——"

"Now hold up, Hen!" Ma screeched, worried over his building

momentum. "It weren't no child or any kind o' live bait that whupper o' Gus's gulped." H2O paused gullibly. "Come on. Tell us 'bout it, Gusser." I shook my head. "Well, then, I'll tell. Hen, that huge bass a Gus's hit the rottenedest, deadest, putridest ol' Oscar Mayer weiner ya ever smelt!"

"Augustine!" H2O groaned.

But Bill Bob perked up, cogitated, grinned and burst out, "Weiners, Weasels, Waffles, Wagons, Walkie-talkies, Wallets an' Woofers!"

Ma looked confused. "What the hell ya tryin' to say, boy? An' git that ketchup off yer forehead." Bill Bob refilled his maw with mash, shrugged his shoulders, swiped at the ketchup (leaving a trail of tartar sauce), slipped a finger into each shirt-pocket to up the volume on his transistors and dropped his eyes to the comic in his lap. Apparently only I appreciated his extemporaneous "Seven W's."

Ma turned back to H2O. "That fish o' Gus's, Hen, looked like the bass 'at come on the Ark. I'm tellin' ya, it woulda knocked yer eye out! 'Ol' Garbage Gut,' they used t'call'm."

"Call who?" he asked, eyeing Bill Bob's overflowing mouth with apprehension.

"The *bass*, ya nitwit!" Ma snapped. "Walkie-talkie, Call Who? . . . What we got roun' this place is a buncha yahoos."

"Pardon me," H2O objected, "but this Natty Bumpo or whatever his name was might also qualify as a garbage gut, in light of the 'seven B's' you cited."

This sounded reasonable to me, but Ma only wagged her noggin. "Numbskulls, nitwits, yahoos! His name ain't Natty Bumpo. It's *Stevie*." (H2O and I exchanged baffled expressions.) "Gnat Buckley's jus' what we *call*'m. An' Gnat don't *eat* all seven B's. He only eats, let me see, he eats or drinks, uh, three of 'em."

"I see," said H2O, clinically indulgent of these deranged computations. "Let's consider, then: he must eat and drink, um, bass, beans . . ."

"Nonono!" cut in Ma. "Ya started right off on yer left foot. Gnat eats bait (crawdads from the lake, that is), Jim Beam, an' bullshit. Wouldn't touch beans or bass. Seen so many o' both they turn his stomach."

"Of course, how silly of me," smirked H2O. "Of course your friend eats, er, cattle droppings. I can envisage him lifting a finely wrought linen to brush a clot of it from his lips."

Ma smiled a little. "Well, I'm only speculatin', he bein' s'full of it."

"A reasonable speculation," agreed H2O, practically purring at the ululations of his own voice. "It was Brillat-Savarin, was it not, who said, 'Tell me what you eat and I will tell you what you are.'"

"Which brings us back to Gussy's bass," Ma stated.

"Ah. I'd wondered where it was bringing us," said H2O.

"OK. Come on for once now, Gus, an' tell us 'bout ol' Garbage Gut."

I refused.

"Then I'll tell," Ma said, as if she hadn't tried more than once. "That big bass, Hen, was one o' the smartest critters there ever lived . . ."

"What about the *two B's?*" Bill Bob burst out.

"Pull them plugs if ya got somethin t'say, boy."

Bill Bob pulled his radios.

"Now, what ya talkin' 'bout, these two B's?"

"ME!" he cried.

Ma shook her head at H2O. H2O shook his head at Ma. In unison they turned and shook their heads at Bill Bob. Ma said, "Shuttup now, son, an' plug yer ears back in."

Bill Bob turned on, tuned in and dropped out.

"Ever been t'Blue Lake, Hen?"

"If I have," he replied, tossing off his after-supper Scotch, "the brain cells recollecting it have been destroyed by this merciful beverage."

"Well let me picture it to ya, then. All along the north shore is a park, and they built these little concrete peninsulas that poke out in the water with a steel picnic table rivetted down onto each one. . . ."

"A scene to delight the John Muir in us all," H2O remarked. Ma ignored him:

"When the city slickers get out there an' picnic they most of 'em git t'chuckin' food an' trash an' shit in the water the way they oughtta be shot, an' that's where ol' Garbage Gut comes into the picture."

"Ah yes, our friend Mr. Stevie," said H2O, knowing damned well she meant the bass, but hoping she wouldn't know he knew, which she didn't:

"Good Lord, Hen! Ya musta bribed the teacher fer yer first-grade diploma. I mean the *bass*, ya stupe. An' we call'm *Gnat Buckley*, not Stevie. Tell yer nitwit dad about it, Gus, come on!"

I'd harvested a headache from Ma's false starts; if I didn't tell it, the story would go on getting half told forever: I gave in. "All right. OK. I'll tell. But let me finish before you butt in, either of you." Ma nodded. H2O smirked. I started in: "Gnat named this bass Garbage Gut, Dad, because it was a sort of self-appointed janitor for the lake. See, when the picnickers threw their trash off those concrete peninsulas the bass would slip up through the weeds and watch, and as soon as they left he'd glide out of hiding and suck in anything edible and some things that weren't, so there I went like a dumb shit and killed him, and now nothing's gonna keep that stinking lake from filling with trash . . .." I paused, trying to calm myself, but Ma butted in,

"So, Hen, how do ya s'pose our bright boyo fooled that wise ol' fish 'at seen ever' lure an' bait known to basskind an' had a brain like a fishin'-gear catalogue an' not even Gnat Buckley ever got it t'strike? Why Gnat only told Gus 'bout that swimmin' trashcan so he'd go git hisself all flustrated tryin' t'catch'm, an' Bingo! Gus nails'm dead! Ha! I'd give a case a Blitz t'been there an' seen Gnat's face! Come on now an' tell it right, son, how it . . .."

"*Shuttup!*" I shouted. "Shut your mouth and I will! Listen. Both of you!" They shut their mouths, though their eyes gaped. Bill Bob turned down his radios and listened too. "Gettin' dressed this morning I happened to think how fishermen usually wear quiet clothes, and how this fish must be used to watching people who fished for him and people who just sat and ate, so I went to a junk store and got some gaudy, ugly picnicker clothes. When I got to the lake I went and searched the garbage cans and found the rotten weiner still in the package; I left it that way so the plastic would help hide my line. I used a ten-pound test monofilament handline—figuring the bass'd spook at sight of rod or reel—hid a treble-hook in the weiner, stuck the line in my lunchbox, and strolled down the cement peninsulas like your average litterbugging nerd. At the second table I came to, there he was, hovering out in the weeds. . . .

"I sat down and ate some lunch, then started throwing crap in the lake; I threw in half a cupcake, orange peels, some boiled egg and the booby-trapped weiner. Then I walked up toward the cottonwoods sloughing line as I went, hid behind a tree and sat tight, waiting for my line to move. . . . And it did move. I jumped up. The bass saw me coming and shot into hiding but my line went with him. I waited a long time to be sure he swallowed the hook, but I didn't need to: he'd gorged it. Then came the sickening part: when he felt the hook deep inside him he just gave up—didn't fight, didn't try to get away, didn't even dive in the weeds and hide. It was like he couldn't believe what I'd done to him, like I'd betrayed him. It was like he was thinking 'If you can't leave me in peace, if you can't even let me go on cleaning up *your* garbage, then it's time to die!

"I dragged him in like a toy boat on a rope. And I saw what a helpless little thing he was. Less than eight pounds. Hell, people act like eight-pound bass are some kind of monster, chasin' 'em around in PT boats with radar and depth-finders, calling 'em 'hawgs' . . . Christ. Who are the hawgs? Eight pounds is nothing. It's the size a newborn baby is. It's a damned small janitor for a lake the size of that one. So. So I felt like shit.

And I was going to let him go. I held him real careful and still in the water, hoping the hook hadn't torn up his insides. He just lay there staring at me. . . ." I tried to steady my voice, hating to tell how it ended.

"Well. A crowd of people started to gather. All kinds of people—kids, teenagers, grown-ups, a couple fishermen, one real old guy—all of them looking at me like I was some kind of genius and at the fish like it was a sea serpent, or maybe a naked mermaid the way they started lusting after it. I couldn't find my knife so I asked if someone would lend me one, and somebody said 'He wants to cut the line,' and somebody else said 'Shit, he's gonna let it go!' and a bunch of them started arguing and shoving and shouting 'I'll take it! Keep it! Give it to me! I asked for it first! Are you crazy? Fuck you, I'm takin' it! Give it to me, me, me!' and then Gnat Buckley came running over and bulled his way through everybody and started screaming and hollering about what a great fisherman I was and how Einstein himself couldn't have caught that bass, and he grabbed my line and jerked hard up on it, and now the bass started thrashing because the hook was tearing through his insides, and Gnat grabbed a rock in his other hand and started hitting at it and some kids started cheering, but the bass fought like crazy now, and broke Gnat's grip and started swimming away. . . .

"But it was stunned and bleeding, and it didn't swim far, and its compass was busted, too, 'cause it kind of half-circled back toward shore. And one of the kids jumped in and grabbed the line and this time when Gnat got hold of it he jammed his fingers deep into its gills, and this crazy old man lent Gnat his cane and Gnat cussed the fish while he killed it, and everybody shouted and laughed and egged him on, and I was alone by the water, dressed like an asshole picnicker, and when I started crying it made me feel stupid, so I just walked away. . . ."

I ducked to hide my face, feeling water welling in my eyes again.

Ma clucked with mock pity, then turned to H2O: "Gnat phoned up'n'give a report. Listen what they found in Garbage Gut's gut!" She pulled a scrap of paper from her apron and read, "A candy bar, two bullfrog tadpoles, rotten hamburger, two cigarette butts, a crawdad, a plastic tip off a White Owl cigar, cellophane, two minnows, a salamander and a carrot!"

"Loathsome!" H2O blustered. "Disgusting! And people call these creatures 'Game fish'! Augustine did well to rid the lake of it!"

Ma clapped her hands and cackled and H2O raved on, but their racket grew muted as something surged up in my blood like a tide: the room went red; wild energy pulsed through me; to commit some outrage would be such a joy, such a release. Something snapped inside me—some rope or tether—I literally heard it break and fall away. I jumped up, leaned into H2O's face and some calm eye inside me watched with pleasure the flecks of spit that flew with my words into his eyes as I roared, "*Do you know what you are?*"

Aghast, he shook his head.

"*You're a fucking fishing Fascist!* You're a flyrod Nazi, and every fish but trout or salmon and everybody but flyfishermen are niggers and Jews and wetbacks to you! You're a diarrhea-mouthed bigot blind to anybody who doesn't drool at the sound of your suave fucking voice! You've never loved anybody but yourself, and you've had your head jammed up your butthole so long it's gone soft and reeks of it!" I almost danced as I screamed: I was in ecstasy! All my life I'd suppressed this: at last I let it fly like lava from a fissure, like sewer from a suburb, like hot green manure from a cow's ass. H2O's eyes bulged amid the red flannel of his face. He smacked at his lips and gurgled, speechless. Ma zoomed to his rescue—

"Gus Orviston! That ain't no way to talk to yer father! What the hell's got into . . ." But I leapt to her end of the table and shrieked, "*And do you know what you are?* You're a greedy, gloating, murdering shrew! You'd butcher an elf or an angel if you could catch one! You'd blast a hummingbird if you thought there'd be a drop of blood left to lick! You're a grease-sucking weasel and you don't know shit about fishing, or living, either of you! You're both buried in ruts so goddamned deep there's mud in your . . ." With a lightning left, Ma caught me flush on the jaw, but to her amazement and mine, it didn't even faze me: I shouted, "Can't hit a girl!" and before they could move I'd slapped H2O across the face so hard it left a white hand-hieroglyph on the crimson of his cheek. Outraged, they staggered to their feet, but I ran in the living room before they could touch me, grabbed my mounted fish and casting trophies and started smashing them on the floor. My parents stopped in the doorway, afraid to approach. Then my eyes fell upon the Sears Roebuck rod and the mummy of Nijinsky. *There it was: the source of all the bullshit!* Ma screamed "No!" and started for me, but I'd stomped rod and fish into the phony gas fireplace before she even got close. Nijinsky flared up as if soaked in diesel. We all froze where we were, watching him burn like Miss Havisham.

Quick as it had come, my anger departed. I felt fuzzy-headed and weak and wasn't sure what had happened. Bill Bob came and put his arm around me. There was no sound but the crackling flames. Then something strange happened. It started when I glanced at H2O and saw, beneath the print of my hand, quick twitches at the corner of his mouth. Then Ma looked at him, saw the twitches, and her mouth started twitching too. Pockets of preservative in the old fish cadaver caught and shot flames, and something inside it emitted eerie whines like shutters creaking open to free spooks from a haunted house. Then the thing caved in on itself. Nijinsky was no more.

No one moved or spoke till H2O, still twitching, let out an involuntary little snort, like a horse saying hello. Ma followed, not with the usual mulish Carper guffaw, but with a genuine musical little-girl giggle. Then it was all over: she looked at H2O, he looked at her, and they exploded into real, relieved, belly-cramping, face-contorting, uncontrollable laughter—a kind I hadn't heard in that house in all my life. Bill Bob joined in, and when amazement allowed it so did I. We stood there rocking and reeling and holding our stomachs while the tears streamed down our faces, and when the uproar finally died, H2O snickered, pointed at the fireplace, and it started all over again. It was ridiculous. It was bliss. Bill Bob disappeared, then reappeared with fifths of Glenfiddich, Christian Brothers and a fistful of glasses. He frowned at Ma and H2O and demanded, "What'll ya have?"

"What'll you have, Ma?" said H2O. "I'll have that."

"Why then I'll jus' try that unblended swill o' yours, by jorj!"

"I'll have the same," I said.

"Me too!" said Bill Bob, and he poured three ponderous snifters and one tiny pony glass to order. We clinked cups, H2O toasted All-for-one-and-one-for-all, we swigged a swash—and Bill Bob choked and bolted for the refrigerator and a huge orange-juice chaser. Then we just sat around sipping, grinning at Nijinsky's ashes, whowhooing like loons on a lake in summertime, H2O and Ma beaming at me like they'd never been more proud and pleased, like they liked getting called Fascist and Weasel. And I think they did. And they *loved* seeing that accursed mummy annihilated at last. I apologized about fifty times for slapping H2O, but they said it was nothing. Ma said she was glad I had some fire in me. H2O said he'd had it coming. I told him no, no he didn't have anything like that coming, but he kept filling my glass and saying forget-it forget-it, and by jorj, I forgot. Then I told them about my cabin at the coast and about being ready to leave and all, and they weren't even surprised; they said they'd miss me, and that if things didn't work out I could come back any time, and that they'd like to help me move. So when I departed the next morning, Bill Bob was on the seat beside me and Ma's dingy camper and H2O's Rover, both loaded with a hodgepodge of housewarming gifts and provisions, followed down the road. Three-fourths of us had hangovers, but our spirits were soaring.

We got to the cabin and unloaded all the gear, then strolled down along the river—Bill Bob too, since none of us carried fishing poles. H2O expressed approval over a nice flyfishing drift right below my back door, and Ma commented favorably on a deep eddying pothole a little distance downstream. Bill Bob stood off by himself imitating the deep knee bends of a water ouzel on a rock in midriver. When they left they all hugged me, even H2O, and Bill Bob presented me with a huge stack of Lone Ranger comics, solemnly explaining that I, too, was now "lone."

Then they were gone, and I was surprised by my sadness. So much of my reason for coming here had been to escape them—but our last bizarre night seemed to have altered all that. Well, I knew one good cure for sadness: I took up my flyrod and turned to the river, and to a new life devoid of every obstacle between me and my beloved art of angling.

Book Two

The Undoing of a Scientific Angler

. . . when first
I came among these hills . . . like a roe
I bounded o'er the mountains, by the sides
Of the deep rivers, and the lonely streams,
Wherever nature led: more like a man
Flying from something that he dreads, than one
Who sought the thing he loved.
. . . I cannot paint
What then I was. The sounding cataract
Haunted me like a passion.

—William Wordsworth

1

Where I Lived And
What I Lived For

I want to walk around in the woods, fish and drink.
I'm going to be a child about it and I can't help it, I was
born this way and it makes me very happy to fish and drink. . . .
Water will never leave earth and whiskey is good for the brain.
What else am I supposed to do in these last days but fish and drink?

—*Jim Harrison*

SOUTH OF THE COLUMBIA and north of California, scores of wild green rivers come tumbling down out of the evergreen, ever-wet forests of the Coast Range. These rivers are short—twenty to sixty miles, most of them—but they carry a lot of water. They like to run fast through the woods, roaring and raising hell during rainstorms and run-offs, knocking down streamside cedars and alders now and again to show they know who it is dumping trashy leaves and branches in them all the time. But when they get within a few miles of the ocean, they aren't so brash. They get cautious down there, start sidling back and forth digging letters in their valleys—C's, S's, U's, L's, and others from their secret alphabet—and they quit roaring and start mumbling to themselves, making odd sounds like jittery orators clearing their throats before addressing a mighty audience. Or sometimes they say nothing at all but just slip along in sullen silence, as though they thought that if they snuck up on the Pacific softly enough it might not notice them, might not swallow them whole the way it usually does. But when they get to the estuaries they realize they've been kidding themselves: the Ocean is *always* hungry—and no Columbia, no Mississippi, no Orinoco or Ganges can curb its appetite. . . . So they panic: when they taste the first salt tides rising up to greet them they turn back toward their kingdoms in the hills. They don't get far. When the overmastering tides return to the ocean, these once-brash rivers trail along behind like sad little dogs on leashes—past the marshes with their mallards, the mud flats with their clams, the shallow bays with their herons, over the sandbars with their screaming gulls and riptides, away into the oblivion of the sea.

The river I lived on is on the northern half of the Oregon Coast. I promised friends there not to divulge its real name or location, so I'll call it the "Tamanawis." The cabin was situated at the feet of the last forested hills—the final brash rapids just upstream, the first cautious, curving letters just below. There were a few fishing cottages near mine, empty most of the time, and upstream nothing but rain, brush, trees, elk, ravens and coyotes. A quarter mile downstream and across the river was a dairy farm, my nearest permanent neighbor. The farmer had 120 cows to take care of; he had it pretty easy. His wife had the farmer and their six kids to take care of; she had it tough. The farmer, wife, kids, and cows had an orange and purple and black house, two red and green and yellow barns, and a clearing of tree stumps where their yard should have been. (I used to thank Fathern Heaven for the trees that blocked that place from view. Something about those stumps and colors. Made me feel I'd been living on TV, Coca-Cola and doughnuts.) Below the dairy the Tamanawis Valley got more populated—a few farms, sportsmen's shanties, here and there one of those antennaed, yarn-floored boxes poor dumb suburbanites call "contemporary homes"; then a sawmill, a huge poultry farm, and a trailer court defacing the edge of a nice little town at river's mouth. (We'll call it "Fog.") Highway 101 runs through Fog, and the chuckholed asphalted Tamanawis River Road takes off from one of the five intersections in town, running up past my cabin, turning into gravel upstream, then into mud, and dead-ending in a maze of logging and fire roads. The only people who use the River Road are fishermen, loggers, hunters and an occasional mapless tourist trying to get back to the Willamette Valley by a "scenic route." The latter folk drive by my cabin all shiny-autoed and smiley, and two or three hours later come spluttering back with mud and disgruntlement on their cars and faces, hell-bent for 101 and screw the scenery. The Coast Range Maze does that to people.

Across the road from my cabin was a huge clear-cut—hundreds of acres of massive spruce stumps interspersed with tiny Douglas firs—products of what they call "Reforestation," which I guess makes the spindly firs en masse a "Reforest," which makes an individual spindly fir a "Refir," which means you could say that Weyerhauser, who owns the joint, has Refir Madness, since they think that sawing down 200-foot-tall spruces and replacing them with puling 2-foot Refirs is no different from farming beans or corn or alfalfa. They even call the towering spires they wipe from the earth's face forever a "crop"—as if they'd planted the virgin forest! But I'm just a fisherman and may be missing some deeper significance in their strange nomenclature and stranger treatment of primordial trees.

The river side of the road had never been logged. There were a few tremendous spruces, small stands of alder, clumps of hazelnut, tree-sized ferns, fern-sized wildflowers, head-high salal, impenetrable thickets of devil's club, and, surrounding my cabin, a dense grove of cedars—huge, solemn trees with long drooping branches and a sweet smell like solitude itself. The cabin was made of fir logs squared off Scandinavian-style and joined so tightly that I could light a cooking fire on a cold winter's morning, fish all day, and find it still cozy when I came home at dark. There was only one room, but it was big—twenty-two by twenty-eight feet—with the kind of high beamed-and-jointed ceiling that made you want to just sit back and study the way it all fit together. The bedroom was an open loft above the kitchen; the kitchen was the table and chairs, stove, waterheater and sink; the refrigerator was a stone-walled cellar reached through a trap-door in the kitchen floor; the bathroom was a partitioned-off corner so small you had to stand in the shower to take aim at the toilet, and if you bumped the shower walls they boomed like a kettledrum—so I took to voiding my bladder in the devil's club outside.

The cabin was dark, thanks to the grove, but some gloom-oppressed occupant had cut one four-by-four window in the south wall overlooking the river: I set up my fly-tying desk next to it, partly for light, partly so if something swirled as I worked I could be out there with a loaded flyrod in seconds. I didn't miss electricity at all—even preferred the absence of it—but H2O, convinced that I'd go blind tying flies by candlelight, left me three Coleman camp lanterns that blazed about as subtly as search-lights, and Ma, appalled by the lack of racket, bequeathed me a big battery-operated AM/FM radio: both earned an early retirement on a remote shelf. Bill Bob voiced no concern over lack of sound or light, but he seemed to have reservations about my proposed life of sheer solitary angling. Though he said nothing more than that I was "lone," upon his return to Portland he borrowed H2O's electric Remington and com-posed the first of an erratic flow of letters; it began,

> I will write and write you all the time Gus. Becase your not a lone by your slef before. So you wont get to lonesome, will you? Are you reading your Lone Rangers? Remember my friend at school? From Mexico, Pedro? He says in Mexican TONTO calls LONE RANGER kemo sabe because it means HE WHO NOBODY KNOWS. But I know you dont I. And dont forget it! And watch out for TONTO, becase Pedro says in Mexican

TONTO means stupid or crazy so when your are too alone write me a letter and I will come stay with you. But I will keep writing anyway to̸ ke̸p̸ep you compnay. . . .

The most outrageous housewarming gift was from H2O: a fifty-gallon aquarium. He keeps one of these monsters by his fly-tying vise and in his books recommends them to all serious fly-makers. The idea is to catch water bugs and larvae on fishing trips and stick them in your tank to use as living models; you can also test an imitation by tying it to a light leader, lowering it into the aquarium and jerking it around among its live prototypes: if it is attacked or raped you may conclude it a sufficiently deceptive fly. I've always thought this more than a little extreme. Trout are not entomologists; they don't care what your fly's Latin name is. I've suckered summer steelhead, brookies and bluebacks on a fly I call a "Bermuda Shorts"—an abstract imitation of a fat tourist on a golf course in a Caribbean travel brochure; my "Headless Hunchback" may one day be famous as a trout killer, and it imitates a thing that attacked me in a nightmare brought on by devouring half a box of Bill Bob's Sugar Pops just before bed. H2O and his pals rigidly adhere to the Imitation of Natural Food School of Fly Tying, but the truth is, trout are like coyotes, goats and people: they nibble, chew and bite for all sorts of reasons; eating is only the most common one. Sometimes Northwest lakes and streams are so rich in feed that their bloated denizens would sooner bite an Alka Seltzer than a natural imitation; sometimes a bored old whopper, like any decadent, affluent creature, prefers gaudy titillation to more of the mundane stonefly-mayfly-caddisfly crap. (Remember Walton's "piece of cloth" and "dead mouse"?) Piscine ennui can arouse a taste for the bizarre that will skunk a Purist who insists on floating sacrosanct "name patterns" over his congregation all day. Bourgeois trout are like bourgeois people: after a week of three dull meals a day a man will empty his wallet and risk his life bombing belly and brain with rich restaurant food and eight or ten cocktails. The corresponding mood in trout is where the Bermuda Shorts comes in handy: of course it doesn't look like food; neither does a Double Margarita; and trout don't have to drive home afterward.

For a time I stashed the tank with the lanterns and radio—but soon, as Bill Bob predicted, the unaccustomed solitude began giving me fits of melancholy. So I set up the aquarium by the south window, rigged hoses to keep a fresh flow of spring water moving through, filled it with gravel, algae, snails, sculpins, crawdads, periwinkles, the works; then I took an ultralight six-foot flyrod, tied on a barbless #28 Midge and went fishing for the smallest fish I could catch. When I had fourteen or fifteen in a bucket I selected two silver salmon, two cutthroat trout and two steelhead for my tank. I ended up watching this liquid zoo so much I gave the inmates names and soon had a favorite—Alfred the Great—a steelhead smolt of about three inches.

The little salmon and trout were straightforward fish, behaving the hungry, swimmy, nervous way one would expect. But Alfred and the other steelhead, Sigrid the Small, were very unusual minnows. Sigrid was less than two inches long—the smallest fish I ever caught on a fly—and she was frail and quiet and beautiful. All she ever did was hover on the side of the tank overlooking the Tamanawis, watching the river slide by below: I don't know if she really saw it or knew it for what it was, but her eyes were unwaveringly aimed toward the wild waters of her home—and in time the sight of her made my heart sink. She was so small, yet so full of longing. Somehow that two-inch creature made me ashamed, or maybe envious—for I, a seventy-two-inch creature, had no such discernible longing, and knew of no true home to long for. But I wouldn't release her. Not yet. She was so pretty, and she was safe in the tank, so I kept her there against her tiny, unwavering will.

As for Alfred, I've never encountered a more gregarious, high-spirited creature—ouzels, otters and chickadees included—if you take into account that he'd only a finger-length, limbless body to express his exuberance. One might think friendship with a steelhead smolt awfully dull potatoes—maybe the sort of neurotic, one-sided thing some lonely old ladies have with their poodle-dogs. But my friendship with Alfred wasn't that kind of thing at all. Ours was a relationship founded on the truth that a fish just doesn't give a damn what you say to it and will never say anything back. It lives in the water; it has no voice box; it is encumbered with neither a large vocabulary nor a large brain, and should you shout at it loudly enough to vibrate its water, it is unlikely to take such utterance as a sign of friendship. Neither is it the kind of pet you can ride, take on walks, set on your lap, dress in a sweater, take pheasant hunting or cuddle; it is not likely to lick your face, and if it did there are teeth in its tongue. But its compensatory virtues are overwhelming: it keeps itself exceedingly clean; it won't jump up on your Sunday suit; it won't shed, won't bark you into an asylum, won't climb onto your roof and scream bloody murder all night as it engages parades of furry gentlemen in the carnal act; it will never roll in dead-salmon rot, never scratch you, never bite the neighbor's toddler in the face; nor will it puke on your bedspread, piss in your shoes or hump the leg of an important dinner guest. A fish maintains its silent, orderly existence within the confines of its tank. All you need to do to befriend it is discover some form of interaction that will create intimacy. Obviously, the key is food.

In state hatcheries the steelhead smolts are kept in huge concrete pools and fed pellets by the bucketful. This is a necessity born of their great numbers, but it is also a great aesthetic waste—for a steelhead smolt is an artist as it feeds. Anybody who enjoys basketball knows that there are dull ways and awesome ways of putting the ball through the hoop. Alfred the Great knew that the same was true for ways of putting fish pellets in his gullet. I won't go so far as to call him the Doctor J of pellet swallowing, but it should be remembered that Doctor J has a hundred or so moveable joints to work with, and that Alfred's "hands" are his mouth: fasten Doctor J's hands to his mouth and how many points will he score in a season?

The surface of the aquarium was nine square feet. If a pellet hit in any of eight of them, Alfred beat the trout and salmon to it every time; only in Sigrid's little corner would he concede—and perhaps this was chivalry. He could see food approaching while it was still in the air; he learned to react to hand-fakes I'd make high above the surface; sometimes he'd take a floating pellet and his upward momentum would carry him six inches into the air; sometimes he'd charge one that floated next to the glass, tucking at the last second like an Olympic swimmer on a turn, thumping the wall with his tail and vanishing in a blur to reappear motionless in the center of the tank; sometimes he faked the other fish so fast so often they began gliding around in baffled little circles; sometimes he jived them so bad they swam smack into the glass. Watching Alfred eat was a joy. He had the kind of moves that cried out for instant replays.

It took some time to get settled in the cabin: a day to stash gear, a day to build a fish-smoker, a day to set up and stock the aquarium, a day to clean, and salt in supplies, two days to cut three cords of wood. But on June ninth I hung the Ideal Schedule on the wall by my bed and began to live it: I proceeded to fish all day, every day, first light to last. All my life I'd longed for such a marathon—

and I haven't one happy memory of it. All I recall is stream after stream, fish after fish, cast after cast, and nothing in my head but the low cunning required to hoodwink my mindless quarry. Each night my Log entries read like tax tables or grocery receipts, describing not a dream come true, but a drudgery of double shifts on a creekside assembly line.

After two weeks of "ideal" six-hour nights and sixteen-hour days I got an incurable case of insomnia. It hardly mattered: sleeping I dreamt of fishing and waking I fished till there was one, undivided, sleeplike state. There was fishing. There was nothing else. A Kiluhiturmiut Eskimo song tells of a man like me—

> Glorious was life when standing at my fishing hole
> on the ice. But did standing at my fishing hole ever
> bring me joy? No!
> Ever was I so anxious for my little fishhook
> if it should not get a bite, Ayi, yai ya. . . .

Like the Eskimo, my last thought before going fishing was "Won't it be glorious!" And like the Eskimo I then stood by the water, a needy, nervous wretch too anxious to wonder how "glory" could be so dismal. Ayi, yai ya!

In mid-afternoon on the Fourth of July my family showed up. I invited them in and made a lunch, but Bill Bob, knowing the inevitable topic about to arise, took his food, radios and crayons and disappeared in the cedars. H2O, Ma and I settled over coffees, and though H2O included the phrase "How are you" in his greeting, we all knew he meant "How's the Fishing?" So I started to tell them—and discovered that a month of solitude had raised havoc with my ability to speak: I muttered and stuttered, repeating short, meaningless phrases, my trains of thought uncoupling in mid-sentence. I was so startled by my performance that I lapsed into grunts and handed over my Log to serve as a surrogate voice. The Log so fascinated them that they seemed not to notice my handicap, and soon they were happily mucking around in a typically tedious Izaak Walton Controversy.

They left after supper, but Bill Bob stayed on. He turned in early, and once he started snoring (like a logger) I lit a lamp and made the following entry in my Log:

> July 4; 9:30 p.m.—after one month of Id. Sched. have caught roughly 1400 fish, 90% native cutthroat, largest 16 inches, average 7 inches, 60% on flies, 40% on bait (mustn't tell Ma this). have read 8 fishing books, 2 manuals, built one 8′ flyrod, tied 29 flies. was unaware till today of certain unexpected results, however: one, find it difficult to speak; another, find it difficult to think; another, am constantly hearing and seeing water, for instance NOW, I shut my eyes—water. I plug my ears—water. don't think I quite like this. Bill Bob brought up some nonangling topics today; could think of no reply or comment; couldn't respond at all; hoped he wouldn't notice; he noticed; don't think he quite liked it.
> —12:30 a.m.—another Id. Sched. result: insomnia. positive I don't like *this!* and tonight Bill Bob asked Are you happy, Gus? and I didn't know, didn't think so, couldn't say. not sure of relationship between fishing and happi-

ness; not sure of much of anything; must consider further. . . .

—3 a.m.—still can't sleep. still seeing and hearing water, even with pillows on head. beginning to feel illogical distress. read three Lone Ranger comics, tried to relax, got drowsy over and over but jerked awake—keep thinking I have a bite. Bill Bob woke and saw me do it, asked What's the matter? said nothing; said felt like reading, said flea bit me. perhaps should experiment with alcoholic beverages. . . .

I faded just as it grew light. I didn't wake up till 10:30—five hours later than I'd slept since coming to the Tamanawis. I got dressed and went to find Bill Bob.

He was sitting on a stump by the woodpile behind the cabin, a bag of peanuts in his lap, a transistor plug in either ear, staring at the cordwood like it was a television. I thought he was getting pretty spacy till I saw heads poking out of his TV screen: chipmunks. Funny I hadn't noticed them before. I sat in the sun and watched: Bill Bob was putting nuts on his knee and the munks were taking turns climbing his leg and grabbing them. I supposed I should consider the scene cute, but they were nothing like fish. I had a headache. I was bored. Bill Bob finally spotted me, took one look at my face and threw me his canteen. Orange juice. I drained it dry—and was suddenly able to see that there is no reason on earth why chipmunks should be like fish, which brilliant insight enabled me to see that what they were like was pudgy people in gaudy furs at a close-out sale, using their cheeks for shopping bags. One particularly saucy shopper hopped out of the TV, climbed Bill Bob's leg, grabbed the peanut, stuffed it in his face, sat down on his haunches and demanded another; Bill Bob complied—and it wanted another; so he kept handing it nuts and it kept stuffing its cheeks till it looked like its head would explode; with three unshelled nuts in each half of its face it even satisfied my obsession by beginning to resemble a fish: a blowfish. Somehow it grabbed a seventh nut and shelled, chewed and swallowed it. Then it vanished. . . . Its cohorts in the TV were first stunned, then frantic. Five at once shot up Bill Bob's leg, clawing him, raising hell, lambasting my headache—but my brother just smiled benignly, dishing out his prasad till the bag was empty, the music of two worlds swirling through his head.

After breakfast we set out for Tamanawis Mountain—a five-hundred-foot ridge reached by crossing Coke and Doughnut Dairy. We wore backpacks. Mine had the lunch. Bill Bob's had dud firecrackers, bent silverware, a cheesecloth butterfly net, a magnet, a compass ruined by the magnet, a watch ruined by the magnet, rusty pliers stuck to the magnet, orange juice, drawing pad, crayons and the two radios. I felt all disoriented as we started out: it was weird to walk slowly after a month of maniacal barging from hole to hole and creek to creek, and my right hand felt naked without Rodney (thus had I dubbed my favorite flyrod); but mostly I felt odd because I walked beside a person who loved me yet took absolutely no interest in anything I'd done for a month, and would be certain to ignore me should I mention any of it. It made me feel as if my recent past and my likely future were illusory—because for Bill Bob they didn't exist. I began to get used to the present, though. The further we walked the quieter the hallucinatory water got, the better I could talk, the less my head ached; I even began to understand Bill Bob—who jumps from topic to topic like a squirrel from branch to branch. . . . At first we were Edmund Hilary climbing Everest, then we were Mountainy Men climbing up to our secret cave-house; then he said that if *he* was a Mountainy Man he'd live year-round in his Giant-Round-Glass-Hut and wear a pair of ancient glasses that let him see every direction at once; then he said there used to be a race of peoples who had a ring around their heads like the ring around Saturn, only this ring was their eyeball, only it wasn't a ball because it was a ring. I interrupted to point out that a Giant-Round-Glass was hardly a hut either, but he ignored me and said that the ring-eyed peoples could see every direction at once, including inside out, because the pupils of their eyes weren't just little holes in the iris like *our* pupils: they were black bands running all the way around the rings. I said they must have been powerfully intelligent folks with such efficient vision, but he said nope, they weren't, they were idiotic as could be, because the trouble with the ring-eyed peoples was that their ring-eyes weren't connected to their heads, so even though they could see everything they didn't know it because there wasn't a single connecting nerve to clue their brains in. I asked how a ring-eye stayed in place if nothing held it there and he said it just spun round and round like a hula-hoop held up by its own speed. He said the ring-eyed peoples eventually grew so stupid that God had to change them by connecting their ring-eyes to their heads, but then they were always getting poked in the eye because their eyes were so big, and sometimes, since there was nothing but eye material connecting the top halfs of their skulls to the bottom halfs, the whole tops of their heads would get jarred off and smashed like a lid falling off a teapot. I said it was hard to imagine what a ring-eyed person looked like. He said the Space Needle in Seattle was modeled after them. Then he said that when he was a baby he didn't know he had eyes or a head and believed he was whatever he was looking at. He said he could remember looking at me and thinking he *was* me, and he couldn't figure out how come I could walk out of the room when he didn't want me to, since he was me; he remembered wondering what good it was to be a thing at all if the thing you were could just wander off some place where you couldn't even see it or know what it was up to. He said he finally figured out he wasn't the thing he was looking at on the day H2O hung a fish mobile over his crib. He said that fish mobile terrified him. It made him think he was underwater. I told him I could remember how he'd cried and cried when we hung the mobile there, and kept on crying till we took it down, which is true. He said he remembered, too, and the reason it scared him was because once he lived in a big city that got covered with water and everybody drowned. I asked him if he'd heard of Atlantis. He said yes, the Yankees burned it down during the Civil War. And so we walked and talked on up Tamanawis Mountain.

As we walked I noticed some things about the way I was feeling: for the first time in a long time the peacefulness and greenness of things was pleasing, and the lack of a rushing stream was a balm to my nerves, ears and eyes. I saw and heard and felt all sorts of things I'd missed all summer thanks to the Ayi-yai-ya's—the paintbrush and fireweed, raven calls and cricketsong, light on meadows and wind in trees. But most of all I noticed this: for the first time since leaving home I felt sort of happy.

We reached the top at noon. There was a wonderful view of the river valley up there, and a soft wind to cool us down. I sat on a log, ate an orange and soaked up the view. Bill Bob got quiet and businesslike with his crayons and pad, drawing maps of the four directions; when he finished them he taped them together end-to-end and said that now we at least had a picture of the sort of view that ring-eyed peoples used to get. The maps weren't much for detail, but they were accurate in depicting the lay of the land. I particularly liked the one facing south since it had my cabin and the river in it; nothing was scale-size, but every bend of the Tamanawis was right where it should be.

When we got back home I obeyed an urge to take down the Ideal Schedule and put Bill Bob's four maps in its place. He seemed inordinately pleased—so pleased that I got the feeling he didn't think much of my Schedule. He even said he liked the Tamanawis River, especially the way it was shaped. This was something he'd never said about any stream, puddle or glass of water before. I asked him why. He laughed and said that that was exactly what the river was asking me. I'd no idea what he was talking about.

We spent the evening at the seashore, watching waves and sunset, talking, roasting weenies, taking a walk after dark to watch the wet sand phosphoresce. That night I slept soundly for the first time in weeks. I took Bill Bob to the bus depot in Fog early in the morning. When the bus drove away I felt all hollow inside; there was a lump in my throat, and the idea of going fishing was repugnant. Before driving home I stopped by the local grocery and, hiding my age behind my beard, scored a couple half-gallon jugs of tawny port. If insomnia should revisit, I vowed to at least bung up my wakefulness.

A Digression

excerpted from the monograph *What is Water?*
by Titus Irving Gerrard

> Human beings were invented by water as a device for transporting itself from one place to another.
>
> —*Tom Robbins*

Life and water are inseparable: 70 to 95 percent of all fresh fruits and vegetables are composed of water, 70 percent of all human beings, and the chemical reactions that sustain the lives of every organism take place in aqueous solution, most involving water as a reactant—photosynthesis constituting but a single example. Eighty percent of the earth's surface is covered with water in solid, liquid and gaseous forms, its total amount being estimated as 1.33×10^{24} kg—or 5 percent of the planet's total mass.

Water is a thing so familiar to us all that we fail to appreciate its remarkable properties. To a massive extent it is the eccentricities of water that make the earth inhabitable. On the moon, temperatures vary from 120 degrees Centigrade at noon to negative 150 degrees at midnight, but on earth, water's high specific heat prevents such drastic deviations of surface temperature, because oceans and lakes absorb solar heat throughout the day and release it into the atmosphere at night. Water's boiling point is some 260 degrees higher than that of methane, though both compounds sport comparable molecular weights; and water's vaporization point is, on a cal/g basis, greater than that of any other liquid: as a result, one-third of the solar energy that strikes the globe is dissipated by vaporizing water from oceans, lakes and ice fields, thereby keeping the earth's temperature relatively constant. The same mechanism keeps the temperature of the bodies of humans, plants and animals within astoundingly narrow limits—because much of the heat generated by metabolism is consumed by the vaporization of water through the pores of skin or leaf, or by panting. If water had the same vaporization point as n-heptane (another molecularly analogous liquid), we would have to consume seven times as much of it to keep from stewing in our juices on a summer's day.

Another mystery: water is one of the few substances whose solid form, ice, is *less* dense than its liquid. If it were otherwise, ice would form on the bottoms of lakes in winter, would melt incompletely in summer, and our planet would soon enter a permanent—and fatal—ice age. Nor would a bourbon on the rocks tinkle so pleasingly.

Even more bizarre is the volumetric behavior of liquid water, which *contracts* when heated above 0 degrees Centigrade, reaching a maximum density at 4 degrees! No structural analyst, no physicist, no scientist of any kind has ever been able to account for this conundrum. It makes no sense. It thumbs a runny nose at every known chemical law. And to those scientists who pride themselves on their gray matter it is an unpleasant reminder that the brain is 92 percent H_2O, and that therefore a frozen scientist's brain is less dense than the same scientist's brain at 4 degrees Centigrade!

Water consists of two units of hydrogen per single unit of oxygen, glued together by what is called a "hydrogen bond." This much we know. Yet no scientist, ancient or modern, has ever managed a quantitative description of the thermodynamics of water, nor indeed of any liquid. Not that they haven't tried. Water is to the structural analyst what Waterloo was to Bonaparte. For many years analytically bent souls believed that liquid water consisted of H_2O molecules with a geometry identical to that of a small portion of ice crystal. But in time more astute scientists pointed out that if water consisted of "microcrystals" of ice and vapor, how was it possible that pure water could be cooled to minus 40 degrees Centigrade without freezing? Stubborn proponents of the ice-crystal theory took to calling water's structure merely "ice-crystallish" or "icelike," but among those scientists unsatisfied with this semantic sophistry a second school of thought arose:

This second, most recent and most widely accepted account of water's "structure" involves what is called a "Flickering Cluster." Poetically dubbed doodads, "flickering clusters" are said to be "open clusters of H_2O molecules" united by hydrogen bonds and "swimming in a sea of relatively 'free' water molecules," like fish. These clusters come in an infinity of shapes and sizes, and each cluster is constantly disintegrating, metamorphosing, forming new alliances, falling to pieces—hence "flickering." Indeed, they "flicker" so fast that the analysts say their average life span is *ten to the minus tenth of a second!*

This is hardly enlightening. If the next-door neighbor should solemnly announce to us that once an hour on the hour he is, for one one-billionth of a second, transformed into a kumquat, we shall—with our eyeballs and wristwatches—be unable to refute him. Nevertheless it would be reasonable, if not scientific, to tell him that what goes on during ten to the minus tenth of a second is of little moment. We must say the same to our structural analysts—whose flickering clusters are in fact an expensive, necromantic way of saying what man has always known: *water has no structure.* Tens of thousands of years ago our wise forefathers shared myths wherein water was said to be the primal, chaotic substance from which all forms proceed. It is clear that our forefathers have not been refuted, clarified or improved upon.

end of digression

2

Water on the Brain

After the doctor's departure Koznyshev expressed the wish to go to
the river with his fishing rod. He was fond of angling and was apparently proud of being fond of such a stupid occupation.

—*Tolstoy*, Anna Karenina

THE TOO-BRIEF COMPANY of Bill Bob helped me see beyond doubt that I
was disintegrating as a result of constant fishing, yet I didn't plan to do
anything about it: falling apart as I fished was depressing, but *ceasing to
fish*—that was terrifying! The rings of Saturn were no more alien to me
than those portions of earth that did not border trout streams. So I
continued my Ideal Schedule and was soon exhibiting more bizarre
symptoms: besides the insomnia, tangled tongue and water hallucinations, I began to hide or even flee when I encountered other fishermen; to
avoid human contact I began stockpiling groceries and bought a fifty-
gallon gas drum; soon my communications with fellow humanoids consisted of an occasional Thank you, Hi, or Fill-er-up, and that was it. Like
many an addled hermit, I started yacking a blue streak, but not to myself.
Oh no. I talked to my flyrod, Rodney. As expected, we became almost
preternaturally skillful at extracting fish from coastal streams ("we" being
Rodney and me). We caught cutthroat in staggering numbers, often over
a hundred a day. I kept only enough to eat and my appetite shrank with
my ability to sleep; still, I ate trout twice a day and grew no more tired of
it than an anteater grows tired of ants, he with his long snout and sticky
tongue, me with my Rodney and flies.

By mid-July I was no longer in pain. I was totally bamboozled; I was
chicaned; I was necromanced; I was stuffed and nonsensed. I no longer
saw anything wrong with my life as it was. Rodney fished because I fished
and I fished because Rodney fished. We had an understanding: we were
two pieces of fishing gear—smash us, lose us, wear us out, fishing gear will
never question your judgment.

In late July, after a week of unseasonable rain, Rod and me undertook an inspection of the Tamanawis starting at the mouth, watching for signs of summer steelhead or sea-run cutthroat. There were steelhead in other coastal rivers, but we only fished the Tamanawis now; saved gas and time, plus we figured it was ours. I was really slavering for a blueback or steelhead; I'd had it with doinky trout; I told Rodney, "You'n'me catch big fish, everything'll be hunky-dory"—and in my condition this Cro-Magnon notion seemed a sage piece of self-analysis. A mile above tidewater we pulled over to scan a big eddy called "The Shakespeare Hole"—named not after William but after the rod and reel of one Crawdad Benson, a ramshackle old geezer of seventy-some who lived in a ramshackle shack overhanging the pool, and who had fished it almost daily for decades with a ramshackle rod and reel manufactured in the Dvapara Yuga by the Shakespeare Tackle Company. Despite his gear Crawdad nabbed a good many fish, some of them literally off his back porch—living proof of Walton's adage that it's the fiddler and not the fiddlestick that makes the music. The Shakespeare Hole was vacant this morning, the hot blue smoke pouring out Crawdad's stovepipe proving him busy with breakfast—no doubt a batch of the red-shelled crawdads from which he derives nourishment and name. Glancing toward the tail of the hole I was surprised to see a good fish roll. (It's funny how, fishing the anadromous runs, you think there isn't a fish in the river till you see one, then you think there's a fish behind every rock; no matter what, you're wrong.) Leaving my truck door open so Crawdad wouldn't hear me, I snuck down for a cast. The fish rolled again. Hurriedly I stripped line, leaving on the weighted Muddler I'd used the night before, explaining to Rodney that it's better to get any fly out there quick than to waste time calculating the "proper pattern" as H2O would have done (I'd been drilling my superiority to H2O into Rodney for days). I made a roll-cast to stay clear of the brush behind and got the Muddler drifting nicely toward where the fish had shown. When the floating line stopped floating I struck . . . and a big blueback went flying across the rivertop in a noble but whimsical attempt to escape its plight by transforming itself into a bird: it entered the air over a dozen times, but each flight was shorter, the longed-for wings remained fins, and at last I hauled it ashore— a beautiful 3½-pound cutthroat, the sea lice still clinging to its sides.

Soon as I had it in my clutches I found myself pitying it; its leaps were so graceful, its drydocked thrashing so dismal. But a gurgling curiosity centered in my belly wanted to compare its flesh to the flesh of the natives I'd been eating. Despising myself, disobeying myself, I grabbed driftwood and killed it.

I was readying for a second cast when Crawdad's door creaked open. He couldn't see me but he knew my pickup. "You! Gus Orviston! You keep outta them traps!" (Ma liked to raid his crawdad traps, and Crawdad figured theft was hereditary.) "Speak up boy! Gus!" As he shuffled down the bank I circled round the brush, jumped in my truck and gunned down the road, cackling like a redneck in a hot-car movie.

I cleaned the cutthroat in the kitchen sink, discussing fishing plans with Rodney. We decided to take Sardine (my aluminum canoe) down to the estuary to try for more sea-runs on the incoming tide. Remembering I hadn't fed Alfred and company, I threw the blueback's guts in the garbage, grabbed a handful of pellets and tossed them in the tank—but soon as they hit the water it began to churn: the fish went berserk, even the bullheads, but especially Alfred who was everywhere at once, lashing down into the gravel, flying up into the lid, slamming the sides of the tank with his tiny body. I was baffled till I noticed my hands—the big trout's blood! I'd thrown in food laced with the gore of a deadly enemy. I grabbed a strainer and tried to net the pellets, but the fish didn't slow. Alfred the Great kept ramming the walls, and the soft, desperate thuds panicked me: he was destroying himself. Suddenly he was in the air and I lunged, trying to catch him, but he bounced off my hands, hit the floor nose-first and slithered out of my grip again and again. When I finally got him back in the water he slid to the bottom and lay there, a little string of blood hanging from his nose. I netted out the rest of the pellets, increased the flow of water to purge the tank of the sea-run's blood, and the other fish calmed down and recovered; but Alfred stayed keeled over on one side, finning the aimless way old spawners do once they've gone rotten and blind. Then he began to turn belly up. I tried to massage his sides to keep his gills working, but he was so small he kept sliding from my fingers; he'd turned a dull green hue, with gray blotches where his protective coating had been scraped off; his mouth slowly opened and closed, as if he were trying to speak. I kept rubbing. After maybe fifteen minutes he wriggled weakly from my hands and balanced upright in the weeds; I caught the crawdads and threw them in the sink so they couldn't claw him. The other fish were all right; Sigrid had resumed her sorrowful pose, staring down at the river; but Alfred lay stunned on the bottom, the thread of blood still hanging from his nostril, and watching his uncomprehending eyes, remembering the same look in the eyes of the dying janitor-bass, tears came threading down my cheeks. I was broken up . . . at first. Then I was disgusted. Hadn't I killed thousands of fish without a qualm? Why was I wasting time watching this one? He would live or he'd die, and if he died there were millions like him thriving in every stream on the coast. I left him to his fate, gathered my fishing gear, fried up the blueback, choked it down without tasting it, loaded Sardine in the truck and headed down to the estuary.

I fished until 10 P.M., trolling spinners and bait, drifting nymphs and streamers, throwing wet flies and dry, plunking ghost shrimp and crawdad tails; I didn't see another blueback; all I caught were smolts, most of them steelhead, and every one reminded me of Alfred, making me angrier at my mushy-heartedness and all the more determined to stay where I was. I got home exhausted at 11:30. I unloaded the canoe and gear, lit lights and a fire, cooked and ate dinner, loaded a pipe. Only then did I go to the aquarium. . . .

Alfred the Great was on his side on top of the water, fins and gills barely moving. All that time he'd fought to stay upright and breathe—such a tiny creature to cling so long to its spark of life. I turned him over and started massaging, but whenever I let go he would glide down again. I knew that had I stayed with him he would have recovered, but now he was too feeble. He lived for another hour, then his gills stopped moving. I started blubbering, cursing myself at the same time: "You jerk! Snivelling over one damned minnow . . . like a ferret deciding to cry over a dead rat." But my poor little Alfred, my only animate companion, the only fish who'd ever trusted me, who'd swum alongside my finger, who'd nibbled the crawdad's feelers but darted away before he got pinched, who'd cheered me more than Scotsmen with his dancing. Then Alfred, Garbage-Gut, all the fish I'd ever killed began to haunt me, and they expanded inside me till all the things that suffered—every bleeding and dying creature in the world, every blighted plant and miserable man—every bit of it haunted me. How sad and ludicrous the runniness of our noses in the face of sorrow; how sad the shabby meanness of our meaningless fishy lives. I put Alfred in a bottle of water, just in case, then held him by a lamp: his pitiful little nose was mashed down into his lower jaw; he was beat-up, dulled, and still. I could see us all—Ma, H2O, Bill Bob, me, every being born—stiff as cardboard, belly-up. . . . I found a flashlight and stumbled down to the Tamanawis, trying all the way to make myself angry, to quash this upsurge of sentiment, to be cold and hard and alone and uncaring—and I thought I was succeeding till I poured Alfred into the river and heard myself say, "Goodbye, Alfred the Great. You were just a fish, but you were my friend."

Back inside I climbed into the loft and collapsed, leaving a candle burning to stave off the water visions. But when I lay down and stared at Bill Bob's crayola map of the Tamanawis Valley its water began to flow; I could even hear it; I could even see a silver speck in it—Alfred's tiny corpse—drifting down the crayon river, glinting in the greenblack water, washing round bend after bend, through riffle, pool and eddy. And I found myself urging him, hoping he made it clear to the ocean—as if this were terribly important somehow; then I saw myself in the drawing, a crayoned stick figure throwing pinecones in the water, and toy boats and bottles, galloping along beside them, coaxing, conjuring, begging everything that drifted to make it clear to the sea, the sea would make it all right, the sea was big, it was great and wise, it was the final abode of drifting things, so sail, Alfred, sail down, down, down the long valley, down to the sea where you'll be all right, you'll be part of the, part of....

I sat up in bed.

What the hell was I turning into? *sail Alfred?* What nautical gush was this? Hell, Shirley Temple was thick-skinned as a rhino, next to me. Alfred! *Alfred?* What in blazes was I doing naming a fish Alfred? I was as bad as H2O. Nijinsky. Sigrid. Alfred ... horseshit! That's what I'd name my next pet minnow: Horseshit.

I jumped down from the loft, got dressed, grabbed a pen and port jug and began measuring out six-ounce mugs of wine as I wrote in my Log, telling myself I'd review my efforts later for scientific evidence of the effects of each cup—and knowing damned well that the quintessential pith of the thing was an excuse to get rotten drunk. I began with an account of the day's fishing, but two mugs later was jabbering aloud to my friend Rodney, writing everything I said in a crabbed scrawl interspersed with blots of wine dripping from my moustache:

... OK Rodney, get that fly over that fish.... No, not in the alders! Can't you watch what you're doing? (Rodney nods his tip up and down: "Sure Boss, I can watch. You bet, yes sir, what am I doing, sure, yeah, you bet!") ... All right then, try again.... No! Not the bushes on the back-cast! Can't you do anything? (Rodney wags his tip from side to side: "No sirree Boss, you know me, nothing right, you bet, sure, thanks, nope, not Rodney!") time on mug #2: .25 hrs. Assignment for 1:30 a.m. July 22 Mug #3 Slurp #1: Describe in five billion words the appearance, behavior and history of Rodney T. Flyrod:

First thing I noticed about Rodney back when he was just a dumb blank in the fly-shop was his nudity: him and the other blanks were all naked as noses, standing in a barrel there. Didn't bother him though. He still don't wear nothing but a little cork, a few wrappings, and some see-through varnish, so it's lucky there's no members growing off him or I'd be ashamed to go fishing with the guy. I'm not even sure which end of him his face is on; he's like me—a poker face, a wood Indian. Unlike me, he's eight feet tall, and according to A.M.A. body charts should weigh about 300 lbs, so at four ounces he's a little on the skinny side. But he won't eat—refuses meat,

drink or vegetable—and he's muscular for a beanpole. (Mug #4 Pipe #2)
Rod is your basic Strong Silent Type, but he's sensitive too: he'll twitch his
head at the peck of a trout 50 or 60 feet off. And he's awfully damned
devoted to me; never goes noplace without me. And I like Rodney a lot. I
guess I do. I must, carrying him around every day all day dawn to dark
Rodney and me all alone in rivers too cold under sun too hot watching water
so bright it engraves my brain, keeps me awake, fills my ears, my eyes, my
dreams, my (Mug 5) me and Rod out there watching that bright water
because, because? because our little fly is on or in it, why else, and we're
curious, Rod and me, wondering which silvery unseen how-big critter outta
nowhere's gonna slash that helpless little treacherous little fly me and Rod
are watching out for, which is why we stand there, feet two pilings, back
cramped, arms leaden, flesh fried, blood mosquito-food, eyes dazed, glazed,
mesmerized, hypnotized and ears by streams and creeks and rivers and we're
Busy the Rodney and Curious the Gus, proud keepers of a unreal insect
strolling long the rivertop like a dog on a leash and let one fish touch our
doggie and we'll yank its brains out the way he wishes we'd leave off, me and
Rodney, making pretty line-patterns in air nobody sees catching fish nobody
knows we catch except the fish who never admit it till we catch them again
and make them sorry they lied and dead like Alfred and what kind of game
is this we're playing here, Rodney? What are we doing? Yeah, we don't
know, yeah, you bet, sure boss, OK, and we keep on walking miles for the
sake of it, being hermits for it, losing sleep over it, going hungry because of
it, crazy thanks to it, no better than dead men at the hands of it and WHY?
who makes us? the fish? the river? the stupidity of our selfs? no. I make
Rodney and curiosity makes me and Who makes curiosity is probably Who
makes us, or maybe I just probably don't know why. so what? does it matter
(Mug 6) if I made rod or he made me, in whose image, what for, on what
day, or rested or did or didn't see it weren't worth meadow-waffles or alfred
or what fish think or people or if there's a god or gog or magog or hell no it
dont make no difference. it's just fishing, chug a mug (7), just fishing, plain,
dumb, and simple like god intended and huge ugly handwriting here and
untold crockheaded whirlies but me and by god Rod are gonna get this
thing hashed out: here's what: I made Rodney and he made me and god
made us and we made him sorry but here we are anyway, tough titty, two
terrible drinks a water altogether designed for the torment and education
and destruction of trouts like public school teachers for little kids, that's
what. we give them fishes what for right in the mouth, that's what, cause we
been around, me and Rod, we know their abode, and their going out, and
their coming in, therefore do we put our hook in their noses as a sign unto
them, and rodney don't sleep why should I? he dont talk why should I? he
dont think or drink or write or go all crazy and alone in a cabin all alone why
am I? Why amn't I snoozing instead of this water whirling whirling letting
me not any sleeping why? mug 5 or 9, why amn't I happy fishing here I
wanted where like this is what I wanted my ideal always angling schedule I

always always wanted and if it kills me it kills me how I wanted to die, so there, goodnite rodney. all hashed out...

[I staggered to bed with jug and journal]

but why rodney, why god in bed can't see nothing but waterrunning in my eyes out my eyes my ears my cabin gone all watery water head to foot to fireplace and wont stop and wont stop and wont and O don't I stick my foot in my mouth's mind sometimes floating around sideways bellyup like poor poor Alfred trying not to let this thing hash out but by god we'll get it figured oh oooh now driffing down down cockeyed, down, hard to write, so hard gliding down but no bottom nowhere dont hit no bottom and O if only my nose'd bust on some lowest bottomest fundamuntelly groundedest thing, then I'd know... where. why I was. am. For. Why i so am what, some day. SO THERE! so where? so sleepy so tired so come O numb night, and cradle this soggy lump till dawns bright dawn dawns...

except, jesus, i mean, maybe he was just a fish, but he Alfred, he *was* my frend.

3

Anvil Abe and the
Phantom Fisherman

Allah, Who payeth the disbeliever his due . . . is swift at reckoning.
. . . There covereth him a wave, above which is a wave, above which is
a cloud. Layer upon layer of darkness. When he holdeth out his hand
he scarce can see it.

—Koran XXIV : 39, 40

AFTER A FEW HOURS tossing in the throes of drunken nightmares I awoke,
bladder bursting. It was dawn. I sat up slowly to the worst headache of my
life, crawled down from the loft and crept outside. As I was splashing the
devil's club I heard a different kind of splash and whirled in time to see
the second consecutive leap of a big sea-run cutthroat in H2O's drift. Had
I believed in some Deity, even in a rivergod, I would have turned around
and gone back to bed; the thing was just too pat; obviously that fish was a
lure wielded by some hungry unseen Intelligence; obviously I was the
prey. Sick, shivering, still half-drunk, I belonged nowhere but back in the
sack. But when the trout soared high a third time I took the bait. I
lurched to the cabin, threw on some clothes and in ten minutes had
Sardine ready to go. Fisherman-consciousness usurped my brain: the
sea-runs *had* to be in. I'd float down to Eaton's Landing on the estuary by
early afternoon, hitchhike home, return in the pickup for the canoe, and
catch up on my sleep . . . sometime. After I died, maybe.

I made a quick cast to where the blueback had sounded. The instant
the fly touched the water the fish smacked it, and after a good fight I
landed it—the spitting image of the trout I'd killed yesterday: the one
whose blood bought Alfred's demise; the one that inspired the delirious
night; the one that got me this damned headache. Warning upon warning. But I suspected no setup. I'd no one and nothing to suspect. I

believed in nothing I couldn't see except air and fish, and the lust for sleek silver bodies was upon me. I killed this blueback, too, then hopped in the canoe and shoved off.

The air was chill for midsummer, but a brilliant pink-tinged sky in the east promised an early end to that. Mist clung in patches to the trees on Tamanawis Mountain like herds of amorphous timber-grazing sheep; a jet squadron of mergansers roared past looking for gook fish to bombard; a great blue heron wheeled by, squawking like an airborne limousine with a dying transmission. But the sky and its residents were lost on me: my eyes were all for the water. In a canoe you don't just float down a river: you're part of it—a silent water creature responsive to every surge and flex of current, gliding like a fingertip over a naked green body. And because you're silent you come upon the watering deer, the bent and laborious beavers, the sleazy muskrats and gossiping ducks you seldom see walking the banks. But what did I do when I rounded a bend and came upon a drinking doe and her two spotted fawns? Turned to a seductive riffle on the opposite shore. My one-pointedness was rewarded with an eleven-inch native whose neck I broke as if twisting off a beer cap while the extraneous-to-angling fawns pranced and stumbled on spindly legs, swivelled outsized ears, twitched wet black noses and flicked ragtag tails, all for the benefit of the numbered hairs hanging off the back of my head.

In a way this July morning was the culmination of my life's work. Fishing with total absorption despite my splitting head, employing a half-dozen well-chosen flies, a dozen kinds of casts, and a hundred fine technical nuances, I created—with Rodney's help—an almost-living creature out of every fly. And the sea-runs *had* come in: we duped fourteen with our insectile artificing, landing eleven and killing five ranging from 1½ to nearly 4 pounds, filling in the under-12-inch portion of my limit with five natives of 10 to 11½ inches, selected from twenty deceived and netted. By 10 A.M. I had the kind of creel full of trout that would set most fishermen drooling, and still I persisted, releasing them now, but performing the ritual to perfection. The few bank-anglers I passed would hail me and ask "What luck?," and I'd nod ambiguously, mutter "Middlin'," and gloat to Rodney over the undoubted paltriness of their catch.

At noon I pulled up on a gravel bar just above tidewater. The fishing had finally slowed, so while I devoured a baloney and banana sandwich I rigged a spinning rod with a small Doc Shelton and worms. When I was ready to shove off I glanced toward the bay—and was shocked to see an enormous wall of fog rolling inland, right for me, like a slow, titanic tidal wave.

Summer fogs are common on the Oregon Coast: inland heat waves drag them from the Pacific as a man with a fever pulls the blanket to his chin. But something about this fog bank made my heart sink—the way it covered the entire sky; its density and darkness; its magisterial, inexorable approach. . . . I tried to ignore it, telling myself the fish would start hitting again in the cold dark beneath it.

But they didn't. I reached tidewater just as the fog engulfed me. The tide was full, the current dead. I let the boat hang and tried the spinner, but somehow in that fog the repetitive cast/retrieve, cast/retrieve seemed stupid, out of place, bootless. And I was cold. As soon as the blanket touched me the air went chill, my throat turned sore, my breath made smoke, and even quick paddling didn't warm me. I trolled the spinner a while longer, but when it snagged I broke off and began paddling for Eaton's Landing.

The fog was incredibly thick now. I could only see the nearest bank, though the river was quite narrow. The air was dank, and unearthly still. I saw and heard no wildlife—not even the inevitable riverside wrens. The world seemed to have shrunken and died, turned shapeless and color-less—nothing but monotonous lumps of green and gray. I began to shiver, and to feel afraid. There had been no sign that the world I'd drifted into was inhabited at all. I listened carefully to my weary brain's assurances that Eaton's dock was less than two miles downstream and impossible to miss; the boats enshrouded at sea, they had something to worry about, but I was three miles even from the bay. I got hold of myself.

Even without fog, the stretch of river upstream from Eaton's Land-ing is humdrum; there are no riffles or pools, no variations to the brush-choked banks; it's more a tidal canal or a slough than a river. I began to lose all sense of distance, and I recognized no landmark: the river bends, the pilings, the few old trees—all strange. I heard a small outboard puttering toward me. I made out one of the old green and black wood boats they rented at the Landing. I read the chipped white number on the bow. I tried to make out the men riding in it, but there were only two shapes, faceless, manlike, hunkered on pewlike benches. I would have called to fishermen, asking how far to the Landing, joking about the fog, or the fishing—but I couldn't make myself call to those shapes. The old boat glided past like a hearse, trailing the reek of menthol cigarettes. Then, when it had disappeared, a disembodied voice that sounded so close it made me start muttered, "You see somethin', Ray?"

A second voice growled, "Not sure."

The first voice said, "Musta been the Phantom Fisherman." The two shapes found this humorous, apparently; at least both voices snorted and coughed up mouthfuls of phlegm—I heard the spats foul the river. I was glad the tide began to ebb: I wanted the hell out of this silent slough. I paddled hard, but thanks to port wine and no sleep my body was no longer heating itself: the fog seemed to flow right through my head and chest. Many more hours in this stuff and I *would* be the Phantom Fisherman, but there was nothing for it now but to shiver and keep paddling.

By and by I heard a muffled shout far up the opposite bank—a man's voice, shrouded and strained, calling, "Abe! AAAaaaaabe! *Abe! Where are ya!*" It was a voice not used to shouting, forced for some reason to holler like a scared kid calling a lost dog. It gave me the willies. Maybe Abe *was* a dog, lost in the brush. Or maybe a couple of old plunkers got separated. The poor guy's partner was probably up snoozing in their car. . . . "Abe! AAaaabe! Jesus, ABE! AAAAAaaaaaaaabe!" A seagull swooped down from the murk and right over my head screamed its most mournful sea-cry—I ducked, nearly swamping the boat, then paddled away with all my strength. I wanted that hollow voice way out of earshot.

My arms grew leaden. I laid the paddle across the gunwale and rested, staring at my rucksack to keep from having to stare at the damned fog. Then I realized I was staring at a bulge in that rucksack, and that the bulge was a pullover slicker. Of all the stupid . . . freezing to death, and a slicker sitting under my shoes. I fished the thing out and pulled it over my head but the zipper at the throat somehow caught in my hair. I cussed and fussed around, struggling like a halibut on the floor of a dory, clattering tackle, almost capsizing again before I managed to pull the hair out and the slicker on. Then I reached for the paddle. . . .

It was gone. Knocked in the water. I looked around the boat—nowhere in sight. I hand-paddled downstream, thinking it might have drifted faster—didn't see it. I back-paddled—still didn't see it. I hand-paddled forward and sideways, this way and that till my arms went numb and my back was breaking, then sat up, muttering the obscene old standbys and inanely computing how many flies I'd have to sell to pay for a new paddle.

Then I saw something floating near the bank. I worked toward it, but was so tired I quit when I saw it wasn't my paddle. What the hell was it, though? An animal of some kind? No. A submerged log? Yeah. And something pale rolled on the surface next to it—a good-sized fish taking a fly, looked like. I eyed Rodney. I was all-in and limited out, but what the hell? Seemed like a way of saying Screw-you to the fog. . . . I tied on a #12 Light Cahill and laid it lightly, right where the fish had shown. Nothing struck, but I waited. The fly got waterlogged and sank. Still I waited. Just as I started to work it in I felt a tug too soft for any cutthroat—I thought "Summer steelhead!" and was careful not to raise the tip too hard. The rod bent, but there was no vibration—just a dull, steady pull . . . snag. I brought the rod up harder,

and a white hand rose from the river.

A man . . . a man floating on the tide, face down, my fly stuck in the sleeve at his wrist.

I didn't move, but unconsciously kept an even pressure on the fly-line, so the canoe slid up alongside the body. I put down the pole and just sat, unable to think. The man's pallid fingers were curled under, undulating like feeding slugs; one sported a gold wedding band. Gray hair fluttered off his head like algae off a rock; his ears were a hideous white. He wore a checkered shirt like one of my own, and he had on suspenders, or no, wader straps. Yes, he had on waders. The man was a fisherman.

He drifted vertically, feet sunken, arms outspread, head lolling on the surface—an outlandish, waterlogged crucifix. In my fished-out condition I found myself wondering what the trout must think of him, even imagined myself a fish on the bottom watching him hang like an icon in the fog overhead. "Christ," I thought, "no wonder the bite is off." I began to grumble at him for wrecking the fishing. My mind was gone. It was a long while before I saw I had to do something. Couldn't just let him drift out to sea. I started to grab him: the canoe tipped; my hand pressed his cold head, forcing it further under. I gagged and lurched back.

To gather my wits I started talking with Rodney. "What to do, huh, Rod? Wouldn't help to grab him. Can't get him in the boat. Got to tie him on and tow him away someway or other." I considered snagging him with my fly-line and pulling him to shore, but a glimpse of the shoreline ended that notion: at high tide the brush overhangs both banks and the water is immediately deep. I couldn't climb out of the canoe for the brush, and I couldn't get the corpse in without me getting out, because to pull him up would swamp me. "Don't matter," I told Rodney. "No fight left in him anyhow. No fun for us once they're all played out, huh, Rod? Well, how 'bout that bow-rope then? Sounds like a plan."

I lurched toward the bow and again nearly capsized. I clutched the gunwale, the thought of being in the water with the body sickening me. Creeping into the bow, I turned and steadied the canoe, then watched vacantly as the man drifted down, head-foremost, and thudded into Sardine's shiny side. "Same noise Alfred made on the fish tank yesterday, remember, Rod? He's like Alfred, ain't he? Wants outta there. Nobody likes it in the water with them big sea-runs. . . ."

Another gull passed over and, when it saw us, screamed and wheeled away like the first. This time I was too far gone to be frightened, but I remembered the fog-bound voice: *Abe*.

"So you're Abe," I whispered to the downward-gazing face. "Well let me tell you something, Abe, your wife's gonna be pissed. I mean it. She never liked you takin' off goin' fishin' anyhow. Shoulda stayed home and mowed the lawn, Abe. You've gone and done it to yourself this time. No joke. There won't be no explainin' yourself out of this one." I thought of the frightened voice, the ring on the finger, the shirt like mine—a gift, I figured, from kids or grandkids—and started to cry. "OK Abe. Steady now. No tricks. Let's get you down to Eaton's."

I looped the rope through his wader straps, touching him as little as possible, fighting off the revulsion when I did; I tied a square knot, let go, and watched. The canoe sped up. The rope came taut. Abe hove around slow in the current, one arm slothfully flailing, his face turning toward me as he bobbed on the tide; the mouth and eyes gaped at me—the same astonished expression I'd seen on the faces of a million spent fish. I turned away. My intestines writhed in a dry heave.

After a time I heard a car creeping through the fog on the River Road. I considered hollering for help but the knots in my stomach—and the recollection of the way Abe's friend sounded—stopped me. The tide was flowing strong now anyway; I should reach Eaton's before long; maybe somebody with an outboard would come and help out.

I hand-paddled hard for a while, trying to reach the south shore where the dock would be. It was arduous: Abe was like a sea anchor, and with my throat and gut all twisted together I couldn't get much thrust. I sat up to rest. "We're not moving so fast," I told Abe; "Damn fool that I am. Lost my paddle just before I found you. Loss is gain, huh?"

Abe's mouth gaped its one reply as I stared against my will, mesmerized by the kelplike flapping of his arms, the unalterable incredulity on his face, and suddenly that expression, the lack of sleep, the fog, the eeriness of our plight—all of it joined to swamp my mind. I burst into uncontrollable, choking, weeping laughter. "I swear to God, Abe. You're the worst swimmer ever was. I don't know, maybe it's those waders, but I swear, I never met nothing could swim the way you can. Unless maybe it was an anvil . . . Anvil Abe. Anvil Abe and the Phantom Fisherman, huh? That's us, Abe. That's us."

My head swam; I grew disoriented, unsure of how Abe and I met or where we were going; fog swirled all through me now and I babbled like a creek, sloshing with affection for my ungainly fellow drifter. "Hope them bluebacks aren't peckin' at ya, Abe. I've seen 'em hit streamers not much smaller'n you, so watch out. . . ." Abe peered down into the Tamanawis, watching out. "Abe, I'll tell you what. When me and you get down to the dock I'm gonna give ya a present, damned if I'm not, Abe. But what the, why not give it to ya now—got it right here in the boat, and, and you can—it, it's my life jacket, Abe. I'm givin' it to ya and would have sooner and anyhow it's all yours now. Yep. This big orange sucker right here in the boat. Maybe it'll, it . . . hell, it'll even float an anvil like you. No sweat, Abe, I mean it. I don't need it. Take it. Keep it with ya and this sorta thing won't happen no more." I picked up the life jacket. I held it out to him. Mind stopped, teeth rattling, I held it out, waiting for him to take it. "Come on, Abe. It's yours." He didn't take it. "Goddamnit, Abe, *here!*" He ignored me, just peered down in the water. That hurt me. I held it out as long as I could but he never looked up. I put it back in the boat when my arm gave out. "OK. OK Abe. I'll give it to ya later."

I started back for the south bank of the river and was making some headway when the canoe jolted to a stop and heaved around sideways. I turned. Abe's feet were tangled in a sunken tree. I tugged on the rope but he didn't come free. I was afraid to pull hard: might capsize, or break the wader straps and lose him for good. Gently as I could I pulled Sardine up toward him till I could see, down through the green flow, his left foot wedged in the crotch of a limb. "OK Abe . . . enough's enough. You kick loose now."

Abe looked at his foot; he waved his arms; he didn't kick loose.

"It's not funny anymore, Abe. Really. Let go."

Abe didn't let go. The tide ebbed faster; the oceanbound river tugged harder at his straps; Abe just rolled a little, side to side, looking down, looking deep down into secret parts of the Tamanawis. So I prayed—for a boat to come, for the limb to break, for the current to free him, anything. . . .

No boat came, no limb broke, no current freed, nothing: that was how my prayers had always worked. I saw there was only one way to free him: dive down and loose his foot myself. I started pulling off my clothes. By the time I'd stripped, my teeth were banging till I thought they'd break; tension, cold and fear had my body knotted and the thought of what I was about to do weakened me. But there's only one way of getting out of a canoe in deep water without overturning it: I took a careful, gasping gulp of air—and dove.

I opened my eyes. It was green and calm under the water, neither as cold nor as turbulent as I'd feared. I swam slowly at first, wary of cramps, but with each stroke the tension flowed out of me till my body felt loose and comfortable, more at home in the river than in the air. I surfaced and swam back alongside Sardine. Seeing how light and high it floated I realized how hard it would be to get back in. Didn't matter. It was better in the water and would be easier to guide the canoe.

I swam to Abe and grabbed his shirt to keep from drifting away, but the boot came instantly free and the current drove him into me so hard he seemed alive and swimming: I shot away in revulsion. But I didn't want Abe to think I didn't like him so I acted like I'd been going to get the life jacket, pulled it out of the canoe, swam back and wedged it under his chest. It buoyed him up well. Returning to the stern of the backwards canoe, I guided our course downstream, looking up now and then for the pier at Eaton's landing. I couldn't see more than twenty feet, but hugged the shore so I wouldn't miss it, sliding once in a while through sunken algae-covered trees whose slick dead limbs now stroked, now gouged my legs, forcing myself to stay calm, knowing I'd drown if I didn't.

After a time the dock was suddenly right there. I let the canoe wedge itself against the pilings and turned just as Abe, arms undulating, scudded into my chest and trapped me against the dock. I shot out of the water, ramming a big splinter into my thigh. Then I just lay there like a beached tortoise, turning numb, feeling spent enough to welcome it. . . . But a sudden rasping voice hollered, "Jesus Christ!" I looked up into the prune face of old Ralph Eaton. "No," I said. "I think his name is Abe."

4

Fainting
Before the Duel

Oh! you should have seen him shiver
when they pulled him from the river!

—*Heinrich Hoffman*

NUMB AND WASTED though I was, I didn't fail to remember that wherever
Ralph Eaton is, Maggie Eaton can't be far behind. So my first desperate
act upon gaining dry land and a few shreds of consciousness was to fetch
my trousers and cover what Adam covered with the leaf. A retired
veterinarian, Maggie Eaton was a rock-hard raw-boned old woman whose
Christian piety kept her bustling around Fog and the surrounding farms,
serving her fellow humans in a kind of medical capacity. Unfortunately,
her Philosophy of Healing was derived from her vet experience and
consisted of what sounded like six words: *Man Ain't No Differnt'n'inny
Other Critter*. So it was that prospective patients attempted to conceal
even grievous wounds and terminal diseases to avoid her charitable min-
istrations; I grovelled for my trousers, propelled not by any Edenic shame
of nakedness, but by the certain knowledge that if Maggie spotted the
splinter in my thigh she'd be at it with a needle the size, sharpness and
cleanliness of a used railroad spike.

Once covered I turned toward an ungodly thumping on the dock
behind me: old Ralph was sitting on the drowned fisherman's stomach,
slugging him repeatedly in the chest. I said, "What the hell ya doing,
Ralph. He's already dead."

"Got t'help," he gasped, none too sanely. "Got t'git 'is 'art a-goin'."

"Day or so late," I murmured, too spent to argue. I thought maybe
Ralph agreed when he left off punching, but once he caught his breath he
began to pick the dead man up by the ribs and drop him back onto the
boards, over and over and over, Sflup! Sflup! Sflup!

"Got t'git 'im breathin'," Ralph explained. "My Maggie shown me
how."

The sloppy thuds sent the blood to my feet. I reeled toward the store, wondering how far I'd get before my knees buckled, the thought of what Maggie might do to revive me making me queasier yet. Halfway up the gangplank the boards began to look so soft and inviting I had to stop and try them out. . . . Next thing I knew, powerful hands were yanking me to my feet. "No, Maggie!" I groaned.

"The name is Titus," said a voice even deeper than Maggie's.

I looked into the grim face of a stranger, taller but not much older than me. He said, "Let me help you," and wrapped his coat around my shoulders and my arm around his neck. I saw he had on some kind of nineteenth-century suit, with waistcoat and knickerbockers: it made as much sense as anything that had happened since the fog set in. As he dragged me up toward Eaton's store he murmured, "'his gory visage down the stream was sent. . . .'"

I said, "Huh?"

"Milton," he replied. "A Puritanical old goat, but the line seemed apt."

"Thought his name was Abe," I mumbled, wondering how this dandy could criticize a man or his religion when he'd only just drowned.

"I refer to the poet," he said.

"Dressed more like a fisherman," I pointed out.

"Easy, friend," he whispered, helping me along. "Let's go thaw you by a fire." I'd have agreed with this plan if I hadn't fainted first.

When next the world intruded upon my consciousness I wasn't surprised to find my fortunes had plummeted still further: I was sprawled on my back on an ice-cold concrete floor, and Maggie Eaton was straddling me as Ralph had straddled the dead fisherman, or as Walton's cowboy-frogs had straddled pike. But instead of attempting any type of respiration she seemed to be going for artificial suffocation: she was crushing my lungs with her weight, pinching my nostrils together and glaring at my closed mouth like it was a cigarette machine that had eaten her change but wouldn't cough up the smokes. When I started to ask why she was misbehaving in this manner she tried to ram a huge pill down my gullet. I bit her, spat the pill in her face and clamped my teeth tight, but she only cursed and pinched my nose till the tears ran, waiting for the moment I'd have to gulp air. I started to black out—but a heaven-sent hand yanked her claw from my nose and her carcass from my chest and she cursed again, at Knickerbocker. While he and she engaged in a Ma-and-H2O-like debate over the applicability of horse tranquilizers to my condition, I played possum and marshalled my strength, hoping to punch her and run for it if she straddled me again. But Knicker must have won—because Maggie abandoned the pill and began trying to break my toes off for some pious first-aid purpose. I was considering returning the favor by doing some dental work on her with my heel when Knickerbocker intervened again, relieving her of the instrument of torture—a pair of wool socks—and sliding them over my feet quite painlessly. I fell back into a stupor or faint or whatever it was. . . .

When I came to, my fortunes had improved beyond my wildest hopes: I was slumped in a wing chair and wrapped in blankets before a blazing woodstove in the corner of Eaton's tackle shop; on a table to my right was a bottle of brandy which I began transferring first into a glass, then into myself. Then a door slammed: Maggie swaggered in. I started to feign hibernation, but remembering the glass in my nonsomnolent-looking hand, I figured the jig was up, so I upped the jigger to fortify myself. Maggie came marching toward me looking a lot like Napoleon, which left me feeling something like Moscow—but the door slammed again and my knickered guardian angel hollered in that Ralph was rifling the dead man's pockets and wallet after an arduous but successful attempt to pull his waders down. Maggie rushed off, dragging a string of oaths behind her. My benefactor stepped in with a saucepan, poured in several healthy glugs of brandy and set it on the stove to warm. "I'll help you dispose of that soon," he said, and was gone before I could thank him. Through the window on my left I saw him rush across the parking lot to greet and direct two policemen and an ambulance driver who'd arrived simultaneously. When they left my field of vision I sat back and stared at my brandy glass, enjoying the tiny police-blue and ambulance-red flashes on its side, which coupled with the hot drink and warm room to make me feel like Christmas; then, out the window, people passed bearing strange gifts—one policeman and the ambulance driver a loaded stretcher, Maggie my pack and poles, Ralph and the second cop Sardine, Knicker my creel, Abe's life jacket, and the rest of my gear. The corpse went into the ambulance, my canoe and gear in and onto an ugly old '59 Plymouth—Knicker's car. As he loaded the gear he paused to peek in my fish-stuffed creel, and even at that foggy distance I perceived astonishment—the first genuine emotion I'd seen on his face: I knew from that moment that his was the heart of a true fisherman.

A fancy camper drove up and an hysterical man jumped out. He was led by the police to the rear door of the ambulance; when the blanket was lifted he hid his face and sobbed so hard I heard him through the window. So. His was the voice I'd heard calling in the fog. Poor bastard. The authorities and the Eatons all stood gawking at him, stubbing their feet in the gravel like bad boys in a principal's office. But Knickerbocker approached him like an old friend, led him away from the others, talked with him a while, and he calmed down. He answered questions and signed papers for the police, then he and the ambulance drove away.

The Eatons crept inside and went to their living quarters upstairs. The cops and Knickerbocker came in by the stove and Knicker offered them hot brandy; they eyed him as if he had horns and a tail. "Oh!" he said. "Oh of course, you're on duty. I'm sorry," and with that he downed a half-glass at one throw. One cop frowned; the other licked his lips. Then they turned to me and started asking questions—who was I, where did I live, when and where did I find the deceased, why didn't I just load him in the canoe, was he cold when I found him, was he stiff, were his eyes open, did I know him—and each question echoed in my head, answers, half-answers, shades of meaning and unmeaning rendering me near-incoherent: who *was* I? where *did* I live? when? when the fog came. where? in the river. cold? I don't know, ask *him*, ask Abe. Did I know him? I knew his shirt, knew his waders, knew his thin hair and white fingers; he was a fisherman and I knew fishermen. "No. No I never met him. No, I'm not trying to be funny: I really did hook his sleeve, yes, a #12 Light Cahill. Sorry, don't mean to laugh; lost my paddle; haven't slept; thought he was a fish, his hand I mean, I mean I was pretty drunk last night. No, yes, I'm sorry he drowned, I'd have given him my—I mean, he should have had a life jacket . . . or something. Yes, brushy banks. Deep water. Right. Used the bow-rope. OK. Sorry. Goodbye."

Poor cops. They shook their heads and rolled their eyes, glaring at Knicker when he tried to interpret, scribbling on pink and yellow slips when my utterances made some sense to them. They looked even gladder to leave than I was to have them go. I watched their blue light disappear from the side of my brandy glass.

Knickerbocker drew up a chair. At his urging I emptied my glass and let him refill it, but I was no match for him: he worked at that brandy like it was his profession. On his fourth glass he started patting his pockets, then frowned, turned to me and asked, "Warm enough?"

"Me? Yeah, sure."

"Might I borrow my coat back, then?"

"Oh! Sure. Forgot I had it."

Knicker started patting coat pockets as he'd done with shirt, vest, and knickers. Not finding what he was after, he started emptying his clothes: he pulled out pens, notebooks, pipes, snuff, beef jerky, fly boxes and a chunk of Dutch chocolate, then scowled and moved on to obscurer pockets—thigh pockets and rib pockets on his knickers and coat; a stomach pocket in his shirt; back and inner pockets in the lining of his vest.

He pulled out two tobacco pouches, three packs of foreign cigarettes, a half-dozen boxes of matches, a pipe tool and reamers, wallet, keys, coin purse, agates, a compass, bookmarks, sunflower seeds, a silver flask, a telescope, snail shells, a magnifying glass, a mechanical pencil, vitamin pills, two little leather-bound books—muttering as he labored: "'To his horror he recollected that he had left both coat and waistcoat behind him in his cell, and with them his pocket-book, money, keys, watch, matches, pencil-case—all that makes life worth living, all that distinguishes the many-pocketed animal, the lord of creation, from the inferior one-pocketed or no-pocketed productions that hop and trip permissively about, unequipped for the real contest . . .'" Then his gaunt face brightened: he reached up a sleeve of his coat, I heard a zipper unzip, and out came a thin glass tube from which he pulled a tapered brown cigar. He lit it, manufacturing a cloud that smelled like putrescent forest fire, then sighed with immense satisfaction. "That, I'm afraid, is my last cheroot, but help yourself to anything that strikes your fancy."

"Glad that's the last," I said, covering my sore nose, "and it was that pocket speech that struck my fancy, Mister . . . uh. . . ."

"Toad. Toad of Toad Hall."

I was confused. I didn't want to laugh if his name was really Toad, but, well, *Toad*? "Didn't you say your name was, um, Tyrone, or, uh. . . ."

"Let's clear this up," he said. "The 'gory visage' was John Milton's; the many-pocketed animal is Toad; Toad is Kenneth Grahame's; and I am not Tyrone, but Titus—Titus Irving Gerrard, at your service."

"It's clearer than that outside," I protested. "The cops said he was Abe Mayfield, and he wasn't gory, just drowned. And *you're* the many-pocketed animal, not Toad Gramkin or whoever you said. That leaves John Milton and Tyrone Irving Jiwhoozits, neither of which is you if what you said before counts for anything. And no sense saying At-my-service now when you've been at it all day: I might be dead by now if you hadn't fought off Maggie Eaton. I like all the pockets, by the way. The knickers too, though I wouldn't be caught dead in . . . wouldn't wear 'em . . . myself." A wave of nausea washed over me.

Knicker lit a cigarette. When the coal was brilliant orange and an inch and a half long he used it to relight his cheroot, which had fizzled in its juices. When its stench had us hopelessly surrounded he looked satisfied. "I can see that further clarification is required, you being apparently unfamiliar with the employment of quotations in conversation. I concede the dead man's lack of gore; the line wasn't apt after all, which typifies Milton, whose verse (they say) renders the English language resonant and (they fail to say) attempts to stand us on our metaphysical heads. I, Allah be praised, am not Milton, at least not at present. Nor am I Kenneth Grahame, from whose fertile head Toad hopped. There remain the dead man in waders—apparently an Abe Mayfield—and the live man in knickers—certainly a Titus Gerrard. And if the Eatons tell me truly, you are Gus Orviston, son of the famous Henning Hale-Orviston, whose *Summa Piscatoria* I abandoned for boredom in midstream. But if in its tedious pages it contains the key to such catches as you have made this day, I'll take it up again and read it ten times over. More brandy? Cigarette? And tell me why you'd hesitate to wear a kind of clothing you admire, which is comfortable, practical for its pockets, long wearing, and was, moreover, worn by Theodore Gordon, the Father of American Fly Angling?"

Trying to keep hold of the dozen loose ends, I replied, "We got the names right. I'm Gus, me pap is H2O, his book is tedious and you are Titus. But no book contains the key to catches like I caught today: the trout I got on wet flies; the corpse I caught on a soggy dry. And you can take the trout with you if you want because, well, I can't, I don't . . . I wish I'd stayed in bed this morning, or was there now, I mean no I don't, I mean I like to yack with you here, Titus, but I uh, don't let me keep you though. I mean, I don't mean I want you to, I don't want, I'd rather not be alone in my cabin yet, or, I'm fine though. I'm fine I'm fine . . . sorry, uh. . . ." As I stuttered to a standstill Titus just smoked and waited as if I'd said nothing, as if I weren't a pathetic fool. I drank more brandy and watched him nervously, wondering what he was waiting for. The knickers and waistcoat clued me in: he must be like two old English flyfishermen who'd once visited H2O—two of the few I'd met and admired—men whose eloquence at first struck me as outrageous, because I'd never met men for whom conversation was an art. Or a sport. I saw then that Titus was waiting for me, hoping to engage in a spot of good sport while I thrashed through the bushes, scaring off our quarry. I shook myself, straightened up, and said, "I digress."

"Don't mention it," he said with a wave of his hand.

"Consider it de-mentioned," I said, then took up the threads: "I'm as familiar as I want to be with quotations trashing a conversation—my parents are great slingers of quoted mudballs. I'm also familiar enough with guys like Milton, Pope, Dryden, Carlyle, Donne and Company to know I prefer the Lone Ranger. I'd like more brandy, and maybe one of those black cigarettes if they don't smell like your cheroot. My magpie mother is why I wouldn't be caught dead or alive in knickers, but if you expect me to believe that your six-foot several-inch self is wearing a suit once worn by the five-foot three-inch Theodore Gordon, you measure inches like a true fisherman."

Titus smiled, tossed me a cigarette, filled my glass to the brim and sucked hard twice—once at his cheroot, once at his drink. He said, "I concede my suit to be similar to Gordon's only in cut. I wonder how familiar is 'familiar enough' with the authors named. I also wonder at your mother, that remarkable clairvoyant, who being neither here nor at your avowedly empty domicile is nonetheless capable of perceiving you in your hypothetical handsome knickers and transmitting her derision over the miles, through untold mountains, fogs, trees and walls. As for your second catch today, I see no cause for regret or dismay. You've done the man's family some service by capturing his remains. And since we're all bodily destined for corpsehood and spiritually possessed of immortal souls, I see no reason to let the proximity of corpses alter our appetites. Nevertheless I'll gladly disburden you of a brace of cutthroats."

Completely caught up in our convolutions, I took a swig and made this reply: "If we are possessed of immortal souls, I'd like to see them. And 'familiar enough' means almost totally ignorant of every English author on earth except Izaak Walton, with whose *Compleat Angler* I may be more familiar than anybody—and familiarity bred contempt. I'm content to be ignorant because Walton alone brought me more trouble than you would ever believe. In these parts, the plural of cutthroat is cutthroat, not cutthroats: to catch 'em you gotta call 'em what they're used to. As for my mother, she's not clairvoyant, just invisible—she just now stomped on your left foot."

Without a moment's pause Titus responded, "Addressing ourselves to the essential first: I can't visually exhibit my soul, but I can and do intuit its existence through occasional pneumatic detonations and wordless intellections, as well as through insights obtained by pondering the words of sages, saints and scriptures. But any discussion of immortality had best be postponed to a time when our energies are up to them. Thank you for correcting my cutthroats. As for your mother, I must assume that she is impudent and weightless as well as invisible, if what you say about my foot is true. And contempt for Izaak Walton I find akin to contempt for friendly dogs, shade trees, flower gardens, sunsets and the like: such misanthropy being incommensurate with your apparent good nature, I intuit factors distorting your judgment that have not yet come to light."

Summoning all the brain and brandy I had left, I took a deep breath and said, "I'm too tired to ask about your rheumatic detonations and wordless infections, but you have my condolences. I know two saints—Nick and Valentine. I know one sage—brush. But I did read a scripture called the Holy Bible and found it confusing and cross-grained and capable of starting but not ending feuds and wars, and some of my contempt for Walton's book comes from the fact that it stars a Character the Bible is full of—a Character with all the invisibility, weightlessness and impudence of my mother. A Character Who has no more to do with Compleat Angling or with fishermen like me than fish have to do with theology. And I apologize for the fact that I doubt I'll hear you and I'm sure I won't understand you if we keep on like this just now, but I'd be glad to go on some other time." I ground to a halt for sheer exhaustion, my Cinderella intellect turning all to rats and pumpkins.

Titus grumbled something about throwing down the gauntlet, then fainting before the duel, but he helped me across the parking lot and loaded me in his car—a vehicle worthy of its owner. It was a rusty, dented, yellow-brown '59 Plymouth dubbed "The Carp" for the simple reason that it looked like one—not a healthy one either. But it had huge fins, a rod rack on the roof, and it glided carp-quiet through the fog. And inside it was a castle: sheepskin seats in front, and—where the back seat should have been—cupboards for food, for tackle and for liquor, a cooler for beer, and a Coleman stove for heating up coffee, soup or numb fragments of fisherman during winter steelhead season; it had a maple pipe rack and bookshelf built into the glove-box space, a row of carbon-crusted briars hanging above some twenty hardbound volumes—most of the latter in languages I didn't even recognize the letters of. And stationed in the back window was a plastic Jesus who raised his arm in benediction every time the brakes were applied—but Titus had glued a flyrod made of three joined toothpicks to His hand, with an ephemeral line of monofilament ending in a #20 Royal Coachman: each time the Carp came to a halt the Good Fisher hauled back, set the hook, and somewhere in the world a saved sinner lay gasping on the planks of His boat, a transmundane dry fly dangling from his spiritual lip.

I made it from the Carp to my loft with Titus's help, but how or when he took his leave I can't say: I slept before my head ever touched the pillow.

5

I Reckon

Think of the man
who fell from his fishing boat in the fog off Alaska. He
heard the motor
slowly trupping away, its cargo of vain fish under its wing.

—*Sandra McPherson*

WHEN I AWOKE my Timex was still ticking, but the 8:45 on its face was of negligible value since I didn't know whether it was A.M. or P.M. The same morbid fog wrapped the cedars in murk so thick I couldn't see the river, and the cabin was danker, darker and more desolate than I'd ever known it. I got lanterns and a fire going, fed the fish and started breakfast, but it took a ridiculous amount of effort. My throat was sore, my bones, my joints, even my teeth and hair ached, and when I sat down to eat the day grew dark: I'd slept twenty-some hours and cooked the wrong meal. I downed it anyway, but had just climbed into bed when it came back out: I filled a handy creel with used-trout-and-eggs which dribbled through the wicker all the way to the bathroom. Then I spent an eventful hour kneeling in the tympanic shower stall, uneating every last bite.

I crawled back in bed, my throat raw, my head on fire; I stayed there for three days. I guess I was delirious—at least there was water rushing around everywhere and Abe's corpse bobbed in the gray air of the room whether I woke or slept. I tossed and writhed like a worm on a hook, inhabiting a region that couldn't have been far from that locale my great-grandmother called 'The Bad Place.'

Finally the fever broke and I settled into a comparably pleasant exhaustion. But the fog remained without, and the ghastly fisherman within, and the stronger I got the more aware I grew of a blackness filling me—a depression so rancid and vast I wanted to stay delirious rather than face it. But I always was a resilient bastard. Try as I would, I got well.

On what I guessed must be one of the last days of July I kept down my first meal. To celebrate, I bundled on winter clothes and waders and crept to the Tamanawis with Rodney. After a few half-assed casts I realized I was too weak to fish, but the fresh air was welcome—except for that damned fog—so I hunkered down on a boulder at water's edge to watch what world there was to watch.

In the world I watched there wasn't much to see: little waves lapped at my rock and boots, the fog lay gray upon green water and trees, and moss lay green upon gray logs and rocks. That was outside my head. Inside my head, gray-faced Abe kept lolling by in a flow of imaginary green water, and I envisioned myself, green-faced from flu, in green waders and gray coat on the green moss of the gray boulder. Appalled by the present, I scanned the future for encouragement: I saw I had a day, a week, a month, a year, maybe even sixty years to live before my green face turned gray and died. Green and gray people grubbing around in a gray and green world. That was all there was. Monotonous, meaningless, dog-pound depressing—but so very simple. "Simplify," said Henry Greenjeans Thoreau. "OK" said I: *"Life is a lot of green crap inexorably turning gray. The examined life ain't worth chub."*

The cold from the rock was seeping up my spine. It was a terrible sensation, but I didn't move. At least *cold* wasn't green or gray. I reckoned that when it reached my head I'd become a rock, too: there'd be flashy newspaper headlines ("Metamorphic Angler Unearthed on Oregon Coast"/"Lot's Wife Drama Reenacted"/"Son of Famed Fisherman Found Permanently Stoned") and an extensive scientific investigation. Then H2O would want to bury me, but of course Ma wouldn't hear of it: "Waste not, want not," she'd say as she set me out in the front yard to scare off Avon and Amway pushers. So there I'd sit in the suburbs, season after season, living the slow, thoughtful, lifeless life of granite as they all died and rotted and disappeared. When you're going to hold a pose for a few thousand years you tend to get a little vain: I combed my hair and straightened my beard a bit with already numbed fingers, held up Rodney in a good casting posture, knit my brows toward the river as if spotting a nice rise. While waiting to petrify I fell to calculating how many centuries would pass before moss and algae reduced me to grains of grit; I supposed my upraised arms would drop off first, like on Greek and Roman statues; if they left me on the river maybe deer hunters would blast my nose off like Napoleon's troops did to the Sphinx's; if they took me home to the suburbs no doubt vandals would scrawl a few obscenities on me somewhere; little green plants would start creeping from my crevices. . . . I got to thinking about how green things are always eating gray things. Then I got to thinking about how a food chain could be constructed based on color: I made it as far as "gray rock gets eaten by green moss gets eaten by black snail gets eaten by red crawdad gets eaten by silver fish gets eaten by blue heron. . . ." Then I got stuck. Nobody eats herons but mangy coyotes—which are gray—or marsh Arabs—who are brown—or starved maniacs—who come in assorted colors; then I remembered how red mergansers eat silver fish and black crows eat baby bluebirds and Americans and goats are multihued and eat any damned thing and my whole food chain went to hell like every other thing in my life had done. That was the thing about Nature: make one lousy rule to describe it and it'll contradict you even if it has to transmogrify and metamorphosize and bust its ass to do it. And so what? If anybody grew wise enough to grasp the real immutable laws of Nature, Nature'd only rear back and strike 'em dead before they got anybody to understand them. Maybe Abe knew. Maybe Abe had just figured the whole world out and was about to tell me as I floated past, but God caught wind of it, stuck out His invisible foot, tripped and drowned him. Abe. . . . blast him! If the fool had only known how to swim there wouldn't be any of this seething in my brain—this What-is-death/What-is-life/Why-am-I-here/What-am-I-for stuff. What use were such questions? Hobgoblins—that's all they were—noisy abstract swill good for nothing but scaring and depressing hell out of everybody they occurred to. . . .

But a fisherman was dead. Everyone I knew would one day be dead. This was no abstraction. What could it mean? What should I do about it? Was there equipment to purchase to protect myself from it? Was there reference material to peruse that would make it comprehensible? Pills to pop to make it bearable? Calesthenics to make it fun? I didn't know. I didn't know anything about anything. Everything in my head came from fishing magazines, fishing manuals, fishing novels. And what did these works have to say about the meaning of Life and Death? I perused my semiphotographic memory: I recalled sentimental paragraphs wherein authors bootlessly lament departed fisher friends; I recalled adventures wherein some angler meets his death by some unfortunate outdoors accident, or, more frequently, adventures wherein some angler hears of another angler who heard of an angler who met his death by some unfortunate outdoors accident, thus keeping the Grim Reaper at a pleasant distance while we readers, like overstuffed cattle in the slaughterhouse corral, ruminate the cudlike morals Death's victims leave as their legacies to Angledom—pithy maxims like: "Don't make Fred's mistake: wear a life jacket" or "Don't pull the fatal boner Arnold pulled: carry that compass in the woods at all times" or "Don't be risky like the late Ronald: put felt soles on those hipboots today." Who hasn't heard—particularly from flyfishermen, who flaunt their literacy more than their bait-fishing counterparts—references to anglers as the most meditative of sportsmen? We feather-daubers love to echo Izaak Walton's characterization of our pastime as "the contemplative man's recreation," yet in none of the thousands of pages of modern fishing prose I'd ingested had I encountered even the most rudimentary philosophical speculations. It seemed that scarcely an angler since Walton's time gave a thought to what the death of an old fishing buddy might *mean*. Suddenly it hit me what a pathetic lot we fishermen were. We sneaked, pursued, teased, deceived, tormented and often murdered the objects of our obscure lust; we compounded our crimes by gloating over them; and we committed them so mindlessly and so often that as soon as we'd done gloating we commenced grumbling and griping and cursing the luck till the moment we managed to commit them again. What were our "contemplations" but odes to fish-lust, scientific explications, more unnatural technologies and more convoluted techniques to help us sneak, pursue, tease, deceive, torment or kill more effectively? And when one of us great *rishis* dies, what rites do the survivors perform? With sacerdotal solemnity we pass the jug till we can't see it and console one another with aphorisms such as "Old fishermen never die. They just smell that way."

Racking my brains on that cold foggy rock, I recollected at last the two most contemplative responses to the Angler's Doom that I had encountered in any angling prose penned since 1900. They were these:

1. We went into the bar at the lodge for the usual round of Opening Day Eve drinks, but among the countless calls for martinis, bourbon and scotch there was one voice missing: Big Jake's solitary bellow for rye whiskey. Nobody could stomach the stuff but Jake. *"Gimme a shot o' Ol' Overshoes!"* he'd cry in a voice like a Yukon wind. But big Jake was no longer with us that season, and the rye whiskey sat untouched behind the bar. I thought of ordering a shot myself—just to remember him by. But then it didn't seem right somehow. Seemed like Jake might be there watching. If he was, he'd want that rye for himself. Nobody could stomach the stuff but Jake, God bless his hide!

2. I drove up to Three-fingered Johnny's to pick up a few extra dry flies. But Johnny's little cabin was all boarded up. There were weeds among his prized dahlias; there was no Nipper or Blue barking to announce my arrival. Johnny had lost the Big Fight. His opponent was a fella named Mr. Cancer. Not many enter the ring with that gentleman and come back to tell the story: he's no clean fighter! Poor Three-fingered Johnny. But what a fly-tier he was! And not even the stub of a thumb or pointer-finger on his right hand! I still had a couple of bucktails I'd bought from him last season; I took

them gently from my fly box and stuck them in my hat to remember him
by. Old Johnny. Now that he'd crossed that Other River, the boys and
me couldn't help believing he still wore the same patched-up old pair of
black waders and was busy catching trout on the Other Side.

There were no references to death or dying in the *Summa Piscatoria*
or any other of my father's works; seldom were there even references to
killing fish—except in the form of admonitions not to. One might expect
in such a pacifistic angler some "contemplative" motivation—perhaps a
Gandhian reverence for nonviolence, or a secret membership in the
Vedanta Society. But H2O took pains to point out that his freeing of fish
was "inspired by no soft-headed mysticism of any kind"; he released fish
for just one reason: "A dead fish will never strike a fly." By restoring fish to
the river and advising others to do likewise, H2O was doing his best to
immortalize the ancient art; the immortality or mortality of the artist was
of no moment to him or his friends. Life and Death were, according to
H2O, "abstractions to be viewed in a scientific light," and he published
more than one caustic review of books by angler-authors who allowed
themselves such "tear-jerking liberties" as the two quoted above. He once
drew me aside to explain the Scientific View of Life and Death:

"Life," he began, "evolved from certain obscure enzymes in the
Primordial Days. Competing for food, for mates, for favorable habitat
and so forth, these minute slimy substances grew incredibly complex after
aeons of evolution, and Humanity resulted! You see, Augustine, the
thing we call *life* is, in any individual creature, nothing more than a unit
of Energy borrowed from the Sum Total. This Borrowed Unit remains in
the creature until such time as its body becomes an unfit container for life
energy, at which time 'death'—which is really nothing more than the
moment when the borrowed unit is sucked back into the Sum Total—
occurs. This Sum Total goes on progressing and improving and getting
more sophisticated, while dead units only decay till there is nothing left
of them but inorganic material that will eventually be reconstituted, by
the Sum, into a new creature. Now, this Sum Total is precisely what
primitive and superstitious people call 'God,' and though you and I will
cease to exist when our borrowed energy units are returned to this 'God,'
we may console ourselves somewhat with the thought that Angling will
very likely continue to exist as long as 'God' does. So, through the art of
Angling you and I can, in a way, partake of eternity!" He stopped here,
apparently too moved by his explication to go on.

I'd found this Sum Total business incredibly depressing at the time
he explained it, and on my riverside rock it was worse: why should the

first piddling enzyme bother to exist in the first place when its destiny was nonexistence? Why should the bloody Sum Total give a hoot whether it "progressed" or not? What's the difference between an undeveloped Sum Total and a developed one? And why throw back fish if Death refused to throw *us* back once he caught us up out of the Stream of Life? If H_2O was right, then the whole blasted creation was a ridiculous ado about nothing. But I'd seen this the day he delivered the Sum Total Sermon. I didn't try to refute him then, and felt no need to refute him later. I had *confidence* in H_2O. I was *glad* this was the philosophy he'd picked out of all possible philosophies—because H_2O had an unerring knack for being dead-ass wrong about anything that really counted. I confidently rejected the Sum Total Theory without giving it another thought.

Ma's ideas about Life and Death were interesting. She claimed to have no Philosophy of Life at all and insisted that there was nothing anybody could know about death until they died, at which point it was too late to share one's discoveries. One might expect a person with such indefinite opinions to take little interest in the metaphysical speculations of others, but this was just where Ma got interesting: she believed there was nothing to know, so there was nothing to say, therefore she could not *bear* to hear anybody, however learned or qualified, advancing theories of life and death. The Scientific View, the Christian View, the Existentialist View, the Oriental View—they were all one to her: Hogwash. I once heard her say that "talk 'bout croakin' is fer preachers in churches, an' preachers in churches are fer idiots with nothin' more constructive t'do but set an' listen to somebody 'at don't know nothin' standin' in a podlium talkin' 'bout somethin' nobody don't know nothin' about. Why Izaak Walton hisself says on the very last page o' *The Angler*: 't'beget mortification we should frequent churches.' Now what the hell'd a sane person wanna waste time gettin' hisself mortified fer?"

The day H_2O endowed me with his Sum Total Theory, Ma had been doing laundry in the basement—yet through the din of washer and dryer, she sensed Croakin' Talk on the wind. Springing into the study just as H_2O concluded his dissertation, she commenced ranting and shouting that his theory was "a commie plot t'turn healthy kids into mixed-up zombies in food-stamp lines thinkin' their great-grand-kin was nothin' but talkin' wads o' snot in a stinkin' swamp somewheres, an' ever'one an' ever'thing is headed fer a big black basket in the middle o' no-goddam-where!" H_2O protested, insisting that his were merely the most advanced scientific postulates and that he labored not to disillusion but to enlighten—but to this Ma replied, "An' what are yer scientists these days but a bunch o' undersexed communistic heaps o' shit with teeth? All they do is set around cookin' up bombs an' nerve gas an' giant Trojan Erections t'wipe us all abso-damn-lutely off the face o' the friggin' world ferever!" (The last weapon in her list was a reference to the Trojan Nuclear Plant on the lower Columbia River; named after the popular prophylactics, its cooling tower was designed by bawdy-witted engineers to look like a decapitated male member.) H2O always had difficulty replying to rejoinders of this sort; he retreated without comment.

Ma made two exceptions to her No Philosophy Allowed maxim: she let GG rattle on about Heaven, The Bad Place and the Second Coming ("'cause GG's old, an' anyhow she don't mean nothin' by it"), and she let Bill Bob, who was the apple of her eye, say anything he liked about anything at all: unfortunately she never understood him.

Maybe Knickerbocker and his saints and scriptures knew something worth knowing about death—he had calmed Abe's friend down. But I didn't even know Knicker, so I couldn't know what he knew. My personal comprehension of this enigma called "dying" consisted of one fact: someday I'd do it. . . .

So on the rock in the fog I went fishing: I fished my head and heart for the least shred of a wise or consoling notion about death. I cast about in all the eight directions—and all I reeled in were enzymes, Big Jakes and Three-fingered Johnnies while the unstoppable, unanswerable, unbearable questions kept lapping, lapping, lapping at my brain like the green waves lapping at the gray rock. My angling craft had smashed upon the reefs of incomprehension. I was marooned.

At last the cold crept up my spine; at last it filled me from foot to head; at last I grew so chill and desolate that all thought and pain and awareness came to a standstill. I wasn't miserable anymore: I wasn't anything at all. I was a nothing—a random configuration of molecules. If my heart still beat I didn't know it. I was aware of one thing only: next to the gaping fact called Death, all I knew was nothing, all I did meant nothing, all I felt conveyed nothing. This was no passing thought. It was a gnawing, palpable emptiness more real than the cold. I was a hollow, meaningless nothing, entranced on a rock in a fog. From that moment I was haunted by the drifting corpse no longer. I didn't need to be haunted by it any longer: it had done its work.

6

Anamnesis

In the green world we carry with us
like a secret illness from a city
we've escaped,
know, too, the shadow suspended in green space, . . .

—*Henry Carlile*

I DON'T KNOW how long I stayed on the rock. When I finally crept down it was dark. I fell twice as I stumbled up the bank, but made it to the cabin. Inside I built a fire and huddled near the flames, and as the fire grew, as my rigor mortis dissipated, I discovered one of the gifts of desolation: a hollow nothing endowed with senses becomes the thing its senses perceive. Thus I became the fire, and as fire my only wish was to flame, to consume, to grow. Dazed and burning I roamed the room, throwing on logs till the fireplace was a wall of flame and bright tongues flickered forward, blackening the mantelpiece; I threw on the fishing books, magazines and manuals that abandoned me in the presence of death, threw on old fishing journals, notes and charts, threw on the Ideal Schedule—and the fire laughed and devoured. Then, as I bent for the last few scraps in the bottom of the woodbox, I found a pitchy knot and started to throw it in—but it reminded me of something; nighttime; a room full of shadows; this knot; I'd known them all before, somewhere, and somehow they now threatened the gloom and desolation.

The overstoked fire faded quickly, but I lit no lantern: I put the pine knot in the tongs, lit it in the coals, set it on the hearth stones and watched it burn. When the light dimmed to a faint gold cast more by the knot than by the dying coals, a word popped up—one of Bill Bob's inventions. I said it aloud: "Dreefee." And in a flood the night in a dim room, the ritual I'd shared with my brother, the mystery revealed, but since forgotten, came back to me. . . .

When Bill Bob was small he had a going-to-bed ritual Ma called Tuckin' Time—a quiet piece of time when Ma or H2O sat on his bed listening while he conducted a rambling discourse that would fade to muttering, and finally to sleep. He was as addicted to Tucking Time as was H2O to his nightcaps (the one he drank and the one he wore). But often when my parents presided at his bedside they'd been squabbling, and all around them was a squabblesome aura that got mixed up in Bill Bob's aura and woke him right up. After a few dozen Tuckin' Times spent listening to him ramble for fifty or sixty minutes with no sign of slowing, Ma and H2O realized they just didn't have the tuckin' touch. So I was made the official tucker-inner.

Given the crass lullaby repertoires and cacaphonous vocal apparati of us older Orvistons, it's no wonder that Bill Bob found his own voice the most euphonious for a send-off into sleep. And given the unaffected spontaneity of a worn-out child at bedtime and the cosmologic calm prevailing at that hour, it's no wonder that some of the most amazing extemporaneous stories, soliloquies and songs ever sounded on this planet come out of such kids in their beds at night. When Bill Bob was relaxed and talkative and the calm was just right, sometimes for seconds, sometimes for long minutes his kid-accoutrements would fall away and a squeaky-edged but bardic voice would launch off on free and easy wanderings, and he would astound me with words that weren't only beyond his years, or beyond mine, but were beyond anyone's—beyond the kind of time that ticks away in this green and gray world.

Most kids have a special stuffed animal, ratty blanket or dog-eared book they take to sleep with them—and a lot of kids, lacking this talisman, go berserk and scream themselves to sleep. Bill Bob had no one special talisman: Bill Bob had *dreefees*. None of us ever quite figured out the etymology of that word, but when I asked him years later Bill Bob thought it might be an amalgamation of "dream" and "feed"—food for dreams you might say. The dreefee itself was always some carefully selected relic of the day's adventures, so he had a different dreefee every night. And every bit as important as the dreefee was its placement: some hung from the ceiling, some he stuffed in his mouth, some he taped to his hair and so on. But if the placement was altered before Bill Bob fell asleep it had the same effect as having refused him his dreefee altogether. He didn't fuss, didn't protest, didn't seem to take notice: he simply didn't go to sleep. If the dreefee was never put back where it had been he would lie in bed in the dark all night long—wide awake. Ma and H2O were surprisingly lenient toward this idiosyncracy; Bill Bob had always been self-sufficient and well behaved, and they appreciated it enough to indulge a few peculiarities. But I can recall four times when Bill Bob didn't sleep all night due to dreefee problems. One time the dreefee was a dried-out two-dimensional garter snake that had been run over by a car; Bill Bob wanted it under his pillow as he intended to ask the Tooth Fairy to blow it up like a balloon into three dimensions again, but H2O spotted it before the Fairy and it ended up in the garbage disposal. Another problem dreefee was the skeleton of a baby rabbit found while digging for treasure in the woods; Bill Bob wanted it hung among the shirts in his closet for reasons that remained obscure, but since it wasn't entirely decomposed it went the way of the snake. The third troublemaker was a dried dog turd bleached white by the elements and shaped incredibly like a tiny sleeping polar bear; Bill Bob said that it *was* a tiny sleeping polar bear, that it had been eaten by a dog, that it had proven indigestible, that it had been eliminated, that it was in a coma thanks to its unmentionable experiences in the dog, and that he planned to invoke the powerful Tooth Fairy again, who would restore it to life, resulting in his acquiring a pet even more remarkable than a certain surgeon's Doberman rat . . . but Ma threw the poor polar bear out the window without a question or a glance at its miraculously sculpted bearness. (So fine was the canine-colon craftsmanship that I snuck outside with a flashlight and found the thing; its head, like a ring-eyed person's, had been jarred off, but I glued it back on, lacquered it and placed it on my fly-tying desk where it stands to this day.) The fourth banned dreefee was a wad of Silly Putty that Bill Bob wanted on his forehead, intending for it to spread evenly over his face in the night so he'd wake with a perfect putty mask of himself which he would peel off and hang on the wall for the aesthetic gratification of friends and family; H2O confiscated this one, stating reasonably enough that, were the plan to fructify, the mask would suffocate the maskee long before dawn. But on the days that followed these dreefee disruptions Bill Bob would drag about the house with dark circles under dulled eyes, able to operate only two or three toys, games and radios simultaneously instead of the usual five or six, and Ma and H2O's hearts would ache. So with each refusal and ensuing sleepless night Bill Bob silently, non-violently and successfully lobbied for greater parental liberality. They eventually allowed such startling dreefees as a bucket of thistle down stuffed in his pillowslip, a gunnysack full of scarlet vineleaf maple leaves scattered all over floor and bed, a stray dog coaxed under the covers (which left him—after Ma took it to the pound the next day—with a commemorative case of ringworm that he flaunted like a black arm band) and a live scorpion he captured under a rock on the Carper Ranch and placed on his nightstand. This little monster mysteriously escaped its plastic container (and impending execution by Ma) during the night and proceeded to make appearances in every room in the house week after week; it was last sighted scuttling across the living-room floor some six months later during a fly-angler's conclave, which conclave broke up directly thereafter despite H2O's assurances that it was the only scorpion ranging his home, that it was shy, and that its sting was no more potent than a bee's. It may inhabit the house still, though H2O once suggested during a squabble that the unfortunate creature had doubtless bitten Ma and died of blood poisoning, to which Ma replied that, no, it had found and fallen in love with one of Hen's mayfly imitations and died of lover's nuts trying to figure out how to screw the thing.

As I sat alone in my cabin before the dying embers, I remembered a night when Bill Bob's dreefee had been a pine knot like the one I now held. He'd lit it, set it in a cast-iron pan, and we watched it burn in the dark. In those days he had a pair of lensless horn-rimmed glasses he would don for the purpose of dreefee-inspecting; he wore them as he lay on his side, intent upon the flickering knot. Our conversation at Tuckin' Time invariably began with the same four sentences:

"Gussy?"

"Bill Bob."

"I got to tell you somethin'."

"Tell me somethin'."

Then he'd lie there a while trying to think what it was he had to tell me. This night he seemed to have an extra hard time thinking of anything, maybe because it was so peaceful just being quiet and watching the little flame. Finally he said,

"You like my dreefee?"

"That's askin', not tellin'," I said, thinking to pin him down.

"That's 'cause I'm not tellin' ya yet, dummy."

"Oh." I said. He always was tough to pin. "Yeah, I like it. Makes a real nice night-light."

"What's a night-light?"

"You don't know what a night-light is? Come on, you're kidding."

"I'm only seven," he protested. "I'm not 'sposed to have a big vocabulary at my age."

"Oh."

"So what's a night-light?"

"It's just what it says it is: it's a light that lights the night, just like your dreefee's doing."

Bill Bob seemed to mull these words as if they constituted a grand conundrum. Flames framed in horn-rim burned in both his eyes. I said, "For somebody who has to tell me somethin' you sure do a lot of asking."

But he didn't hear. His eyes had stopped blinking; he hardly seemed to breathe. He was lost—in thought, in recollection, in whatever it was he so often got lost in. It was the same expression he'd worn as a baby, staring at the 7-Up bottle. In an absent whisper he asked, "Know what a light night is?"

"No," I said.

"It's just what it says it is: it's a night that nights the light."

"Oh."

"Understand?"

"No."

"It's a night—like a night in shining armor—except his armor is black and makes everything darker all around him."

"Oh, a *knight*," I nodded. "The kind with swords and shields and lances."

"Yeah. It's a knight that nights the light."

"How does he night light?" I asked.

"By making it darker," he said, "like the world's shadow does to the sky at night."

"Oh."

"So now do you know who your light-knight is?"

"No."

"Dummy."

"Whaddya mean, 'dummy?'" I grabbed his foot and tickled it through the covers, but he pulled it away. He was serious about all this.

He said, "It's your *shadow*."

"My shadow? Then why call it a 'light knight'? My shadow is dark."

He said, "It may be dark, but it's way lighter than you are."

"Come on," I said; "I'm a whitey, same as you."

"Whiteness don't matter," he said. "Skin weighs more than shadows."

"Ah, *that* kind of light!"

"Yeah," he said. "But the other kind too, because know what your shadow *really* is?"

"No," I confessed, wondering if he'd been studying some old riddle book on the sly, "not unless it's the thing on the ground the sun makes, or according to you, my 'light knight.'"

He said, "It's both those things, but it's something else, too. Know what?"

"No. What?"

Leaning toward me, he whispered this secret: "It's your Garden Angel!"

"Oh," I said, figuring he was mispronouncing it, "Guardian Angels" being an institution GG often referred to.

"Know what your Garden Angel is?"

"I don't think so."

He smiled. "Told ya I had to tell ya somethin'."

"OK, OK, so tell me."

He leaned toward me again and whispered, "Your Garden Angel is your twin."

"My twin?" (This was not GG's brand of angel!)

"Yeah," said Bill Bob.

I began to suspect he didn't know what he was talking about. I said, "How can he be my twin? I thought he was my shadow, and my light-knight, and the thing that nights the light."

Without the least hesitation he explained, "He looks like your shadow, and he looks like the thing that nights the light. But really he's your twin."

"I get the picture," I said sardonically. "I had this twin brother, born when I was born, but nobody in the hospital saw him come out so he just snuck off and . . ."

"He wasn't born when you were born!" cut in Bill Bob. "He *died* when you were born. And he's *born* when you die."

That stopped me. This was getting complicated. I said, "Wait a minute, Bill Bob. What's the difference between what my Garden Angel *looks like* and what he *is*, for starters."

He shook his head at his hopelessly dull pupil. "What your Garden Angel *looks like* is what you see. What he *is* is what he is. Lots of junk don't look like what it is."

"Oh yeah? Name me some of this junk."

"Dummy," he said. "Like the world isn't flat and the sun don't go around it and the moon ain't bigger than the stars and shooting stars aren't stars at all and . . ."

"All right already!" I said. Hmmm. The kid was on top of it. So far, anyway. "You got a point there Bill Bob, but I'm not letting you off the hook so easy. How can my Garden Angel be my twin when he's one-dimensional and black and gets tall or short or deformed depending on what the light is doing to him, and dies when I'm born, and is born when I die? What kind of twin doesn't look or act like a twin at all? What good is he? What's he got to do with me?"

Bill Bob shook his head sadly. "That's *edzackly* what your Garden Angel says about you."

"But he's the weird black wavery deformed one, not me!"

Calm and certain, Bill Bob replied, "Not in the place where *he* lives. Where he lives you look just like he looks here where you live."

I had to stop and think about this one; I could feel battalions of brain cells mustering in my forehead, not about to be routed by a seven-year-old. I said, "But my Garden Angel lives on the ground, or wherever the light happens to throw him. Anyone with eyes in their head can see that."

He said, "Anyone with eyes in their head can see the sun going 'round the flat world and the moon way bigger than the stars."

I mumbled, "You got a point there."

His mouth stayed still, but his eyes grinned a little through his glassless glasses. "I told ya twice I had to tell ya somethin'. Now I'm tellin' ya: See, every person in the world has their Garden Angel, and every Garden Angel has their person."

"Yeah?"

"Yeah. And every person thinks their *Angel* is just their shadow, and every Angel in the Garden World thinks their *person* is just their shadow."

"Hold on a minute! Garden World? What's this about a Garden World?"

"Sure, the Garden World—where the Garden Angels live. We live in our world and they live in theirs. But if we learn the right things and they learn the right things, then finally we get to be each other's friend and go back and forth to both worlds wide awake forever, which is funner than you can shake a stick at."

Wonderfully confounded, I thought I'd better confuse him before he lost me completely: "But Bill Bob, if our shadow is on the ground, then we should be able to dig a hole and get into the Garden World whether we did the right things and met our friend and all that or not. Now you and me have both dug enough holes to know there's no world down there, right?"

"Wrong!" he said, disgusted and utterly unconfused. "Listen, ya big dummy: I told ya already, *you* are your Garden Angel's shadow, and he's yours. You think you're standing up. He thinks you're lying flat. He thinks he's standing up. You think he's lying flat. Look at your light-knight now. . . ."

I looked at my shadow: it was sitting on the closed bedroom door. Bill Bob said, "Go out that door you're in the hallway, not the Garden World. You don't get into the Garden World by *walking* there."

Again I mumbled, "I guess you got a point."

Bill Bob said, "The trouble with people *and* with Garden Angels is *they just don't know they're twins.*" (This obviously struck him as a regrettable state of affairs.) "We think we're growing bigger and older. They think they're growing younger and smaller. We think we're . . ."

"Hold it!" I cried. "They think they're getting *younger and smaller?*"

He nodded, very solemn now, eyes riveted on the quivering flame. He said, "You see, Gussy, Garden Angels come from the ground, like carrots, into their world. That's one reason they're called Garden Angels. When they first come out of the ground into the Garden World they're very old, or hurt, or sick, or crippled or sad, but the other Angels help them out and they get better bit by bit, and they're real happy to be there in that world because it's all so pretty and nice, like the nicest garden in this world 'cept the whole place there is like that, and everybody's so friendly and there's nothing to make ya scared or hurt nowhere like in our world. It's such a wonderful place to be that the longer those broken ol' Angels live there the younger and smaller they grow and the friendlier and happier they get, so the ones who have lived there the longest are the kids and babies. And the very longest ones are tiny, and so bright and happy they look like flames burning up out of gladness—like *that* one!" He pointed at the dreefee: a bubble of pitch had ignited inside it and was sending out a minuscule but brilliant white torch that glistened and hummed as it burned . . .   but after a time it consumed itself and vanished, so I asked,

"What happens to the oldest, smallest little babies when they burn all the way out? Is that the end of them?"

"No," he said. "They don't ever burn *out*. Sometimes they burn *up*. But most often they just get so bright and small that nobody can see them anymore, and they disappear out of the Garden World and enter our world, and we trade places."

"We *what?*"

"We trade worlds with our twin: we go there and our twin comes here. See, all the time our twin is growing younger and happier, we're growing older and more crippleder, till finally we die, and pass through our shadows, and get buried in our ground. Then we journey up and up through a long, black tunnel till we reach the Garden Angel ground, and then we sprout up through it like carrots, and there we are, Garden Angels now, not people—but the big, crooked, sad, new sort of Angels that haven't been there long. And our twin, who has disappeared in a little bright speck too small to see, passes through his shadow and comes here and gets in a lady's stomach and turns into a baby. So it's really not *our* world or *their* world. We trade back and forth. Both worlds belong to both of us. We're twins. The shadows we pass through are each other, us and our twins, swapping places."

This was mind-boggling information! I mulled it over, comparing it to GG's Heaven and Hell System and H2O's Borrowed Energy Units and Primordial Slime, and the Garden World struck me as not just more pleasant, but also more plausible. It accounted for where we came from before we were born—which GG's formula didn't—and it accounted for where we went when we died—which H2O's formula didn't—and any fisherman would like the sense it made out of releasing fish, for after a blissful sojourn in the Garden World you could come back here and catch the great-grand-fish of the ones you'd spared. But then a problem occurred to me:

"Bill Bob, what about this? Let's say a guy like Chunky Chuck . . ." (Chunky Chuck was an obese buddy of Bill Bob's) ". . . gets run over by a car and killed. Now his Garden Angel couldn't have been in the Garden World very long because Chunky's only seven years old. So the Angel must still be tired and beat up from his last life in this crummy world, and he must be pretty darn big, too—huge even, if he's anything like Chunky. So how is this Angel going to be able to disappear and come here and get in a lady's stomach right off the bat?"

Bill Bob had been nodding his head with suppressed excitement as I'd set him this problem, as though the solution to the Chunky Chuck Difficulty was a thing he'd always known and delighted in, as an old metaphysician delights in the thorniest of paradoxes. In an intense whisper, he said, "Remember, Gus, how I told ya that some Garden Angels burn *up* even though none burn *out?*"

"Yeah, I remember."

"Good. Let me tell ya, then."

"Good. You tell me then."

"Sometimes in the Garden World a full-sized, new Garden Angel—wrinkled and beat-up and not very bright or happy yet compared to the little ones—will be walking in the woods, or in the hills, or out in the country somewhere way away from everybody else. And while this Angel is walking along he'll hear a sound, and he'll look behind him, and the Queen of the Garden World will be there on her white horse! And she's so very very beautiful, and he's so happy to see her, that what usually only happens to an Angel after years and years in the Garden World will happen to this Angel *in an instant:* watching her and seeing her smile and looking at the beautifulness and niceness and love flowing out of her reaching to every corner of the whole Garden World and even every corner of the sky, he starts to shrink like crazy and turn brighter and brighter, then Poof! He goes off like a million flash bulbs! and at the same instant his shadow—like Chunky Chuck—goes splat in this world because the car hit him! And they swap worlds just like that!"

"Incredible!"

"Yeah, it is," he agreed. "And you could say that Chunky got hit by the car because his Garden Angel saw the Queen, or you could say that the Angel saw the Queen because Chunky got hit by the car. Either way it comes out the same, and they swap, because they're really really really *twins*, and every single thing one of them does, both of them does."

"I see what you mean," I said. "Can't get any twinnier than that."

"Nope," he said.

We were silent for a while, watching the dreefee. I don't know what Bill Bob was thinking, but I was thinking I'd like to get a look at this Queen. Somebody so beautiful she made you pop off like a million flashbulbs . . . wow! I was liking his cosmology more by the minute. Then I thought of something else: "Bill Bob?"

"Gussy?"

"What about animals, like fish for instance? And what about trees and plants and bugs and all those kinds of critters? They all got Angels?"

He looked me in the eye and said, "Everything that gots a shadow gots a Garden Angel."

"What about a river, then? A river doesn't have a shadow."

"Dummy," he grumbled, shaking his head again. "A river does, but a river's shadow is on the bottom of the river."

The varmint was right; I remembered the strange, vague shadows of waterfalls I had seen. Bill Bob yawned, smiled, took off his horn-rims and said, "I'm gettin' sleepy, Gus."

I sure wasn't. Not with these Garden Worlds and Angels and twins running around practically in plain sight. "Just tell me a couple more things," I begged.

"OK" he sighed.

"Doesn't everything there is have a shadow?"

He shook his head again. "Dummy."

"Whaddya mean, 'dummy'? Name me three things that don't have shadows."

Fool that I am, I thought I had him this time. But he stared at the dreefee and in a calm, soft voice that sent three chills dashing up my spine said, "Fire. Air. Light."

He was seven, and he knew more than five of me put together. Trying to save face, I said, "I know another."

"What?"

"The lenses of your glasses."

He laughed sleepily. Trying to wake him, I added, "And shadows, Bill Bob. Shadows don't have shadows."

"But they think they do," he said sadly. "That's why we don't know we're twins. That's why we get frightened."

I scratched my head to help it along, but it didn't help enough. "I don't get ya, Bill Bob."

He said, "There are no shadows, Gussy. Not really there aren't."

And that's all the explanation he ever gave.

After a long silence he yawned, then said, "We're using another shadowless thing."

"What's that?"

"Words."

Words. The kid was way too many for me. I thought about our family as I watched him watch the pine knot: if it had just been Ma and H2O and me then maybe energy units, enzymes, genes and chromosomes would have accounted for us, for I was a plausible offspring. But this little one we called Bill Bob—such theories could never account for him. Most of the things I knew were directly traceable to Ma, H2O and Angling, but almost none of what Bill Bob knew was traceable to anyone anywhere. He knew things nobody told or taught him. He was a most implausible son. To account for the things he did, for the way he was, for the words he spoke, you needed a Garden World, or something very like it. But he was going to sleep and I had more questions to ask . . . "Bill Bob?"

". . . Gussy."

"I got to ask you somethin'."

"Ask me somethin'."

"Does my Garden Angel like to fish?"

"Just as much as you do," he said.

Fantastic, I thought . . . then up cropped another problem: "What happens to Garden Trout when I kill a trout in this world?"

"The Garden trout your twin catches sees the Queen and bursts into light," he stated as matter-of-factly as if he'd said "Let's play checkers" or "What's on TV."

"But doesn't my Garden Angel see her, too, then?" (I had a crush on this Queen: I wanted to get a look at her!)

"No," said Bill Bob.

"Aw, why not?"

"Because if he did, he would burn, too. And you'd have to die, and you and your twin would have to swap worlds. She don't show herself to nobody 'cept who she chooses. She's usually careful and quiet about it, but when she wants to she can pick one Garden Angel out of a thick crowd of 'em and show herself only to that one, even if the rest seem to be looking in the edzack same spot."

I'd kind of expected this. It was consistent with the laws of Bill Bob's worlds, but it sure put the kibosh on my hopes to sneak a look at the lovely Queen. Beauty that kills. Now what good was a thing like that? I began to suspect the convoluted hand of God at play in the background somewhere. If she was the Queen, then who was King? And if there was a King, what chance was there for us piddling light-knights? Jealous and disappointed, I shrugged off my infatuation with the Queen and cooked up an abstrusity intended to bushwhack Bill Bob and his fairy-tale world but good:

"Bill Bob."

"Hmmm. . ." (he was dozing.)

"What about this: Suppose I kill a trout on the Metolius while somebody kills a deer in Montana while somebody else runs over a mouse in Minnesota while 8,000 people in 8,000 places all over the world die all at once of 8,000 sudden causes while 8 million animals and 8 trillion bugs and 8 zillion tiny organisms with shadows all do the same, all in an instant, which is about what happens all the time, you'll have to admit. . . . So, how can this fancy Queen of yours and this horse of hers be in all the corresponding umpteen-quintillion places in the Garden World all at once? Huh? Answer me that!"

Far from impressed, farther from dismayed, Bill Bob eyed me with the sleepy exasperation you might see on the face of someone whose cat wanted in or out for the tenth time that day and had roused him from a snooze with obnoxious meows. He said, "Dummy. The Queen is *everywhere, always, all at once.*"

"That's impossible."

He shook his head, sighed, and patiently explained: "Gus, you don't understand how *beautiful* she is. There's no way I can say it. Even sunlight covers half the world all the time, burning through thick clouds, making it light underneath. And it don't compare to Queenlight. Sunlight shines *on* things. Queenlight shines *through* things—through *everything*. It's everywhere at once, and everywhere *it* is the Queen is. . . ." He paused, leaned toward me again, and said, "The Queen is right *here*, right *now!*"

I looked around nervously. "I don't see her. Don't see her light, either. . . ."

Bill Bob sat up very erect and looked slowly, mournfully about the dreefee-lit room. "Me neither," he croaked, seeming suddenly on the verge of tears. "I used to . . . when I was real real small . . . but I can barely remember. . . ." his voice trailed off.

Exasperated with her elusiveness I blurted, "If she's there, why *can't* we? It doesn't make any sense. It's not fair!"

Bill Bob glared right through me and snapped, "Why can't we jump off cliffs and fly? Why can't we move chess pawns like queens? Why can't baseball batters just run to the pitcher's mound and back 'stead of havin' to go clear around all the bases?"

I felt ashamed. I said, "Sorry. Guess I'm sounding like the guys who cast lures that horrify fish into the river while they stand there moaning 'Why can't I catch a fish?' as if it's the fishes' fault. I guess if they could catch fish *that* way, fish wouldn't be worth catching. Is that sort of how the Queen is?"

Bill Bob nodded, turned to the dreefee and murmured, "The Queen's the most beautiful thing there is. She's where all pretty things come from. When we can't even look at something as pretty as the sun without shuttin' our eyes, how could we look at the Queen?"

He was right, and instantly I was enthralled with her again. Bill Bob saw by my face that I was beginning to get the picture. He said, "See, Gus, the Queen has to wear lots of thick robes to cover herself up with. She makes the robes herself, 'cause nobody else can make somethin' Queen-light don't shine through. It's not like she *likes* wearing all that heavy stuff. She does it 'cause of us. The Queen is *here* . . ." (He sought my eyes to be sure I understood how literally he meant this) ". . . she is right here in this room, and if it weren't for her robes, we'd be going Poof! See the Queen before you're ready, you die. . . ."

I turned to the dreefee—which somehow continued to flicker and burn though there seemed to be nothing left of it—and was lost for a time in thoughts of all he'd told me. When I turned to Bill Bob again he was curled in a ball. I had so many more questions!

"Bill Bob!"

"Gsshmm. . . ." he mumbled, eyes closed.

"Don't go to sleep yet! I have to ask ya some more . . ."

"Ask me."

"Can you really remember the Garden World, and the Queen, and all what you've been telling me? I mean, *really* remember?"

He frowned a little, opened one eye and said, "How could I tell ya somethin' if I didn't remember nothin' about it?"

"Then you *do* remember, really and truly?" I wanted to make sure of this place. I wanted to *go* there one day. Heaven and hell and nothingness were none of them my cup of tea.

Bill Bob nodded very sadly: "I remember. Not as much as I used to, but I couldn't say it good enough to tell ya somethin' then. Now I can say it, I forget. But what I tell is all what I remember. Except what I remember is lots lots better than anything I can tell . . . but Gus . . . I'm sooo sleeeepy. . . ."

"One more question?" I begged.

"OK" he mumbled.

"Why don't some things have shadows?"

"Some things don't need Garden Angels."

"But why?"

"That's two questions," he grumbled, alert even in his sleep.

"Please. No more, I promise. Why don't some things need Garden Angels?"

He smiled, sighed, and kept his eyes shut tight. "Dummy," he said, turning away toward the shadows. "Some things never die."

And he was asleep.

I stayed on, watching the last remnants of dreefee burn, lost in the labyrinth of shimmering images his Garden World had inspired: I saw loggers felling towering firs in our mountain forests while in Garden mountain forests Angel-loggers gaped as the trees they cut exploded, before they fell, into blinding pillars of light; I saw salmon and steelhead caught and killed in our rivers while in Garden rivers Angel-anglers watched their catch suddenly burst and blaze away to nothing in their hands. . . . And I saw that to die here was to begin to live there, which meant we never died, which meant there was nothing anywhere to be very much afraid of.

Questions continued to flood my mind: what must I do to meet my twin? What about the King, Garden animals, Garden rivers, cities, birds, fish, bugs? And what must I find or learn or love in order to see the Queen as she really was, without being consumed by her beauty? . . . but Bill Bob was asleep. And in the morning I'd be fishing.

The pine knot burned utterly away. I waited till the last coal faded, then asked the light-knights blackening the room, "You like my brother's dreefee?"

I'd no doubt they answered. And I'd have heard them, if only words had shadows.

In my cabin on the Tamanawis the pine knot crumbled and vanished. I was alone. It was pitch dark. And at once there came a vision of Abe the Drowned Fisherman, vivid as dreefee-light before my eyes. His head was rising from a green surface, but the green was not river water: it was grass—a wild, unending lawn. His gray hair was still sodden, his eyes still astonished, but the gaping mouth was closed. Behind him rose a verdant ridge, like Tamanawis Mountain, but unlogged and a hundred times higher, and all about him the plain of meadow grass so green it glowed. He seemed to be looking toward me, and the once-filmy eyes were clear now, and alive. The soggy shirt rose into view, then the waterlogged waders that drowned him, and when at last he stood free upon that wide meadow he smiled, then chuckled, then laughed and laughed, holding his hands high above his head and turning in slow, joyful circles, turning, turning, turning upon the meadow as he faded from my sight.

Book Three

Characters in Nature

You will often meet with characters in nature so extravagant that a discreet poet would not venture to set them upon a stage.

—*Lord Chesterfield*

Allah hath created every animal of water.
Of them is a kind that goeth upon its belly
and a kind that goeth upon two legs
and a kind that goeth upon four.
Allah hath created what He will.
Lo! Allah is Able to do all things.

—*Koran XXIV : 45*

1

The River Writes

... sounds, then a sentence, then just sound.
It's an odd place wherever I sit,
this fluid speech around me,
liquid vowels, purling,
consonantal patter ...
                 a word, then sounds.

                         —*Kevin Oderman*

WHEN I AWOKE, the first thing I saw was the morning star, bluegreen and brilliant between black silhouettes of cedars. I felt very strange, but very good; I'd no desire to do anything but watch—no schedule to keep, no fish to catch. I scarcely recognized myself: the fanatical fisherman in me had died, and what remained was a stranger. I was someone I barely knew, lying on my side, watching a star. The fisherman left a pair of binoculars on a peg at the window. He'd used them to watch for trout rising on the river; I aimed them at the star—and was amazed: brilliant greens, violets and blues eddied through it as it glittered and shone like the Queen's own dreefee. My naked eye had seen nothing of this whirling spectrum, and even now, through binoculars, I saw little of the beauty that must really be there. Then it struck me: trees, mists, mountains, flowers, fish, stones and streams—all these must be the robes saving my eyes from the Queen's searing light; yet they refracted and colored that light, and it shone dimly through, making them beautiful. Such beauty as the Queen's *must* exist. My heart pounded that it be so.

Not till the star began to fade and the sky to brighten did it dawn on me that the heavens were mimicking me, or I them: the fog was gone! Vanished in the night without a trace. Old fish-crazed Gus might have scoffed the notion that he was a microcosm mirroring the world, but whoever I now was smiled: it was almost contrived the way the two fogs, inner and outer, had dispersed simultaneously.

I got dressed, threw fruit in a rucksack and tore out the door to race the sunlight to the top of Tamanawis Mountain. As I ascended the beams descended, winning the event by a wide enough margin to warm the rock I collapsed on—the same rock Bill Bob used the day he'd drawn maps of the four directions—but I confess I gave north, west and east only a cursory examination before turning south to the river valley, in case too swift a weaning from my water addiction should bring on a withdrawal delirium. But just looking south and finally *seeing* something of the place where I lived aroused all the delight I could contain: as the sun went about its business of waking and warming the wooded valley, as its beams crept deeper, rousting lascivious mists from their tree-and-fern bedrooms in the draws, as its warmth spurred thousands of birds to cascades of song or flight, as it finally touched the Tamanawis and set the waters poppling and burning I felt the touch of a Garden World joy, and wondered what would become of my twin if I, instead of he, blazed and diminished into an ecstatic point of light. Letting my eyes flow down the river's sun-silvered bends, I began humming aloud what seemed to me the pronunciations of the random eroded letters those river bends formed, intoning—in the deepest, wettest voice I could muster—words like "yreeeee . . . yroooo . . . yriii . . . fwoooowrlwrlwrlwrlyryooooo. . . ." Then a long rapids ending in a pool: "krshrsh**KRSHKRSHKRSH**krlkrlkrorrkrorr-krorrrrsssshhhhhhhhhhhhhrrrooooooooo . . . ." Then I stopped, gaped, and burst out laughing as the morning up here with Bill Bob came back to me: he'd said he liked the Tamanawis River—he, the dryest of the dry—and when I asked *Why*, he laughed and said that was exactly what the river was asking me. Not till now did I catch his drift. There were the letters, there was the word: plain as water, in a flowing, utterly uncrabbed hand, current, erosion, gravity and chance had written *why* upon the valley floor! Billions of ever-changing, ever-the-same gallons of gurgling sun-and-moon-washed ink, spelling forever, in plain English, *why* . It was incredible. It had to be kidding. Rivers can't write, let alone ask questions.

why it said. It had a point. What did I know about what rivers could or couldn't do? But granting it literacy, what did it mean by *why* ? And was it asking *me*? I didn't know. I looked upstream and down for a clue, but all I saw were the random scribbled curves of runs and rapids. Yet right below, in quarter-mile letters it had taken centuries to form, water—my favorite element—asked in the only language I could read, *why* .

The word began to make me nervous. I swivelled to the northeast to escape the sight of it. But today the earth was talkative; today it gave no respite: my newly opened eyes fell upon a smooth almost head-shaped mountain. Within the past year it had been clear-cut on the right, clear-cut on the left, scraped, bulldozed, burned and 2, 4, 5-T-ed to rock and poison soil—but a single-filed swath of mangled, uncut firs had been left to straggle over the summit in a line. It looked like a green-haired Mohican, buried to the neck, beaten, tortured and left to die. It was hugely pathetic. An *entire mountain*—not just scalped and maimed but made ridiculous, robbed of all mountain dignity by the absurd surviving swath. "Seed trees," they're called by the men who leave them—men who claim they'll sire forests of the future, men who claim there will be no difference between that future forest and the primordial groves that have been killed. As if an ancient, ever-beautiful and mysterious virgin is no more desirable than choked rows of "easily harvested" clones. As if devastation, mass murder and forced mutation, when wrought upon plants and animals, are not crimes but a kind of farming! How could loggers or their employers or whoever the hell was responsible be oblivious to such a sight? The forests gave them incomes, homes, furniture, baseball bats, tool handles—and in return they treated it like an enemy in a bitter war. Granted, trees had to die. But couldn't men show some shred of gratitude or reverence in the way they killed them? Couldn't they see the difference between a murder and a sacrifice? I wanted to get a chainsaw and down the swath myself, saving the mountain its shame; I wanted to find who had done this thing, club him cold, give him a Mohican haircut and bury him to the neck . . .

until I looked back at the Tamanawis. *why* it asked me, and the question slowed and confused me just enough to let me remember myself down there fishing, maiming and murdering trout like enemies in wartime, ticking them off in my Log by the thousand, robbing them of all dignity at death by stuffing them, still thrashing, into my creel, or tallying them like downed bowling pins before flinging them back in the water, pierced and bleeding from my hooks, weakened by my clutching hands, stunned by the too-rare air. And never a thought about the suffering they endured for my amusement. Christ, I was nothing but an aquatic logger; Rodney my chainsaw, trout my trees, I had clear-cut many a pool. I hung my head, waiting for some river-god to give *me* the Mohican. . . .

But nothing happened. I guessed the gods didn't mess with petty vengeance. Not with haircuts anyway. Maybe they'd drown me later. Or maybe the shame twisting in my gut was the brand of vengeance in which they dealt.

I wanted to make amends. My first impulse was to build ponds and raise fish—like the penitent loggers who spend their twilight years planting trees. I mentioned this plan to the river. You can guess what it replied. . . . And again the question slowed and confused me: *why* plant fish only to watch them die at the hands of jokers like myself? Or if they lived, how would new fish undo the damage done to the maimed or dead? And just what *was* the damage done? I had to understand my crime before I could amend it. Maybe what was needed was participation in that activity Izaak Walton so long ago recommended to fishermen: maybe I ought to *contemplate*.

I tried. I'm not sure that what I did was proper "contemplation," but whatever it was, I did it long and hard. Was it the death of the fish that bothered me? Was *killing* the crime? If fish-death was the crux of the issue, then I should start telling fishermen to stop killing fish. But I'd watched H2O at this for years, and I'd seen that such sermons were suspect: for him and his friends more fish meant better flyfishing, better stories, prettier color glossies, a greater reading public, hence a greater income. With ham sandwiches and beer in the cooler at camp, how great was their need for the flesh of fish?

But I'd once watched a kid named after his own diseased breath eating stolen relish from a styrofoam cup because he was hungry and had no money. So here the issue grew complex. Dead fish are food. Live fish aren't. People have to eat, so fish have to die. At its roots, the matter was that simple. And a moral condemnation of fish killing doesn't get far before it runs smack up against Jesus himself, who fed fish to the multitudes, and who helped his disciples to the hundred and fifty and three, and who kept fish-breakfast warmed on the seaside fire *after* the Resurrection. If Christ didn't know *then* what a fish was for, who did? And according to him, you caught fish, you cooked them, you ate them, you thanked his Father from your heart, and that heartfelt thanks made the deaths of fish acceptable, made it a sacrament. My father's arguments against the killing of fish were based on an inability to understand Sacrifice. . . .

But what was the difference between need and greed? How many fish could a man kill without his killing becoming wanton? Which fish could he rightfully kill, and when? And what was the extent of each man's sacrifice on the day he *stopped* killing? For a lifelong commercial fisherman it meant the end of a way of life, the separation of men from boats and rivers and seas. And even in "sport" fishing, when a no-kill law leads a weekend plunker to stop fishing, it cuts one of the last little links the man had with the natural world and its wonders. It seemed justifiable to censure greed, but it didn't seem to be greed that was censured when fishermen were flatly condemned for keeping a few honest, hard-won victims. No, it wasn't simply the death of fish that bothered me. The thing I found offensive, the thing I hated about Mohican-mountain-makers, gill-netters, poachers, whalehunters, strip-miners, herbicide-spewers, dam-erectors, nuclear-reactor-builders or anyone who lusted after flesh, meat, mineral, tree, pelt and dollar—including, first and foremost, myself—was the smug ingratitude, the attitude that assumed the world and its creatures owed us everything we could catch, shoot, tear out, alter, plunder, devour . . . and we owed the world nothing in return.

I found myself thinking of a man I knew when I was small—a friend of Ma's; a Warm Springs Indian. He was known as Thomas Bigeater—hardly a promising name. He fished the runs of salmon and steelhead at Sherar's Rapids on the Deschutes, and at Celilo Falls on the Columbia before it was buried by the Dalles Dam. Ma took me when I was six to watch Thomas fish the last run of chinooks to challenge that falls. . . .

Ma is a rabid hater of dams and did her best to instill that hate in me: I remember her carrying me to the control-reservoir dam below Lake Simtustus on the Deschutes, just as the summer steelhead run was waning. She stood me on a rock, pointed and said, "Watch." Hundreds of steelhead fought the man-made white water blasting over the spillway. Most were battered and dark, growing weak. I'd seen many Deschutes steelhead in my short life, but none like these; I asked what was wrong, why their mouths gaped, why some had gone blind, why they wore the look of fish with hooks in their gullets. She said the dam was new; the fish couldn't understand it; they'd been battling that torrent for weeks; she said they'd come 300 miles inland, surmounted Bonneville dam, climbed hundreds of rapids, leapt a dozen falls, but the ill-designed ladder leading to their birthplace and spawning grounds eluded them. So they fought till the blasting water broke them, then drifted back down the river they'd climbed—unable to spawn, unable to return to sea. There was an island not far downstream covered with tall cottonwoods: the trees were black with vultures too stuffed with mouldering steelhead meat to fly.

. . . But that day at Celilo the chinooks had only gill-netters and Bonneville to contend with. They still came in good numbers, though they were but a shadow of the runs of Thomas's boyhood. Ma and I sat on the basalt cliffs, watching the old Indian in the distance, dwarfed by the magnitude of the falls. I'd expected a loin-clothed spearman, so for a time I was bored with this fat, dark man in white-people's clothing. But when Ma handed me the binoculars I saw that his fishing gear consisted of nothing but a leather thong, a totem club and a handmade net; and when Ma told me the carved club was sacred, handed down from ancestors; and when he dipped the first chinook with the impossibly long-handled net, my boredom died. Thomas was in his seventies, and he was obese, but he ranged along the rickety platform jutting over the froth with light, sure feet; and when he lunged to take a salmon he was sure-handed, fish-quick, strong. Once he'd captured a chinook he would hoist it up, then kneel over it: as it struggled in the net he would put his face to its face, rub it, speak to it . . . it would cease to thrash. He would look at the sky, at the falls, toward the sea to the west, then turn back to the salmon. I had no idea why he did this. When it was done he killed the fish with the ancient club, and as he did so his face was solemn—none of the pride or giddy jubilation I'd come to think was inevitable on a successful fisherman's visage. His corpulent agility, his aged youth, his sad success, his undignified dignity, his ugly beauty, his clothes, his name—all of it baffled and fascinated me.

While we watched him two young men, muscular and loud, strutted out on a platform just below us. The rocks around were covered with tourists, and whenever one pointed a camera at this pair they would scratch their butts or crotches, take dramatic swigs at a whiskey bottle or flash their middle fingers. I laughed. Ma didn't. The water beneath them was churning with chinooks. As the pair thrust barbed spears at them they cursed at each miss and whooped at each hit. The salmon they took they ripped from their spears and stuffed, still writhing, into gunnysacks. The ones they missed were "smart fuckers," the ones they hit "dumb fuckers." They missed twenty for every one they hit, and maimed many for every one they caught. Ma said spears were illegal, that the two were drunk, and that she didn't blame them—but I was six and had little idea what these remarks signified. I was accustomed to obnoxious fishermen. I was more interested in watching Thomas.

I asked Ma why he was named "Bigeater." She said it was because he ate big. She said Indians always had names that told you a little something about them, plus another name that was their real name. I asked what Thomas's real name was. She said we'd never know. I asked what her and my real names were. She said we didn't have any. I asked what "Gus Orviston" meant in English. She said, "Nuthin'." I said I wished I was an Indian. She said she used to, but no more. I asked why Thomas knelt so long over every fish when he could be catching more, like the guys below us. She said Thomas was praying for the salmon's spirit, and that if I counted I would see that the drunks weren't catching more. But they were wounding more. Thomas wounded none. She said Thomas Bigeater was the greatest fisherman in his tribe. He alone fed five big families. I said, "So do you, Ma." She smiled, but the smile was odd. Crooked. Maybe embarrassed. I asked what spirits were and why she and H2O didn't pray for them. She said she didn't know what they were, which was why she didn't pray for them, that Hen would have to speak for himself, and that she hoped to hell she didn't have to listen. I asked if Thomas could tell me what spirits were. She said she thought he could if anyone could. I asked if she'd ask him for me. She said, "You ask him. He's comin' this way."

I looked up. Thomas was crossing a frail wooden trestle, lugging his net, club and five chinooks threaded on a thong and slung over his shoulder. The load must have weighed 160 pounds. The trestle jounced and swayed with each step and he'd no free hand to hold the rope railing. The river below him was a stone-crushing, blinding mass of white. I said, "Thomas is brave." Ma shook her head the way that meant *yes*.

When he spotted us, Thomas Bigeater smiled and came up; I felt honored and eyed the tourists to be sure they noticed. They noticed the fish and that was all. I too ogled the fish, overcome with admiration; but when I looked at Ma's and Thomas's eyes meeting, there was a sadness in his and an anger in hers that I didn't understand. He laid the catch down carefully, sat beside me with a loud grunt, saw my confusion and smiled again, but so sadly. He said, "These are the last."

"AAEeii! A big fucker!" screamed one of the drunks.

"God damn dams," muttered Ma.

But Thomas had turned to the two men below, his expression as heavy and dark as his body. He said, "It is not the dam. It is *they* who are to blame!"

Ma's face twisted. "Come on, Thomas. I'd get shitfaced too if some three-faced white bureaucrat broke treaty an' sunk my fishin' an' burial grounds ferever!"

Thomas shook his head. "This is not forever. Dams break. Rivers never do. Two salmon can spawn a thousand. The salmon are an old and patient people."

"Well you an' me sure as hell won't be 'round t'see 'em returnin'," said Ma.

"Fuck! Missed the fucker!" bellowed a drunk.

Thomas's face terrified me. Emphatic, he repeated, "It is *they* who are to blame."

Now Ma shook her head. "I just don't get ya, Thomas. You mean they're the ones 'at let the white bureaucrats buy 'em out?"

Thomas said, "Who pays money, who accepts money, this means nothing." He pointed to the drunks. "It is for their actions that the people must suffer. So it has always been."

"But *you* didn't want no money!" Ma argued. "An' no white power company's got the right to swagger out here wavin' greenbacks in poor folks' faces! Nobody's got the right to wreck a way of life!"

Thomas regarded Ma's pinched expression through one cocked eye, then he looked at the ground for a while. Finally he said, "You are angry, little sister. You want to fight. But who is there to fight? What weapons would you use?" Ma pursed her lips and frowned, and it was odd to me how powerless and petulant she seemed—like a coyote pup growling at an old Kodiak bear. "I used to fight for the old ways," he said. "I used to try to defend them with my fists, and my strength. But the old ways of my tribe were not the ways my people wanted."

Ma looked confused. I looked at Thomas's fists, disbelieving that they would fail to defend anything they chose to defend. He said, "Finally I saw that most of my brothers were dark-skinned whites. Old cavalry men come back to suffer as Indians, maybe!" He laughed, then fell solemn: "I stopped fighting. I stopped because I saw that the old ways needed no defending. I stopped because the old ways are never killed, never lost. They are only forgotten, sometimes."

Ma's face was bitter. "I don't get ya at all, Thomas."

He said, "It is not white against Indian that causes suffering. It is the Spirit Father who sends down suffering when the old ways are forgotten. To remember this *is* the old way. Once I remembered this, I remembered that suffering had been sent down many times before—long before the whites came among my people, hopping like fleas in a drought . . ."

"Haii! Got 'im . . . Agh! stupid little fucker. . . ." One of the drunks had speared a jack and, seeing its smallness, kicked it from his spear; he watched with contempt as it flopped into the river to bleed to death.

"You see!" Thomas growled. "That is what I am saying. He kicks himself! He kicks our people! He brings down the anger of the Spirit Father. He helps build the great white dam."

But Thomas's anger vanished as quickly as it had come. He looked downriver toward the dam site; he closed his eyes; he began to chant. And at the blend of deep voice and booming falls I moved closer to Ma for comfort. But she was fidgeting.

"Sorry Thomas," she said, "but if ya want me to understand ya gotta give it to me in English."

Thomas turned to her: his face made me want to hide. He said, "I sing the story of the young men of the Nass River People. It cannot be sung in English. English will not sing. Do you scold the geese flying over in autumn because they sing in their own language!"

Ma blushed and turned away: it was the first time, the only time, I have seen her utterly abashed. Again she said, "Sorry." But this time she meant it.

Thomas extended his tree-branch arm out over the falls and bellowed, "Celilo! Stop your roaring! Roaring is not English!" Then he chuckled like a kid who'd farted in a car and chucked Ma in the ribs. She giggled and hugged the huge brown arm. Thomas said, "I will tell you this tale in *your* language, little sister and brother. Stiff and ugly as it is."

I thought he winked as he said this, but I wasn't sure. I didn't know Indians winked. I thought winking was in English.

Thomas's eyes grew vacant and he hummed for a little. All the while he told the tale he stared, but seemed not to see, across the river. . . .

> There was a place in a canyon, near a great mountain, where the Wolf Clan of the Nass River People lived. There was a pool there, below a falls, where many salmon came in spring and autumn. Much game was there, too, and berries. In this place it was easy to live, as it once was here. . . ."

Thomas extended his hand in a circle around us.

> But in this place the young men of the Wolf Clan grew foolish. They began to leave carcasses unburied. Later, they began to kill the small forest animals only to test their skill, letting them lie, after. And they began to kill more deer and elk than they needed, keeping the choicest meat, wasting skin, bone, entrails. And they bragged of their hunting prowess, killed for the sake of mere betting. No longer did they recite the sacred prayers over those they killed. No longer did they purify themselves before the hunt. No longer did they give their kill to the elders, to share with those who couldn't hunt. So the elders began to warn them. They warned of the Spirit Father's anger. And the young men laughed.
>
> One autumn they went to the fishing grounds and stayed after night came. Then, to amuse themselves, they caught salmon, slit their backs, placed burning torches in the slits, let the salmon go in closed-off shallows. They laughed as the salmon swam madly about. When the torches burned out they left them to die and returned to their lodges.
>
> An old tamanawis man found the salmon in the morning. Some had beached themselves in their pain and confusion, spraying red eggs and milky sperm upon the dry stones. Some swam till they died of exhaustion. Others bled to death. All but one were dead. This elder knew, then, that great trouble was to come. He returned and warned the people. He told them they must pack and leave that place. But the young men scoffed him. They ordered him to be silent before they slit his back and put a torch in it. To the people they said, "Winter is coming. The salmon are drying on the racks. It is time to make ready for the winter ceremonies, not to listen to crazy old fools."

But the tamanawis man said, "A fire is coming." And he packed and left that place. Only his wife and one daughter went with him.

Before many days passed, the Spirit Father began to voice his anger. For a little time each day the ground would shake and rumble. The other elders were worried now. They asked the young men to try to appease the spirits of the salmon people they had tortured and badly killed. They said the young men should fast, pray, offer gifts to the angry spirits. But again the young men laughed. They said the rumbling came from the ghosts, waking to join in the winter ceremonies. They said that ghosts like feasting and celebration, not fasting and prayer.

Then, for a time, the noises in the ground stopped. The words of the tamanawis man were forgotten. Even the elders thought the trouble might pass. But one day a sound like a thousand Celilos was heard, and from the mountain poured rivers of fire, and they streamed down every canyon, and fiery rocks flew through the sky like leaves in the first fall winds. The village and its people were devoured.

But those young men of the Wolf Clan saw the fire-river coming. They ran swiftly in their terror. They left their children and parents and they ran like wolves. . . . but the forest watched as they escaped to high ground. The forest had not forgotten who they were. Forest told the hazel to lean into the fire river, and the hazel leaned, setting itself aflame. Then Forest called on Wind. Wind came, driving the fire madly from tree to tree. The fire chased those bad men down.

All were destroyed but one. That one was badly burned. And he knew why his people were destroyed. He thought then that it would be better to die, and he sat himself under a smoking tree to wait. But the old tamanawis man came to that place and found him. He was a doctor, that old man. He brought him back to life.

The Wolf Clansman married that elder's daughter. He became known as Nothing-But-Scars. And he lived for many years, singing his story each winter as a warning to the other clans.   That is all.

I shivered and watched the river, fearing it would leap and snatch the drunks from their perch, and maybe Ma and me, too. Thomas said, "Then it was the river of fire. Now it is the white man's dam. These are the Spirit Father's weapons. Always it is the same: it is the greedy, the cruel, the ungrateful that bring down suffering upon the people."

I never asked Thomas what spirits were. I felt they must be even greater than he, and just his greatness made me afraid, there, beside the falls. A month later Celilo was silenced and the dam began to roar—in English. The ancient fishing and burial grounds were submerged.

Not long after, Thomas Bigeater died while fishing at Sherar's

Rapids. He was the first unconverted tribesman to be buried in the new Christian Indian cemetery high above the reservoir. A few zealots grumbled, but there was nothing to be done: the ancient burial ground, like the converts, had to undergo baptism. Until its immersion ended there was nowhere else to put an old fisherman.

On Tamanawis Mountain the sun had grown hot, but Thomas's tale chilled me—for comparing my fishing to Thomas's, resemblances were all too few. I hadn't descended to calling trout "fuckers," but I fished for and fed only myself. My angling was a contest—Gus Versus Coastal Streams—and throughout the contest my opponents flowed, undefiled, undefeated: I was a flea screaming challenges at a hibernating bear; I'd die of old age before my "enemy" yawned or stirred. The only consolation was that my Fishing Log had gone the way of the Wolf Clansmen— ashes now.

That greed, cruelty and ingratitude brought down suffering on the people, this I understood. But that I personally might be bringing suffering to something or someone besides my catch or myself—this possibility appalled me. Who would I be hurting? Who were "my people"? And if I found them, what could I do to help them? I guessed I wouldn't mind attempting a little friendliness if I had some friends, but who did I know? Nobody. . . .

But by choice. Was this my mistake? Avoiding all anglers and neighbors, fishing for and by myself—was this my crime against the people? I wasn't sure, but the thought left me uneasy.

The Spirit Father business was getting to me, too. I'd reckoned once that if He was so blasted important, He would make Himself less scarce. But how scarce was He? It was beginning to seem like everybody I respected—Bill Bob, Knickerbocker, Thomas—had some kind of secret Deity they worshipped, but who mostly just confused me. Yet everybody without a Deity looked a tad pedestrian beside those three.

Well, gods or no gods, I knew I wanted to annihilate all similarity between the Wolf Clansmen and me. The question now was *How?* And as I pondered it, who should come puttering into my mind but those long-winded god-fearing plunkers, Piscator and Venator, acting out a scene on the TV screen in my mind: *Compleat Angler;* Third Day; fourth chapter; Piscator and Venator out on the riverbank, plunking, munching, gassing away the day. . . .

"Look you scholar!" cries Piscator. "We have a bite!" (He means *he* has a bite: Venator can't catch a cold at this stage of his career.) "O' my word I have hold of him. Oh! it is a great loggerheaded chub. . . ." Piscator keeps his distance from the repugnant creature, but he orders Venator—who likes chubs—to land it and thread it on a willow branch. Then, already loaded down with trout (none of them Venator's), the jolly pair elects to head for their lodgings, Piscator spouting verbosities about harmless lambs and the swollen udders of bleating dams, Venator listening patiently, as if this Freudian flubdub will somehow make a fisherman of him.

They don't get far before they encounter a handsome milkmaid, Maudlin by name (and by behavior, as Walton depicts her), and her mother, who is not handsome and therefore remains anonymous. Piscator bellows at old Anonymous, "God speed you, good woman!"

But God doesn't speed her. Instead she stops in her tracks. Maudlin stops in her tracks as well. In fact, Maudlin and her mother do everything alike throughout the scene, like moms and daughters in Post Grapenuts and Ivory Liquid commercials—except that nobody would mistake Anonymous for Maudlin. (Then again, Venator might.) The picture of politeness, Piscator eyes Maudlin but addresses Anonymous: "I have been a-fishing, and having caught more fish than will sup myself and my friend, I will bestow this upon you and your daughter, for I use to sell none. . . ." With that, he opens his creel. Maudlin and Anonymous crowd close and gaze longingly at the trout. Piscator and Venator crowd close and gaze longingly at Maudlin. Then, lo and behold! Piscator hands over the great logger-headed chub!

The naive ladies act delighted. Piscator probably told them the thing was a baby pig, or a new species of trout. Or maybe he had Venator recite his famous Ode to Chub: "'Tis as good meat as ever I tasted!"—cutting him off before he can explain that he was raised on fried rats and boiled dog.

Anonymous and Maudlin give the two anglers some "fresh red cow's milk" (red? perhaps it was blood!). Then lovely Maudlin sings them a song that tells how milkmaids don't die of consumption and gout at the least provocation like upper-class ladies do. When she finishes, it's Venator's turn to get generous. Piscator has taught him well. He grins at his master, at old Anonymous, at the lovely young girl, and enthusiastically blurts, "I'll bestow Sir Thomas Overbury's milkmaid's wish upon her, 'That she may die in the spring, and being dead, may have good store of flowers stuck about her winding sheet.'"

Maudlin is so moved by the thought of dying the next spring (for wasn't it a backhanded way of saying she was upper class?) that she and Anonymous sing another pretty song together, moving Piscator to say,

"I'll give you another fish one of these days."

"Full of maggots, I'll warrant," thinks Anonymous.

"Come scholar, let Maudlin alone," says Piscator. (Walton doesn't tell us what the lout was doing to her.)

And so they go their separate ways, the anglers to gorge on trout, the ladies to gag on great loggerheaded chub. . . .

The memory was an inspiration: I couldn't do worse than that! I looked down the Tamanawis Valley. Pillars of blue smoke rose up here and there; beneath each pillar lived folks I'd never met, never sought out, never even greeted unless I had to. Whoever they were, they'd better watch out! A latter-day Piscator was about to attempt a little friendliness.

2

Neighbors

Most of the good men who lived along that shore
Wanted to be in love and give good love
To beautiful women, who weren't pretty,
And to small children like me who wondered,
What the hell is this?

—*James Wright*

WHEN I REACHED MY cabin I rifled it for potlatch gifts: smoked trout, salmon and steelhead; flies and fishing tips; tall tales, and a Timex to give away the time of day. Wasn't much, but it beat chub and death poems. I tossed it in the pickup and struck out for the first column of smoke. It rose from Coke and Doughnut Dairy.

I was greeted in the dairy driveway by six kids and three dogs, the former chattering with the comprehensibility of starlings in a fir at dusk, the latter arfing and snapping so enthusiastically I had to stay in the truck. I introduced myself, gave the kids some smoked fish (a little of which wasn't inhaled on the spot by the dogs), offered them free fishing lessons, told them where to find me and started to depart. But they yelled "WAIT!" and vanished in six directions, returning from various hideous-hued buildings with fresh and frozen fruits and vegetables, a dozen fertile eggs, a couple of steaks, a jug of raw milk, and their parents—Ernie and Emma—who took turns reaching through the window to shake my hand till it hurt as they discoursed about the weather, the kids, the impossibility of my refusing any of the gifts they'd just buried me with, the wonderfulness of my reputation as "the fella 'at saved the life o' that poor corpse outta the river," the crops and cows, which discourse was conducted at a full shout interspersed with an assortment of slaps, kicks, curses and threats directed at various heads among the encircling war party of dogs and kids.

The next smoke column rose from a forbidding, weatherbeaten, gray-boarded farmhouse half a mile down the road. At the head of the rutted dirt drive was a multicolored hand-painted sign which announced "CANDLES FOR SAIL," nailed to what had once been a fence post. What had once been front yard and garden was now a kind of insect-and-weed sanctuary, and what had once been a barn and chicken coop was now a kind of huge lean-to leaning on what had once been an International Harvester tractor. But what had once been a house was still a house, and a network of well-worn paths wove through the thistles, tansy, wild rose and daisies, betokening signs of vigorous life within. And sure enough, as I hopped out of the truck four seemingly angelic beings emanated out into the insects-and-weeds. The leader was what had once been a surfer and was now a candle-maker—a beaming, ephemeral, un-dernourished-looking person featuring a brown beard and yellow braid that shared the remarkable distinction of reaching to his woven jute belt. He was followed by a consort named Satyavati—a quiet, dark-skinned, very pretty, very skinny woman with a braid just like the candle-maker's, only black. Bursting past them were two yellow-braided sons, aged three and five, named Rama and Arjuna. (The candle-maker's name was Steve.) Rama was the smaller son with the ax. Arjuna had a hatchet. These two greeted me with identical dour nods, then set upon a formidable clay embankment with their weapons, apparently intending to hollow out a cavern (into which, perhaps, the family would move when the house too became a lean-to). Their excavations weren't faring well. Rama's yellow braid unravelled after one swing and his ax, though missing his head, was driving the ends of his hair into the bank at each stroke; to lift the thing required a violent backward snap of his entire being, but often as not it was only ax-pinned hair, not ax, that he pulled out of the bank. "Thwack. Youch! Thwack. Youch! Thwack," said Rama and his ax. Arjuna's braid was faring better but his hatchet wasn't: he'd selected a several-ton boulder to extirpate from the clay, chip by chip by chip.

Steve and Satyavati's matching pants and shirts were of baggy white Indian cotton. Rama's and Arjuna's were of the same cut and material, no longer white. They were a pleasing sight in the morning sun, the four of them there in the weed sanctuary in their cotton and braids and skinny bodies and Oriental names (except Steve). The ax and hatchet worried me for a while, but the longer I stood there with them the more I began to feel like growing a braid that hung to my butt and not worrying about anything forever. Like, it was what it was. Like, the hatchet hits Arjuna and it hurts for a while. Or it doesn't hit him and doesn't hurt for a while. Like Rama hacks off a toe; sew it back on. Like Arjuna puts out an eye; use the other one. Like they lop off their hair—plenty more where that came from. Like yin or like yang, what happens is what is. Like we stood around looking at each other and at the weeds and bugs and trees and ax and hatchet and clay bank and kids, and it was what it was . . . until I offered them smoked fish. Then it wasn't what it was. Then it was thanks man but creatures are to love not eat. Like meat in our temple goes nowhere, man, closes the gates, grossness and decay, man, Constipation City. So I gave them the fresh vegetables Ernie and Emma gave me, and it was what it was again. We left Rama and Arjuna yanging away at the boulder and clay and went yin to the candle shop at the back of the house.

There were hundreds of candles in there. Steve gave me a huge sand candle shaped like a flounder, a calendar candle guaranteed to burn a notch a day for a fortnight, and a half-dozen squat tapers in tintinnab-ulatious colors. That's what the sign said: "Tintinnabulatious." I asked what it meant. It meant what it was. Talking to Steve was a bit like talk-ing to the Tamanawis.

But I could see the guy worked hard at what he did, and he did it with great skill. I told him so. He smiled and said, "How it is." There was a table covered with big cloud-shaped multiwicked monstrosities in grays and whites and sunset colors, called "Cumulonimbustibles"; there were a couple of shelves of green and brown treeish-looking little chaps called "Leprechaunatious." And there were "art candles"—complicated, beau-tifully sculpted things, some of them selling for three or four hundred bucks and, if you were interested in that sort of thing, actually looking worth the price. Some had a dozen or more wicks coming out of various parts of them, and when I asked why, Steve left off leaving things "how it is" long enough to explain that some giant candles are rip-offs because after burning and melting for a while they just turn into piles of waxy garbage. *His* masterpieces didn't just fall to ruin: they "did things to your mind." He showed me a series of snapshots of one art candle that had changed from an office building into a mosque as the wicks were lit, extinguished and relit according to the detailed instructions. Then he showed me a massive conglomerate that looked like a dull row of subur-ban split-levels, but which melted away into a Tillamook Indian village: the cars turned into canoes, the telephone poles into totem poles, the split-levels into lodges, and the wickless wax dogs stayed where they were. This was his masterpiece to date. We wandered among the fabulous candles, me exclaiming, Steve disclaiming, till I was struck dumb by one of a naked woman lying on her back, and her breasts were in her hands, and each breast had a bulbous, goggle-eyed face peering out from deep under the watery flesh, with wicks coming out their noses, which were also her nipples, which were surrounded by her fingers, which were each shaped like thighs, under which were these, these uh, well, you'd have to see them. I didn't make the mistake of asking what it was. I did invite them all to come see me whenever they liked. Steve said they'd like to soon, but that it would be when it would be. He wanted to see my hand-built rods and seemed to know a surprising amount—considering he was a Sutra-thumping vegetarian—about flies as well. He explained, "I'm into hands." I gave him a #6 Bermuda Shorts, a #12 Coachman (I do tie an old classic now and then), and a #24 I invented, the Flea. He looked the Flea over, nodded, laughed and said "Flash." I realized that this was, coming from Steve, strong praise.

The next smoke signal came from Eaton's Landing. What it wasn't was fun. What it was was they gaped at me like I was the Grim Reaper come to harvest. What it was was I gave them a couple of flies (knowing they didn't flyfish), thanked them for helping with Abe, and split. I made another half-dozen stops—including the local grocery store, cafe, gas station and library—and in trying to give away flies, fish and fishing tips I got a free oil change, apple pie and coffee, pamphlets and books on Tamanawis Valley and county history, two quarts of pop and a huge bag of corn chips. I had found my people. And I had found that Thomas Bigeater, Piscator and I weren't the world's only proponents of friendliness.

When I returned to my cabin it had undergone a subtle transformation: I'd left behind a solitary structure on a lonely river; I'd returned to the home of someone the locals called "Gus the Fisherman"—a home just up the road from Ernie and Emma's, not far from the candle-makers, Crawdad Benson, Eaton's Landing, the "Fogged Inn Cafe," and all those folks that made the valley and town a valley and town full of folks. I *had* "saved the life o' that corpse outta the river"; that corpse was me. And with my de-fished eyes I really saw my home: I couldn't get over the sight and smell of it—the almost drinkable gold beams filtering through green glowing cedar, the thickness of the moss, the clarity of the river, the lupine, paintbrush and daisies in the clearings, the songs of birds and chippiting of chipmunks, the sweet, watery fragrance of the glade. . . .

I spent the afternoon purging the place of the crasser vestiges of the dead me, introducing tin cans of wildflowers, Steve's candles, Bill Bob's rock and junk and dreefee collection, pinecones, water-sculpted sticks and a bright red mushroom, in place of strewn fishing gear. As I worked I let the radio blare for the first time—and on a band Bill Bob had selected, where rock and roll from Seattle, baseball from Boise, Gospel from Medford and static from the stratosphere battled for my ear.

At dusk I fed the fish and chipmunks, poured a mug of wine, and sat at the four-by-four window, sipping and pondering what further deeds of reconciliation with the world might be accomplished before dark. And there, before my face, hovered Sigrid the Small—longing as always for her beloved river. I fetched a bucket, filled it at the sink, then took the minnow net and moved it slowly toward her, explaining that I had to capture her in order to set her free. She seemed to grasp the paradox, for she stayed in the corner—fins beating like hummingbird wings—till the net enclosed her; only then did she struggle, but once in the bucket she again hovered patiently as I lectured on the dangers of mergansers, kingfishers, raccoons, mink, herons, big fish and *fishermen*. By the time we reached the river I was frazzled with worry, but I recalled a knee-deep pool in the spring-creek my cabin water came from—the same water she'd lived in most of her life. There had never been fish in that tiny stream, so predators would exclude it from their rounds; she'd be safe until she moved down to the river. I waded in and immersed the bucket, but she stayed in it, hovering in the hummingbird pose, as if reluctant in the end to leave me. Bending over her, I noticed for the first time a greenish crescent on her back, almost a moon—probably a scar from the day Alfred went berserk. She never moved, so at last I drew the bucket away; she lingered a moment, then was gone. I scanned the pool, glad I couldn't spot her because her enemies wouldn't either. Just as I turned to leave she darted out of hiding, caught her first wild midge and, after the splash, vanished.

It was a lonely walk back to the cabin; just a day among my people left me longing for more. Before coming to the Tamanawis I'd believed that solitude was a cure-all, a psychic panacea, an invisible knife certain to cut me clear of all the parental debates, the wasted time, the drivel of school, the unending parade of cars and machinery; I'd believed that solitude would free me and, alone and independent, I would make myself into the person I wanted to be. But solitude, I found, was no guarantee of anything. Day after day I stood alone on whispering streams, tranquility and beauty on all sides, not a city nor a suburb nor a soul within miles and Presto! a swarm of hobgoblins came scuffling into my skull, hunkered down like hobos under a bridge, and proceeded to yammer at the tops of their lungs! One voice would belt out some facile ditty from a TV commercial; a second would join in with obscene or idiotic scraps of doggerel, trying to drown out the first; the third was my critic, pitching me shit, calling me names, giving me grief over every treed fly, missed strike, stubbed toe, telling me I should be on another creek, using a different fly, wearing different clothes; this one had a brother, the

Whiner: "I'm sleepy, I'm hungry, I'm tired, I'm bored, I'm lonely, I'm horny, My back hurts, My stomach aches, Why are we doing this, What are we doing here, When can we go home, When can we leave home? . . ." And most obnoxious of all, the Gloater: "HA! What a cast! I'm the greatest! H2O couldn't have laid that fly in there if his Scotch depended on it. now . . . Haii! I got him! Who but * * * ME * * * could have hooked that fish under those conditions? Walton, Cotton, Gordon, Ritz, Brooks, GUS ORVISTON—the true greats!" I was free. I was alone. It was hell. The confusion, the misery, the stupidity—all of it followed me from Portland to the Tamanawis, and in the quiet it grew fecund and multiplied. It came from nobody but me.

And so I learned what solitude really was. It was raw material— awesome, malleable, older than men or worlds or water. And it was *merciless*—for it let a man become precisely what he alone made of himself. One needed either wisdom or tree-bark insensitivity to confront such a fearsome freedom. Realizing now that I lacked both, I let myself long for company. Unashamed, I let my heart ache for someone more substantial than my shadow, someone less hidden than the Queen, someone willing to share jokes and junk food . . . and I hadn't reached my back door before I heard whispering, looked round the cabin, and there were the Doughnut Dairy kids with six ratty poles, six rusty reels with rotten line in bird's nests, brown paper bags of popcorn and bottles of pop, wanting their first lesson in the ancient art of angling. We paraded inside, lit the new candles while taking turns attempting to say "tintinnabulatious," scarfed munchies, fixed tackle, told tales, chortled and learned till I took them home in the pickup long past the small ones' bedtimes. For the second night running I slept peacefully, and the water noises came not from my head, but from the Tamanawis.

3

The Warble
of the Water Owl

In our aquarium we may witness all the cruelties of an embittered
struggle for existence. . . . Before the glorious male, the modestly
garbed female lowers the flag . . . and, if she is unwilling to mate, flees
immediately. . . . The male must never obtain so much as a glimpse of
her flanks, otherwise he will immediately become . . . unchivalrous.

—*Konrad Lorenz*

I AWOKE BEFORE DAWN. The morning star was twinkling through the
same opening in the cedars and the world was too wide and lovely to
leave unexplored. I jumped up, got dressed, dashed to the truck and—
empty-stomached, shivering, and the stars still out—started down Highway 101 with no particular destination.

After an amount of time I can't disclose (lest it hint at the location
of the Tamanawis) I pulled into Otis for a depth-charge breakfast of
pancakes and coffee which I choked down in huge quantities for the
inane reason that some loggers were sitting by me and I wanted to impress
them. I think one *was* impressed; at least he gave me a crooked little smile
as he stirred his piping-hot coffee—with his thumb! I was glad to find an
early-opening grocery in Lincoln City: I bought ten pounds of oranges,
figuring it would take at least that to flush the batter from my bowels.
Then I headed up into the Coast Range to explore the Siletz River
country.

By early afternoon I'd wandered well into the mountains. The sun
was hot, the pickup dusty, and I was finally getting hungry, so I thought
I'd eat oranges somewhere along the river, bake in the sun, then go for a
skinny-dip. It is a strange fact that I had never deliberately been swimming in all my twenty years; I'd fallen in fishing, but I'd never gone
swimming for swimming's sake. Since I am, like most hermits, modest, I

picked a place where the river wound away from the road into a canyon. There were deserted places all along that hundred-mile river; there was nothing outstanding about this place: but this was, inexplicably, the place I picked.

A Digression: Inexplicabilities

There appear to be, generally speaking, two explanations for the inexplicable. One is logical, crediting the random operation of a principle known variously as Fate, Destiny or Chance. Fate, Destiny or Chance, in its extreme manifestations, is said to be capable of descending upon a room full of monkeys playing with typewriters and causing one monkey to type *an entire Shakespeare play*—provided the number of monkeys and the amount of time are sufficient to allow for those frustrating cases wherein a monkey types its way clear to the end of *Hamlet*, only to conclude, ". . . Take up the bodies: such a sight as this becomes the field but here shows much amiss. Go, bid the soldiers sh&$bznx¢ ¼grntnokyirt."

The other explanation of inexplicabilities is *mytho*-logical, crediting (or blaming) various mischievous, machinating gods with names like Pan, Cupid, Kama, Khizr, Coyote, Raven and even Narayana Himself for the stranger experiences we endure. I ask the reader to remember these two explanations, and to ask which of the two most plausibly accounts for my selecting that nondescript parking place on the Siletz.

end of digression

Lugging five of the ten pounds of oranges, I hiked down a hellish incline through firs, alders, salal, devil's club and cooties, and came out by a rapids. I've never liked lingering beside rapids: they're noisy, you can't catch fish in them, and if you fall in you die, so I wandered upstream till I came to a long, slow glide. Above the glide was a big quiet pool with a massive broken-topped alder hanging out over it and a number of moss-covered sunlit boulders just past, any of which would make an admirable picnic table for my oranges and me . . .

but before proceeding I happened to glance once more at the broken-topped alder—————and there was a person in that alder. Way up in the top. Way out over the river. I scrambled closer, hoping the person in the alder wouldn't see me. Finding the five pounds of oranges inconducive to furtivity, I set them down, thinking to return for them soon after . . . but I returned for them neither soon nor ever after—and the reason I didn't was up in the alder.

I stopped a spin-cast or so below that alder and looked again. The person in the tree hadn't seen me. In fact, the person in the tree hadn't moved a muscle. I didn't know why the person was so motionless, but I did know this: it was no ordinary person up in that tree, way up in the top, way out over the pool, all alone in that desolate canyon. No. It was a *girl* up in that tree. A barefoot girl. A full-grown one. One who wore the top tenth or so of what had long ago been a pair of blue jeans. One who wore a short, skin-tight, sleeveless sky-colored t-shirt through which I could see the, which showed the, which revealed the shape of the . . . well, I really couldn't see her very well through all those branches. Not as well as I wanted to. I crept closer, stopping a fly-cast or so below the broken alder. I looked again. What was that girl doing up there? Why didn't she ever move? Why did she hold her golden right arm before her like Moses had done waging war against the Amalekites? My angle-ridden memory supplied me with a Biblical verse:

> Thy rod, wherewith thou smotest the river,
> take in thine hand, and go.

And I saw it—the dangling line, the rod in the extended hand . . . of course! The girl was fishing. I slunk closer, stopping a mere roll-cast below the broken alder: I could see her very clearly now. From where I stood it was impossible not to observe that there were no problems pertaining to her appearance. None at all. Because, well, she was fishing. It would, um, it would be, uh, *interesting*, yes, it would be interesting, I told myself, to unobtrusively observe the way the girl in the tree fished. A kind of research project. A study in fishing methods. Nothing voyeuristic about it. It would simply be best not to disturb her concentration and sense of privacy. Clearly, there was much to learn. Take, for instance, the innovative and utter lack of waders and vest and and every sort of cumbersome clothing. This interested me very much. More freedom of movement and so on. Something to consider. Very practical and so forth. I could hardly have been more interested. . . . Her fishing equipment was innovative also: she appeared to have no creel or equipage or container of any kind apart from her pole and line and whatever was on the end of it. There was the possibility of a few spare hooks or leaders in the pockets of the fraction of blue jeans, certainly, but given their fit, given the fact that from my excellent vantage point there were only anatomical contours discernible within their sparse confines, the spare-hooks-or-weights-or-baits theory grew tenuous. As to the possibility of fishing tackle concealed within the sky-colored t-shirt, this was even less likely. Nevertheless I considered the problem long and carefully, scanning every least curve of the thin material, reluctant to give up the search. All in all her angling costume was so thought-provoking, so fundamental yet satisfactory, that it was difficult to proceed to an examination of pole and line. There was something so pleasing to the eye about it. I wasn't used to looking at such things, let alone in trees, let alone fishing, let alone slender and golden-skinned and young and blond and solitary and, um—the pole. It must be mentioned that the pole and the line and the whatever-was-tied-to-the-line were the only other tackle to be considered: there was *no reel* on the pole. I'd never seen anyone before without a reel like her in trees dressed like she was fishing up there ever ever before that way, for which reason I couldn't help but feel she must be an extraordinary person, well worth watching, well worth meeting, well worth thinking about, an exceptional fisherman, and I was, what was I, I was learning, yes, *learning*: I was learning like crazy. I'd never learned so much so fast before, all sorts of new things about my sport, for instance how important it is to learn by watching others, how valuable it can be to meet other fishermen and share ideas, get to know them and so forth, after watching them for awhile up in the tree, fishing like that, in those clothes, with, um . . . the pole. I should describe it: it was a *huge sucker*. That's not slang: that's a literal fact. It was a huge hazelnut sucker, fourteen feet long, with the bark and even a few leaves still hanging on it. It had two wire guide-loops and a third loop attached at the tip, but there were no real guides. And there was no reel: what line wasn't in the air or the water was coiled in her left hand, which also clasped a branch for balance while her right hand held the rod high. Which brings us to her posture. It was a superb fishing posture. Extremely alert. Among other things. Lots of other things. I could only see the edge of her face. Fishermen's faces can tell an experienced observer a lot about the fishing and all, so I craned my neck to see it as clearly as possible. It was an excellent edge of a face—lips the color of silver salmon roe; long lashes curved like the hind legs of mayflies; a nose that gave you the same sort of feeling a baby cottontail rabbit's nose gives you. Not that her nose looked like a baby cottontail rabbit's nose. That would have looked ridiculous. Just like *her* nose would have looked ridiculous on a baby cottontail rabbit. I just meant the *feeling*. You know. How baby cottontail rabbit noses, the little fuzzy ones, make you feel? You know, how when they scrunch them up to smell something, how cute it looks and everything . . . Oh forget it.

Anyhow her nose was nice. It was a part complete unto itself. Which was the sort of parts all the parts of her were: you saw one part—just a nose, or a foot, or a t-shirt—and you'd no desire to look elsewhere. But you did look elsewhere anyhow, because you didn't want to miss anything going on up there. Those sorts of parts. To me, anyway.

But when I kept looking all over her not to miss anything, watching how she was getting along up there—the *entire her*, that is, apart from the parts—I realized something: there was something more going on, something on the wind, some impending thing impending. My native intelligence, enfeebled though it was by fractions and parts, still sensed it: something spectacular was afoot—

because she never once moved. She hadn't budged since I first laid eyes on her. It was remembering Moses that clued me in. I don't know why I remembered Moses, but I did. I remembered how when the Israelites battled away against the Amalekites ol' Moses held his arms extended so the Israelites would win, and his arms got "heavy as stones," and Aaron and some other guy had to come hold his arms up for him. I always felt sorry for the Amalekites, whoever they were. Seemed like Moses should have had to hold his own dang arms up. Like the girl in the tree was doing with her arm. And with five or six pounds of hazelnut sucker at the end of it! Her poor arm must have been killing her, but you'd never guess it by the edge of her face. I could think of only one thing that would inspire such strength in a fisherman and put such a feeling in the wind: Big Fish. There *had* to be a big fish in the pool down there, and judging by the signs it must be watching her bait about as closely as I was watching her and she was watching it. . . .

Suddenly she flexed, and O! the entire up and down of her rippled like a zephyr across a lake. Her line began wandering slowly upstream: something big had taken the bait! Like a ballerina she leaned and twisted, extending the rod out over the water as far as she could reach. Then, savagely, she struck! and sang out like a meadowlark as a bright summer steelhead of eight or nine pounds took a tail-walk across the top of the river. It tore upstream on a powerful run and would have her handful of line in seconds so I figured the game was up, but still her face was undismayed. She let the coils fly from her fingers as though she expected it. What came next took maybe ten seconds, but as those ten seconds contained the three most spectacular and profound fish-fighting maneuvers I have ever witnessed, I will take some time to describe them:

First she pulled some sort of release string and the three guide-loops fell into the water. Her line was now attached only at the butt, so the long rod would be useless for battling the steelhead; yet her expression was still undismayed. . . .

Next, she leapt to the very tip of the snag, turned the rod around backwards and *threw it*, like a javelin, upstream after the speeding fish! The hazel disappeared in the Siletz, then surfaced, speeding along butt-first like a whale boat on a Nantucket sleigh ride! Seeing in a flash that the attachment of line to butt made the hazel a truer-flying spear, a straighter-gliding sled, and a more resistant barge for the fish to tow, I felt for the first time in my life that I was in the presence of a fishing genius exceeding my own. It seemed no tactic could possibly surpass the two I'd just seen. *But they were nothing. . . .*

When I looked back up in the alder my eyes met with a sight beyond hope: the small fraction of blue jeans, the t-shirt, and a pair of blue panties fluttered from a twig. . . .

And the lithe and blinding figure of the naked girl was airborne, soaring out in an arc and flashing down through the leaves in a swan dive next to which the gliding flight of swans was a sorry, lumbering sight. She shot through the tree—sun and shadow streaking across her body—flying more than falling through the blue-green air, past glowing leaf and dark deadly limbs, vanishing with a fish-soft splash in the pool. Surfacing far upstream, she struck out after the speeding rod in an otter-swift crawl stroke. I scrambled through brush and boulders, gashing slits and gouging holes in my person, not about to take my eyes from the girl for a purpose so mundane as watching where I was going.

The hazel stopped at the head of the pool. I ducked behind the long-forgotten picnic boulders. She waded up and grabbed her pole then started for the far shore, but the steelhead turned and ran downriver so she launched the pole again, but gently, like a toy boat, and breaststroked after. The fish jumped twice more, but sluggishly; then the line slackened and the steelhead wove, weary and confused. She waded o my god into thigh-deep water. She detached the line from the rod butt while the fish rested, tied it to the tip, then backed toward shore. When the line came taut the steelhead reacted with a last, slow-motion leap and a few short runs, but she'd calculated its strength perfectly and now used the length and suppleness of the rod to keep it from gaining line. She led it into the shallows, and by the time she'd beached and killed it my bloodstream was pulsating with so many outrageous romantic goads that I had to turn away to stave off the head-staggers. When I caught my breath I turned back—and she was swimming, rod and fish in tow, right toward me!

I ducked behind a boulder and looked madly for a way into the trees. There was none. Any way I took would expose me, and the conglomeration of heat, scratches and emotion must have had me looking like the Mad Rapist of the River. I heard her wading toward me through the shallows. I heard water dripping from her body onto the rocks. I heard her quick, soft breathing as she climbed onto a moss-topped boulder *very* near mine . . . then I heard nothing. She must have seen me! I could picture her face—gaping in horror, too terrified to begin the screaming sure to follow. I didn't move a muscle: huddled in a ball, head in arms,

arms round knees, I vowed to stay that way for a day, a week, as long as it took. I wouldn't move for anything. Sooner or later she'd take me for dead or crazy and go away.

But after an eternity of silence I heard a low humming. It was not the low humming of a horror-stricken nude. With a furtiveness that far surpassed any fish-stalking furtiveness I have ever accomplished, I peeked over my boulder. . . . She was sunbathing on a stone not a flyrod's length away, in an utterly unsuspecting, utterly alone pose of poses.

O ye frogs and fevers, ye coots and constellations, the fisher-girl was the loveliest of lovely sights! On the sunbaked boulder, on green moss she lay, the quicksilver trout, rose-hued and stippled, glimmering by her side, glistening by her side, a pale, paltry thing by her gleaming side. As she ran a slender finger through the moss, over the stone, along the wretched fish, only Heaven and myself knew the pain that I was in. And when at last I remembered to breathe, that breath came, that breath went, with a fall and rise of rose-tipped breasts. Birds flew, crickets sang, stone and river spoke together in the shallows, and her music low and lovely and the beauty of her body and the wind's soft singing and the beauty of her body O the beauty of her body beat upon me like a storm. Ah, what became of my mother's boy as he watched beside the river? What became of her fisher-son gazing on the gleaming girl?

> The warble of the water owl poor Gus became.
> A salmon in a gill-net little Gus became.
> The ouzel's cry on a frozen creek,
> the field mouse in the kestrel's clasp,
> the otter whelp weeping in the nettle patch
> poor Gus became.
> The grass blade growing in the asphalt slab,
> the baying of a lone hound in bare winter,
> a gnat in a cobweb,
> a trout in a creel,
> a child in a night wood without a trail
> poor Gus's heart became. . . .

At last she stirred and I hid again. I heard her slide off the boulder. I watched her return to the alder and climb it with the grace and agility that marked everything she'd done. She dressed in her fishing perch. As she climbed down I broke at last out of hiding, striving hopelessly to feign innocence, ignorance and a fresh arrival. To give her fair warning I crashed through the underbrush like a great landed nabob, whistling, mumbling, resolved on an attempt at bluff gruff fishermanly good humor. Just as I prepared my jolly hello I saw her face full on for the first time . . . Piteous Christ it was beautiful! I croaked, "Wet luke!"

She froze, and said nothing. I tried to laugh: what emerged from my gullet was the death rattle of a wen-headed Hoosier. Attempting to explain my initial utterance, I gave vent to these sounds: "Oh! Me, I say Wet luke but A meant to snay 'What muck,' I mean 'Lut,' orm, um. . . .'"

That did it. Still silent, the lovely girl leaned over and picked up a big rock. Grinning my face off, I blurted, "AWrr! Yore rock hown!"

O ye hodags and ye ditzels! I imagined what she must be going through. . . . Just got her clothes on—what few she had—when a blubbering Sasquatch comes heaving out of the underplants making incomprehensible mating gurgles in its hairy throat! I imagined my beard full of lint, my teeth yellow, my fly open and undershorts showing there the color of my teeth, and thick green boogers clogging both my nostrils. I stared at the ground: there was a wee little snail crawling peacefully along down there. O ye Newark New Jersey how I wished I was that snail! How softly I'd sneak under the nearest rock and die! She stood before me, terribly beautiful, terribly frightened, while I gawked on, helpless to hide, feeling my face was the size of a billboard. I had to do something. "Don't get scored," I burbled. "Me gog peech inspediment. M-m-my-I juss a marmless fissamren!"

"Oh," she said, clutching the rock tighter, lips quivering, eyes the size of ripe blue apples.

It was too awful. I gurbled, "Ope! Got go now . . . Goodo, mmm, Good lerk! Bye." I stumbled to the river, waded in, and kept on wading till it swallowed me alive. I swam and swam along the very bottom where the slime and mudsuckers and fish-shit lived, hoping I'd black out, take a deep lungful of river, get it over with then and there. But I came unexpectedly to the far shore and surfaced against my will, gasping for air. Then I waded up the bank and barged into the brush on a beeline, refusing to veer to either side for anything; I tore though devil's club, briars, wildrose thickets and choked, evil copses; I left a legacy of flesh and clothing on stickers and snags; then I came to a cedar—a great stinking monster of a tree—and since I wouldn't move for it and it wouldn't move for me I jumped up, caught the lowest branch, shinnied it to the trunk and started climbing, intending to keep on climbing till I ran out of tree.

As I labored up I encountered a red ant laboring down and was moved by my misery to interrogate it: I asked it why I was ever born, why my parents lacked the sense to expose me at infancy on some icy mountain, why I failed to drown, why some compassionate disease didn't ravage and kill me, why some rabid squirrel didn't come open my throat, and other questions of similar description. But the ant, like the girl, took one look at me and began to brandish its tiny pincers. I climbed on alone.

4

Eddy

Sweeny the thin-groined it is
in the middle of the yew-tree.
Life is very bare here,
piteous Christ it is cheerless.

Grey branches have hurt me,
they have pierced my calves.
I hang here in the yew-tree above,
without chessmen, no womantryst.

I can put no faith in humans
in the place they are;
watercress at evening is my lot.
I will not come down.

—*from a medieval
Irish poem*

AS I ASCENDED the cedar a plan formed in my mind in somewhat the way
scum forms in an abandoned cup of water. This plan was an agenda—a
program to carry out for the remainder of my scurvy incarnation. It went
like this: #1 Climb till you reach the top of the tree. #2 Cling there till
you become too weak and starved and thirsty to hang on. #3 Fall from
top of tree. #4 Smash and splinter countless bones as you fall. #5 Burst
your head and break your neck when you hit the ground. #6 Lurch,
writhe and bleed for a few moments. #7 That should do it.

I liked this plan. It seemed like one of the few types of plan a person
with my particular abilities and attributes could manage. I adopted it and
commenced carrying it out. According to plan I reached the treetop. Not
according to plan I looked back across the river: the girl was still there!
Poof! went the plan.

She had gathered her rod and fish and now sat with them, cross-
legged, atop the same boulder that couched her during those eternal
moments that reduced me to idiocy. She looked like a dryad bodhisattva

there on the moss, every bit as beautiful but not so devastating as she'd been face to face. The river between us eased my panic; my tongue stopped writhing like a trout in a puddle; I could see she was no longer frightened. She called, "You all right up there?"

Purified by water, mortified by devil's club, I told the naked truth: "No."

"Are you hurt?"

"Yes," I said, for the pool carried her voice straight into my heart and convinced that heartless organ to start pummeling the rest of my innards mercilessly. At least the scratches and gashes didn't hurt: I forgot I had a body the moment I saw hers.

"Can you get down?"

"No," I said, thinking *no* a nice word, easy to conjure, easy to pronounce.

"How come?"

"Because," I said, wary of any more syllabulous explanation.

"Because why?"

"Just because."

"Why just because?"

"Just because just because."

"All right, Mummy-mouth. If that's the best you can do I'll see you later." She started up. . . .

"No don't go!"

"Why not?"

". . . . . ju . . . just . . .because," I croaked, and we both started laughing. But the laughter died, a silence began, and no one broke it. A breeze came and played in her hair, and her hair came and played in my brain, and the breeze crossed the river and played in my cedar, then it died, too. The silence grew thick. I ought to say something. *Mummy-mouth?* I *had* to say something. But to her I could only say something beautiful, and my brain was full of her hair and my tongue was a trout again and for a trout to speak hair-thoughts beautifully was just not possible. Desperate, I took another tack: scanning my trusty rote memory, I pulled a passage from that controversial volume, *The Compleat Angler*, and with all the H2Oratory in me boomed, "No life, my honest scholar, no life so happy and so pleasant as the life of a well-governed angler!"

"Prob'ly not," she said. And she smiled.

God what a smile! Craving nothing on earth but the sight of another, I poured forth another Waltonian passage: "Indeed, my good scholar, we may say of angling, as Dr. Boteler said of strawberries, 'Doubtless God could have made a better berry, but doubtless God never did'; and so, if I might be judge, God never did make a more calm, quiet, innocent recreation than angling!"

"I don't s'pose He did," she agreed, smiling some more.

Dizzy with bliss, I recited, "And now, I think it will be time to repair to your angle-rod, which should be left in the water to fish for itself—and it is an even lay it catches!"

"Why not?" she laughed—and she hopped down from the boulder, stepped into the shallows and commenced turning stones till she spotted a big red crawdad; one fearless swoop and she had it in her hands—and I wished I was a crawdad till she gave it this brief sermon: "Life is short. It's God's fault. Sorry." with which she tore off its tail, crushed its body into compost and soul into the Garden World, shelled the tail, baited her hook, cast into the head of the pool, propped the hazel and climbed back onto the infamous boulder. I was moved to encourage her with this from *The Angler*:

"Let me tell you, scholar, this kind of fishing with a dead rod is like putting money to use, for it works for its owner when she do nothing but sleep, or eat, or rejoice, as you know we have done this last hour!"

"So that's what we've done," she said. "I thought I'd been catching a steelhead. And I thought you'd been up to even weirder things—like turning from a harelip into a harebrained bard, maybe."

"Trust me scholar," I recited. "I know not what to say to it. There are many country people who believe hares change sexes every year."

She smiled again, but this one faded into a frown. "Look, pal," she said. "I don't want to, uh, bring you down—so to speak. But are you afraid of something? I mean, like, did you run away from somewhere— an, uh, asylum, maybe? I won't tell on you or anything, but maybe I could help. What are you doing out here? If you're a fisherman, where's your gear? What's the story with you?"

Suddenly clammy and weak, I abandoned the words of Izaak Walton and said, "I *am* a fisherman, but I only came here to swim. My gear's at home—on the Tamanawis. And I *did* run away from something. And I *am* afraid of something, but it ain't an asylum. But I *am* in trouble, and . . . and nobody but you could possibly help."

"So OK," she said. "What did you run from, what are you scared of, how do I help?"

Caution tried to stop me, but when my heart saw the opening the words leapt out: "It was you! It was you I ran from. It's you that's the . . . you I'm scared of—I mean, I was scared you were scared of me. I mean, I couldn't stand to scare you again. And to help, just don't go away. Just stick around a bit. I'll stay up here. Heck, I like it up here. Just don't go away . . . not yet."

She said nothing for a long time. When she spoke her voice was puzzled, but so soft and pretty. "I was scared at first. I'm not now. But what do you mean, *I'm* the trouble? I didn't do anything to you."

"Yes you did."

"What?"

"I don't know. Nothin', maybe. But nothing will ever be the same."

She made no reply. I was afraid I'd gotten shlocky then, so to cover my tracks I shook the tree and filled the canyon with these lines: "'Some waters being drank cause madness, some drunkenness, and some laughter to death. . . . One of no less credit than Aristotle tells of a merry river that dances . . . for with music it bubbles, popples and grows sandy, and so continues till the music ceases, then presently returns to its wonted calmness and clearness. Dolphins love music, and can swim as swift as an arrow can be shot out of a bow . . . but now let's say grace and fall to breakfast. What say you, scholar?'"

She said, "Say grace if you like, but don't fall to breakfast."

"Why not?"

"You'll break your neck before I find where that lingo of yours comes from."

God what a smile! I said, "Comes from Zizik Waltlick—blaf! Zike Walston—brroff!"

She laughed. "You're doing it again! Did you mean 'Izaak Walton'?"

God, what a laugh! "Yast," I said, melting like butter in a frypan.

"What's your name?"

My name! She wanted to know my name!. . . . . . ohoh. What *was* my name? Oh yeah! Gus. I blurted, "Gorse Vordlestine, er, Orffle-Orvisdit . . . dammit! What's yours?"

"Eddy," she said. "Glad to meet ya, Gorstlevorkerdorkt."

"Eddy, like the swirlzles in riverd wattle?"

"I wish," she said, laughing again. "But it's Eddy like my dad, Edwin. But what do they call you for short, Orgdwartstilldiftergraft?"

"Crall me Gust," I moaned.

"Sure thing, Gust," she said.

"There's smumthing I ought tolled you, Eddy."

"What's that, Gust?"

"You gite a bite."

And she did, so to speak. She pounced on the hazelnut, slammed home the hook, and away down the river shot a second steelhead, towing her pole behind. She dove in and struck out after it while I half fell, half climbed down the cedar, hoping to help out, tearing myself into finer tatters in the devil's club, reaching the riverbank breathless and bloody—but only the pole was veering about the pool. Eddy was gone!

I spotted a blue and gold blur dashing through the woods on the opposite shore. She was running away! "Wait!" I shouted. "I'll grow brack up tree! Just wanded to helpt! Crum back! Come brack!"

But the louder I shouted the faster she ran. I didn't want to scare her, but if she got away before I found out something more about her—where she lived, her license number, *anything*, I'd never see her again! I plunged into the river and swam as fast as I could (which was incredibly slow). I struggled out of the canyon, fighting brush, exhaustion, heart attacks. I was a mess when I reached the road but I staggered to my pickup and started after the telltale dust cloud rising from the road downriver.

I kept it floored all the way. If my truck wasn't such a turkey I'd have killed myself on the curves. As it was, I overtook the car after a mere half-mile chase. I honked and waved: the car pulled over. I drove alongside—and peered into the furious face of a fat old woman. "You're not Eddy!" I screamed, and leaving her gaping I tore back the other way. I drove a maniacal, fish-tailing ten miles, passing at least twenty turnoffs, any of which Eddy may have taken. My nerves began short-circuiting, my gas gauge slipped toward E, I was shredded and wasted and my heart was jumping rope with my intestines. Admitting defeat, I turned and drove slowly back to the Broken Alder Pool.

I limped down into the canyon and began searching the river for the hazel pole and its steelhead, hoping against hope that it would bear some clue by which I might one day find her. I started at the head of the pool and worked downstream, but found only the dead steelhead lying on the boulder, and the mangled remains of the crawdad. The pole was nowhere; the river wore a poker face; I might have believed the afternoon a dream if the sweat weren't stinging the hell out of my cuts and scratches.

I climbed into the alder and huddled in a stupor as the sun sank and the air grew chill. The evening star came out and I thought of dreefees and my twin, but how could they cheer me now? Death was no longer the thing I feared. But to live without ever seeing the beautiful fisher-girl again . . . God, what a miserable prospect!

I stayed in the tree as the day turned to dusk, salt in my cuts, cramps in my gut, metamorphic numbness in my mind. . . . Then something stirred on the surface of the Siletz, down at the tail of the pool: a derelict V-wake, wobbling slowly toward me. I plunged into the river in a kind of goose-dive that was an insult even to those ungainly birds and struck out in a spent dog paddle toward the wake which, thanks to my splashing, now moved in the opposite direction. Seeing it outdistancing me, I scrambled ashore and straggled after, adding bruises, cuts and gashes to the unreckonable total. Sure enough, it was the hazel.

It stopped at the brink of the rapids, but the steelhead at the end of the line was so utterly spent that the pull of the pole was more than it could resist. The hazel washed downriver, dragging the luckless, thrashing fish after—a strange and pathetic sight. I followed and finally waylaid it in a shallow gravel run, pulled the steelhead to me and bent to release it. But there was blood streaming from its vent and gills, and it couldn't right itself. Then, for the second time in my life, I wept for a fish, thinking it and me the most regrettable pair of fools that ever swam a river. I took a rock and released it into the waters of a better world; its body, the deadly hazel and I trudged back to the alder, picked up the first victim, struggled out of the black canyon and drove slowly, sadly home.

5

Jesus Keeps Fishing

> After she left me and I quit my job and wept for a year and all my
> poems were born dead, I decided I would only fish and drink. In the
> river was a trout and I was on the bank, my heart in my
> chest, clouds above, she was in NY forever and I, fishing and drinking.
>
> —*Jim Harrison again*

AFTER A NIGHT OF fitful sleep and fits of sighing, dawn found me covered
with iodine and band-aids, my bottom atop a rock beside the Tamanawis, the Tamanawis atop its own rocky bottom. Iodine, band-aids,
rocks and bottoms—that's what Life was made of. For the thousandth
time I sighed, then grumbled "Good morning" to the river. It gurgled an
incomprehensible reply. Then I remembered that its gurgles came from
the tip of the *n* in its *why* . So *that* was its reply.

"You're right," I said. "It isn't a good morning."

why

"Because I'll never see her again."

why

"You know, River, you're stupider than I thought."

why

"Because I thought any water knew what every water knew, because there's only one water and it's been around forever, but if all being
around forever teaches you is how to say why why why why why I guess
immortality ain't all it's cracked up to be."

why

"I don't know, dammit! And I don't know why she ran away, or why
I had to see her at all when I'll never see her again, or why she smiled but
ran, or laughed but ran, or talked to me but ran, or asked my name but
ran, but God she was beautiful, and she fished like, like, like Thomas and
Ma and H20 and Piscator put together, and I think I might go crazy if I
never see her again!"

"Why?"

"Because I'm in love with her."

"Why did she scratch you all up like that?"

"The brush and stickers . . . Hey! Who said that?"

I turned around. It was Steve. And Rama and Arjuna. And their braids. And Arjuna's machete. And Rama's white India-cotton monkey doll.

"You look terrible," said Steve. "She's beautiful, huh?"

"Yeah," I mumbled, embarrassed.

He shook his head. "It is what it is."

"Yeah. Sure. I guess. What's the monkey's name, Rama?"

"Hanuman," said Steve.

"Whitey," said Rama.

"Hanuman Whitey or Whitey Hanuman?" I asked.

"Just Whitey," said Rama. "Mama and Papa call him Hanuman. But he's my Whitey."

"Hanuman," teased Steve.

"Whitey!" shouted Rama.

why said the Tamanawis.

"Because he's white," I said.

"Yeah," said Rama.

"What it is," said Steve. "We're going up the mountain. Want to come?"

"Yeah," I said.

We started out, me and Steve with walking sticks, Arjuna with his machete, Rama with Whitey, Whitey with three long strands of yarn sticking out the top of his head like antennae.

"Hey Rama," I said. "Why's Whitey got those funny hairs? Makes him look like a bug."

"Mama made them," he said. "I show you. . . ." He twisted the three hairs into a braid and stuck a rubber band like his and Arjuna's and Steve's rubber bands on the end to hold it together. Then he kissed the monkey's grunjy face and said, "Oh Whitey, you looks bootiful!" Then he unbraided the hairs, and a while later braided them again, said the same thing, unbraided them, braided them again, and so on, clear up the mountain. Meanwhile Arjuna macheteed stickers, Steve showed me edible plants, and I nodded and mumbled over each plant, seeing nothing but the fisher-girl.

We reached the top and sat around looking at the view. I showed Steve the *why* in the Tamanawis. Rama and Whitey and Arjuna fought some monsters that looked more like rotten logs to Steve and me, hacking their limbs and fangs off with the machete. Then we walked back down and ate the other five pounds of oranges. I told Steve I'd rather show him my rods and flies when I was feeling a little better. He said, "How it is." Then it was time for them to go. That's when I noticed something wasn't quite right.

"Hey Rama, where's Whitey?"

Rama held his two smudgy, empty hands in front of his face and stared at them incredulously. "Whitey!" he cried. "You're gone!"

"You left'm up there," growled Arjuna, pointing at the mountain with his machete, "when we was killin' monthters."

"Whitey!" cried Rama, looking up at the mountain. "*Whitey! Whitey!*" It was like Anvil Abe's friend in the fog, the pitiful way he called.

"I'll go get him," said Steve. "Mind watching the boys, Gus?"

"Glad for the company," I said, and meant it.

Steve left. Arjuna and Rama and I stayed by the river. It was an hour-and-a-half wait. Arjuna started worrying after a while about getting home for lunch. I started worrying after a while about Steve, in between my constant worries over Eddy. And every few minutes Rama would sigh and say, "O, Whitey, O Whitey, I hope he finds you!" The three of us were a whiny mess.

Finally Steve returned. Empty-handed. Rama moaned, "Whitey!"

Steve grinned and turned around . . . Whitey was riding piggyback, woven right into Steve's braid. "Whitey! you're back!" cried Rama. Steve untied the monkey and handed it to its master. Rama hugged it for a while, then commenced braiding its three crummy hairs. I don't know, for me it was a moving scene—the three of them there with their cotton clothes and braids, Steve smiling about how everything was how it was, Arjuna scratching his stomach with the hilt of his machete saying "I'm hungry," Rama fastening the rubber band on the end of the monkey's lousy little hairs and crying, "O Whitey, you looks bootiful!"

I was sorry when they left. I went back to my rock by the river and watched the eddies, wishing I had a Steve to fetch my lost one for me.

After a while I saw a guy way downstream, flyfishing. That reminded me of the fourteen-foot hazel—all I had left of Eddy. I fetched it from the pickup and returned my bottom to its rock, then sat there like a lump of mud, fondling the fish-murdering thing and moaning Why? Why? Why?, the Tamanawis commiserating with me for a change.

But who was that joker down on the river? Holy Izaak, what a parody of a Piscator! He had on a huge, flop-brimmed Amish-style hat pin-cushioned full of dozens of the gaudiest Taiwanese flies imaginable; his torso was buried in a cram-packed fishing vest, pouches, landing net, creel, camera and binoculars; his face was raccoonish in some kind of welder's goggles doubtless guaranteed to lay bare every fish in the river; his waders were three or four sizes too big in the chest and one shoulder strap was broken so that his fly-line fell into them and refused to come out—and no wonder: it was a terribly ill-used line. Most flyfishermen spend their fishing time drifting imitations at the current's sweet pace through the likeliest looking water in the stream. This angler obviously held no truck with so simple a process: *his* method was to lurch through the deepest water flagellating the river fore and aft before slashing his mutilated fly into ankle-deep shallows where it sank and died—an advertisement to minnows, a curiosity to crawdads, and an item ignored by the angler himself, who was busy pulling fly-line from his waders and gear. In fact "angler" was no name for him: transplant him and his outfittings to the streets of New York City and he'd pass for a wandering bag-lady.

When he reached the riffle below me he waved. I nodded and watched. He began making fabulous mock casts with outrageous vigor, possibly to impress me. "Crack! Whoosh! Crrack! Whoooosh! Crrrrackk!" went his line. After thirty or forty Crack-Whooshes I was more than impressed: I was hiding behind a log. When he'd let out too much line to keep airborne he tried to force a cast—the line piled into the back of his head, he roared "Sacajawea Argeiphontes! I am wounded!" ... and I recognized the voice and vocabulary of my friend Titus.

Ensnarled and sweating, he waded ashore, pulled off the goggles, tossed down the hat, pointed to the #10 Mosquito freshly hung in the lobe of his right ear and said, "The Sufi, Attar, has written: 'One tiny fly which entered the ear of Nimrod troubled the brain of that idiot for centuries.'" He fished a fingernail clipper from his vest, then added, "Please, Gus: spare me Nimrod's fate!"

I clipped the barb from the Mosquito, invited Titus to say *Tintinnabulatious*, and yanked the fly from his ear on the fifth syllable. "How's it feel?" I asked.

"Eerie," said he.

While we untangled him from his gear I invited him to stay and fish (or *learn* to fish) all weekend. He accepted, and I proposed we begin with a good meal—but he said, "I'll find it hard to digest in peace until you answer a few questions."

I said, "I'm hungry. Ask away."

He pointed to my gashes and iodine: "Was it odious harpies or house cats that attacked you yesterday? How did you escape? Why'd they do it?"

I blushed, and it burned every scratch. "I'm not hungry anymore," I mumbled.

"That's no answer."

"It's a long, dull story."

Titus lit a smoke and eyed the hazelnut pole. "What is *that?*"

I shrugged. "Part of the long, dull story."

His eyes narrowed and his tone turned serious. "Trust me, Gus. You look like a dam about to burst. What happened?"

I said nothing. He said, "Unless I'm much mistaken, I've seen that look before. Is there a woman in this?"

I turned crimson, but I'd always trusted an intuitive ear: I said, "If I'm gonna tell what happened I'm gonna need help—the bottled variety."

He nodded. "There's bourbon in the Carp."

Ezra Brooks bourbon proved a fine tongue-loosener, and Titus a sympathetic listener: I started at the beginning—the evening after the Anvil Abe episode—and as the whiskey got to flowing, so did I. I talked for hours without a break, pouring out all I'd thought and felt and seen, and throughout the sagas of fever, fog and cold, light-knights and Garden World, *why* and Wolf Clan, Titus smoked pipe after pipe, nodding and grunting now and again, keeping our cups full, soaking it in. He didn't interrupt or cross-examine, didn't counsel or question, but the nods and grunts were oddly eloquent, and at the light-knight chapter, at the *why*, and again at the tale of Thomas Bigeater his eyes flickered and the pipe went out for neglect. When I reached the Siletz the going got tough, but I chugged my pride with a whiskey chaser and told the unexpurgated edition of my fool performance. Titus laughed a little, but mostly just kept nodding and grunting. Sometimes grunts are just the thing you need to hear. When I'd ended with Rama and Whitey he shook his head and said, "Gus, you've lived a lifetime in a week!"

I smiled bitterly. "Yep. Nuthin' left to do but drink till I die."

He pursed his lips so hard they vanished, took another slug of bourbon and said, "I admit there's no cure for a soul in your situation. But there are three consolations."

"Let's see," I said. "Suicide . . . amnesia . . . and Lone Ranger comics."

He said nothing, so finally I had to say, "OK. What are they?"

"One is hope. You may one day find her."

"Shit. Fat chance!"

He shrugged. "I admit the odds are not obese, but there *are* odds. Why would she ask your name if she didn't like you?"

"For the fun of hearing me bite my tongue off!"

He shook his head. "No, you made a horrendous first impression, but an excellent second one, I'm sure of it. When you fled to the tree you earned her respect—maybe more."

"How?"

"Chivalry," he said.

"Chivalry-shivery-shittery," I burbled, adding, "Oops. I'm crocked."

Titus loaded a pipe and handed it to me; when the tobacco had cleared my head he said, "Listen, Gus: if she's as beautiful as you say she . . ."

"She's *twice* as beautiful as I say she is!"

"All right," he said. "If she's twice as beautiful as you say she is, she's accustomed to reactions to her far worse than yours: the world is full of proctological-headed orcs who leer at and torment beauty. She thought she had you pegged when she picked up the rock. But then you took your inspired plunge and tree climb."

"So what?"

"So she realized you meant her nothing but good but were too stunned by her to speak. That *had* to flatter her. And I doubt your treetop recitations hurt your cause either." He pointed at the hazel. "Quotations to match her pole: arcane but likable period pieces."

"But why did she run!"

He shrugged. "Shyness. A little fear. I don't know. Mohammed the Prophet said that men must accept women as they are, 'with all their curves.' She knows your name; she knows your river; she might guess you have her pole and fish; she might come to get them."

"We might grow wings," I muttered.

"We might," he said hopefully.

I took another drink. "What about these other consolations?"

"You've put down a healthy dose of the second already." He gave his glass a tap. "The third takes more aptitude."

"What sort?"

"A sharp mind. Some erotic mania of the soul. Maniacal stamina. Ever hear of Boethius?"

"Nope."

"Meister Eckhart?"

"Nope."

"They wrote books about the consolation of philosophy—good books."

"Goody gumdrops," I said. "Hells bells, Titus! I know as much about philosophy as you know about fly casting."

"Then you're no philosopher," he said calmly, "and are therefore unfit to judge its consolatory powers."

"You got a point," I admitted.

"I know this must sound like a dehydrated scheme to a creek addict like yourself, Gus, but if I were you I'd get ploughed tonight, and in the morning I'd start philosophizing."

"I just told you, Titus, I don't know *how.*"

He smiled. "And *I* don't know how to fish."

"So?"

"So if you're willing to risk your life initiating me into the mysteries of fishing, the least I could do in return is introduce you to the forgotten science of philosophy. What do you say?"

I shrugged. "What have I got to lose?"

"Your unhappiness," he said.

"Is that so!"

"It depends on you," Titus said. "But a saint named Gus once said, '*Nulla est homini causa philosophandi, nisi ut beatus sit.*'"

"For shame!" I said. "Did they wash his mouth out?"

Titus smiled. "It means 'Man has no reason to philosophize, except with a view to happiness.'"

I took another swig. "You sure it's better'n this stuff?"

Titus took a swig too. "If it's not," he said, "I'll buy you another bottle. . . . But look, Gus—" he was pointing around the cabin, "this is a fisherman's domicile. My flat in town is more fitted to our needs. What say we migrate tonight, philosophize this weekend and fish the next?"

"Back to *Portland*?" I made a face.

Titus cleared his throat for another recitation: "'The Way into the light often looks dark. The Way that goes ahead often looks as if it went back.'"

"The Way into the Garden World looks a lot like croakin'," I extemporized. "I only leave this cabin if Ezra rides in my lap."

Five minutes later Titus and I were in the Carp chugging down the road toward Portland while ol' plastic Jesus cast his dry fly in the back. By the time we hit town the Ezra Brooks was totally drunk, and so were Titus and I—but Jesus just kept on fishing.

6

Descartes

For already have I been
a boy and a girl, a bush
and a bird, and a mute fish
leaping out of the sea on its way. . . .

—*Empedocles*

Creatures never rest till they have gotten into human nature; therein
do they attain to their original form, God namely.

—*Meister Eckhart*

I AWOKE ON A COUCH in a strange room with walls of nothing but books.
The outraged condition of my cranial arteries forbade the assumption
that Titus could be anywhere but asleep in his room: no one could
recover very speedily from that much Ezra Brooks. I pulled myself out of
the sack, dressed, collapsed in a nearby rocker and addressed myself to the
hard business of blinking: my eyes felt like bruised balls of sand. I
staggered to the bathroom, primed the dry ducts with faucet water, tried
to swallow a little—and nearly choked on the stuff. I was glad I wasn't a
fish this morning.

Returning to the rocker I sank into a revery of green pools and
moss-topped boulders. Just as the broken-topped alder was shimmering
into focus, my native intelligence butted in to tell me I was being
scrutinized: I raised reluctant lids . . .

and stifled a scream! Two horrible albino eyes glowered into my face
from a massive black visage not two feet away! My terror was only slightly
alleviated when I realized the visage belonged to a dog. I tried to smile.

"Good boy," I told it.

The dog didn't smile, didn't wag, didn't move, didn't blink. The
white eyes had a turquoise tint: I felt as if I could see through them,
straight into his head, and there were miles and miles of empty blue sky in

there. This notion would have intrigued me—if the dog had had a muzzle. "Titus?" I called softly.

No answer.

The glower deepened. There was command issuing from those eyes, or from the sky behind them. The sky was ordering me to do something, but I was too dumb to understand. The eyes were saying, "Understand, or *else!*"

"Titus!" I called louder.

No answer. Not from Titus anyway. But the dog began to rumble—like a volcano. It was a mountainous dog. I thought of the Wolf Clan. I thought of the thousands of fish I'd killed. I watched the empty blue expanses inside the dog's head and thought of a sky god, a nature god, a hard god of retribution.... "Nice boy," I whimpered, leaning as far backward as the rocker would allow, slowly raising my hands to shield my face and throat.

The front door flew open—I cringed—and Titus entered from outdoors, bearing a bag of groceries. "Ah, you're up!" he called with that briskness so repugnant to the unbrisk. The dog didn't move, didn't even glance at Titus—who amazed and disappointed me by passing directly into the kitchen without taking the least notice of my plight.

"Titus!" I whispered desperately. But he was clattering among dishes and pots and sinks, calling in that he'd soon rescue me from my hangover with some strong black tea. Black tea! What was that to me? A liquid to pour in my mouth and watch run out the fang gashes in my throat!

"Titus!"

"Yes?" he called at last.

"Is this your dog?"

"Yes."

"Well, he's . . . he's looking at me!"

"So?"

"So he has me trapped. What does he want? Does he bite? Can I move? Why won't he go away?"

Titus hollered in, "He doesn't bite without cause. But you *should* move. You're in Descartes's chair."

"Eeeeasy, big fella," I whispered, remembering that these brutes sense fear and attack it mercilessly. "Easy now. Your ol' buddy Gus'll just shuffle on over to the couch there, and your friend Descartes can have his silly old chair. . . ."

The dog continued to glower but remained motionless as I crept to the couch. I sat down gently. The dog waited till I was settled, then hopped into the rocker, sat back on his haunches, kept his wild sky eyes glued on me, and by the unnerving device of nodding his awesome head up and down, up and down, commenced rocking himself in the chair.

"Titus!"

"Yes?"

"The dog's in Descartes's chair now. And he's rocking himself! Should I tell him to get down?" (I only added the question to impress Titus; I really wouldn't have dared to tell that dog anything.)

Titus replied, "No, you shouldn't. The dog *is* Descartes."

"Oh," I said.

The sight of the creature bobbing its head in the chair made it difficult not to laugh, and the sight of its eyes made it difficult not to scream: teetering between these verbal extremes, I managed to say, "Good morning, Descartes."

The dog nodded in reply, allowing his tail the liberty of two curt, courteous wags before resuming his vigilant rocking. Although I didn't yet know it, we'd just made friends.

Descartes was a ghostly-looking but handsome mongrel graced with as unnerving a pair of eyes, in their way, as Anvil Abe's or Eddy's—eyes that glared and glowed with wild, unpredictable intelligence. His genealogy was obscure: I would have guessed him to be one part blue-eyed border-collie and two parts black European wolf, but Titus preferred to classify him as one part dog and one part man. In any case he was, like most Americans, a mongrel—and his skull was of as remarkable a size among dogs as was his master's among men. The intelligences housed in both their heads were ponderous to a degree bordering upon the preposterous. Descartes's sage nodding in the rocker was one example of this. An even odder example was Titus's avowed ability to understand Descartes's thoughts.

Titus took from his dog what he called "Psychic Dictation"—a silent form of dog-to-man communication which he translated aloud into English (employing as his "dog voice" a mode of articulation several shades slower and deeper than his own), affording eavesdroppers an unprecedented opportunity to hear a dog brain in action. But as I was not familiar with Titus's talents in this direction, was likewise unaware of his adherence to a metaphysical doctrine holding that the goal of animals is to attain human form and emanate thence to Godhood, and was also ignorant of how literally Titus put this doctrine into action—constantly exhorting his hound to transcend animality and start conducting himself "like a civilized man, and I don't mean an American"—I was in for a surprise:

As I watched Descartes tranquilly rocking I made some enthusiastic exclamation and asked Titus how he'd managed to teach the brute such a trick. . . . He burst in from the kitchen, glowering à la Descartes, raised a hand to shut me up and said, "Please, Gus! Don't make a stew about it. You'll confuse him. Descartes's immediate goal is humanity as surely as ours is Divinity. We should no more gawk at a dog behaving like a man than at a man behaving like a saint."

"Hrnk?" I responded. Having been raised in the orthodox Fido-Rover-Fetch-Rollover School, these arcane precepts were Greek to me.

Titus announced that he was preparing oatmeal for me and tea for all, the latter's imbibition being a custom observed daily in his household at about noon. When he returned to the kitchen the dog and I proceeded to eyeball one another, he nodding gravely—perhaps in keeping with profound inner deliberations, perhaps just to keep on rocking—and me fidgeting, wondering how to comport myself toward this formidable fellow. Titus rescued me by striding in with a silver tray laden with a gigantic teapot, cream and sugar containers, a steaming bowl of oatmeal with raisins, sunflower seeds and honey, and three cups and saucers. Intuiting the party for whom the third cup was intended, I emitted a nervous giggle that dematerialized in my craw when both my companions furrowed their capacious brows: this was no Lipton Quickie; this was a High Tea. Giggles were not kosher. Titus set the tray on a low coffee table, filled the cups with some of the blackest tea I'd ever seen, turned to me and asked, "Cream?"

"No thanks," I said.

"Descartes?" he asked, holding up the pitcher.

Descartes panted slightly and gave a quick wag of the tail; Titus responded by giving his tea a substantial lacing.

"Sugar?" asked Titus, turning back to me.

"No thanks," I repeated, stifling another inane giggle.

"Descartes?"

Descartes repeated the pant/wag gesture with an added intensity indicative of his love for this unwholesome substance; Titus stirred in a heaping spoonful. I started to sip my tea to keep from tittering again, but Titus said, "Wait." I waited. He placed Descartes's cup at the edge of the table near the rocker, bowed his head (and the dog bowed his) and prayed,

"O King Eternal, Open our eyes, we beseech thee, to behold thy gracious hand in all thy works as easily as we behold it in this excellent beverage. Amen."

At the word "Amen" Descartes leaned forward and began noisily lapping out of his cup, splashing a good deal of "excellent beverage" onto the table in the process. My relief was considerable: had he raised the cup to his lips and sipped, my infant mind might have collapsed. Even so, the formality of dog and master had me feeling like a hick in homespuns at a bourgeois ball, making my confusion the more profound when Titus—in an unusually ponderous voice—observed, "Today, as it is sunny but cool outside, I suffer from an acute case of unsublimated rambunctiousness. I would very much enjoy a brisk trot to the park after tea, pausing frequently upon the way to smell fresh dog-berries and pee on shrubs and hydrants. . . ."

I hawhawed unstably. "What are you talking about, Titus?"

But he stared at Descartes with invincible concentration, continuing in the same sluggish voice: "To explore a few alimentary apertures beneath the tails of cringing comrades would be gratifying, and the company of a bitch in heat would not detract from the excursion. But I suppose we'll sit here all afternoon while Master and the stranger talk and talk. Ho hum. Master might at least toss me a piece of the Hershey bar on the desk behind him."

"Well," said Titus in his normal voice, "at least your last request was human. Here you go." He tossed the fellow a chunk of chocolate; then his voice turned lethargic again:

"I'd like to bolt this insignificant tidbit in one massive inhalation, but Master has expressed displeasure at such sensible eating habits and urges a disgustingly *feline* pace, so I'll make some small display of chewing."

With that Descartes snatched up the chunk, masticated a sedate and undoglike number of times and swallowed.

"Good fellow," said Titus.

Descartes smiled, wagged his tail, and according to Titus rejoined, "Yes, I am a good fellow. But even the best of fellows have bladders; I think I'll ask to go into the backyard and void mine before Master and the stranger light their noxious post-tea pipes and cigarettes and destroy my olfactory efficiency for days to come."

And sure enough, Descartes climbed down from his rocker, sauntered into the kitchen, scratched on the back door, and in his own voice said, "Rowf!"

Titus stood up.

"Good. Here he comes," said Descartes via Titus.

"There you are, my friend," said Titus, opening the door.

"Thank you," replied Descartes. "Next incarnation, God willing, I'll have hands and won't require human assistance with doorknobs and such hindrances."

"So you may," said Titus, "if you can overcome certain inhuman foibles."

"Which foibles might those be?" asked Descartes.

"Snacking on cat feces, attacking the mailman, chewing up small dogs, to name three."

Descartes flattened his ears and retorted, "The mailman has no sense of territorial propriety. He struts uninvited past bushes I've sprayed with a thousand warnings. His audacity infuriates me. As for smaller dogs, if you could smell the unwarranted insults some of them give me you'd cudgel them yourself. I never attack mutts that acknowledge my obvious superiority, and I treat my rare equals with respect. Your ignorance of the subtleties of scent language really make you incompetent to judge."

Titus considered his defense, then asked, "What about cat shit?"

Descartes looked a bit sheepish. "Ah, well, yes, uh, as for cat feces, I confess my weakness, though their fragrance and flavor are far more informative and interesting than you humans could possibly realize. Don't you ever wonder what a passing man or woman has had to eat for the past few meals?"

"Not to the point of wanting to sample their emissions!" snapped Titus, "and cat dung gives you worms."

"But your vices—alcohol, caffeine and tobacco—destroy your liver, kidneys, adrenal glands and brain cells," Descartes replied.

"Touché," said Titus. "Allah have mercy on us both."

"Amen," said Descartes, walking out the door and whizzing on a geranium.

"Hey, knock it off!" squeaked a high, angry voice from the vicinity of Titus but which I came to comprehend was the geranium's. "I'm not a WC!"

"My apologies," said Descartes.

7

Philosophizing

He said, "They are feeding on drowned yellow stone flies."
I asked him, "How did you think that out?" . . .
"All there is to thinking," he said, "is seeing something noticeable
which makes you see something you weren't noticing which makes you
see something that isn't even visible."
I said to my brother, "Give me a cigarette and say what you mean."

—*Norman Maclean*, A River Runs Through It

WHILE I QUEASED my way through the bowl of oatmeal Titus inhaled four
piping cups of tea then strode to his desk, rammed a wad of Oriental
tobacco into a stump-sized pipe, fired it up with a foot-long fireplace
match, obfuscated us both in a swirling weatherfront, and stepped to his
bookshelves. There he paused, as a good fisherman pauses to read the
water before his first cast. Then he folded his fingers, turned his palms
outward, extended his arms till his knuckles went off like firecrackers, and
commenced extracting books—zipping them from their rows with the
deft backward wrist flick he so sorely lacked when flycasting, plundering
his shelves like a master organist pulling stops on a cathedral organ.
When he'd plucked a yard-high stack he heaped them on an end table,
slumped in an armchair, aimed his eagle beak my way and said, "Well,
Gus. Are you ready to fish?"

Being the sort of reader who worried a single thin volume for weeks,
I was dazed. "*Fish?* For what?"

"For happiness; for consolation; for a way of comprehending the
death of an Abe, the *why* in the Tamanawis, the beauty of an Eddy."

I sighed. "Where do we fish for that?"

"Ultimately, *here*," he pounded his chest. "But provisionally we
might peruse the Annals of the Primordial Tradition." He tapped the
stack of books.

"What 'primordial tradition'?"

He reached over and whipped out a silver paperback; he said, "There's only one. It is the perennial tradition proclaiming, with the Sufi, Attar, that

> From the back of the fish to the moon,
> every atom is a witness to His Being."

Cringing against the inevitable pious reply, I asked, "*Whose* being?" But Titus read this:

> "Such a fish that when He breathes He draws
> into His breast the first and the last . . .
> He sweeps away the two worlds, and draws to
> Himself all creatures without exception."

I laughed. "Attar called God a *fish*?"

Titus nodded. "So did the early Christians, insofar as Christ is God. The lovers of God delight in hyperbole, because we *need* hyperbole to talk about God. Poets can't describe Him; scientists can't quantify Him; the sages state flat out that from the disadvantage points of language and logic, *God is a Whopper*—yet from the vantage point of love they say this Whopper can be known." He snatched up a dog-eared Bible. "Attar calls God a fish; Jesus tells where to fish for it:

> If any man thirst, let him come unto me, and drink.
> He that believeth on me, as the scripture hath said,
> out of his belly shall flow rivers of living water. . . ."

"Which reminds me," I interrupted, hoping to ease Titus's intensity, "out of the belly of the pot shall flow the rivers of living tea." I filled our cups as he delved in a tall brown paperback; he didn't even notice.

"Rumi—first and best of dervishes—weaves our fish and river together:

> Every soul that reaches God
> enters the majestic secret,
> turns from a snake
> into a fish,
> leaves solid earth,
> dives into the sea,
> swims in the river of Paradise.
> The soul moves from earthly bondage
> to the kingdom without place. . . ."

He slipped a blue clothbound volume from a silk bag and said, "Listen:

Seen or unseen, I can pass through a wall
or a mountain as if it were air; I can sink
into the earth, or emerge from it as if it were water;
I can walk on water as if it were solid earth;
I can move through the air like a bird;
I can touch with my hands the sun and moon. . . ."

"That's a cocky fellow!" I observed.

"That's the Buddha," said Titus. "Cocky as Christ when he walked on water. Or as Rama when he appeared in the water cupped in Valmiki's hands. Or as Krishna when he told Arjuna, 'I am the savour in the waters, O son of Kunti, and the light in sun and moon!'"

He reached for another book, but I said, "Wait! Wait a minute Titus. This sort of thing is all very fine and dandy, but, well, do people really believe it? Do *you*? I mean, is any of it true?"

He smiled. "Rumi said, 'To the sane, the words of lovers are nothing but stories.' And Lao Tzu said, 'When a man of low capacities hears Tao, he laughs loudly at it—and if he did not laugh, it would not be worth the name of Tao.'"

"But what do *you* say, Titus?"

He looked me in the eye. "I'm not sane, Gus. I believe in the rivers of living water; I believe our souls swim in that water; I believe Jesus and Buddha and Krishna are the savour in that water; I believe in the Garden World and its Queen. I love the ol' Whopper."

I shook my head. "Wish *I* did."

"Well," said Titus, "why don't you?"

I shrugged. "What's to love? Where *is* this Whopper? Or the soul that jumps in the living river—where is it? And where are these sages and buddhas holing up, now that we really need them?"

Titus shot me a look. "Would you know one if you met one? Have you even *looked?* How hard did you look? How easy should they be to find?" His voice was soft, but his eyes were as piercing as Descartes's: the questions hit me like slaps in the face—well-deserved slaps. I hid in my teacup. Titus said, "Look, Gus: why can't a duffer like me catch fish? Isn't the answer obvious? Isn't it because at my present level of skill the fish would have to be so damned dumb and easily duped and utterly *unelu-*sive that they wouldn't be worth catching? How much more elusive should a thing so wondrous as the soul be? It's not a hatchery trout! And are you sure it's never flashed inside you? What was it in you that loved to watch Thomas Bigeater fish? What healed you and made you happy the night you remembered Bill Bob's pine knot and our elusive twins? What nearly jumped out of your rib cage and ravaged your brain the day you met the elusive Eddy?"

I made no reply—because at the mention of Eddy my soul began to ache. Like a tooth. I could feel it, filling me from head to toe. Titus said, "Fishermen should be the easiest of men to convince to commence the search for the soul, because *fishing is nothing but the pursuit of the elusive*. Fish invisible to laymen like me are visible to anglers like you by a hundred subtle signs. How can you be so sagacious and patient in seeking fish, and so hasty and thick as to write off your soul because you can't see it?"

Again his question hit me where I lived: I pictured rivers—December rivers, mist-shrouded and cold—and thigh deep in the long glides stood fishermen who'd arisen before dawn. . . . There they stood in the first gray light, in rain, wind, snowfall or frost; silent, patient, casting and casting again, retrieving nothing yet never questioning the possibility of bright steelhead hidden beneath the green slicks; numb-fingered, empty-bellied, aching-backed they stood, hatted or hooded like rabbis or monks, grumbling but vigilant, willing to pay hard penance for the mere chance of a sudden, subtle strike. What was a fisherman but an untransmuted seeker? And how much longer must be the wait, how much greater the skill, how much more infinite the patience and intense the vigilance in the search for the gift men called *the soul*? "Titus," I said, "I've been walking around for years with my metaphysical dry fly stuck in my ear!"

He laughed. "Let's get it out and go fishing!"

And that's what we did. We drank tea and read and talked all day, and late in the evening I made my first "catch":

We were getting tired and a little giddy, and words like "pizza" and "beer" were beginning to sound better than words like "beatific" or "immortal"; but the sun was just setting and my lifelong experience taught me never to quit the evening rise. So I asked, "Do you think souls strike harder in the early morning and late evening?"

"Could be," Titus mumbled.

"How do you suppose I ought to fish for mine now, then?"

"With a soul-pole, I suppose," he said offhandedly.

"A soul-pole."

"That's right."

"What do they cost, these soul-poles?"

"Whaddya got?" asked Titus, falling into a New Yawk accent.

"Oh, I got some," I said, patting my wallet pocket. "What do they cost?"

"All ya got," he said.

"All I got!"

He nodded. "But not all ya think ya got. All ya *really* got."

"Hmm. What all do I really got?"

"Nuthin'," said Titus.

"Ha! Right in my price range! Where do I pick one up?"

He shrugged. "Right here's fine."

"You got one here?"

"I got one here," he said, pounding his heart, "and you got one there," he added, pointing at mine.

I gaped at my rib cage. "I got to pay all the nuthin' I got for a soul-pole I already got *right here*?"

"You don't *know* you got it," he said. "You got to pay to know."

"OK" I said. "How do I pay?"

He said, "Repeat after me . . ."

I said, "Repeat after me . . ."

"Not yet!"

"Not yet!"

"Never mind. Here goes:"

"Never mind. Here goes:"

"I, Gus Orviston, do here give every last bit of the nuthin' I got . . ."

"I, Gus Orviston, do here give every last bit of the nuthin' I got . . ."

"to the Creator of my soul-pole . . ."

"to the Creator of my soul-pole . . ."

"in exchange for the soul-pole itself."

"in exchange for the soul-pole itself."

"That's it," he said. "It's yours."

I pawed at my shirt front. "Where is it?"

"Shall I show it to you?"

"Can you?"

"By analogy, yes—if you'll answer a few questions."

"Fire away," I said.

"All right. Where is Rodney the Flyrod at this moment?"

"Hanging on my cabin wall—but *he's* no soul-pole. . . ."

"Of course not," Titus agreed. "He's *your* pole. And what do you suppose he is experiencing as he hangs on the wall there?"

"Not a hell of a lot," I said, scratching my head.

"A little weight and mass, perhaps?"

"Yeah, and a little rod varnish and guides and handle—those sorts of experiences."

"And that's about it."

"Yep."

"So Rodney hangs on the wall until you pick him up, then he bends when you bend him, casts when you cast him, fights fish when you hook them. But the electric jolt in your hands, the line singing through the water, the beauty of the riverbank, the taste of the trout—all these wonders are unknown to poor Rodney, are they not?"

"Yeah. I mean, they're not."

"Good. Now, who made Rodney from a nondescript blank into the lovely rod he is today?"

"I did."

"And who controls his destiny, decides whether he will hang on the wall, ride in the pickup, cast for trout or bluebacks? And who will determine when he is worn out or broken and will one day consign him to the closet, garbage can or funeral pyre that is his inevitable end?"

"I do, and I will."

"Yes. Now, who do you suppose made you from a configuration of molecules into the living fisherman you are today?"

"I wish I knew," I said.

"Excellent!" said Titus. "And who controls your destiny, decides whether you shall be happy or miserable, long-lived or short, infamous or famous, erudite or acrimonious and so on and so forth?"

"Wish I knew that, too."

"*Very* good!" he exclaimed. "And who will decide when your body has become an unfit habitation for that which enlivens it and will one day consign it to a crematorium, river bottom or wormy grave?"

"Wish I knew that, too," I said, "but why do you holler 'excellent!' and 'very good!' when I say I wished I knew? Don't you expect me to say 'God does it' or 'My soul does it'?"

Titus looked aghast. "Gus! I'm a philosopher, not an *evangelist*! It's the 'wish I knew' that's crucial. To say 'God does it' and leave it at that is to abandon the search before it's begun. To really want the truth, to long for it desperately, is to reject every formulation and theory and dogma and opinion right up to the time you see and touch and unite with the Being or Thing itself! Nobody ever discovers truth by barfing up sunday-school answers to questions . . . but where were we?"

"We were after my soul-pole."

"Yes. And we agreed that Rodney is oblivious to everything except a bit of weight and mass and varnish, did we not?"

"We did."

"So it follows, does it not, that he is likewise oblivious to the existence of Gus—even though Gus is his maker, the controller of his fate, we might say his very *essence*?"

"Yeah, that follows."

"Isn't it possible, then, that you and I might be just as oblivious to the existence of a maker, a controller of fates, we might even say an Essence—Who wields us even more deftly than you wield Rodney?"

"Sure it's possible."

"Well, there you have it," said Titus. "Rodney is to Gus what Gus is to his Essence. Name the Essence 'soul' and you've got your soul-pole."

"Me!" I laughed. "*I'm* the soul's pole! I like it, Titus, I like it."

"Thank you. Swiped it from Plotinus. What do you like?"

"I like the implication that even though I'm hopelessly stupid compared to my soul or Essence, I'm damned useful: I have a profound purpose!"

For once it was Titus who looked confused. "I don't follow you, Gus."

"You're not a fisherman yet," I said. "But think about Rodney: he may not know much, but I sure can't fish very well without him. I may lay down the law, but Rodney lays out the line; I may strike, but Rodney's body sets the hook; I could live and even catch fish without him, but it's Rodney's bending and bouncing that makes it fun! Rodney may be dumb, but he's crucial; he may not be much of a human being, but he's a hell of a flyrod! So, Mr. Soul or Mr. Essence, wherever you are: I may not be much of a god, but I must be a hell of a soul-pole! And whatever the metaphysical version of fishing is, I know you couldn't do it as well without me! And even though I'm kind of a dumb blank next to you and owe you everything I've got, you have more fun with me than you had without me!"

Titus applauded. "Here, here! A philosopher is born!"

And we went for beer and pizza.

After two exhausting, exhilarating days of Titus's tea and tutelage I left his flat bearing fourteen borrowed books, a monograph he'd written called "What is Water?," a shaky belief in an imperceptible but seemingly inescapable essence called "soul," and an even shakier belief in an Essence of Essences which I took to calling "the Whopper," because the word *God* still brought to mind the glowering white-haired-and-bearded fellow that GG and the Witless so zealously advertised. Titus insisted that God, Allah, Parabrahma, Elahi, Yezdan, and various John Henrys of that ilk all referred to the same Deity, but I insisted that if I was going to learn to respect this Deity I'd have to start by calling It a name I felt a bit of fondness for.

For the first few blocks down the street from the flat I was anxious to get home and read more about the Whopper. But the farther I walked the slower and lower I felt, till I began to wonder whether Descartes's eyes emitted some kind of microwave away from which I had no interest in anything more transcendent than hamburgers. By the time I reached the bus stop I was wilted and desolate, and as I climbed aboard I realized why: the broken-topped alder had returned to haunt me. It struck me, then, what good pals Titus and his dog were. With them I thought of Eddy only with hope. But without them the thought of her filled me with a gnawing and an emptiness and an ache and an itch and a sore botch of the heart that could not be healed. Knowing I'd best find company fast, I transferred busses and rode to the west-side suburbs to see how my family was doing.

8

Little, But Strong

Consider this water which flows toward the city. . . . See how pure and fine it is! But when it enters the city . . . people wash their hands and faces and feet and other parts in it, and their clothes and carpets, and the urine of all the quarters and dung of horses and mules are poured into it and mixed up with it. Look at it when it passes out the other side of the city! Though it is still the same water, turning the dust to clay . . . making the plain verdant . . . disagreeable things have been mingled with it.

—*Rumi*

WHEN I REACHED my parents' house I walked right in, then felt like a housebreaker for not having knocked. Strange that so short an absence had erased my ability to call this place "home." I heard voices in H2O's study—happy voices, laughing and giggling. Nobody ever carried on like that when I lived here. I went in.

The instant the door moved there was a mad scramble: Bill Bob, Ma and H2O all jumped up from whatever it was they'd been doing like I was a schoolteacher and they were punks caught grinding garter snakes in the pencil sharpener. "What gives?" I asked, really feeling like an intruder now.

They wore red faces and foolish grins. Bill Bob recovered first: "Mu--mu--musical chairs!" he burbled. "We was playin' Musical Chairs!"

Ma and H2O nodded idiotically.

"Oh," I said. "Musical chairs. I see. Well well well. . . ." I turned to H2O, whose face is transparent as cellophane in the presence of a fib. "So where's the *music?*"

Ma started humming the "Battle Hymn of the Republic." H2O chuckled convulsively. "Musical chairs! Heheheh! Silly, huhuhuhuhuhu. Felt foolish heheh. Thought you were one of my high-flown fisher-friends. Hee! er, silly. . . ."

He was on the verge of hysterics, and mirth in my father was a commodity so unfamiliar to me that I couldn't tell what to make of it. I looked the situation over. One piece of evidence seemed to corroborate Bill Bob's explanation: nobody was where he or she should have been. Ma, still intoning the "Battle Hymn," was behind H2O's fly-tying desk and there was a fly in the vise; H2O, humming a harmony, was at Ma's rod-building table and a lightweight spinning rod was under construction; Bill Bob, thumping time with both feet, stood in the midst of a rubble of tools, oil cans, spools of line, and an old surf-casting reel in ten or fifteen pieces. "All right," I said. "What the hell's going on here?"

Ma had a tweezers in her hand. She sat down at H2O's vise singing "Glory-glory-haller-lew-yer," grabbled the hackles of the fly with the tweezers, ripped them away and shouted, "How 'bout Musical Sabotage!"

H2O giggled maniacally, grabbed one of the guides on the bait-rod, viciously tore it off, and drowned out the "Battle Hymn" with an operatic "Rule, Britannia."

Bill Bob stared at the floor, grinning at the uproar till his cheeks must have ached and avoiding my incredulous stare.

What hell had my family fallen into? I shook my head, collapsed in a chair and muttered, "So you wreck each other's gear for fun now, huh? Well I think it's pretty damned *pathetic!*"

"Hell yes," agreed Ma. "We always was pathetic, Gus, but we've got patheticker since you ain't been 'round to keep us civil."

H2O nodded enthusiastically. "The Great Izaak Walton Controversy rages on unabated!" he thundered, ripping off another guide. "We didn't realize what a steadying influence you had on us, son."

"Me too," said Bill Bob, smiling placidly. It was *his* acceptance of it all that sent my heart to my socks.

H2O kept singing, but Ma started out of the room, saying, "But ain't this some way to treat the projital son. Come on in the kitchen ever'body an' we'll fix Gus a sandwich."

As she and H2O trudged away I noticed that H2O had lost some weight while Ma had gained some; for the first time it occurred to me that they were beginning to look somewhat alike: it gave me a *crappy* feeling. Bill Bob plugged in his radios and started to follow, but I grabbed him by the wires, disconnected him and demanded, "All right! Cut the bull and tell me, what the hell is happening around here?"

He shrugged. "Nothin'. Nothin's happening. That's all."

"That's all, huh! Since when did *you* start thinking Ma and H2O's squabbling was funny? And what are you doing with this surf-casting reel?

You gonna take up fishin' and turn vegetable on me, too?"

"Nope," he said, sitting down in the reel parts and starting to scrub them.

"So what *are* you doing?"

"I'm takin' up Airing."

"*What*ing?"

"Airing," he said, pointing to a kite kit in the corner. "I send up a kite with a radio receiver on it, and I let it anchor up there, and I put on my headphones and fish for radio waves. Catch lots, too—'specially on that bald mountain up behind Uncle Zeke's. Caught some Hopi Indian music from Albuquerque once, and some hockey from Toronto. But that was with a hand line. I can handle *four thousan'* feet o' string on this reel. I'm gonna try for somethin' from Europe, or China maybe!"

I sighed. At least there was one sane soul in the family. "Let's go get something to eat," I said. And we went, but in the kitchen H2O and Ma were already ensconced in a full-blown debate over whether Charles Cotton had ever angled with worms. I gorged down a sandwich and said I was going for a walk. I would have hitched straight back to the Tamanawis, but I wanted to tuck Bill Bob in that night, for old times' sake. Maybe I could get him to tell me what had really been happening in the study. Musical chairs my ass.

When I headed out the door it was two in the afternoon and drizzling. In that godforsaken suburb there wasn't anyplace much to walk to. I strolled along by some mud puddles for a while pretending there were fish in them. But there weren't, so it got depressing. Not that it hadn't been depressing in the first place. Then I remembered U.S. Grant Creek. It was a suburbanized creek, but it was water. I headed for it.

These suburbs, just a century ago, were a wetland—a wide interlacing of ponds, creeks, sloughs, bogs and meadows providing homes for more mink, muskrat, beaver, ducks, deer and herons than you'd find in all the Willamette Valley now. But gradually it had been subdivided, drained, filled, imprisoned in pipes, buried alive. U.S. Grant was the only nontroglodyte creek left within miles. And before twenty-four hours passed they may as well have buried it, too . . . because U.S. Grant Creek was about to die. I know this for a simple reason: I killed it.

U.S. Grant Creek was almost ten miles long, but that didn't stop me from killing it. I was glad I did it, too—not because I managed to out-macho a thing thousands of times bigger than me, but because I released someone I loved from unending, intolerable misery. I call the creek a "someone" because it was a living body—more a him or a her than an it. But I called it an it after I killed it.

When I was a kid I called it "Sisisicu." It means "Little, But Strong," and it had been that creek's name for centuries. But the white settlers didn't speak Indian. They didn't speak it so well they didn't know the Indians didn't call themselves Indians, and they never found out what the Indians did call themselves. But the Indians and the creek are dead now, so maybe it didn't much matter. It's a funny coincidence that the settlers chose to rename Sisisicu after kind of a "little, but strong" guy—a guy with a stale cigar reek about him, kind of like the creek came to have. It's almost as if the settlers knew that before their grandchildren were through with Sisisicu, "U.S. Grant" would be a damned good name for it.

The corpse was a big, unwieldy thing—impossible to move and too big to bury. But nobody thought of this till I finished it off, and probably nobody but me thought of it even then. Anyhow, it's still lying there in the suburbs of Portland—gallons and gallons of slithering liquid carrion. A creek stiff.

It still looks something like a creek. People still call it "creek." "Don't play in that filthy creek!" mothers tell their kids. But you know how kids are. They play in it anyway, cutting their hands and feet on the broken glass and shredded metal in it, going to the doctor when the cuts start to fester. It's a problem of semantics at this point: "creek" isn't accurate anymore, but there isn't a word yet for what creeks become once they die. I guess the makers of English didn't plan on creeks dying. But I think "U.S.G." is a good name for Sisisicu's corpse. It's almost onomatopoeic: has both the prez's initials and a certain MSG/U.S. Certified Color sort of ring to it.

Slogging along through the drizzle I met the creek in the middle and started hiking upstream. I hadn't seen it, except from a car, in years; hadn't fished it since I was twelve; used to catch some nice native cuts and a lot of crawdads in it. But I saw that those days were long gone. . . . "Water," according to the Random House Dictionary, has forty definitions ranging from liquid H_2O to urine, with cosmetics, adulterated whiskey and tears in between. Poor Sisisicu looked like it was full of all forty of them. By an uncanny but probably meaningless coincidence, "Dead" also has forty Random House meanings—and the bulk of them seemed also to apply to little Sisisicu. Even in the least frothy rapids the creek foamed at the mouth, dull yellow-brown bubbles coating everything they touched with a rabid scum. I put my hand in—and gloved it with a tepid, oily film that smelled like a hot street.

I kept heading upstream, moved now by a melancholy urge to see the worst, to feel and smell it all. I would journey to the source of my childhood creek. I would find, for better or worse, what had become of the waters of my past.

It was tough going. I was trespassing every step of the way, mostly in suburban backyards—incurring the glares and suspicion of every dog and homeowner. But I kept on: the Indians had no word for "trespassing," so the trespasses of their neighbors needed no forgiving. And I had walked this riparian before these candy-coated houses ever stood; I had fished this little water; I had loved it. I figured this gave me the right of passage. This pilgrimage was between no one but Sisisicu and me. Whoever made the laws protecting these backyards from intruders made no law to protect Sisisicu from poison, filth and sewer. They weren't my laws. To hell with them. I trudged upward, resolute.

I had to leave the water when it passed under streets. This was not in keeping with the self-imposed laws of my pilgrimage, but the culverts reeked, and they were dark, so I crossed the streets and continued my trek on the upstream sides. The rain fell harder.

After a slow, sad two hours I reached a big pipe pouring out of an embankment. At the top of the embankment was a four-lane street running through a wide, flat shopping district. I crossed this street, but no creek continued on the other side. Was this the source—squalid square miles of lots and plots pimpled with real estate offices, fast food chains, gas stations, shopping malls, factories, tickytack churches, funeral parlors, concrete schools? I wasn't satisfied with such a conclusion. There was water in the pipe. It was coming from somewhere. I would find where.

In the center of the street was a manhole-cover. When the traffic lights stopped the flow of cars I ran to it, listened, heard a muffled gurgling. Was this Sisisicu, or just a random sewer? I found a grocery receipt in my pocket. I rolled it into a ball, pried up the manhole cover, dropped it in, ran to the embankment where the pipe poured out: there came the paper, covered with greasy scum. I returned to the street and stumped along from manhole to manhole, checking now and then to be sure Sisisicu still gurgled below. Then I came to a place where the manholes ended but the stream at the curb ran strong: obviously a higher tributary. I followed the gutter stream for half a block, then it vanished into a hole in the curb. I turned slowly in a circle: in every direction the suburb lay lower than where I stood. The only thing higher was the three-story bank building there beside me. It was a Benjamin Franklin bank—a true-to-scale replica of Independence Hall. So, the pipe in the curb must come from the bank. I sighed, sniffed, sucked up my courage and strode up the walk into the Benjamin Franklin: like a Burton seeking the source of the Nile, I had to make inquiries of the natives. I was rain soaked and creek spattered; my hair and beard were a dripping mess. But this was no time for self-consciousness. I went straight to the manager's desk.

The manager was a short, broad-beamed fellow with a shiny, good-natured face before he looked me over and a shiny, not-so-good-natured face afterward. He said, "May I help you?"

I said, "Yeah. I'd like to ask a few questions about your building here."

He nodded coolly: his eyes darted round the room, caught sight of the security guard and bulged with meaning. Seeing the guard nod, he turned back to me. I asked, "How many floors you got here?"

He frowned. "Three, not counting the basement. All equipped with multiple alarm systems and cameras. *Why?*"

I grinned as stupidly as possible. "I'm doing a paper for school. About, uh, Independence Hall. This is a model of it, right?"

"Ah!" He smiled like a Sears santa, muzzy with relief. That's the trouble with lies: they're so soothing.

"Is there a, um, bathroom, up in the tower?"

He frowned again. "No. But there are several service stations just down the street."

I turned on the grin. "Oh, I don't need one. I just need to know."

It didn't quite work: he looked at the wet scuz all over me, one side of his face staying where it was while the other side smiled. Out of the diagonal slash of mouth came the word, "Bathrooms." That was all he said.

"It's an architecture class," I lied. "I'm gonna be a plumber."

He was soothed again, and his mouth returned to horizontal.

"Any sinks up in the tower?"

"No, no sinks," he said, helpful now. "No water pipes higher than the faucet on the second floor. Will that be all?"

"Yeah. Yeah, I guess. Thanks."

I went back outside and stood in the rain, looking up at the bank, down at the gutter, back at the bank. The pilgrimage felt unresolved. Faucets and toilets go into sewers, don't they? But Sisisicu had entered that curb, and they don't pump shit from banks right onto the street. Not yet they don't. So where had the creek gone?

Then I saw my mistake, realized the interview with the manager was unnecessary, realized my Second-story-faucet Theory was, like Burton's Lake Victoria Theory, a blunder born of haste. . . . For up on the bank tower was a replica of the Liberty Bell. And rain poured onto that bell, cohered on it, grew heavy, rolled slowly down the brassy sides, off onto the roof, down the roof to the gutters, to a drainpipe, to a drainfield (and perhaps a buried spring, where deer and Indians once drank), then into and out the underground pipe at the curb. Here was the uttermost source of the waters that had been Sisisicu: an imitation Liberty Bell on top of a mock Independence Hall.

The security guard came out the glass doors and lolled nearby. He looked at the passing cars, at the rain, at the sidewalk to my right, to my left, in front of me, behind me. I could see he was embarrassed; I could see that the manager told him "Keep an eye on that guy," so he did, because he had to to get paid; I could see he could see past the muck on me; I got the feeling he might even be a fisherman; I got the feeling he might like walking back into that bank all mucky and sopped himself. I said, "See that bell up there?"

He said, "Yeah."

I said, "It's the source of a creek. I followed it all the way. U.S. Grant Creek it's called. The Indians called it 'Sisisicu.'"

He said nothing.

I pointed at the bell. "Used to catch some nice trout out of there," I told him.

The security guard looked up at the bell. He was still standing in the rain there, looking up at the bell, when I rounded a corner three blocks away.

9

Closing the Door

The fishermen that walk upon the beach appear like mice.
—*Shakespeare*, King Lear

THAT EVENING AT SUPPER Ma and H2O bolted their food till their second helpings, then slowed enough to squabble with their mouths full. I ate fast and cleared out.

I went to my old bedroom to hide till Bill Bob went to bed, but it had been converted into a guest room for visiting Carpers and flyfishermen. It figured. My room was gone; my creek was gone; my parents' minds were gone; Eddy was gone. I left the house and went walking in the night, but there was nowhere to go. Cars and burbs everywhere. If Titus's Primordial Tradition wasn't gone, too, it sure wasn't easy to spot around here. I almost headed for the highway, thinking to hitchhike home to the Tamanawis, but it was raining, I was exhausted, there was still Tuckin' Time, and in the morning I wanted to walk to the mouth of U.S. Grant Creek, just to finish off the inspection. So I returned to the house, but circled around back: Ma's pantry is just inside the back door and it's a lot nicer walking into a room full of drying herbs, fruits, smoked fish, jars of jam and vegetables than into a hollow shag-carpeted hallway.

But before I reached the door I heard whistling. I stopped to listen: it was a slow, melancholy air, simple, repetitive, haunting. Bill Bob was the whistler. I snuck up to listen. There was something odd in the song; after a time I realized that this was the first time I'd heard him in a minor key. It made him seem old; it made me feel sad. And it made me feel *good*. Because sometimes happy songs will make sad people miserable, because they feel guilty that they aren't happy, on top of the sadness. But a sad song talks to the part that hurts, says, Yeah I know, yeah it's bad, yeah it hurts: but I'm with you. I feel it too.

He was standing in a shadow cast by the spotlight on the porch, engulfed in an enormous coat. It was cold out for summer; you could see your breath. The rain had stopped. The sky was half-full of clouds, half-empty, and a half-moon poured down its half-light half the time. Whistling seemed like an odd thing for Bill Bob to be doing—not because he didn't often whistle, but because it was only one thing, and he usually did several.

But I watched a good long while, and in the end I saw he *was* doing several things. I saw that the enormous coat had been mine; I saw that the spotlight on the porch cut a clean, sharp shadow; I saw that Bill Bob stood in that shadow so close to the line of light that his puckered lips sometimes barely touched it, glowing pale and pink when they did; and I saw that he wasn't just whistling the song: he was watching it. Each slow, sad note sent a bright stream of vapor into the spotlit air.... And then I saw that not only was he watching, he was aiming his song: the high notes he blew downward, the low notes he sent high, the middle ones he blew horizontally. I nearly laughed and ruined the sight. My brother the juggler, balancing everything he did. There he stayed at the edge of the dark, bundled up and buttoned down, satisfied—a dry darkness making wet music stream into the light.

Later I tucked him in. His dreefee was the surf-casting reel, loaded now with four thousand feet of kite string; cleaned, oiled, overhauled and ready to nab airwaves clear from China. He placed it on his desk beside a model B-52 bomber and ordered it to spend the night "slurpin' up the bomber's flyin' juices" so the bomber wouldn't be able to bomb anymore, and so the kite would have the juice to fly higher. Then he hopped in bed, lit a candle, flopped on his back and said, "I'm gonna tell you what my friend Pedro saw...." But then he cut himself off, sat up, looked at me closely, asked, "What ya been doin', Gus? How ya been? We ain't seen ya."

I said, "Oh, I've been all right. I've quit fishin' so much. Made some new friends, you'll have to meet them. Been swimmin' a couple times, too."

"Swimmin'? I thought you didn't like swimmin'."

"Well, I don't much," I admitted. "But once this guy, Abe, kind of roped me into it. And another time it was this girl, Eddy...."

"Eddy?" he smiled. "You got a girlfriend, Gus?"

"No," I said. "So what about this thing Pedro saw?"

He said, "Ever seen Pedro's place?"

"No."

"Do you wish your girlfriend was Eddy?"

"What about Pedro's place?"

"You do, dontcha! She's pretty, I bet!"

"Prettier than you're gonna be if you don't change the subject."

"There's eleven of 'em lives in there," he said.

"Eleven what? Where?"

"People, Dummy. In Pedro's place. It's a tiny little house, and it ain't much good. But Pedro's got four brothers and four sisters and a mom and a dad livin' in there with him. And they like it all right. They're poor. They sleep in tripledecker bunkbeds. I stayed all night once; I got the middle bunk. Why'd ya go swimmin' with her if she ain't your girlfriend?"

"Don't change the subject, Bill Bob. And what was this bullhooey today about musical chairs?"

"Don't change the subject," he said. "Pedro's place don't have just people in it either. It gots bats in the rafters, and possums under the floor, and a skunk once, and four goats in the garage for milk to drink and for lawn mowers. And it gots mice. That's what Pedro saw I'm gonna tell you about. A mouse."

I snorted, "A mouse!"

"Listen, Dummy. I didn't tell ya what sort of mouse."

"OK. What sort of mouse?"

He leaned toward me and in hushed tones announced, "A singing mouse!"

"In other words, a squeaking mouse," I said.

"In the *same* words, a *singing* mouse," he insisted. "Pedro woke up in the middle of the night. The mouse was sitting in a patch of blue-colored streetlight light in the middle of the floor. And it was singing its heart out. Pedro said it sounded like a sad canary."

"Really?"

"Really. And while it was singing two other mice came out to listen to it. They squeaked a little, and looked at him, and scratched their heads with their hind legs like they couldn't believe it, and looked at him some more. But they couldn't sing. But that one mouse sure could.

"So first thing next morning Pedro took away all the mouse traps and made his family promise not to set 'em. And he told 'em to listen that night, but they said they'd be sleepin', and the way they said it Pedro could tell they didn't believe about the mouse. But their house is small, so Pedro waited till they were all in bed and he tied strings that went from his finger to all their fingers and told them that if the singing mouse came he'd give the strings a tug. His big brother said what did he think he was, a fish? But he went along with it.

"Just when they were going to sleep Pedro's dad gave his string a tug from the bedroom, but Pedro told him to knock it off, Dad. He was serious. So they all settled down, and pretty soon all the ones that snore were snoring, and all the ones that sucked their thumbs were sucking their thumbs, and everybody was asleep 'cept Pedro, and he was feelin' awful sleepy himself. But about when he was going asleep the three mice came out to play, and there were crumbs Pedro left right in the patch of blue streetlight light, and pretty quick they found 'em and ate on 'em. But when they were done they all went away, and none ever sang.

"The next night Pedro tried again with the strings and all, even though they made fun of him, but this time he didn't leave no crumbs. He said he figured the singing mouse must be like a guitar. Couldn't get music unless the insides was empty and the gut stretched tight. After everyone was sleeping again, Pedro too, by accident, Pedro dreamed he was a fish, and he bit this worm because it looked and tasted like a beef burrito, and it *was* a beef burrito, but it was a worm, too, with a hook in it that went through his hand, and he jumped and woke up and someone was tugging on the string: he heard the singing mouse singing! His little sister, Maria, had heard it first and tugged Pedro, then Pedro gave all the other strings some tugs. The singing mouse was all alone in the blue patch of light, sitting up on his back legs like a graydigger does, and singing his heart out. Pedro tugged and tugged. His littlest brother, Juan, woke up, then his mother, who snuck to her doorway and watched and heard. But just when his dad woke up the mouse stopped singing, and Maria and Juan were so disappointed they went "Aaawwwww . . ." and it ran away. Then everybody woke up and started arguing whether it was squeaking or singing. Pedro's older brothers had undone their strings and tied dirty socks on for a joke, and his sisters besides Maria were so sleepy they never felt anything, so they all said it was squeaking. But Pedro's dad said that even though he didn't hear, everybody who did was sure it was singing, so they won, and Pedro's mom said it was a blessing to their house and a sign of God's grace because she's Catholic.

"Pedro's dad stayed up most of the next night, but the mouse never came. Pedro wanted to stay up, but he'd got in trouble for falling asleep in school, and he was too tired anyhow. Juan heard it one more time about a week later, but it never came back after that. But Maria made up a song about it in Mexican, and the middle part was supposed to be how the mouse sounded, and I heard that, and Pedro and his mom say that it *is* just how the mouse sounded. Maria's real small for her age. She's five and her hair goes clear to her bottom in the back even in a pigtail, except pigtails in real life are short and squiggly, but her hair is straight and thick and pretty, so after the mouse came she started calling it a mousetail.

Nobody else was around when I heard her. She was swinging in the swing all alone, singing the singing mouse song, which told how Pedro heard it but nobody believed him and he got the strings and crumbs but they didn't sing but the next night her and Juan and her mom heard so now everybody believed them, and her voice was real high and small, and when she got to the parts about how the mouse sounded it kind of went right through me. It was exactly the sort of song you'd make if you was the only mouse in the world who knew how to sing. . . ."

I asked Bill Bob if it was the singing mouse song he'd been whistling into the spotlight that night. He said it was. I told him it was very beautiful, because it was. He said he thought maybe when she got older Maria might be his girlfriend, like Eddy was mine. I said Eddy wasn't mine, and that I doubted I'd see her again, but he said he didn't believe it. I asked what reason he had for not believing it, and he said he didn't have any reason except for the way I'd said I'd gone swimming with her. I said that that wasn't a reason, but even as I said it I felt outrageous and unreasonable hope and believed that if a mouse could sing I just might see Eddy again. Then he taught me to whistle the singing mouse song, and when I'd learned it he went to sleep.

The following morning I set out again for the midpoint of U.S. Grant Creek, this time journeying downstream, bound for the mouth. The weather had cleared in the night, which meant that even more people would see me trespassing, but today I'd brought equipment to assist me: I had a bag of beef ribs to keep the canines busy with something besides my calves; I wore a baseball cap, carried a Big Chief 500 tablet on a clipboard and had numerous pens and mechanical pencils clipped conspicuously in my shirt pocket, the idea being to come off as some kind of meter-reader or county official.

I covered the six miles quickly, including all the places I'd fished as a kid, and I saw beyond doubt that U.S. Grant had had it. There was scunge, car bodies, garbage, sewage and shredded plastic everywhere; there were no kingfishers, ouzels, crawfish, not even any skippers. Not even any mosquito larvae. The water was strangely clear, but slick and greasy, nothing alive in or near it. Three hundred yards from where it scuzzed into the Willamette was a hole where I'd invariably taken a cutthroat or two in springtime—a short gravel run ending in a shallow pool created by a log and garbage jam, and in the center of the pool, an underwater spring. I snuck up on hands and knees, figuring if there was a fish left, this was the place. Where the spring rose was an area the size of a bathtub where healthy moss and algae still grew. And lo and behold, there hovered a solitary seven-inch cutthroat. The last trout in U.S. Grant Creek. The last living thing in it. I slipped up to watch how it lived.

It wasn't up to much. It hardly swam at all—just finned in its bathtub oasis. God knew how it got there. There were 300 yards of deadly water between it and the Willamette and nine miles of poison creek-corpse confronting it upstream. It was trapped. It was alone. It was the last. Half-angry, half-brokenhearted, I watched, the singing mouse song singing itself interminably in my head. One trout, one mouse, one kid—they were all that was left of the world I'd grown up in. The rest was all sick and crazy, dying, or already dead. That Bill Bob and this trout had survived intact in their respective environments seemed to me a fact more miraculous than mice humming Beethoven.

Yet when a flying ant drifted over the oasis the last trout rose and took it with all the confidence of its Tamanawis cousins. Which gave me an idea. The idea was to perform euthanasia: this doomed trout was all that let me call the creek *alive*; given the state of the creek, its source, its foreseeable future, it seemed better to save the trout and kill the creek.

I found a gallon milk jug to put the fish in if I caught it. I pulled out the hand line I carry in my wallet. But when I went foraging for bait there was nothing alive in the streamside garbage. All I found was a rotted, waterlogged navy-blue pea coat. Which gave me another idea. I sat on a tire, pulled a long thread from the coat, jammed my #10 bait-hook into a board, held the board between my knees, took up the thread and tied a fly—a #10 Ant of sorts. A derelict ant, in a tiny pea coat.

My fly wouldn't float, I'd no rod to cast with and a direct cast would spook the fish anyway; so I got out my pocketknife, cut an elderberry twig and whittled it into a little boat for my pea-coated fly to ride in—a three-inch canoe, with an outrigger. I readied my line, stowed the fly on board, slipped upstream and sloughed the booby-trapped canoe down toward the trout in the oasis. . . .

> Once upon a time on an afternoon dismal as any afternoon, the last trout in U.S. Grant Creek was treading water when it found itself confronted by a remarkable spectacle: a little elderberry outrigger canoe was floating down into its pool! This trout was a young trout, a trout unacquainted with canoes. Nevertheless it was able to identify this one, through the operation of its Racial Memory. This trout was also a nervous trout. It had had no one to talk to for a year; its creek was filthy; it knew it might be dead by now if a rain hadn't cleaned things up a bit. This trout was, in a word, a *wreck*. And now this—a canoe! When would it end?
>
> The trout's first reaction was to spook, but its second reaction was to recall that there was nowhere to spook to: last time it left its oasis it nearly suffocated before finding its way back. So it stayed where it was. Still, it

didn't like the idea of it—a three-inch outrigger canoe; a three-inch canoe dragging an anchor rope that ran so far astern you couldn't see an end to it. It was a bad business, to the trout's way of thinking. It was about to get worse:

When the canoe was dead overhead it capsized. An ant fell out. "I'll be swiggered!" thought the trout. "I didn't know ants could canoe!" The trout eyed the ant warily; the ant clung to the anchor rope; the canoe drifted away; the ant began to sink; it was sinking right in the trout's face. . . . The trout's mind began to race: it must be an exceptional ant that could teach itself the science of canoeing; should such an ant swim to safety, what would prevent it from teaching countless other ants how to canoe? and if other ants learned to canoe, what would prevent one of them from learning the closely related science of angling? and if one ant learned to angle, what would prevent it from teaching tens of thousands of other ants? "It's a terrible drink of water!" thought the trout, and its Racial Memory pictured dominoes—hundreds of thousands of ominous black dominoes in a row, falling, falling, one after another—ant after ant after ant in canoe after canoe after canoe killing trout after trout after trout. . . . "I've got to stop it!" thought the trout. I've got to *kill that ant!*"

Deploying two troops of teeth, the trout clamped down viciously upon the ant, but just as it did so it perceived another bad business: the ant was wearing a navy-blue pea coat. "Judas Priest!" thought the trout. "The ant can sew!" The trout crunched the ant again and again, but as it did so there came a whole bevy of bad businesses: the trout was swimming down, but it was going up; this sort of thing should never happen. And there was a pain in its mouth which its Racial Memory identified as toothache, a malady the poor trout had believed itself immune to. Then the trout realized the anchor rope was fishing line, and that the ant had a hook; adding one and one together, the trout got three: "Holy Moses!" it thought, "*the ant already has learned how to angle!*"

I landed the last trout in U.S. Grant Creek—a feisty, confused-looking little scrapper less interested in escape than in snapping the pea-coated ant. I slipped the hook from its jaw, dumped it in the water-filled milk jug and raced to the Willamette, noticing as I went a silhouette in a VW bus watching me from a parking lot; I supposed whoever it was would start fishing the creek-stiff after seeing me score—good luck to them! I went far enough upriver to escape the stream's vile outflow and poured out the trout: when it found itself free it hesitated, darting back and forth near shore, but as its gills began to work, as it began to breathe the compara-tive purity of the river, as it sensed something of the vastness of its new home it hung near the surface for a long instant, then darted forward, disappearing like a thought in the marbled green depths.

I sat on a rock and watched the river lap and glide. The sun found an opening in the clouds and began to warm my back, and I smiled, feeling I'd never done a better morning's fishing. . . . But the sun soon vanished. A cold gust and a shadow passed over me. And I was suddenly afraid, suddenly aware that I stood outside an open door. Back through the door was everything familiar to me—this creek, my parents' house, the self-conjured fisherman's world I'd grown up in. But here before me were the swirling greens and grays of a wide, unresting river, and beyond the river a wide and ancient and unknown world that I must now enter. The time had come to close the door—but the wind was gusting, the water was the shade of steel—

Yet the last trout had had no choice. And it, too, was a timid, creek-bred suburbanite. It might have liked its little oasis there in the dead creek. I didn't ask: I forced it to go free. I saw then that I'd no choice either. There was nothing back through that door to sustain me. I stood up, reached into the air and swung the door shut across the mouth of little dead Sisisicu and all that lay upstream. The silhouette in the VW bus was still watching, probably thinking I was crazy. I didn't care: I reached again into the wind, locked the door, threw the invisible key into the river, walked to the highway without once looking back and stuck out my thumb for the Tamanawis.

Book Four

The Line of Light

I went out to the hazel wood,
   Because a fire was in my head,
And cut and peeled a hazel wand,
   And hooked a berry on a thread;
And when white moths were on the wing,
   And moth-like stars were flickering out,
I dropped the berry in the stream
   And caught a little silver trout.

When I had laid it on the floor
   I went to blow the fire flame,
But something rustled on the floor,
   And some one called me by my name:
It had become a glimmering girl
   With apple blossoms in her hair
Who called me by my name and ran
   And faded through the brightening air.

Though I am old with wandering
   Through hollow lands and hilly lands,
I will find out where she has gone,
   And kiss her lips, and take her hands,
And walk along long dappled grass,
   And pluck till time and times are done,
The silver apples of the moon,
   The golden apples of the sun.

           —*W. B. Yeats,*
      "The Song of Wandering Aengus"

1

Hemingway

... Furiously all up an downe doth swimme
Th' insnared fish, til cleane wearied, underneath
A willow it lyes and pants. . . .
Wherewith the fisher . . . takes his line in hand,
And by degrees gets the fish to land.

—*William Browne*

IN THE WEEKS THAT followed, my life began to feel to me more like a toy in the hands of Heaven and Earth than a tangle of tissue and glands in the hands of an idiot named Gus. I quit gabbling at Rodney, forgot my garble-headed parents, wrote once weekly to Bill Bob, and—between visits from Titus and Descartes—read like a fiend, finding it a far more satisfying thing to sally self-effaced through a masterpiece than to mope along creeks all day pricking holes in fishmouths. Titus and I continued to trade fish-knowledge for philosophy, taking turns playing mentor and dunce (during our initial conclaves I accomplished in thought and speech what Titus accomplished in deed the day he ambuscaded his ear with the #10 Mosquito), but our dunce stints made each of us more tolerant mentors, and soon we hobbled toward some semblance of attainment. By mid-September there were rods, reels and fly-tying equipment strewn about Titus's flat, and pens, papers and diverse heaps of literature swamping the desk at my river-view window. As Titus wrestled with backhanded and roll casts, I forged my way through Plato, Rumi, Valmiki and Shakespeare; as I pondered Hindu, Buddhist, Islamic and Taoist mythology and scripture, he intrepidly pursued and finally subdued his first fall chinook, silver salmon and winter steelhead. Scholar though he was, Titus was no academician: accuracy and intricacy of knowledge were to him not just secondary but twentysecondary to the love one felt for the things one studied, so whenever I was unable to love a book, even if I wanted to struggle with it, Titus whisked it away and proffered another. And when I challenged him on this he explained that *philo* meant "love" and *sophia* meant "wisdom," that every book he gave me was full of wisdom, but that in order for my reading of them to be truly *philo-sophic* I must not just read but love them. It seemed to work: at least I soon found myself eyeing the covers of unknown books with the same sense of expectancy I felt when scrutinizing the waters of a new stream.

The same day I killed U.S. Grant Creek I had a little adventure that eventually won me something I never dreamed of seeking: *notoriety*. How I handled it is another story, but how I got it was like this:

From Portland to Highway 101 I rode with a speed-freaking six-teen-year-old in his stepfather's Porsche; from 101 to Fog I rode in a milk truck—not the square white kind full of bottles and cottage cheese, but the tanker type that looks like a giant Lone Ranger silver bullet. From Fog I started hoofing it up the Tamanawis River Road for home, soaking in the sights and sounds and smells of the valley, marvelling—after successive days among the tract houses and condos jammed along U.S.G.'s corpse—at the inexplicable scarcity of people. Which scarcity I took as empirical proof of the existence of some kind of God, because only the unseen but illimitable powers of a God could keep stacking people on top of each other in urb and burb pancake-housing when they could be living on little farms or in cabins or villages in the woods and fields and mountains; I figured God kept jamming them in there because He refused to turn them loose on the Tamanawises of the World until they learned a way of living that wouldn't turn Tamanawises into U.S.G.'s. It was nice to find myself approving of God's behavior for a change.

It was three miles to the cabin, and all of me was satisfied to trudge it except my arms, who had fourteen members of Titus's library to tote. So I suppose it was my arms that started me down the trail toward Noto-riety, since it was the pain they felt that inspired me to accept a ride from Ernie and Emma, and the relief they felt during that ride that inspired me to tell Ernie and Emma to send over their kids for a fishing lesson "anytime you like." They "liked" in approximately 2½ minutes—the puniest "anytime" I'd ever encountered. I hadn't finished chugging my welcome-home beer when all six of them boiled like storm surf into the cabin along with the dogs, a gallon of homemade apple cider, two jars of pickled tomatoes, a jug of raw milk, a pound of fresh butter and (for themselves) a six-pack of sixteen-ounce Cokes. There had been a brief period when the extravagance of Ernie and Emma's potlatch gifts put me to shame, but a few afternoons spent tutoring the half-dozen flowers of their family tree had shown me the justice in their generosity. Today the warm weather had them awfully sped up: by the time they snorted down the Cokes the cabin was quaking. They'd brought their ratty poles and lost no time making it known that they wished to go fishing. When I refused they ignored me and chanted the demand louder and faster and faster and louder, explaining as they did so that this was an occult wish-fulfillment technique taught them by Arjuna and Rama, and that it was called a "mantra."

The reason I'd never taken them fishing was not arcane: they simply didn't know how to fish. And I knew that you don't teach kids to fish by taking them fishing. To take ignorant kids fishing is to take nobody fishing: what it really is is to take yourself on a descent into a watery hell of kid-boogered pools, reels covered with monofilament Afros, heads voodooed full of hooks, and an Akashic Record full of "When-are-we-gonna-catch-one"'s. To teach kids to fish you say, "OK. We'll all go fishing as soon as you can all cast, reel, catch crawdads and caddis-fly larvae, bait a hook, rerig after a snag and promise not to drown." But this day they perjurously insisted that they'd mastered these fundamentals, and when I demanded proof by demonstration they demonstrated all right—with Hollywood Indian war dancing, anti-Gus slogans and threats to mantracize my head with the empty Coke bottles. "You kids can't intimidate me!" I roared . . . as I led them like a mother duck down to the nearest plunking pool to fish.

I've been avoiding some things in my characterizations of the Coke and Doughnut Dairy kids. I have not, for instance, mentioned that they consisted of two boys, sixteen and fourteen, three girls, twelve, nine and seven, and a littlest boy of five. Nor have I mentioned that they were hearty, stocky stock—noisy, happy, not particularly brilliant, but good-hearted and full of an old pioneer-style generosity and ingenuity. But most flagrant of my omissions is their names. I could exercise an author's authority and claim (as is partially true) that names are superfluous to describing what one actually experiences as a six-headed hydra writhing and spewing in fits of abstruse gyrations and unfathomable jabber. But this isn't the real reason I've avoided their names. The real reason is their *names*. Beginning with the eldest, the names are Kernie, Bernie, Darlene, Charlene, Marlene and Ernie II, so it should be evident why, when Kernie dubbed Ernie II "Hemingway," I eagerly clasped and clung to it.

This monotonous, ominous and homonyminous naming system of Ernie and Emma's was not a euphony enjoyed without cost. Seldom did parent summon child by name and end up with the child summoned. Instead Marlene would show for Darlene, or Bernie for Kernie, always with the same old whine: "I thought you said ——lene!" or "I thought you said ——nie!" Emma came up with a cacaphonous but effective solution for herself when she took to calling them Kern Bern Dar Char Mar and Ern. But Ernie Senior understandably disliked these amputations, and more than likely realized from the start that the situation was, for a man of his distinctions, utterly hopeless. One of his distinctions was a remarkably rudimentary power of declamation: under good conditions he mumbled, as a rule he stumbled, when angry he grumbled. Add to this the distinction that he called his wife "Hunny," the distinction that his dogs were named Cindy, Zindy and Bindy, the further distinction that he drinks a six-pack of Burgie beer every evening after supper, and the final distinction that he is infected with Scrabble's Disease—a malady wherein the victim gets an invisible Scrabble board and a can full of wooden letters jammed into his cerebrum somewhere between the Reason and the Tongue so that, when he thinks a coherent word and sends it winging mouthward, the wood letters hit the Scrabble board, clack, slip, rattle, flip, fornicate, inbreed, regroup, and the word shoots into the Great Outdoors, a mutant, full of surprises—and you get some remarkable results. It wasn't so bad that Ernie called his kids "Burplie," "Crundy," "Flartly," "Zernile," "Mirkleak," "Benzene," "Jerkly" and "Bourbon" (though it was a bit unfair that he hit the ceiling when they failed to ascertain which of them he intended with these epithets). No, what really unbalanced the Coke and Doughnut Equanimity were those times, usually after four or five of the six-pack, when he would address his beloved and hard-working wife, Emma, by such sloshtongued tags as "Hunky," "Weenie," "Hernia," "Hurky" and, alas, even "*Burgie*"!

I guess the kids thought I was about the greatest neighbor in the world even before I took them fishing (maybe because I could say their names). After we went fishing it got worse—like when Charlene, Marlene and Hemingway would crawl all over me hugging and kissing and pinching, and other fishermen ogling in the distance; Darlene left me alone, but boy did she make googoo eyes; and worst of all were Bernie and Kernie, who were aces on their high school wrestling team, and who were convinced that no show of affection was nearly so touching as wrestling, and who agreed that wrestling me was twice as fun as fishing and fifty times as easy, and who were right about the ease and wrong about the fun, and who were also *ripe*, disdained deodorant, and delighted in mashing my face into their armpits for the sheer Walt Whitmanesque celebration of it, and who roared extempore Songs of Their Selfs afterward, gloating over how much older and taller I was. And I was. And so is a decrepit heron older and taller than a pair of young pumas.

Hemingway was the only egg of the half-dozen who looked likely to

hatch into a fisherman; he was the first to master the requisite fundamentals, and his grim little factory-worker face lit up and opened wide
when fish stories were being told. So I'd slipped him the best rod and reel
of their shabby lot—a Green Stamps Zebco, better for throwing bass
plugs or jigging for panfish than trying for bluebacks and steelhead; but
the drag worked and it held a hundred yards of ten-pound Stren line. (I
didn't mess with extolling the virtues of light line to this crew: if they
hooked a good fish it would be gunbutts and gravestones, Might versus
Fight. They were a decidedly indelicate brood.)

We quacked along to the big plunking pool at the bottom of their
westernmost pasture, then I showed them how to shuck the shells from
the crawdad tails I'd brought. Everyone managed to get a baited hook
into some part of the river, however unlikely, then they began gossiping,
snickering, shouting, shoving and eating candy—which was what they'd
come for. Except Hemingway. He sat apart, staring at his rod tip, wordless and vigilant, a humanoid osprey. After ten minutes and a hundred
and twelve "When-are-we-gonna-catch-one"'s Darlene landed a four-inch
bullhead which occasioned another ten minutes of hysteria, since three of
them fell in while hauling the leviathan to shore. Hemingway's lip curled;
he reeled in and moved quietly away to a good-looking pocket at the head
of the hole, and this time he didn't prop his rod, but held it, jaw clenched,
eyes squinting, a dwarf clone of his namesake. He was beginning to give
me the fishy feeling.

The sun neared the horizon. The air cooled and calmed. On the far
side a muskrat paddled by. A little mist started rising from the river way
downstream and the light turned to red gold. Mergansers flew from right
to left in military fours and sixes, speeding toward the mountains for the
night. Herons flew from left to right, solitary, slow, coasting down to raid
nocturnal mud flats on the bay. The day melted into buttery evening.
Things grew beautiful. The kids felt the change and left off acting silly.
Trout began to swirl in the pool. Kernie and Bernie sat close to each
other and spoke in muted tones of the one subject solemn to them—
football. The girls encircled me and waxed philosophical, plying me with
questions: "What does *trout* mean?" "Why is water wet?" "Is it wet to a
fish?" "Wouldn't air be wet to a fish and water dry, since air drownds
'em?" "What *is* a fish, anyway?" "What's water?" "Where did the first
water come from?" "Where will the last water go?" They didn't ask a
question I could answer till Marlene wondered what time it was, and I
couldn't answer that without my watch. They finally wearied of my
stupidity and Charlene asked politely just what I *did* know, and would I
like to talk about that. So I did Titus dirty by telling them I knew a guy

with weird clothes full of pockets who could answer any question they could ask. Or make them *think* he'd answered. Provided he had a smoke. And provided they didn't mind not understanding the answers. Then Hemingway started screaming bloody murder.

I thought a mud-dauber had stung him till the steelhead took a tail-walk and the kids let out a sixfold WOW the Russians must have heard on their trawlers, out past the twelve-mile limit. I ordered everyone but Hemingway to reel in fast and was amazed when, despite the clamor, they heard and obeyed. I raced down and checked Ernie II's drag; it was set about right. I would have coached him, then, but when they finished reeling the others chucked their poles and closed in around us, jumping and whooping, so I walked up the bank, sat down and watched. Hemingway was squeaking "GusGusGusGusGus! ..." but he held his rod high and his family at bay, so I just hollered "It's OK! You're doin' great, Hemingway! Keep reeling!" which he did, and kept doing no matter what the steelhead did, which wasn't exactly scientific angling but which served to keep his hands off the line and drag and took up the slack when there was any. Meanwhile Kernie marshalled the mob and issued some peculiar commands: Marlene, Darlene and Charlene he sent to the tail of the hole while he, Bernie and the dogs ran to the head, then all of them waded into the river and set up the war-whoop and water-dance—a strategem intended to confine the fish to the pool. There was nothing but open, shallow, gravelly water upstream and down—water designed by the rivergod to tire and land fish in—whereas the pool was littered with ledges, boulders and snags. But I spectated, saying nothing: they were six berserk beginners, and I trusted sextuple beginner's luck far more than my ability to instill strategy during the heat of battle. Unfortunately Kernie's plan worked: the steelhead started downstream, caught sight of the splashing milkmaids, wheeled and tore upstream, encountered the flailing mainstays of the high school wrestling squad and their dogs, turned back to the hole, dove for the bottom, twisted and sulked. I grew worried then, but still said nothing. Hemingway just kept cranking.

After five minutes the fish wearied; I said, "Tighten your drag a half turn." He did, and the fish neared shore; it would have been happy to slide into a cleverly concealed net, but five kids and three dogs greeted it in the shallows. It plunged away downward, desperate and thrashing. Then, watching Ernie II's rod tip, I saw it had entered a sunken tree; the pulsing in the pole grew less and less vibrant then stopped altogether. Snagged. And in the deepest part of the hole.

Hemingway realized what had happened and burst into tears. I went down to console him and might have succeeded if Kernie, Bernie, Darlene, Charlene and Marlene hadn't rushed to their poles and immediately cast, with unbelievable accuracy, into the very spot where the fish had hung up. Hemingway howled at this stroke and fumbled for his pocketknife—but I snatched it away before fratricide was committed. And soon the five usurpers were also snagged—just retribution, I thought . . . till a startling thing happened: six united lines tugging at one sunken tree generate a lot of pull. First haltingly, then steadily, the six kids began winching the snag shoreward. . . .

My native intelligence flared up. I shouted, "Look sharp, Hemingway! Keep reeling everybody!," then I emptied my pockets, grabbed the net and dazzled them all by diving into the Tamanawis. I swam for the bottom. Maybe forty feet from shore and twelve feet down I saw a silvery flashing, but I grew short of breath; back at the surface I yelled "Keep reeling!" I treaded water and waited, then down I went again. The snag was now in maybe eight feet of water; approaching it from the back (so I wouldn't be skewered if their hooks came loose) I felt my way along it as it crawled toward shore—and sure enough, tangled in the digits of one tree-leg was the exhausted steelhead. I netted it, pinched the net shut, snapped Hemingway's line and shot to the surface. The kids and dogs took one look at the loaded net and KERSPLASH! they were all in the river. Fortunately the ones who could swim had the presence of mind to help the ones who couldn't. We scrambled ashore and the fish and I got hugged and kissed and pawed and licked till even Whitman might have hollered "Cool it!" Suffocated and nauseated, I told Kernie and Bernie that the fish needed to be put out of its misery, figuring that clubbing something to death would be right up their alley. It was so far up their alley that they started fighting over who should get first whack, so I found a priest myself, handed it to Hemingway, and he adroitly dispatched his prize then cradled and cuddled and cooed it like a babe in his arms.

On the way home another fight started over whether Hemingway or I had actually caught the fish; I pointed out that it was their six-poled snag-hauling that raised the fish from the deeps to a place where I could capture it, so technically all of us caught it, but Hemingway caught it most because he hooked and tired it. But Ernie II shrugged off this exegesis, stated flat out that I was the greatest fisherman in the world, and said he'd knife anybody who said otherwise. I asked if he'd knife me if I said otherwise. He said he was sorry but yes he would. He was a hell of a Hemingway. But I said otherwise anyhow, partly because I'm not the greatest, but mainly because he'd forgotten that I had his knife.

It isn't every day a ten-pound summer steelhead dies at the hands of six kids and their tutor. It was a tale they could tell Ernie III one day. And it was a tale they soon spread all over the county, which tale made me famous, and put my cabin on the map.

It wasn't so bad, this fame. It was kids that came first—mostly boys Kernie and Bernie's ages—wanting to see the hero of the tale. But when word got out that I didn't bite despite my hair and beard, and when a few dads caught sight of my rods and flies, the numbers began to swell. Fisherman-pilgrims from up and down the coast began appearing in my driveway, looking mean because they were bashful, but carrying some dairy food, meat, vegetable or other welcome-gift, wanting to browse and get acquainted, satisfied with a fishing tip or a sample fly; then a week or two later some would return to buy or swap for the rod or flies that caught their eye on the first visit. Satyavati painted a sign in Tintinnabulatious colors which I hung from the cedar at the head of the driveway. It said,

> ### HANDMADE FLIES & RODS FOR SALE
> fishing tips free
> some true
> maybe

I started tying more flies, building more rods, and organized a cabin corner into a poor-man's tackle shop. Portlanders started stopping by, and a few Californians, and when word spread among guides and highbrows that I was Henning Hale-Orviston's son the numbers grew some more. By winter steelhead season I was filling my belly with swapped-for food, meeting my bills with profits, salting away a few bucks, and I had half a hundred people I could call friends. It was a kind of notoriety a fisherman can live with . . . until one day it threatened to become much more.

2

Dutch

I refuse to rise
To the tempting fly
Of the message I was sent
Feathered with bright poetry.
I am too wise a fish
To gobble that angler's bait;
These are troubled waters,
But I can avoid being caught.

—*Njal's Saga*

THERE IS A THING my father and his colleagues do which has always baffled me: whenever they find a good place to fish they return as soon as can be with a truckload of friends, take a hundred pictures, concoct descriptions intended to render it as alluring as possible, tell exactly how to fish it, and sell this veritable tourist brochure to the biggest publication they can find. Looking at the evidence we can only conclude that they seek the prompt annihilation of their fishing grounds. This makes a kind of metaphysical sense: the metaphysicians, Titus tells me, say that Time is not *linear* but *cyclical*, and the unprecedented amount of chaos in our day and age is due to the fact that we are approaching the end not just of a Cycle of Time, but of a Cycle of Cycles. Now the fag-ends of Cycles have always meant Bad Times, but compared to the end of a *Cycle of Cycles* they're almost mellow: some day soon, say the metaphysicians, so much cosmic havoc and hockey will hit the fan that the whole damned fan will short-circuit, Creation will go bideep, and Heaven will be forced to play the greatest Ace ever held in the hole to keep us all from biting the dust, which Ace will usher in the New Age. In the meantime, say the metaphysicians, if there's a Name of God that's dear to you, keep it on your lips and you'll be all right. Which is why what H_2O and his colleagues do makes metaphysical sense: by ruining the fishing wherever they go, they speed us on toward the New Age; and by saying "Jesus Christ! What happened to the fishing?" they keep a Name of God on their lips. My bafflement stems from the fact that H2O and his colleagues are adamant *non*metaphysicians and therefore neither perceive nor take pleasure in the esoteric wisdom of their actions. On the contrary, after spilling the beans in spades they return to the fishing hole, find a swarm of anglers, take pictures, write how rotten the fishing has become, concoct descriptions intended to make the place sound like a garbage-heap, and get crocked when no publisher will touch this package with a ten-foot flypole.

At the opposite extreme to this approach is (who else?) Ma and her backwoods buddies—who'd be hanged before they'd reveal the unpublicized and unfished-for anadromous runs they chase up local rivers. But the backwoods boys are schizoid, too, because they kill everything in sight till the fishing goes to pot, then they start cursing too. They curse the northward migration of retired Californians, the Fish Commission, the Army Corps of Engineers, the foreign fleets, and every other fisherman they see; they curse otters, mergansers, belted kingfishers, ospreys, eagles, raccoons; they curse Modern Times, logging companies, road builders, farmers who irrigate, factories that pollute (and for money they log, build roads, farm and work in factories); they guzzle their booze, chew their chaws, look sadly at the river and say "They just don't make 'em like they used ta." To which Ma says "But then they never did." And they nod, hangdog and brokenhearted.

It's a sorry fix for highbrow and lowbrow alike, and I've cursed and drunk many a time, in both camps. But the longer I waged war on the Wolf Clansman inside me, the more obvious the answers became: if you want a river full of fish, it won't help to advertise; it won't help to kill everything you catch; it won't help to work for a fish-killing industry; it won't help to curse and drink and lament. So I cut down on my killing; I tied more flies on barbless hooks; I built more fly- and fewer bait-rods; I told tales more than I gave tips; and I found myself loving rivers and fish and fishing more than ever before.

I'd learned, from Ma and the backwoods boys, of an unpublicized run of bluebacks on a stream not far from the Tamanawis; the same stream has a mediocre run of silvers that gets heavy pressure, but because of the salmon anglers' coarse gear and discommodious tactics the simultaneous superb run of sea-runs moves upstream almost unscathed. It was on this creek (let's call it Shat Creek, in hopes that no one'll want to find it) that I encountered the more dangerous species of Notoriety:

It was late afternoon, mid-September; I'd driven to Shat Creek after a long stint of fly-tying and stopped on a one-lane bridge overlooking a deep pool. An old man stood at the head of the hole flinging a wobbler for salmon, but the water was so low and clear and the salmon so scarce he may as well have been fishing for Roosevelt elk. I didn't know it yet, but this man was my temptor; what I did know was that the slack water in the shadow of the bridge was lousy with fat bluebacks, lying deep, waiting for rain or darkness to move upstream.

The water was too quiet for flyfishing, so I grabbed a light spinning rod and (alas, H2O) can of nightcrawlers, tied on a two-pound leader, crawled on hands and knees to the side of the pool, flicked in an unweighted worm and presto! I was into a seventeen-inch fish. When it jumped the old man whoopied and came running, kicking rocks, stumbling, talking to himself, waving his arms—and boogering every blueback left in the hole. I landed my fish and killed it with a rock, then considered applying the same to the cranium of the old man, who was now trying to shake my hand while shouting what a nice jack salmon my trout was. But the fish were already spooked—right under a ledge at our feet—so in keeping with anti-Wolf-Clan philosophy I tried to be friendly. It wasn't easy. While I tried to explain that the fish was a sea-run cutthroat the old guy nodded like he'd never said it was a jack and sent his five-inch half-pound wobbler crashing into the center of the pool: a couple more bluebacks zipped under the ledge. I said, "What are you doin'?"

"Gettin' skunked, goddammit! Been fishin' my ass off all day and not a bump. Whatcha say ya got that jack on?"

I lit a cigarette and sucked it till my head rang while adrenalin and nicotine ran a footrace inside me: if nicotine won I'd have to sit down to keep from passing out; if adrenalin won I'd push the old fart in the creek. I sat down. Oblivious of nicotine's heroics on his behalf, the geezer kept strafing the pool with his B-52 wobbler. I watched him for a bit then turned away to keep from having to light another cigarette: why should I die of cancer so he could keep spooking the fish?

I heard a sigh and a plunk and turned to see he'd thrown his pole in the sand; he sat on a rock, grimaced and said, "I'm plumb jinxed!"

"Or plumb dumb," I muttered, lighting another cigarette.

"Huh?"

"Nuthin'."

"Been here since early morning and nary a strike, and here you come for ten seconds and ZABBODABBO! ya nail a nice jack! How do you account for it?"

Between my nicotine and his zabbodabbo my head felt like it had a Liberty Bell in it. I stumped out the cigarette, caught my breath and said, "Lampreys."

"Huh?"

"Lampreys."

"Whaddya mean, 'lampreys'? What's lampreys got to do with it?"

I said, "Listen Mr. Dabbo: you need lampreys out there, the way you fish. Lots of 'em."

"How come?"

"Because fish have an organ in their head which we scientists call a 'brain.' It's just a little brain, I'll grant you, but it's a brain nonetheless. But if a lamprey would latch onto a fish and suck its brain out, then the fish wouldn't mind if somebody kicked rocks at it and waved at it and threw a nuclear-powered wobbler on a Transatlantic cable at it. So you ought to make it a rule of thumb always to fish where there's plenty of brain-sucking lampreys."

He said, "Oh," and lit a cigar. Then he sat and watched me. I watched him back. An inch down the cigar he asked, "Why'd ya stop fishin'?"

I nodded toward the water. "No lampreys. Just a lot of trout. In shock."

He said, "Oh," and watched me. I watched him back. Another inch down the cigar he said, "Sorry."

I liked him better then. I said, "That's all right. If we keep quiet a while maybe they'll hungry up."

We fell to gabbing and he turned out to be congenial enough. He knew an awful lot about the fishing around the state—and I mean "awful": everything he said was slightly askew, almost but not quite accurate, so that if you didn't know better you could spend a lifetime checking out his advice, and you'd find it just true enough to have an awful lot of awful fishing trips. When his cigar turned rasty he threw it in the creek (*zipzip* went two sea-runs, ssszft went the cigar), then asked if I knew anything worth telling about "our grand old sport." I said Yes. That was all I said. He waited and waited, then asked what it was I knew. I said I knew that if he wanted a grand old blueback he'd need lighter gear. He said, "I don't have lighter gear." And I amazed myself by saying "We can take turns with my pole." His face lit up like a chain-smoker: he jumped to his feet, sent several chunks of basalt crashing into the pool, and *zipzip-zipzipzipzip* went the bluebacks, back under the ledge. He cursed and apologized so profusely that I began to feel sorry for him; obviously the guy was a born oaf. I sat and pondered for a way to get this stumblebum into a sea-run . . . and had a brainstorm. I said, "Sit tight." He sat.

I went to a clay bank next to the bridge, grabbed a fistful of oozy gray clay, skewered a nightcrawler on my hook leaving lots to wiggle at each end, then squeezed the lump of clay gently around the worm. The old man marvelled at my performance, pulled out a notepad, started to scribble and asked what I called this invention. I told him it was an old Estonian ploy the classical name of which I forgot, but that Estonian immigrants to America's fair shores had renamed it the "Hostess Twinkie." He carefully recorded this flubdub on his pad. I waited for him to put his pen away, then handed him my pole.

We crawled to the ledge on hands and knees (I didn't trust him to walk); I flipped the bail on the reel and set the drag so loose that he couldn't break the leader no matter how hard he struck; then I lowered the Twinkie by hand down to the spooked cutthroat in the undercut; when the Twinkie touched bottom I said "Get ready!"

We lay on our bellies, watching: the clay around the worm began to dissolve and crumble away; the ends of the nightcrawler emerged, writhing like a stripper coming out of a cake . . . the sea-runs went nuts! Four of them assaulted the Twinkie and the biggest swallowed it, mud and all, gulping it so deep that even Mr. Zabbo Dabbo couldn't manage to lose it. It was a nice trout, almost twenty inches; when we landed it he was ecstatic, literally jumping for joy—and sending another avalanche into the pool. But now it didn't matter: we had the formula. Two more Twinkies got us two more fish, then I said, "That's two apiece. That's enough."

He said, "You're right! Anyhow, I gotta rush back to town and write all this up for tomorrow's paper!"

I nearly choked. "Tomorrow's *What?*"

"Tomorrow's *Oregon Reporter.*" He beamed and held out his hand. "I'm Dutch Hines. The 'Fishing Dutchman'!"

Holy Hostess Hohos. Dutch Hines! He was so much more wrinkled and klutzy-looking than the picture at the head of his biweekly column. He said, "You said your name was Gus, didn't you?"

"Huh? Who? Me? Gus? Oh, well, that's just a nickname."

"Well I'd like to interview you, Gus. By golly I would! Haven't had a better day's fishin' since I lost nine steelhead in one morning, on the Kilchis it was, two winters ago, with Fuzz Gramsay."

I told him I remembered that trip. Did I ever—he'd written twelve columns about it! Pen and pad in hand, he said, "So how 'bout that interview?"

Cripes! Dutch Hines. I didn't know what to do. All my life I'd marvelled at his prose, amazed that any man could say so much about catching so few fish; even more amazed by his stubborn use of the editorial "we." He reminded me of a kid in my first grade class, Mikey.

Mikey used to talk about his pencil at Show'n'Tell. It was a fat green
pencil with the school's name and district number stencilled on it. Every
kid in the class had an identical pencil. But that didn't stop Mikey. He
would hold it up for us to see, read the stencilled name and number to
us, tell us it was a gift from his grandma, or his dad, or his uncle, tell us
how green it was, and how fat, tell us how we must be sure to turn the dial
on the pencil sharpener to the very biggest hole before attempting to
sharpen such a pencil, point out to those who'd just joined us that yes it
was a pencil, and yes wasn't it a fat one, and wasn't it green, and he'd
show it and tell it and tell it and show it till children of frailer constitution
started passing out from ennui and the teacher would have to carry him
by his belt, telling all the way, to his desk. The Dutchman's fishing trips
were his green pencil; the *Reporter* was his Show'n'Tell; and the addiction
of America's eyeballs to newsprint constituted the invisible walls of an
inescapable first-grade classroom. . . . Dutch Hines! Crikeys. What to do?
This bozo had easily three-quarters of a million readers. That's 1.5 million eyes, barring cyclopses. And he wanted to interview *me!* My brain
began to lurch and flutter like a moth toward the flame that will cook it.
I knew his writing habits; I knew about the Green Pencil Syndrome; I
knew he would be show'n'telling about this afternoon on Shat Creek,
about the bluebacks, about the Twinkie, about *me*, for many a column to
come if nothing distracted him. And nothing *would* distract him, because
it would be weeks, maybe months, before he caught another fish. I knew
he'd made Fuzz Gramsay a rich man by endorsing him, and that if I told
him that I'd built the rod he'd just used he would do the same for me; I
knew that if he endorsed me I'd get a thousand rod orders before the
month was out; I knew that even if I lowered my prices, even at a meagre
ten dollars profit per rod, that was ten thousand smackers; I knew that
with profits from that first burst of orders I could advertise in every major
sporting magazine in the country, could hire a half-dozen peons to do my
rod-building and fly-tying for me while I became a designer, an organizer,
an entrepreneur; I could open a tackle factory and warehouse in Fog; I
could hire salesmen and financial advisors and marketing experts; I could
automatize and computerize and expand; I could spend my days invent-
ing prototype rods and flies and let the local peasantry hunch over vises,
squinting their eyesight away and snorting rod varnish; I could shunt Gus
Orviston Autograph rods off to every corner of the trout-infested world; I
could put Fleas and Headless Hunchbacks and Bermuda Shorts on the
map; I could buy a floatplane, a fleet of jet-boats, start a guide service,
take fat cats to all the great sport-fishing grounds on earth; I could buy a
jet, make connections in high places, hire politicians, hire accountants,

secretaries, research assistants—all of them women, sleek-thighed and soft-bosomed; I could open a chain of Trusty Gus's Custom Rods and Flies that circumscribed the continent; I could invest, get into real estate, play the stock market, cruise Tahoe and Vegas, start chains of Cutthroat Gus's Seafood Restaurants, Cutthroat Gus's Riverside Fishing Schools, Cutthroat Gus's Trouter's Resorts; I could buy myself a harem to forget Eddy with; I could catch (or buy the proof and claim I caught) record-breaking fish to heighten my repute; I could speculate in land and lumber, subdivide the Coast Range, build private solar-powered hatcheries and surround them with resorts; I could build a geodesic dome over the Tamanawis and control its ebbs and flows with a pushbutton control panel by my half-acre bed where I'd loll with my harem, dictating fish stories into computers that edited and polished and sold them for national syndication; I could buy myself a nuclear aircraft carrier with built-in spas and woods and trout ponds and sail out to sea to escape the rabble on weekends; I could make H2O look like a hick with a cane-pole and bobber compared to me; I could buy the whole blasted coast of Oregon, name it Gussica, secede from the Union, start my own space program, make Titus my Lieutenant Spock and me the Captain of an Intergalactic Winnebago and blast away into space to search out potential trout-planets and go where no fisherman had gone before; I could stock my new planets with Donaldson Rainbows, Montana Black-spotted Cutthroat, or the Salmo-Gussious Titantrout I'd have developed by then in Gussica's solar hatcheries; I could spread my name, face, rods and flies all through the fish-infested heavens, and every resource and river, every hidden treasure and tree, every huge fish and alien queen and natural and unnatural wonder would spread itself before me . . .

and so on.

"Well," said Dutch. "What do you say?"
I said, "Sure, Dutch. I'll do the interview."

The following day the *Oregon Reporter*'s three-quarters of a million readers found the following special double-sized column ensconced in their sports sections:

THE FISHING DUTCHMAN

*Dutch Finds Redhot Cutthroat Fishin'
on Shat Creek!*

Well, we learned yesterday afternoon that there's nothing to the old saw that says "You can't teach an old dog new tricks." By a stroke of dumb luck this old dog learned a bagful of tricks from a young buck he bumped into who just might be the finest fisherman this Great Northwest of ours has seen in many a decade. We were trying for silvers on Shat Creek, but the run isn't what it once was, nor will it ever be until something is done about a problem this writer has pointed out again and again. We do not refer to pollution, overfishing, poaching, clear-cutting, bad management, or any of the things the ecology boys keep raising such a stink about. No, the culprit behind all the lousy fishing is, in our opinion, sea lions. That's right. Sea lions. And here's proof: just twelve years ago we were fishing with Jocko Dreyfus, who runs the excellent charter service out of Yaquina Bay, when we got into a school of silvers, and this writer had hooked a dandy when— you guessed it! A sea lion ate our lunker right off the line! We think every saltwater angler ought to carry a rifle and shoot these creatures on sight. Why, the blubbery monsters are so fat and active, one can easily guess how many salmon they swallow in a single day!

But getting back to the old dog and the young buck, his friends call him Gus, but he told us this is just a nickname and he doesn't know where it came from. His real name is Antoine Chapeau, and he hails, believe it or not, from Palm Springs, California, where he used to manage a beauty salon. In yesterday's exclusive interview, Antoine told us,

"I got awful tired of looking at women's hair all day, Dutch. Most of 'em had hair just the color of monofilament, you know. The healthy ones reminded me of eight-pound test and the ones who wore wigs, once you pulled the wig off, reminded me of 5x tippet or algae or something. I got to thinking, 'This can't be healthy!' So I sold out, pulled up stakes, headed for Oregon, baited my hook and started fishin'!"

And fish he does! With a passion and a skill he claims he learned in the desert around Palm Springs. Chapeau told us he learned to fish by studying books on mesmerism, Indian mythology, behavioral psychology, and by working with a flyrod out in the wastelands. Throughout his youth he diligently practiced an art he calls "Dry Fishing," and it is this that taught him both the incredible patience and the "shamanistic" approach to the sport that characterizes him today. Chapeau told us,

"After a day spent casting hookless flies into mirage creeks among the arid dunes, one begins to sense an order of things imperceptible to those whose minds are unaffected by extreme heat and dehydration. You see, Dutch, fish live in water. If one understands water one understands fish. And it is by craving water that one comes to understand it. Hence, to learn to fish, go to the desert and stay there. When the seizures and hallucinations start, you'll be amazed at what you'll learn!"

Sounds odd to us, too, but you should see the results! One trick he learned in the desert from an aged Estonian immigrant is called a "Twinkie." When the big sea-runs we were after shied under a rock ledge, Chapeau wrapped a wad of clay around a nightcrawler and lowered it down. As soon as the worm started poking out of the clay the big cuts smashed the "Twinkie," and did they ever put up a fight! We caught four in minutes, all fifteen- to twenty-inchers, then Chapeau made us stop. A true sportsman, he didn't want to deplete the supply. While we cleaned the dandies he talked about some of the desert lore he uses to take lunkers by surprise:

"In the first place, Dutch, you got to be superstitious as h_ ll. You got to think like a witch doctor. There's too much science in people's approach to fishing nowadays. Fish don't understand science. But they worship magic!

"Take a trick I use on chinooks. (By the way, Dutch, not many know this, but the best runs of chinooks anywhere are in northern California, not in Oregon. You might go try it come November.) Anyhow, what I do when the chinook run is late is I get out my knife and carve a little salmon out of driftwood, then hook it on my line, cast out and reel it upriver. I do this seven times each in seven different places, and all the while I recite a Nootka Indian incantation, part of which, roughly translated, goes:

> Getting strong now.
> Time to spawn now.
> Time to throng now.
> Won't be long now.
> Getting high now.
> Time to die now.

When I finish this ritual I reel in, replace the totem fish with a conventional lure, cast back into the same water, and before long BINGO!"

Sounds strange, we realize, but Chapeau showed us the very knife he uses to carve those totem salmon! If more proof than this is needed, go try that Twinkie method on bluebacks!

Another interesting technique of Chapeau's is not for the modest! When he knows there are salmon or steelhead in a hole and they just aren't biting, he walks up to the edge of the water where the fish can all see him, props up his pole, pulls out a little line, places his lure on the ground a few feet from the pole, lays his landing net beside it, then retires into the bushes. In the bushes he strips naked, then he moves back toward the water, puffing his cheeks and writhing his nude body in a fishlike manner; he pretends to swim up to the lure, grabs it, pretends to be hooked, struggles for awhile, then throws the landing net over his head and cries out in a loud voice so the fish can hear, "OH! WHAT HAS HAPPENED! OH! OH! I FEAR I AM CAUGHT!"

This sophisticated psychological pantomime serves to condition the behavior of the spectator fish, so that when he sneaks away to the bushes, resumes his clothing and casts his lure back into the pool they mimic his every action to a "T," and a limit is soon lying on the bank!

Sounds a bit weird, we admit, but don't scoff till you've tried it. Antoine showed me how he puffs his cheeks and "swims," and even with his clothes on it was very convincing. Besides, if the Twinkie worked (and did it ever!), why shouldn't these others?

Chapeau promises to share more angling secrets when we meet next week provided we print a message for him here. We don't understand the message, but we can't wait to hear those tips, so here goes!

Will the girl who ran from the guy who recited Izaak Walton in the tree please contact Gus on the other river he named. He has your rod and fish and wants to return them. He is totally harmless, but urges you to bring a loaded gun if frightened, as long as you come. Thank you.

Two days afterward a rash of irate letters poured into the *Reporter* offices accusing Dutch of senility, insanity, homosexuality, communism and other perversions, demanding a new fishing editor and generally raising a stench. Perhaps the most eloquent of these epistles was from one Henning Hale-Orviston. Dutch quoted the least insulting part of H2O's letter in his next column, along with an apology to the makers of Hostess products, and in conclusion admitted that he may have been hoodwinked in part but that skeptics simply *must* try the fabled Twinkie. The same day I received a telegram from Ma. It read,

EVER HEAR OF A FELLA NAME OF CHAPEAU STOP
SOMETHING ABOUT HIM REMINDED ME AWFUL MUCH
OF A SON OF MINE STOP HIGH TIME SOMEBODY
PULLED RUG FROM UNDER THAT OLD FART HINES
STOP NICE GOING BOY STOP LOVE MA

A Digression
(*from the notebooks of Titus Gerrard*)

It shall be a rule for me to make as little noise as I can when I am fishing, until Sir Francis Bacon be confuted; which I shall give any man leave to do.

—*Izaak Walton*

In the time of Lao Tzu and Chuang Tzu, the Chinese—particularly the Taoists—employed a phrase intended to designate all the noteworthy objects, substances and creatures in Creation: "The Ten Thousand Things." Anyone who has given the works of either Tzu a modicum of thought can have no doubt that these were two wise men; it cannot be doubted that such men possessed sufficient intelligence to realize that there were a great deal more than "ten thousand things" located between heaven and earth; it cannot be doubted that both men's mathematical prowess allowed them to perceive the possibility of counting "things" from dawn to dark for aeons and never arriving at a digit sufficiently sumptuous to include all the objects, substances and creatures under the Sun.

But the phrase "The Ten Thousand Things" was the product of minds incapable of counting and cataloguing every particular variety of creature and substance, and this incapability sprang not from an inability to count or catalogue, but from a lack of the stupidity requisite to such numerical undertakings. One's brief sojourn between Heaven and Earth was recognized as being so precious, and one's goal (*called* "Tao," though it was Nameless) was seen as being so worthy of all one's thought and endeavor, that "Ten Thousand Things" were considered a sufficient number to familiarize the pilgrim with the Nature of things. "The Ten Thousand Things" is no childish synonym for "lots and lots of things": it is a phrase that implies horizontal limits to man's comprehension; it is a phrase that implies that these horizontal limits should be self-imposed, and that Tao must be sought through vertical, transrational leaps; it is a phrase that implies that one cannot seek while forever counting; it is a phrase that implies that Tao will finally be found in the *nature* and not in the *number* of things.

Counting and cataloguing grew rampant in the West during the Renaissance. A great man of the Renaissance was Francis Bacon. The great Francis Bacon gave immensely practical advice on how to achieve success in the political and economic arenas; the great Francis Bacon knew how to count. During his lifetime, Francis Bacon became Lord High Chancellor of England; then Francis Bacon was thrown in jail for playing the politically and economically practical game of taking bribes from defendants in cases he was to judge. Ultimately Francis Bacon engaged in stuffing dead chickens full of snow as part of an experiment concerning the preservative powers of refrigeration, only to die of the effects of standing too long in the weather. The great Francis Bacon had failed to understand the nature of a thing called A Cold Day.

Chuang Tzu could count to ten thousand. One day he strolled along the dam of the Hao River with his friend, Hui Tzu. Chuang Tzu said, "See how the minnows come out and dart about where they please! That's what fish really enjoy!"

Hui Tzu said, "You are not a fish. How do you know what fish enjoy?"

Chuang Tzu said, "You are not I. How do you know I don't know what fish enjoy?"

Hui Tzu said, "I am not you, so I certainly do not know what you know. On the other hand, you are not a fish, so you do not know what fish enjoy!"

Chuang Tzu said, "Let's go back to your original question, please. You asked me *how* I know what fish enjoy—so you already knew I knew when you asked the question! I know it by standing here beside the Hao."

end of digression

3

Nick the Convert

You had to suffer shipwreck through your own efforts before you were
ready to seize the lifebelt he threw you. . . . The Master knows you
and each of his pupils much better than we know ourselves. He reads
in the souls of his pupils more than they care to admit.

—*Eugen Herrigel,* Zen and the Art of Archery

BY THE TIME NICK came I was living in a different world: same cabin, same
Tamanawis, same seventy-two-inch vehicle of consciousness, but different contents in each. In the river there were salmon; in me there was a
soul; in the cabin the walls were covered with weird lopsided pictures of
fish and rivers and me fishing, all of them painted by peewee pals of mine
in Hemingway's kindergarten class; books were heaped everywhere; two
pairs of hand-knit woolen gloves with no tips in the fingers hung on a peg
by the back door—gifts from Emma for cold-weather fishing; on my bed
in the loft lay a suit of white India-cotton clothes from Steve and Satyavati—used them for pajamas mostly, but donned them when visiting the
candle-house-and-weed-sanctuary (ducking low in my pickup when passing those logger and fisherman friends who might not understand how
white cotton "did good things to my vibrations," or why my vibrations
needed good things done to them in the first place). Outside the back
door was a tiny stable Kernie and Bernie built, full of hay and feed, and
staked on the bluff overlooking the river was my pet goat, Charles the
Second. Charles ate the briars around the cabin. Charles also gave two
quarts of milk a day. . . . Hemingway was three when he named her. It
seems he'd had a white duck he thought a lot of, a drake, named Charles.
Charles the Drake made a legend of himself one icy winter's day when he
took it into his head to glide down the Tamanawis and paddle away
forever into the wastes of the Pacific—leaving Hemingway disconsolate
till one of Emma's goats bore the untwinniest set of twins anybody ever
saw: one was a big, healthy, airplane-eared, black and white buck, the

other a scrawny, dusty, Lamancha-eared doe that looked like a tiny humpless camel. The duckless Hemingway took one look at the camel and was utterly smitten. He began living with it from dawn to dark, feeding it, dressing it, grazing with it, napping with it. He also demanded that Ernie and Emma retract the name they'd given it; this was easily done because they'd named the twins Mandy and Candy and immediately forgot which was which. Nobody forgot which was which once the girl goat became Charles the Second. Hemingway's adoration of Charles lasted till she was bred and became a mother, then he fell for her son, Charles the Third. That left Emma to milk and care for Charles the Second, and Emma, as anyone might guess, had more than enough to do what with minding the house, poultry, goats and garden, raising the kids and knocking the crap out of Ernie when he called her Hurky, Hunky or Burgie. So when she kept insisting on supplying me with fresh goat milk I offered to buy a goat and supply myself; she agreed, and Hemingway insisted that this goat be his second most favorite, Charles II.

The transformations in my cabin extended to the cellar refrigerator where there were homemade wines and juices, deer and elk jerky, home-brewed stout and steam, canned fruits and vegetables, cow and goat cheese, frequent shrimp or crab, an ominous gallon jug of potato whiskey—all of it caught or made or grown by friends who'd swapped for flies or rods, every bargain struck based on time, materials, and the number of beers drunk while bargaining. And sometimes, when the flies or rods proved true, the swappers would sneak back when I wasn't home and leave more whatever-it-was we'd swapped for.

I guess we hermits tend to be dewy-eyed creatures. I did anyhow. Many a night I'd sit up late looking at the cabin full of swappings and pictures and gifts and candlelight, unable to get sleepy for the fullness in my heart—and the aching in it too, because most people couldn't live the way we lived in Tamanawis Valley; and also because I had so much to share, but nobody to share it with. One nobody in particular. For that particular nobody I made another fourteen-foot hazel pole, then I built a twelve-foot four-piece split-bamboo rod with a medieval sort of look to it, but with real guides on it, a cork handle, and—to match the pole—a belly reel. Belly reels aren't really reels: they're simple boxes or baskets you wear on your belly, with two upright stems inside around which the line is wrapped by hand. My thought was to keep Eddy from having to dive into the drink in cold weather while still allowing the most primitive kind of pole-and-line fishing I knew of. Most belly reels are metal, but I'd a hunch she'd prefer something more archaic, and at a junk shop in Astoria I found a woven basket from Tijuana with a little donkey painted on the front. It was four inches deep and six inches by twelve inches, perfect size; I lined the inside with mink-oiled leather, fitted a maple board in the bottom, drilled two holes three inches apart, glued dowels in the holes, loaded the "reel" with twenty-pound nylon line and a monofilament leader; then Satyavati helped me weave a thick rainbow-colored waistband out of preshrunken lamb's wool and Steve helped me fix it on. Not that fixing it on should have been difficult. I just couldn't stop thinking about it being around Eddy's waist.

I tested it with the cane rod when the jacks and silvers were in and found I could make long accurate casts with little weight and get a sensitive drift through glides too slow to fish with conventional gear. The first evening out I caught three jacks. The second day I caught five, then hooked a nice silver—a hen, to judge by its lunatic leaping—and though the pole responded well I lost the fish when I got to watching a VW bus across the river: there was someone in it, watching me through binoculars. It occurred to me that it was the same bus I'd seen on U.S. Grant Creek. Odd. I went home, finished an extra tip-section, then stashed all the stuff in the rafters to await its golden-haired owner, or—more likely—to turn to dust.

Because of back orders I'd upped my production to 15 rods and 300 flies a month, but I couldn't see a way to improve on that without it turning into drudgery so I reluctantly began to turn orders away. Or, sometimes, not so reluctantly. One day not so long after the Shat Creek episode a portly gray-haired gent in a burgundy suit, pink shirt and matching white tie-belt-and-shoes walked into my cabin like he owned it, announced that he owned a chain of stores in Arizona, said he'd heard I was H2O's son, said he'd buy every rod I could build for the next ten years, make them his top line, sell them for three times what I was asking, and half the profits would be mine. Then he sat in my rocker like he owned it and added, like he owned me, "Whaddya say good buddy?" I said I'd sell him one rod if he wouldn't mind waiting a year and a half for it. He laughed: like a jackhammer. He said I didn't understand, he was prepared to advance me a few grand this very day; he said, "Careful, kid. You're missing the opportunity of a lifetime." I said I hoped it was the only such opportunity I'd have in my lifetime, grabbed my fishing vest and flyrod, told him I was locking up, and opened the door. He sneered then, and in the doorway turned and snarled, "Stupid-ass hippie!" I laughed in his face. But after he left I got the piece of broken mirror I trimmed my beard and hair in. I looked. My hair was not quite shoulder length, my beard a bit shaggy. I grabbed fly-tying scissors and snipped for

a time, then checked again. Still couldn't tell: many a time it had occurred to me that I was stupid, but I didn't even know what "hippies"
consisted of. I didn't care if I *was* one, but figured I ought to know. I could
get a razor and decide that way, but I hate shaving. I had another idea. . . .

Minutes later, as I lurched up the potholed driveway at Steve and
Satyavati's, a rock flew from the weed sanctuary into the side of my
pickup. I gunned it to the house, then snuck down on foot to investigate
(not to investigate the rock; I knew where it came from; I snuck down to
investigate the hippie question). At what I rashly took to be a safe distance I slipped behind a tree, and without introduction or explanation
hollered, "Hey Rama, hey Arjuna! Wait a minute and tell me—am I a
hippie?"

Thok! Thwek! two stones spattered my tree. These were not the
thoks and thweks of forked-stick-and-rubber band slingshots—the crazy
little Kshatriyas were using wrist rockets! And they were both invisible. I
yelled, "Hey, I'm not playing! Just answer and I'll leave."

Eeeeeekreeng! A projectile whined past my head, hit a boulder and
sent shrapnel in all directions. From the salal to the right of the driveway
came a savage snort and a snarl: "You *fish* too much!"

That would be Arjuna. I put plenty of tree trunk between us. Across
the driveway a telltale cloud of thistle-friz betrayed Rama's position
even before his eerie, disembodied cry: "Hippies got loooong hairrrr!"
Sshhhssfft! he sent a rock ripping through the leaves above me. I couldn't
see him, but across the driveway I saw Arjuna rise from the salal and send
a missile screaming. "Look out Rama!" I shouted. Too late! A weird
thunk, then silence . . . then a muffled laugh from the thistles: "Right in
the head!" Rama cried, popping out and streaking for better cover, a
huge motorcycle helmet bobbling about his head and shoulders, the
blond braid bouncing on his buttocks. Arjuna sent another shot ripping
past me, then galloped after his brother, a scuba mask and three of
Satyavati's straw sun hats stacked and strapped on his warlike skull.

I considered launching a lecture in support of the thesis that helmets
are not always an effective antidote to slingshots (witness Goliath), but it
seemed likely that pedantics would only attract fire to my own unhel-
meted skull; and my desire to resort to pedantics constituted a final
proof: I was no hippie. I waited till they carried their war into the distant
briars and ragwort, then slunk to my truck and cleared the hell out.

The next morning I was tying flies when another gray-haired man
came in, mumbled an inaudible greeting and set about scrutinizing every
rod and fly in the entryway display. Expecting another crass business
offer, I composed a bomb reply. When at last he turned to me I needed

only his verbal match to explode the bomb in his face . . . so I nearly choked on my own bile when he smiled bashfully and said, "Nice work. Beautiful work. Good as I've seen in four states. Don't mean to sound pushy, but I'd work for you for no pay if you'd show me a few fine points. Got my own desk and tools; I'm slow, but careful, and won't talk your ear off. And once I learned what I could, I'd be on my way."

My mood slammed into reverse. I looked him over: weather-beaten skin, rough clothes, bright green eyes, a kind smile; yet he had a last-apple-before-the-frost quality, as if he had an old dog that just died and his smile was to keep from crying. Still, it took little native intelligence to see that here was a good, guileless man who'd work quietly, and maybe well. I went to the kitchen, poured two shots of whiskey, handed him one and said, "I'm Gus. You got yourself a deal. When do you want to start?"

He said, "Thanks, Gus. I'm Nick." He clinked my glass, drained his, said "I don't even drink . . . hope I did that right. How 'bout tomorrow?"

I said tomorrow was fine. When we shook hands at the door I noticed a scar on his palm, and for no reason found myself thinking "It's this scar. It's the scar that makes him sad."

The next morning Nick showed with his equipment and we set to work side by side. He proved, as promised, to be slow but meticulous; his first fly, a #12 Renegade, was good enough to sell. But when he handed it to me I handed it back, saying "Give it away for luck."

Nick nodded, sad and smiling. He said, "There's an old Norwegian fisherman's prayer. Put 'fly' in place of 'fish' and it would go,

> The first fly I make
> In the Name of Christ,
> King of the Elements,
> The poor man shall have for his need;
> And the King of Fishers,
> He will afterward give me His blessing,
> and still for me the crests of the waves. . . ."

Something in the words, or in the way he said them, so moved me that I turned away. I finally glanced back at Nick—and was stunned to see his head bowed and tears dripping onto his hands. I pretended not to notice, but it scared me a little: made me think he might be a trifle crazy. But nothing of the kind happened again.

I grew fond of Nick. In the weeks to come all I needed to show him were some tricks with knots, clamps and special tools to speed production, or materials and steps for fly patterns he didn't know. As a rod builder he was as accomplished as me from the start—just slower—so I figured, after a week or so, that each day would be his last. But he kept on coming, 7 A.M. to 1 P.M., six days a week, remaining grateful and enthusiastic about the few meagre pointers I could give. By mid-October we had my back orders filled and I'd laid by a good stock for the future. By late October he could wind guides and tie more perfectly and nearly as fast as I could. If he wanted to. But still he had an odd habit of stopping while he worked—often just after placing a naked hook in the vise—and lapsing into inertia or revery or something; I thought maybe it was some kind of health problem since he didn't seem to eat much. He wasn't much for talking, either, but didn't seem to mind me rambling on or asking him things; I managed to learn that he and his wife were renting a shabby cabin north of Fog, that she was a nurse and a Norwegian, that they had two grown children, that she would finish her present job in November, and that they hoped then to open a small tackle shop on the west coast of Vancouver Island—which was why he'd come to learn.

A week before Halloween Nick came knocking in the evening for the first time, so I knew what was up. When I opened the door he gave me a bashful smile and a gift-wrapped package. He said, "Goin' away present. Wife got off early. We leave for B.C. tomorrow. Can't thank you enough, Gus. It's just an old book, but I thought you might like it."

I opened it . . . and barely managed to thank him without bursting into hysterics: it was *The Compleat Angler*.

Then I told him I'd a gift for him, too, if he'd wait outside while I wrapped it. He left and I packaged up twelve rods and a gross of flies, wet and dry, thinking he could start his shop with them. But when I went out and laid them in his truck he carried them right back in the cabin. I followed him in and we settled down to dickering: I got him to take a steelheading pole, a flyrod, a dozen flies and one of H2O's discarded Coleman lanterns, but only by threatening to chuck them all in the river if he refused. I also gave him a drawing of the cedar grove and cabin that Charlene had done. (I remember it was Charlene because it was in charcoal, not darcoal or marcoal.)

After we wrapped and loaded the stuff we stood by his truck a while. He'd already promised to write; we'd said we'd try and visit each other; it seemed there was nothing more to say. I kicked a rock. He kicked a tire. I said, "Nippy out."

He said, "Frost by dawn."

Then we both said nothing. But the silence didn't settle right. All those quiet hours working together—they'd been good hours. I blurted, "Hell, Nick, this is no way to say goodbye! Just because you're older than three of me and don't drink doesn't mean we shouldn't step back inside for a farewell dram!"

Loquacious as ever, Nick said, "Right."

We stepped inside. Nick started a fire while I poked in the cupboards. I figured if we were going to have a farewell conversation and not a farewell silence he'd need a fair amount of lubricating, so I grabbed a half-gallon jug of burgundy, dumped it in a pot, added cinnamon and clove, heated it, set it on the hearth, dipped two mugs, handed him one and we both pulled up a rocker. To my satisfaction and, judging by the sheepish smile, to his, Nick drained his mug without a breath. He leaned back and said, "Right good." I could see we hadn't quite arrived. I followed suit with my mug, then refilled them while he fed and fired a pipe—and as his hand cupped the flaring match I saw once again the scar on his palm. I'd watched that scar for hours as we'd worked, wondered about it, even dreamt about it. But I'd never asked about it: I'd never lost that initial certainty that the scar was the key to his sadness, his calm, his way. To ask about that scar casually was impossible; I'd watched it too long, seen it too well. It ran clear through to the back of his hand. As if he'd been one-quarter crucified. But I knew this night might be the last chance I'd get; I drained a second mug for courage; I avoided his face; I said, "It's none of my business, but all these days I've been wondering, Nick. What left that scar on your hand?"

I felt the change; felt his eyes; felt him hesitate—like a deer when it first sees you—watching, testing the air. I knew without looking that I *had* pried, and, raising my eyes, half expected anger. . . . But all the softness and sadness in him had blossomed, not just into the green eyes, but into the creased flesh of his face. He said, "I'd like to tell you, Gus. But it's a long story."

I told him I had food and drink enough to last us a month.

He smiled his smile. "There's no story I'd rather tell, providin' someone with ears is willin' to hear it."

I pulled back my hair to let my ears poke into view. He smiled again. We drew our rockers closer, placed our feet side by side on the hearth-stones. It was strange: sitting that close to anyone I knew so little usually made me uneasy, but I liked sitting close to Nick. There was a little cloud of quiet that hovered around him. I'd found it by accidentally bumping his head, again and again, when scrutinizing the fine points of his smaller dry flies. He wasn't just low-key; he was *no*-key, and my head, expecting air, would bang into his.

I lit a cigarette. Nick worked down his second mug, closed his eyes, puffed his pipe, waited for the words to percolate up to a place he could speak them from. He said, "I should warn you. It's a war story. I've seen war stories hit some young fellas like pints of laudanum."

I shrugged. "Couldn't be worse than fishin' stories I've stayed awake through."

Nick frowned. "That's the other thing, Gus. It's a fishin' story, too. But it's one I take mighty serious, and I'd as soon skip it if your tongue's gonna be jammin' sideways into your cheek. Because this story is true."

I said, "I'll let my tongue rest right up to the part about how you and Blackbeard and Moby Dick and Popeye joined forces and sank the *Bismarck*."

He smiled a little, but he didn't laugh. I could see he wanted quiet before he started—quiet not just in the room, but in our minds. He said, "There'll be no pirates, no whales, no battleships. But there *will* be a thing I might have quit believin' myself, without the documentation."

"The documentation?"

He held out his palm like a book: on its one page, the red scar. Then, tentatively, he began his story:

"Happened durin' World War Two. I served on a minesweeper, in the North Sea. You familiar with sweepers?"

I nodded.

"Small boats. An' we were small even for a sweeper. But we had a brave an' rowdy crew, an' we did our work well. If it hadn't been war I might say I enjoyed it. War or no war I figured I couldn't have been on a better boat with better men, except one—the chaplain." He paused and poked the fire, dipped more wine and went on: "Boats our size didn't usually have a chaplain. We reckoned it was our devilish reputation that won us ours. But the other men seemed to like him all right. He was the serious, devout sort, an' since we didn't have a cook he did the cookin'. Not bad cookin' either, though I never told him so. I guess, the kind of religious minds we had, there wasn't a hell of a lot else for him to do. Only times we listened to him was when he said Time-to-eat, and Sundays. Sundays we had to squeeze into a little room in two shifts, sing some hymns, an' listen to Chaplain preach a sermon. He really cut loose on those damned sermons. They were as full of that zeal an' faith an' dead-ass certainty some Christians have as bacon's full of grease. I hated 'em! Still remember 'em. Every week at some point he'd talk about Jesus, always callin' him 'Fisher of Men,' always pointin' out how 'HE' stilled the seas, always hammerin' at how HE helped sailors an' fishermen an' whores an' cripples an' died for you an' me. Then it came time for Allegories—an' time for me to start wantin' to throw up. Every Sunday, the same little Allegories: because the Fisher calmed the Sea of Galilee,

HE'd calm the North Sea for us; because HE fed the multitudes (this really made me barf, since you-know-who was cook), HE'd feed us; because HE did this, that an' the other thing two thousand years ago HE was still doin' this an' that for us men there on the sweeper praise the lord amen. I tell you, Gus, he and HE both made me *tired*."

Nick drank deep and watched the fire. "I couldn't stand that pious crap. It wasn't just the hollowness or smugness of it; it was what it might do to the men. It was scary out there—*damned scary*—an' all of us but Chaplain felt it was our courage an' skill an' the way we did our jobs that kept us from gettin' blowed to Kingdom Come. I felt those sermons could jinx us if jittery men started listenin' an' believin' an' left their work to the Fisher 'stead of carryin' out their duties themselves. An' what did Chaplain care? Gettin' blown up was a ticket to Heaven, to him.

"So one day when he started in on me with his Jesus talk in private, I was ready. It was the chance I'd been wantin'. I said Jesus died too damned long ago to make a difference now. Chaplain said HE was still living. I said alright, maybe he was, but if he was it was worse than if he'd died, because if he lived he was a liar, because what kind of compassionate Saver of Men would create an' rule a world where men were bein' tormented an' mutilated an' tortured an' gassed an' squashed like flies by the millions. Chaplain said it was men who tormented men, an' that Jesus suffered whenever any man suffered, an' that HE suffered more than all men put together. An' that made me *mad*. I cursed him to his face, told him he was crazy, told him it was men who were suffering, and women and children, an' Jesus was either dead or in heaven where he couldn't be hurt or feel pain or pity. Chaplain stayed calm, said he was sorry I believed that way, said he thought I was a good man an' that one day I'd understand that Christ's suffering never ended. And I saw red. I wanted to put my fist through his righteous face. I shouted that it was *man's* suffering that never ended. God didn't suffer. God didn't do anything! What God would allow a thing like the war we were in the middle of? I told him he was a condescending sanctimonious son of a bitch, told him to take his piety and his Bible and go swim down his Death-god's throat! He said nothing after that. So I left. . . ."

Nick was up and pacing, the words pouring out:

"That same damned night a storm come up. Storms spin down out of nowhere on the North Sea faster an' harder than anywhere else I've sailed, an' this was a bad one. We were batted around pretty good. Between the roarin' an' winds an' seas an' my wantin' to go find Chaplain an' toss him in an' say 'Where's your wave-calming Man-Fisher now?' I didn't sleep at all. I was pretty useless when I got up to go on duty.

"It was just gettin' light when I come on deck. We'd set in toward the Norwegian coast to get lee of the mountains an' were idlin' in the wind there, maybe a mile offshore, waitin' out the storm. . . ." Nick stopped pacing, stared at me absently, turned to the fire.

"We struck a drifting mine. It blew the front of the boat to hell in a second. Killed half the crew in their sleep. I was knocked down by the blast, but stayed conscious. I lay stunned on the deck, watchin' men pour out the hatches, but the boat went down so fast most never made it up. No lifeboats were launched.

"A wave washed me over the side. Or maybe the side just sank. I was alert through it all, but spellbound: I felt almost no emotion. As I floated up the side an' over the top of a big comber I looked around: there were maybe fifteen men an' some debris in the trough below. That was all there was.

"If it hadn't been for the daze I was in I'd have panicked an' started swimmin', an' the movement would have squeezed the air pockets out of my clothes, an' I'd have froze an' drowned. But I just floated there, almost peaceful feelin', though a little sad that the water was so cold, because I knew in a vague way that we'd all be dead in fifteen, twenty minutes. Yet I felt no fear,

nor happiness either when, from the top of the next swell, I saw a big trawler bearin' down on us. Six men stood on deck mannin' two lifelines, an' a seventh shouted orders in a voice so powerful I heard him over the seas, though I couldn't understand him. The lifesavers were bein' thrown to our men, sometimes actually hittin' em. But some were too cold to grab hold. I still have dreams about the way they'd quietly sink, or drift away. . . .

"Next time I come to the top of a wave the boat was just one swell off, headin' right for me. Each of us, the trawler an' I, slid off our waves an' met in the trough. Then I saw that one lifeline was thrown for a man on the other side of the boat, an' the second line already had a man hangin' onto it, gettin' pulled in. Those two were all the lifelines they had. I still remember what I said. Just '*Jesus Christ.*' That was all.

"Then I saw the seventh man bellowin' an' wavin' at me, grinnin' like we were at a picnic an' pointin' to a fishin' pole he had in his hand, an' I thought, 'Yeah, that's a nice pole, fella. Thanks for showin' it to me.'

"It was a heavy, stubby pole, but he was handy with it, or I was lucky. He cast way over my head, but the fishin' line fell right on top of me.

"I tried to grab it . . . but I couldn't feel. Couldn't feel my fingers, my hands, couldn't tell if they were open or closed 'less I looked. It was like a dream, all in slow motion: I watched the line runnin' away through my hands as the boat moved off. I *had* to grab that line and hold it, an' all I could do was watch it slide an' trickle an' fritter away. My hands couldn't squeeze it. For all I could feel, it might have been made of air.

"As the boat too slid away the big fisherman on deck bellowed at me. But it wasn't English. I didn't know what the hell he wanted. Maybe he was just cussin' me, or sayin' goodbye.

"The trawler disappeared over the next swell while I still floated up its side. I came to the end of the line. There was a big ring of cork tied to it. Just as I clutched the ring I was washed over the top of the wave. . . .

"When the water cleared out of my eyes I saw the trawler, already near the top of the next swell. I looked at my hands. They weren't together anymore. But then I saw the cork just floatin' there, a few feet away. I didn't get why. Thought maybe the fisherman had chucked his pole, disgusted at my helplessness, but what he'd really done was pay out line to keep the float near me.

"I took the cork into my hands again, but it wasn't much solace. I could never hold it if the man on the deck started reelin' me in. I was too weak, too cold, too stupid. I tried to curl my whole body around that little cork, to hug it to me, to somehow make it part of me—and that's when I saw it!"

Reaching in the neck of his shirt, Nick turned to me, his face flushed; he pulled a string over his head, and something that hung from it, hidden in his hands. He offered it to me: it was a fishhook. Black, heavy gauge, maybe five inches long. And hanging on an ornately woven line, ancient and frayed, but still strong. I knew then what line it was, and how the story ended. Nick said,

"I couldn't feel that hook, *but by God I could see it!* And I knew what hooks were for. Coward that I am, I tried to trap my wrist in the crook—but you can see, it's too small. The boat was atop the next crest. It was my last chance. I took the hook, then, and held the point, steady as I could, right against the palm of my hand. . . .

"The trawler disappeared over the wave. A pain shot up my arm. I was dragged over, then under the water. I began to drown. It scared me at first, then it got peaceful and the awful cold went away. And I knew nothing. . . ."

Nick sat back in the rocker and swallowed his wine. "I awoke in the galley of the trawler, pukin' up water an' wonderin' why whoever was bilge-pumpin' me hadn't let me die in peace." He laughed, frowned, drank some more. "When I started comin' round I saw a big Norwegian, the blond hair all ocean-smatted onto his head, grinnin' an' hollerin' into my face like he believed I'd learn his language if I heard it loud enough. It was the hollerin' I recognized him by: it was the fisherman. I wiped away some vomit, smiled at him as best I could and said, "Don't you ever shuttup?" Another Norwegian started laughin': I realized he had some English, so I'd have to watch it. Hearin' me speak, the big fisherman squeezed my shoulders and boomed another string of babble. The other Norwegian laughed harder. I asked what was funny. He said, 'Gunnulf he say you gives up one hells of good fight!' I didn't know what he was talkin' about till I wondered why my hand hurt so bad. I looked at it—an' started retching. That blessed hook was still stuck through my palm!

"Ol' Gunnulf roared with what seemed to me to be entirely un-called-for laughter. Then he held up a huge pair of pliers. I fainted on the spot. When I come to I was swayin' in a hammock, my hand all bandaged up."

Nick stopped, turned to me, and for the first time saw and held my eyes. He said, "I tell you, Gus. I was right about God. He isn't just. If He was, I'd have sunk there in my North Sea stupidity. But thank God He's more than just. . . .

"It isn't that it would have been so bad for me to drown, an' it isn't that I was salvaged—these aren't the things that make me glad. What scares me, what makes me happy, is what I'd have died believin' then, compared to what I'll die believin' now." He shook his head. "I don't know how to put it. I'm still not religious. Never will be. But since this hook pierced me the world hasn't been the same. I just didn't know anything, nothing at all, till God let me watch that line run away from me, my hands all powerless an' cold. You're young, Gus. I don't know if you've been to that place beyond help or hope. But I was there, on the sea that day. And I was sent the help unlooked for, an' it came in the shape of a hook. An' nothin' will ever be the way it was before that day, not for me it won't. . . ." Nick's voice seemed to fail him, but he stretched his right fist toward me. He opened it in the firelight: in the center of the palm lay the scar, red and waxy. "Behold, son," he whispered. "Behold the sign of the Fisher's love for a wooden-headed ass!"

I gazed at the scar dumbly. He said, "Touch it!"

The skin round the wound was calloused and hard, the scar soft, tender. It almost didn't look healed. And the feel of it set my fingers trembling. "Does it hurt still?"

He nodded. "Sometimes . . . yeah. *Good* hurt." And he grabbed my fingers in the pierced hand and squeezed till they hurt, too. Then he released me. We watched the fire.

After a long silence:

"All nine survivors were in good shape once they thawed. The captain, the chaplain, most of my closest buddies were gone. Anyone wounded went fast in that icy water. No survivor was even scratched, except me." He laughed. "You know, they gave me the Purple Heart! I tried to talk them out of it. Told them just what happened. But they insisted. Pretty damned religious of the United States Navy to give a man a medal for gettin' himself saved, purple ass an' soul!"

We shook our heads and smiled at the fire as if it were the Navy. We rocked slowly, side by side, and slowly drained the wine. I couldn't say if I was drunk or sober: I was aware only of an opening and a light inside me where before there'd been nothing. Then Nick said, "Oh. Almost forgot—that big fisherman, Gunnulf. . . ."

"Yeah?"

"He had a sister," he said, looking sheepish.

"Yeah?"

"She's my wife," he grinned, "and right now she's wonderin' where I'm at."

It was near midnight when we walked again to his truck. The second farewell felt right.

4

The Trek

for every real lock
there is only one real key
and it's in some other dream
now invisible

it's the key to the one real door
it opens the river and the sky both at once
it's already in the downward river
with my hand on it
my real hand

and I am saying to the hand
turn

open the river

—W. S. Merwin

THINKING I WOULD BE slow with wine, I climbed to the loft to sleep. I lay
down, turned to the window, watched the river glint beneath the night-
blackened boughs of cedar. I kept hearing Nick's voice, seeing his face,
wondering what it must be for a man so scarred to handle a fishhook. Or
to fish! Every hook he touched must set his heart and hand throbbing,
must be to him over and over what the pine knot had once been to Bill
Bob. No wonder he would pause, no wonder work so slowly.

I tossed, turned, couldn't sleep. My mind danced and reeled amid
vague, watery images—glimpses of sun or moonlit river surfaces; of lines
reaching from men to water, swinging downstream in long arcs, turning
golden at dusk; of flashes deep in a dimensionless green flow; of sudden
swirls on a still pool's surface; of pierced hands and mouths, gaffed sides,
blood melting away in water. . . . I could connect and order nothing. All
these darting pictures encircling me, fishslick and swift: they felt important. But what did they mean? And how to catch them? Despite their
elusiveness, despite the fact that they nibbled and teased and darted

down, vanishing under too-close scrutiny, I couldn't rest: a once-empty-and-dark current was alight with intimations; cold deeps had warmed and shallowed. I was feeling things I'd never felt, and I knew—these things were of the soul. I had to act, had at least to try and glimpse them, whether or not they could be caught.

At 2 A.M. I arose and fixed breakfast—pancakes, eggs, coffee. I knew that eating was a risk; I'd heard and read of the sages fasting. But I wanted to be strong and sober. I was no fakir. I was a fisherman. Fishermen eat before going fishing.

The meal removed the last traces of wine. I sat and pondered. These quiverings and jolts inside, they were not indescribable: they did to my head and heart what striking fish had always done to my hands as they held the rod. But these jolts came from an inner stream other than the obvious red one; these were waters my five senses could never ply. What waters were they? To fish them, I must learn them. But learning new water takes time, and in the morning there would be kids and customers, work and words to do and speak that had nothing to do with this stream, nothing to do with these glimmering rises. "Well," I thought, "inner waters must be portable: where I am, there they must be also." So I put on my winter coat, filled my pockets with fruit, pipe, tobacco, knife and leftover pancakes, then I fed the fish, fed Charles the Second, hid the Flies For Sale sign in the bushes and set out walking.

I headed up the River Road with no more specific destination than a remote and quiet place, choosing upstream instead of down because I'd no human neighbors in that direction. It was still dark—a moonless, one-dimensional shade. I walked quickly for warmth but quietly for hearing, and over the heel/toe crunch of gravel came the changing speech of the Tamanawis, the rasp of leaves, the flutter and flit of sleeping birds my steps had disturbed. When those steps grew loose and my breathing easy, the glimmering began again; but when I'd make a stab at the thing that caused it, try to name it or even to guess at its nature, then the glimmering abruptly stopped. So I called it Nameless.

What was it in Nick's story, what was it in the image of hook and hand that set me off inside? What had it been in the pine knot that set Bill Bob off? I didn't know. All I knew was that I'd set out walking in the dark of the night, without destination, and with no more cause than a glimpse of a stream flashing secrets. What in a scarred palm could cast such a spell? Who cast it? I didn't know. But I felt that the one I called Nameless was trying to speak to me—had long been trying. And his "words" were silent, spoken in a language of images: the drowned fisherman, the pine knot, the *why* in the river, old Thomas, Eddy in the alder, the scar in the palm—these were the signposts marking both my inner and outer journey. They were not much like the usual sacred signs—but fishing was hardly an orthodox faith. . . . And these things had been given as gifts—like rain, like rivers—unlooked for, unasked for: I had to follow the signs that I was given, as rivers follow valleys, as spring follows winter, as leaves turn and salmon spawn and geese fly south in October. I couldn't trade the trail these images blazed for me for a straight and narrow way—not when water's ways, meandering and free flowing, had always been my love.

Dawn came up behind the hills, extending her old fingertips of rose. I plodded on toward the outstretched fingers and the glimmering continued; fish-bites, birth-pangs, I didn't know what they were. But the further I walked, the less I cared. It was enough to feel them.

I trudged on, helpless to catch hold of things, but hopeful. And when the first sunlight lit upon the tallest ridge's highest vineleaf maple, when the rosy fingers faded into blue behind the mountain, when the vineleaf's leaves shone out in scarred and blazing scarlet atop that wave-like ridge of dull alder gold a chill shot from my thighs to the top of my head, surged up my backbone, again and again—for in that moment I felt as though an oldest, greatest, longest-lost Friend had come to walk the road, unseen beside me. . . .

When the dull alders brightened the moment passed; the chills subsided. My thoughts began again. Because I watched the changing trees I thought the word "botanist"; and because thoughts are like starlings (they usually come in flocks; they can sing, but would just as soon chatter; they can fly, but would just as soon walk; they're English exports, but thrive almost anywhere) my thoughts swerved to botanists, telling how deciduous leaves in autumn reveal their truest colors. . . .

The colors come when the life-giving water and chlorophyll take their green wet business elsewhere, the leaves turn ghost, and we're left looking at shades—shades of minerals, sipped in secret from the earth all spring and summer. But what the botanists never tell is: *who* told the alder and the vineleaf growing side by side on a single ridge each to sip, separately, only the minerals that would turn their leaves dull gold, or blood red? And *who* told the neighboring firs never to die for the sake of a change of season? And *who* told the vineleaf and alder always to do so, but only for the sake of the change men call October? What the botanists never tell is why each tree, leaf and needle obey. Not that botanists are at fault in this—for mustn't it be that same *who* they failed to tell of who decreed what a botanist would and would not know? Decreed for example that they *would* know the phylum/genus/species of any plant a man might hope to see; decreed for example that they would *not* know why the dying leaves of the tree called "vineleaf maple" must turn the same blood red as the once-silver salmon that journey up the Tamanawis to give birth and die—and at the same time of change: *October*; decreed for a final example that they would extend their analysis no deeper than to discuss the effects of water on the mineral Iron to explain why leaf skin, salmon skin, palm-of-hand skin must be made scarlet in order to reach the ends they must reach. Nor may a botanist wonder, within the confines of his discipline, what those ends are, or why they seem to be reached only by those who suffer, who know pain, and who learn in pain that it is this scarlet end and only this scarlet end that can free us from pain. "So is it Iron?" I asked my Friend as we walked, "is it Iron that gives the blood its beautiful color? And to learn to love that color will I somehow be wounded as Nick was wounded, and so come to know what hooks are, what they are, what they really are?"

I walked slower (there was sun now for warmth) but stayed quiet, and over the heel/toe crunch of gravel came the speech of the river, the rustle and rasp of deciduous leaves, the water-shush of conifers, the sudden cries of bright birds you only see flushed and flying, and the quiet calls of dark birds you hear but never see, since they never fly, only flit through the shadows of the deepest thickets. I still believed the one I'd called "Friend" walked somewhere near me, but still caught nothing I could keep hold of. I just walked, watching as the sun made and melted prisms over the stairs of white water.

Twelve miles, fifteen miles, the gravel road branching into dusty fire roads, the river dwindling, the air turning heavy with heat. My body, too, grew heavy. First my feet, then my mind began to lurch. I thought of turning home. I looked at my watch. It had stopped. It lay dead on my wrist . . .

and there was my hand—tanned on the back, pale on the palm, its few small scratches not scar enough to guide me. So I made my fatigue into a scar: I kept moving upstream, thinking of the relentlessness of salmon. And in time a fisherman's patience crept up from behind, tramped past the fatigue, gave me heart, led me forward.

At about twenty miles I sat down on a log and emptied my coat pockets: two oranges, two apples, some cold folded pancakes; I ate them all, smoked a pipe, resumed walking. I passed the middle fork when the sun was just past zenith, later the south fork: this left me climbing the north fork, which was the longest and carried the most water—and when I tried to think why this should matter to me I realized I'd had a vague goal from the moment I set out in the dark: I was heading for the source.

The source of the Tamanawis. No banks or mock Liberty Bells this time. I'd never been there, knew no one who had. I'd heard it lay ten miles past the last fire-road; I'd heard it was reachable only by deer and elk trails; I'd looked at it on maps: they showed a marsh, then beaver ponds, and at last a mountain at whose foot the river ended. Must be a spring there. What would happen if I reached that spring and drank? Would it quench my thirst? I walked on, my feet grumbling in the dust.

Passing a hemlock grove I was lured by a bed of moss; I lay down. . . .

When I awoke the sun had turned toward evening. The air began to cool. At thirty-some miles the fire-road branched: a well-worn fork turned northeast, but the disused needle-strewn way that paralleled the Tamanawis headed due east. I stepped onto the needles.

My footfalls fell silent. It struck me, then, how far I'd come. I was a long day from home, bound to be spending a night in the wilds without food, shelter, sleeping bag; there would be frost, and the October nights are long. I started feeling hollow and weak, and loneliness began to gnaw—but I tried to make these feelings into another scar. I walked on, and on, and on.

At about forty miles the fire-road ended. In a clay cul-de-sac, sun-hardened deer and elk tracks funneled into a gap between trees, narrowing to a hoof-cut trail, meandering but sure. I followed it. Maybe ten miles to go.

On the deer trail the evergreens joined over my head. They made it dark, though the sun still shone on their tops; it weakened me to think how close the night was, and how long it would last. Two miles up the trail I came to a clearing full of late huckleberries. They were small and red and bitter, but I nibbled them for an hour—because where they grew sunlight still fell. When the sun sank the sky turned pink and the air golden. In that light my hands turned the red of fresh-cut cedar: I could almost see the blood, streaming like groundwater under the pale earth of my flesh. I could almost see the scar.

When the sun set I continued on the trail, the forest nothing but silhouettes now. There was no wind. The air was cold, and full of the spiral watersongs of towhees: they sifted through hazel clumps, watching me with crazed red eyes. Why had I come so far, carrying so little, the cold and the night coming on? I didn't know. I kept walking as the trail grew too dark to follow. I lost it once—had to feel for the cloven tracks with my hands—and as I crawled along, groping, I began to laugh: I laughed louder and louder; I was insane! Crawling through black brush forty miles from mankind, carrying nothing, heading nowhere . . . but the thickets ate my laughter as the sea eats a stream. I got a grip on myself. I crept on.

An Indian could have walked this trail at night. Clatsops, Nehalems, Tillamooks, Chinooks—they had lived here once, walked here, eaten the bitter huckleberries, hunted and fished. Now they were gone. How was it they had vanished so quickly? Perhaps to be red-skinned in this country—like the vineleaf sprays that white-skinned women pluck for decoration, like the spawning salmon that white men club for their eggs alone—is to come soon to an end. I remembered my own hands in the last sun of the clearing; I felt my way faster, wanting a camp.

I found a grove of cedars more by smell than by sight. I gathered wood beneath them by crawling and groping till my hands hit on fallen branches. They were red cedars—like the ones around my cabin. Their fragrance made me homesick, and cedars were saddening trees—doomed, most of them—each worth an easy five thousand of the man-made leaves called dollars. Three hundred years to grow, three minutes to be felled.

The Indians, too, had cherished them. They used the biggest for whaling boats and totem poles, the smaller for dugout canoes. Each tree took weeks to fell: they worried the wood with stone blades and hatchets, let fire and time do the rest. Each vessel took years to build: stone adzes and small fires to hollow and temper the wood; stone axes and chisels to shape and sculpt body and bow. Each bow was given a totem head and face, all the long length of body a bright winged design; each vessel was given good food, was instilled with charms, was spoken to as man speaks to man, and when the whalers and fishermen set out to sea the boats came to life: they helped find, follow and catch the quarry.

I lit my fire of dead cedar. The encircling trunks glowed red by its light, the boughs an eerie green. Birth-green and dying-red, the Christmas colors. The Indians carved and painted heads and wings and bodies on boats to catch the fish; I wound feathers and thread into wings and heads and bodies on hooks to do the same. Maybe on the Tamanawis things hadn't changed so much. My work was old work, good work: if only I could find the old reasons for it, the good reasons. . . .

When a young Tillamook was ready for manhood, he was led to a fire by the elders. He was made naked. His boyhood name was taken and burned. The people of his village then closed round him like trees round a clearing. He was given a blanket, a knife, and a pine knot. The pine knot was lit. He took the knot and departed; his people sang him away.

The nameless boy carried his knot into the mountains. He walked slowly, protecting the flame from wind or rain as if it were his soul, shielding it with the blanket, moving inland for as long as it burned. The knot burned long; he had to walk far. When the knot burned low he found the nearest stream. He made a camp, gathered wood, lit a fire before the knot could die. . . .

I used a Diamond match. I built my fire high, and by its light found more wood—lots of it: it was going to be cold. With my pocketknife I cut ferns and fresh cedar boughs to cover myself with and to lie on. Then there was nothing more to do. No food. No one to talk to. What was I doing here? Why had I come? Something to do with hooks, scars, hands, glimmerings; something to do with these things; that was what I was doing here. And something to do with a Friend who by the way where was he? He'd been gone for hours. If he'd ever been there. Christ it was cold. I threw on more wood.

The Tillamook lit his fire and huddled down beside it. Then he waited. The night came on. He paid it no heed. He knew he'd be waiting a long time. He'd nothing to eat. He'd no clothes but a blanket. He felt the cold, the hunger, the loneliness. He knew he'd be feeling these things. These things were not important now. He had come to meet them, to journey past them. So, as each came in turn, the Tillamook greeted them: Ah, hunger! You have come. Good. Sit down by the fire. Sit down in my belly. Twist and writhe, make awful faces! Good. But how my belly growls at you! How it complains! Go ahead, belly, go ahead, hunger: fight! To fight each other is your work. Me, I am not hungry. To fight with you is not my work. You will both grow tired. You will leave me in peace. . . .

The October night closed down. I found a short, thick log and dragged it close to the flames to reflect heat and rest my back. I shivered a little, but not from cold. I heard an owl, and maybe a coyote. Thought of Bill Bob and Ma, owl and coyote. Musical chairs? What had they been doing? Didn't matter. I thought of Titus slumped in his easy chair, Descartes nodding in his rocker, the warm flat, the walls of wonderful books, far, far away. And Eddy. Where had she come from? Where did she go? Did she see the Fishing Dutchman notice? What if this very night she came to my cabin and I was—don't be ridiculous. I thought of my friends down the river—Steve and Satyavati, Arjuna and his machete, Rama and Whitey, Hemingway, Charles the Second. Nick. All far away now. I'd walked a hell of a long way. How come? God I was tired. But the hook, the hand, the dark water inside me—what did they mean? If they had no meaning, why did they keep floating up in front of me? If this walk into these woods had no meaning, how did I come to be here?

The Tillamook stayed by his fire. Cold sneaked up behind him and gnawed his back and legs, so he turned them to the fire; then cold gnawed his face and knees. He turned first one way, then the other, but it gnawed his shadowed side, whichever way he turned. He built up his fire and spun slowly, like a planet, but cold stayed. The Tillamook grew tired of turning. He said, Ah, Cold! You are here. Good. Sit down by the fire. Sit down in my shadow and make awful faces. Gnaw at my skin and bones. But how my skin and bones fight you! Go ahead cold, go ahead bones: fight! You will grow tired. But I am not cold; I am not bones or skin; I am not tired, and to fight you is not my work. You will leave me in peace. You will leave me in peace. . . .

The owl I'd heard came closer. It came closer and closer. Once I thought I saw it. It didn't hoot or who. It had its own language—tree-consonants, wind-vowels. I didn't understand, but I listened. Then it fluttered through the dome of red my fire made, landed on a dead limb close by. It was scruffy and gray and small. Its eyes were nothing but pupil: the entire eye could do nothing but see. And it was watching me. It spoke its wind-tree word and watched. It was scruffy and gray and small and alone. It lived here all the time. Way out here, all the time. Sometimes out here the sky turned gray and it rained for weeks on end: even then it lived here, that owl. We shared the fire dome. We watched each other. We kept each other company.

I never heard the coyote again. I suppose it smelled me and ran. I suppose this was wise. I had no weapon; I wished it no harm; neither had I wished Alfred the Great harm. Neither had many people of my race wished trees or Indians harm. Coyotes, fish, trees, Indians—if anyone had the right to hate or fear, on sight, a man of my color, they did.

In the blackness just beyond our dome, twigs cracked. Deer maybe. I thought of a Sasquatch, and felt foolish. I doubted the young Tillamook thought of a Sasquatch. Or if he did, I'll bet he felt foolish. The twigs cracked again. . . . Whatever was cracking those twigs, it wasn't a Sasquatch. Deer, maybe. Bear, maybe. No, not a bear. Not a cougar either. They're too smart, bears and cougars. And too rare. Deer, maybe. Whatever it was, it wasn't a Sasquatch. To hell with Sasquatches. City-slicker yarn. Cootie of the mind. Cootie-stories. City folk in the wilds are full of 'em: I'd been with H2O on excursions where every night, as the campfire died, the women did nothing but gasp and squeal as the men did nothing but laugh and guzzle and tell about people (usually women, usually comely, sleeping women) who got mauled by bears, or screwed by cougars; or earwigs or centipedes crawled in their ears and ate into their brains; or leeches painlessly, silently sucked their blood away; or sleek rattlers glided onto their sleeker breasts and coiled, tongues flickering, hooded eyes gazing, hour after hour, till with the fading night and the fleeing snake fled their sanity, and at dawn friends found them, giggling and slobbering and chewing their lips forever; or spacemen came on kidnapping expeditions, or woods-zombies cruising for snacks of fresh flesh, or wildmen with horse-sized members, looking for mates—and always, in the end, the horrible sexy death, happily ever after. Cootie-deaths. Creepy crawly nasty deaths that waited in the wilds . . . that really *did* wait in the wilds: that waited in the wilds of a man's mind.

To hell with Sasquatches. To hell with cooties. The twigs kept cracking: to hell with them. They were just deer. . . . Maybe. The screech owl watched. It wasn't scared. I turned to the fire and forgot the twigs. I lay down in the cedar boughs. I covered myself with branch and fern as best I could. I watched the coals till my eyes felt hot and the lids slid down to cool them. The cedar smelled good. I fell to sleep. . . .

. . . and the dreams came so thick and fast the end of one was the middle of the next, and I tossed, squirmed, became a man on a dump—a huge dump, a small man, scruffy and small and alone. And the dump is alive! It's moving! It heaves and writhes and it's full of fragments of man and splinters of man and ghouls and cooties and cooties, and the small man lies on the dump, rides it like a cowpoke, stays in the saddle, rides and rides, and how can a cowpoke lie down and ride? because the saddle is on the ground, by the fire, by the coffee pot, by the lariat, the guitar, the boots, the hat, the chiggers, and it's the man's head and not the man's butt that's in the saddle, and the saddle is cinched to the dump, so he keeps on riding, rides and rides. . . .

Brrr! Too cold . . . hard ground . . . fire's down. build it back up. lie back down. fire flares up, eyes close, head sinks, twigs crack, don't care, back in saddle, back on the dump, ride and ride; hard to stay on, impossible to fall off, keep on riding . . . brrr! fire's down, ground's hard; more wood, lie on other shoulder, flames and saddles, heave and writhe; cold and fire and can't keep covered but wahoo! keep on! ride and ride . . .

Gettin' a little light, maybe. No. Too early to tell. More wood on fire. Brrr! Christ! Both shoulders ruined. Lie on back. At last, no dump: just hard, sound sleep. . . .

It got light. The air was gray. The grass was white—frost. The fire was dead.

I sat up, stiff, sore, smelling of cedar. My head had stopped fishing: no bites, no strikes, no glimpses, no Indian, no nothing. Just morning. A few clouds. And the owl—there in a vineleaf maple, stating its wind-tree word.

I stood, groaning, my bones years closer to an arthritic old age than they'd been twelve hours before. Gathered more wood, made another fire, got warm. Walked back to the huckleberries, ate for a solid hour, got diarrhea. Different dump. What the hell was I doing here? Hooks, hands and sources . . . got no coffee, no food, no car, forty miles on foot from home, and why? Buncha goddam malarkey, that's why.

I walked back and checked the fire. It was still smoldering, but safe. But I thought of Smokey the Bear and his broad-brimmed hat and shovel and belt-buckle and big brown eyes so I kicked dirt in the fire, stirred the fire, stomped the fire, spat in the fire, pissed on the fire—PHLECH-HRBLRBLRBLT! What a stench! . . . damned Smokey! He's practically a cootie!

To escape the smell I walked. But I walked upstream. How come? Aw hell, I'd come this far. May as well see the rest. I'd at least know every inch of the Tamanawis. I stayed on the deer path and walked till walking warmed me. I drank water at a spring; ate a little sorrel; sucked some clover tips; smoked a pipe; felt better. I came to the marsh but skirted it, passing along a ridge, keeping my feet dry. I snuck up on the beaver ponds at the same time as the sunlight and saw five beaver on three different ponds. You don't often see beaver; they haven't forgotten the jokers who made them into hats. Ma says you've got to go a good piece and get there early to see a beaver.

Saw some big cutthroaty swirls on a beaverless pond that made me wish for the first time for Rodney. Saw two deer—doe and fawn—and a seaward-coasting eagle who would glide in an hour to where I'd been a hard day-and-a-half's walk ago. I saw seven ravens, flapping toward the sun singing Cro-awk, Cro-awk, trying to look portentous and mythical but coming off kind of scruffy-headed and up to no good. Still, except for the logging roads way up on the ridges, it could have been any century you'd care to name. Even the raven-worshipping Indians only came here ten thousand years ago: I saw *any* century, barring deluges and ice ages.

Trotting away across a high slash-clearing, five elk, one a fine big bull. Watching them I nearly stepped on a blue grouse; it flew fifty yards up the trail and froze as I walked by. Could have kicked it in the head. Would have, too, if I'd something to cook it in. I'd seen Ma do it with sticks: she just clubbed 'em, plucked 'em, spitted and broiled 'em, ate 'em, laughing, right off the stick. Made H2O sick when she'd tell about it. I could have done the same. Should have. Would have . . . well . . . maybe I wouldn't have. Damned thing. So dumb it was cute, squatting right under my boot, thinking it was invisible. Opposite of my yesterday's Friend.

Clouds were rolling in fast off the Pacific, but it looked like it might be a day before they meant business. Watching them, I spotted an osprey shopping the ponds for breakfast. And beside the ponds, a mink or muskrat—couldn't tell which. They let me see them, these animals, way up near the source: empty-handed, I saw them. Not so easily would hunters see them; it's not just the guns: it's those red hats. Nature doesn't take that color lightly. I envision a man up here hunting, sometime around the turn of the century. He wears a fluorescent red hat—the first red hat of them all. The deer and elk see him . . . and stagger away into the brush, cramped with laughter.

But at this altitude I was running out of rust-colored subjects: the salmon didn't climb this high (the river was just a screech-owl creek now), and the vineleafs and alders on the ridges were already naked, waiting for winter. An odd strategy, this stripping down for winter. And the trees looked as if they liked it no better than a human would, rattling and groping at the air; bony fingers begging for sunlight; shirts in tatters, rotting at the wrists; wearing crows for jewelry.

I kept on walking, watching for animals. Hunger pangs would come and go, but I'd come far enough that I was beginning not to care.

> The Tillamook, with his pine knot, went to no source. He had been told by his elders that the source was everywhere, so he made his encampment on the first waters he found once the knot burned dim. Then he waited, naked as a winter tree, to make his elders' words come true.
>
> By night he kept his fire going. By day he rested in sunlight, rain or shadow. Twice daily he would bathe in the icy water, scrubbing his flesh with evergreen boughs. The boughs hurt, he was weak, and the water was bitter cold. But hurt, weakness and cold were none of them the one he waited for. He let them do their work. They left him in peace.

The river twisted and shrank above the beaver ponds. It neared a mountain. It was small and quiet here, full of snake-bends, oxbows and small cutthroat trout. It entered a grove of virgin Sitka spruce, and the hoof cut-trail entered in beside it.

The grove was like a vast lodge, barked pillars rising to a high mosaic of green and black and sky. A watery light filtered down, as if through stained glass. In the center of the lodge was a hollow, bordered by sword ferns and fallen logs. In the bottom of the hollow was a broad, rocky bowl eerily paved with moss-haired, head-sized stones. Among the stones was a quiet spring. And from the spring brimmed the water, old and clean and untiring. I had reached the source of the Tamanawis.

5

The Raven and the ∿∿∿

The layman Ho asked Basho, "If all things return to the One, to what does the One return?"

Basho said, "I will tell you, as soon as you have swallowed up all the waters of the West River in one gulp."

Ho said, "I already *have* swallowed up all the waters of the West River in one gulp!"

Basho replied, "Then I have already answered your question."

—*a Zen legend*

A TIN CUP SAT on one of the stones by the spring, half full of red rust and fir needles. So—I had predecessors here at the source. I wiped the cup clean, filled it, shut my eyes and drank. Then I leaned back against a log, smoked a pipe, scratched my chin, wondered what to do next.

I decided not to do anything. I just sat by the water and watched it brim. . . .

For three, four, maybe five days the Tillamook waited. If the waiting grew very long, his people came to find him. All of them came, filling the woods with chatter. When he was found, they gathered a little distance downstream. Then they just stood there, peering, craning their necks, calling to him, laughing or crying—whichever might work best—begging him to come home . . .

but he raved at them. He threw rocks at them, reviled them, drove them all away,

just as they'd hoped he would. They knew that they were not the one he waited for. They knew that his long wait was the sign of a powerful spirit's approach. They knew, when he hurled stones at them, that he had not grown sick or feebleminded. They left him in peace.

He waited alone. Bones and stomach, hunger and cold, weakness, pain and people, they all left him in peace. The young Tillamook grew still.

Because he stayed still, the animals began to come. For days they had watched him. For days he had taken no notice. From the fasting and bathing his scent had grown faint, and from the long wait it had become familiar. At night they came close to his fire and watched. They sensed that nothing that stayed still for so long would harm them; nothing that sat so quietly could be a man. Maybe this was one of the strange shapes they sometimes found in abandoned villages—a discarded totem carving, a broken tool or weapon, a caved-in canoe. Maybe this Tillamook had become a kind of tree. Maybe he had become a spirit.

The small animals came forward first—wren, chipmunk, mouse, jay; then raccoon came, and squirrel and raven; later deer came, and elk, and wise coyote; even old honeypaws, old black bear came. Some would circle his waiting-place, just watching. Others would pass through that place, pretending to ignore him, treating him like an old stump. Later, some flew just over his head, tousling his hair with the air of their wings, but still he did not move. Still later, some walked right up to him, touched his skin with paws or wet noses, sniffing, looking into his eyes. He smiled then, and spoke to them softly. He said, "Even you, my friends, even you are not the one I wait for."

But in the end, the one for whom he waited came. Crept up in silence, with all its power sheathed—yet the motionless boy knew, and his heart danced. His spirit-helper had come!

The spirit made no sound, yet the boy could hear it—and its voice was kind, for he had waited well. It told the boy his man-name, and it told him his true name. It told him what his life's work would be. And, whether boat-builder, wood-carver, hunter, shaman, fisherman or chief, it promised him help, and told how that help could be summoned.

The animals watched while, in silence, the boy sat with his spirit-helper. The animals did not see the two sitting as friends sit, nor as brothers sit, nor as fathers sit with sons. The animals saw one being sitting—not the spirit, not the boy. It was simply a man they saw sitting, then rising, then returning to his people to take up the tools of his vocation. Later that man would hunt them, to feed and clothe his people. And the animals could sense, in that hunter, the boy who had waited so long by the water: that hunter would *sing* them to him, would kill them quickly, and would speak softly to their spirits. And there would be no violence in their deaths.

I stayed a long while at the wellspring, staring at the water. But, once I reckoned that there was nothing left for me there but the nitty-gritty waiting and cleansing and fasting, I began to realize I was two hundred years late and the wrong color. I had no elders—not really, not like the young Tillamook had them. I barely met Thomas Bigeater. Except for Nick, Titus and Bill Bob my people knew next to nothing of sources and spirits. And just a day and a half of huckleberry-fasting left me weak and sick. I pulled off my boots and tried soaking my feet in the spring—just my feet—and in seconds they ached so bad I had to yank them out. Yep. Looked like "Gus" would have to be name enough and fly-tying and rod-building vocation enough for me. . . .

But that was all right. It was good work, and the name would serve if people laid off the "Augustine." I'd never quite figured what I was seeking at this source anyway. I wasn't sure I'd know a spirit-helper if one bit me on the nose. If I was sure of anything at all, it was of what I'd find no matter how many layers of Gus-ness I scrubbed and fasted and sloughed off: *more fisherman*. I had hidden laminations and substrata and sinkholes of fisherman in me I hadn't even begun to tap. God knows, I wanted to know my soul, I wanted to befriend Whoever it had been that walked with me on the road, yesterday dawn. But when I stuck my feet in the source-spring I could feel too well the limits of my own unguided yearnings: I would never make it. Not alone. I would never make it to the real source of things unless or until Ol' Nameless chose to come and find me fishing.

I stayed on at the spring for a time, not waiting and fasting now, but just resting and feeling hungry. There's a difference between the two. I can't explain that difference, but I know it's there because as soon as I quit waiting and fasting I was filled with relief. It's a damned tough business sitting around trying to force yourself to force God to forcefeed you a revelation or vision or spiritual assistant or something. But it's A-OK to just sit around sitting around, especially in a spring-hearted moss-headed Sitka-roofed grove that looks like a place where any Irish grandma could win arguments about whether the Little People exist. And though my stomach was knotted with a hunger that wasn't about to leave me in peace, the knots loosened some when I left off searching for spirits and made another meal of tobacco smoke and water. I found myself feeling the same loose, relieved way I'd felt the few times I'd been in churches and had snuck out the back into the open air. And no wonder: I'd been trying to make a church out of the source of the Tamanawis. Thank God I failed. It would have been a hell of a note to have to hike fifty miles up into this place every time I wanted a word with my spirit!

I remembered the Tillamook elders' saying, *the source is everywhere.* And I began to appreciate their meaning, maybe not on any very profound level, but at least on some kind of meteorological and geographical level—which was profound enough for a hopeless case of a hungry fisherman sitting in the woods there smoking. What I realized was that a mecca isn't worth much if it's not a place inside you more than a place in the world; what I realized was that this mecca-spring here in the Sitka lodge was to the Tamanawis only what my birthplace was to me—a tangible starting point, but not an ultimate source; what I realized was that the real Tamanawis was the *entire* Tamanawis, and the source of *that* river was rain, groundwater, dew, snowmelt, fog, mist, animal piss, no-name trickles, podunk swamps, hidden springs, and the source of all these sources was the clouds, and the source of clouds was the sea, so the river running past my cabin literally did have its source "everywhere," at least every where that water has ever visited—which includes all the Space and Time in the world. . . .

Then I remembered a story—the best I'd ever heard concerning the source of rivers. The Indians told it—the India-Indians, that is. I don't know if they're related to the Northwest Indians, but I know it's a story the Northwest tribes would have gone for, because there's copulation in it. Northwest Indians have more stories about copulation than anybody I ever heard of. Anyhow it was an India-Indian story that came to me there in the Sitka grove, and the music from the spring brought the story to life, and the cool air made it dance. And even though to hear it in English without the water-and-air accompaniment is about like having Walter Cronkite read the lyrics to your favorite song, it meant too much to me to leave it out. It's the story of the time that Sun's light first touched Ocean. In English, it might go like this:

A long, long time ago the old man in the sky, name of Sun, fell in love with the woman named Ocean, and straightaway made love to her, and, for a time, that was fine. But in his gung-ho solar affection Sun kept staring, staring, staring at her lovely blue-green body before and after and during their love-making till she began to feel transparent, sunburnt, over-exposed—and this was not so fine: Ocean, like a human, was made almost entirely of water, and so like a human she shied from such bald, brilliant adoration. But there wasn't much she could do, so she tolerated his hot gaze. Then she bore him children—

and he beamed so brightly that they were blinded at birth! After the fifth child—all daughters, all blind—Ocean had had enough. She gathered her daughters around her. She changed them into clouds. She said to them, "Help me. Hide me from your father!"

The five daughters did their best. It even worked for a time—Ocean looking very like the planet Venus, swathed in a thick layer of cloud. Sun tried to brazen his way past the daughters, but all that heat and light only fattened them up. So he called on his brother, Wind, and Wind got mixed up in the affair by blowing the cloud-daughters inland. Ocean saw what Wind was doing and kept changing more daughters into cloud, but she couldn't keep herself covered.

That's when it became plain that she had made a big mistake. If she had been lovely naked, she was *ravishing* now, for now she was garbed in billowing cotton robes and thin veils of swirling mist, and at her dawn and sundown borders these garments flamed scarlet, auburn, pink; and all day long the robes and veils fluttered and slipped away from different parts of her body so that poor Sun would see a bare shoulder here, a naked breast there, a pale throat up here, a smooth thigh down there, so that now he was constantly aroused. And constantly gratified—for now he made love to her without ceasing, moving gently across her undulating body as the planet spun....

Ocean got used to it. She realized in time that her daughters were no less beautiful for their blindness, and she came to see that Sun was a skillful and prolific, if tediously brilliant, lover. And she gratified her dark, restless side by keeping a little flirtation going with Moon on the sly. (Sun got wind of this, but didn't mind, figuring what good looks old Moon had were borrowed from him.)

As for the five blind daughters (their names were Ice, Snow, Fog, Rain and Dew), Wind did his job well: he blew Snow to the distant mountains, Ice to the highest, coldest places, Fog to the headlands, swamps and river valleys, Rain to the ends of the earth, and little Dew right down into the dust itself. But the five daughters were simple-hearted, and they loved Ocean very much: their only desire was to do her bidding, and her bidding, as far as they knew, was to shield her from Sun. So as soon as they touched the earth they began trying to return to her. Being blind, they couldn't tell north from south or east from west, but they could feel the difference between up and down. Knowing only that Ocean lay somewhere below them, they turned into water and began to grope their way downward.

Since they couldn't see where they were going, they brushed against or crashed into just about every plant and creature on the face of the planet. The plants and creatures grew accustomed to them, and learned to stay away from the places where the daughters ran fast and strong; they became fond of their soft, yielding, almost apologetic touch—so fond that in time no plant or creature could live without that touch. But this meant nothing to the daughters: seeing nothing, they were distracted by nothing. They moved on downward with the relentlessness of their father, merging in the valleys and canyons, gaining power, speed and surety, unwittingly benefitting every least plant and creature as they won their way back to the sea....

I dipped a last cup from the spring, toasted the daughters, drained it dry, pocketed the cup for a keepsake and started down the trail toward my cabin. Miles later, stopping to pee, I was still so taken with the Ocean tale that I peed directly into the Tamanawis, believing I was helping a little blind girl home.... It's a good thing it started raining: I might have sat down and smoked up some mythologically auspicious ecologically atrocious deposit for my next attack of the runs.

It was a soft rain, descending in the same windless way a spirit-helper might descend. But it was a wet rain and a cold fall rain and I was hungry and tired and on foot fifty miles from home. Walking fast, I made it to the end of the deer and elk trail by dusk. The rain never increased, but never stopped; it was only a drizzle, but it clung to the brush till the brush soaked me through. I decided to try for the logging road before making camp, in hopes that some late-returning hunter or fisherman would offer me a lift.

When I reached the logging road I was stumbling, sopped, all played out. The night was black and the sky still leaking—in revenge, I figured now, against my pissing in the river. I gathered wood, thinking to build my fire right on the shoulder of the road so that any passing vehicle would be sure to stop. I pulled out the book of Diamond matches: the cardboard fell to pieces; the match-heads were mushed together, useless. Like many a sorry camper before me, I summed up the situation with a single shouted word: "Shit!"

I was shaking with cold and hunger; I couldn't stick it out in the woods; I started walking to get warm and I realized before long that I would have to keep walking until a car came. . . .

No car came.

I made some discoveries that night. I discovered that in addition to the well-known "second wind," there are third, fourth and fifth winds—each a little punier and shorter-lived than the one preceding. Then—still hours before dawn—I discovered that last of all comes a windless wind that lasts till you drop. You experience this last wind more in your gut than in your body, heart or lungs. You know it has arrived when you feel certain essential parts of your anatomy start to chew and ingest the less essential parts. You walk along, digesting yourself, no longer able even to pretend to understand or to enjoy or to desire or to seek anything whatsoever. You forget everything that ever happened to you. You come to believe that nothing but this interminable dark wet walking ever *will* happen to you. You cease to think, cease to feel, cease to exert, cease to do anything conscious at all. You just wash down the road on your two dumb feet like a dead leaf washing down a river.

You do this all night long. The darkness makes you stumble, and the night lasts far longer than any three nights you've known combined. You don't care. You just keep doing it. You keep doing it as at last the sky turns a dull dead gray and no warmth comes with the day and the drizzle never stops and your boots weigh forty pounds apiece and incomprehensible trees close dripping over the road and there isn't an unaching unwet bone in your body and you feel the little campfire inside you that is your life start to sputter in the damp so that you have to walk with head and body bent to shield it from wind and rain. But you don't care. You just wash down the road like a dead leaf washing down a river.

From somewhere along the road ahead you hear the morning cry of a lone wet raven. You think, "Raven is an Indian god." But you don't care. You spot the raven, perched high in a snag overhanging the road. You look at the raven. The raven looks at you. The rain falls on you. The rain falls on the raven. Then suddenly you are the raven, perched high on the snag, watching yourself trudge past below. You don't care. You just keep going. One you watches the other you down there, forlorn, sopped and laborious, slogging along a rutted mud strand, too stupid to grow wings and fly. You wait till the other you passes beneath, then you pluck a twig from your snag, hop into the air, flap over his head. You drop the twig, sing out "Cro-awk!" and fly on. You look back over your shining black shoulder and see the twig just miss the other you's ear. When he picks it out of the mud and puts it in his pocket you sing "Cro-awk!" again. This is your laugh. It is also your cry. If there is a difference, you don't care.

You fly down the corridor the man-road makes through the trees as the other you grows small and gray in the drizzle behind. You fly swiftly, effortlessly on your untiring wings. In all directions you see an unending sea of gray-green hills, rags of mist twisting along their sides. The man-road and the river cut two pathways through the trees. You fly low down these pathways, weaving from one to the other, watching for food. Higher hills stand behind you. The ocean lies far ahead. It is raining. . . .

But just before you pass beyond the other you's range of vision something in him wakes and panics, fearing that if you pass beyond his sight you will be separated and he will lose you. You are never lost, but he forgets this and feels afraid. And so he calls you back into himself. The raven flies on without you.

The raven is out of sight now. Your body feels heavy as stone. Your wings are hands now, stuck in your pockets. One wing holds an old tin cup, the other the twig the raven gave you. There is a water in your eyes that is not sweat or rain; you feel you must laugh, or else cry: if there's a difference, you don't care. An unending ocean of gray-green hills surrounds you, rags of mist twisting along their sides. The road cuts a path through trees. You wash down this path on your two faithful feet like water winding down a river. The sea lies far ahead. It is raining. . . .

If the raven keeps flying seaward it will soon be over the *why* . It will look down and see the same curves you saw from Tamanawis Mountain—but now you know that the raven will see no word, no question, no order—because there is no need for word or question, because there is no disorder. The raven will see the *why* as the river wrote it—as a simple, bending statement: the rivery intricacy from source to sea, the life and lives the water supports and contains, the infinity of facets it welds into one, all of this is not asked, but stated. Stated, as it is created, in a language so simple, so pure, so primordial, that it is not accessible to our inspection or understanding; not at the mind's disposal, nor at the tongue's. All that can be said of it in English is that *it is* . . . yet thanks to the raven you have glimpsed it. You have seen that the answer to the ᴡʜʏ was the word itself: the Tamanawis was not questioning. It was sculpting and painting and humming seaward with all it touched and fed and carried and concealed, singing, "*This—all of this—is* ᴡʜʏ ."

6

Googler and Mangler

But I will lay aside my Discourse of Rivers, and tell you some things of
the Monsters, or Fish, call them what you will, that they breed and
feed in them. . . .

—*Izaak Walton*

FOR THREE DAYS IT rained, almost without sound, almost without ceasing.
It was the first good rain since the August showers, and the first rain I had
ever watched and listened to without fishing: it was a rain that soothed
and softened everything it touched as the river rose, taking back into its
glassy Indian-summer eye the cat-eye greens it had lent to the leaves for a
summer; it was a rain that hummed on the river pools and pattered on
new puddles, washing the songbirds south, but bringing newcomers from
the north—rain birds, water lovers—eared, horned and western grebes
with wild, scarlet eyes; varied thrushes, ruddy ducks, hooded and red-
breasted mergansers; birds bearing the rufous sides or iron-red markings
the autumn demanded of survivors. It was a rain that plucked the last
leaves from the trees, turned stone gullies into streams, set the water
ouzels singing; it brought long, undulating V's of geese to the smoky sky,
brought whistling swans to the dune ponds, brought juncos and chickadees to the tiny cones clustered high in the naked alders. It brought the
last bluebacks, summer steelhead, silvers and jacks and the first fall chinooks to the Tamanawis, yet while the rain fell I didn't fish—only watched
and rested, and I was lulled and cradled, caressed and enveloped in a cool,
mothering touch that washed away the wounds of the summer; and my
old, unmitigated longings—even the longings for fish, for Eddy, for the
Friend—were changed from gnawing, aching dissatisfactions into a kind
of sad, silent music, and the hollow place those longings had carved in me
became a kind of sanctuary, an emptiness I grew used to, grew satisfied to
leave unfilled. Reckoning up these transformations, watching the rain
that began the day I sat at the source, I realized I *had* been given a
spirit-helper: I had been given this rain.

The sky cleared—perhaps in answer to the prayers of trick-or-treaters—on Halloween day. Hoping for visitors, I made a dozen caramel-coated apples and carved six jack-o-lanterns to brighten the black and crooked walk down the driveway to my cabin.

All evening I listened for footfalls, figuring at least Bernie and Kernie would come soap my windows or t.p. the trees. I waited and waited, but no one came. I tried to write a letter to Bill Bob but couldn't make it go; tried to read, made me sleepy; tried to sleep, made me jumpy; tried to eat, wasn't hungry. When I finally slumped on the couch I found myself staring up into the rafters at the poles and belly reel I'd made for Eddy, and the peace of the last few days spilled like milk and threatened to turn rancid. I had one unexplored alternative: the Halloween Party at Coke and Doughnut Dairy. I knew damned well that that was where the trick-or-treaters were: houses in Tamanawis County are too scattered for efficient trick-or-treating, and the older kids too randy to be trusted among the abandoned fodder-sheds and thickets, so parents let kids throw parties. When I'd gotten my invitation to this one I'd convinced myself I was too old for a kid party—but after several hours of fidgeting and fretting I realized that what was keeping me cabin-bound was a libidinous fantasy that Eddy would come trick-or-treating in her cut-off jeans and sky-blue t-shirt. I quit kidding myself, threw together a costume and stormed out the door, kicking in the faces of the jack-o-lanterns as I tromped up the driveway.

When Kernie, Bernie, Charlene, Marlene and Darlene join forces, they do it up big. (Ernie II won't help: he hates parties.) For the Halloween fiasco they had scoured and decorated the haylofts in both their barns, called for a potluck/potlatch, invited a hundred and fifty souls, and postscripted each invitation with the warning that anyone lacking a contribution or costume would be "wrassled" by Kernie and Bernie. I brought the caramel apples, dressed as a wino, and refrained from explaining to the chaperones present that my clever slur was the result of the fifth of Cabernet I guzzled on the way over.

The dairy was a madhouse by the time I arrived. The distribution of people was approximately thus: Emma and a cluster of responsible moms and dads hung out on the front veranda, dispatching occasional deputations to maintain a PG rating in the barns, or to take flashlight-lit strolls past certain R-rated stalls and parked cars wherein furtive postpubescent ghouls and witches might be tempted to gather and breed; Ernie Senior and a couple of veiny-nosed pals stayed in by the Z-rated TV with a cribbage board and three cases of Burgie; almost everyone else crammed into the G-rated haylofts, which sported the apple dunks, spook houses, peanut races, arm wrestlings, costume contests, flirtations, spoonings, dirty jokes, guffawing, overeating, belching and farting we associate with such gatherings. I paid my respects at the veranda, then annihilated Ernie in a quick game of cribbage—but I paid for my victory by contracting a sudden fit of Scrabble's Disease, thanks to the Cabernet and to listening to Ernie contagiously counting out his "flifteen tool, firfteen flour, sixteen sick" hands; I then strolled through the seething barns, trying to shout Hi to kids I knew without spitting the pumpkin pie I was scarfing as a Scrabble's Disease antidote into their faces. Unfortunately the pie sobered me up a bit and I was able to see that I was either ten years older or twenty years younger than most of the people present: in the barns I felt like a crow in a flock of starlings, on the veranda like a crow in a flock of domestic geese. I wandered into the stump-filled yard, feeling depressed and lonely and having a hell of a time staving off visions of the Broken-topped Alder . . . then I spotted Arjuna and Hemingway:

Midway between the two barns one of the biggest yard-stumps had been drenched with diesel and ignited for the occasion; Arjuna and Hemingway (without costumes, but armed with knives in case Bernie and Kernie tried to wrassle them) had dragged hay bales up by the flames, hunkered down with bags of popcorn and a jug of cider, and proceeded to exhibit—via a variety of leers, sneers, snorts and gestures directed at passing guests—the most flagrant antisocietal sentiments. There, by the fiery stump, with the hard-bitten, world-weary five-year-olds, I found my niche in the natural disorder.

I pulled up a bale, flopped down, glowered at the barns, the house, the sky, spat in the fire and grumbled, "Evenin'."

They grunted in unison and, with barely a glance at me, passed along the popcorn and cider. "Dumb party," observed Hemingway.

"Stupid pigs," added Arjuna, nodding toward a covey of acneed girls feeding by the barns.

Never having seen these two together, I'd wondered how they hit it off. Arjuna had spent his first four years on the streets of L.A., whereas Hemingway had been a farmin' fumin' fishin' an' huntin' North Coast mossback from the day he could toddle and tote a BB gun. When I'd had my fill of popcorn I asked them how they met. . . .

They said it happened at lunchtime, on the first day of kindergarten, just over a month ago. Hemingway was a rookie in the school-going field, but Arjuna had been the terror of the Wilshire Boulevard Montessori School and had brought to Tamanawis County some very undairylike ways of looking at things. It seems he and Hemingway sat side by side at the lunch table, nodded wordlessly, and proceeded to ignore each other—till Hemingway reached in his brown bag and pulled out a greasy steak sandwich. Arjuna ogled it, then glowered, then gritted, "*Meateater!*"

Hemingway was taken aback: as far as he could see there had been no insult in the stranger's words, yet the challenge in the voice was unmistakable. He frowned; he checked out the newcomer's baggy white India-cotton clothes and long blond braid; then he sneered and growled, "*Girl!*" Here was a proper insult: nothing ambivalent about it.

Arjuna's glower darkened. He said, "*You'll* be the girl, if ya keep eatin' meat!"

Hemingway's sneer faded. He scratched his head. What was this freak talking about? He didn't make good sense. Trying to stick to the more comprehensible issue, he said, "You're the girl, *Girl!*"

Arjuna shot him a condescending smile. Smug as a Witless, he made this pronouncement: "My *dad* says that meat gots hornmones in it that turns men into women, *Girl!*"

Hemingway was flummoxed, but he forged on ahead, snarling, "Betty didn't got no horn-worms in him! And your *dad's* the girl, *Girl!*"

Arjuna flinched at this shot. "*My dad ain't no girl!*" he hissed—but then he too started to feel confused. He scratched his ear. "Who's Betty?"

Hemingway pointed at the meat in his sandwich. "Betty was our steer."

"Oh," said Arjuna, pondering. "But ain't steers men-cows?"

"Yeah," Hemingway nodded. "I thought he was a girl 'fore he was born so I named him Betty but he came out backwards but we left his name that way anyhow, like Charles the Second, 'cause Pop said we was gonna castrate him sooner or later so he might as well be a Betty."

"Oh," said Arjuna, utterly bemuddled. "Who's Charles-a-second?"

"She's our goat."

Arjuna just shook his head. Hemingway watched his braid swing from side to side, trying not to admire it but privately wondering how he'd look with one.

"What's *castrate?*" Arjuna asked.

"That's when Pop cuts their balls off," said Hemingway offhandedly.

Arjuna gaped. "He cuts off their balls—like, their *nuts?!*" He couldn't believe his ears.

"Sure," said Hemingway. "Makes 'em fatter and taste better. But what's *horn-worms?*"

"Hornmones," Arjuna corrected. "They're stuff in your blood: boys got boy-hornmones and girls got girl-hornmones, but cattle blood gots girl-hornmones that makes boys into girls when boys eat cattles."

Now Hemingway was gaping. "I don't believe it!"

"*Why not?*" roared Arjuna. "*You* cut off their *balls*!"

Hemingway tried to sort this one out as he eyed the stranger's white clothes and braid, but there was too much for sorting: five minutes of talk with this city-bred hippie and he was no longer sure of the difference between a boy and a girl!

They sighed and sat at the lunch table there, each kind of admiring the other's rugged, cocksure style, but each kind of wondering what planet the other came from. Finally Arjuna remembered their unfinished business. He said, "You called me a girl."

Hemingway tried to refocus. "Oh. Yeah. You called me one, too, cause of, um . . ." (he dropped his voice in case he got it wrong) ". . . 'cause of Betty's whore-gnomes. . . ."

"Well," said Arjuna, trying to simplify matters, "wanna fight?"

Hemingway thought it over, shrugged, said "Sure," and without further ado punched Arjuna smack in the nose. It was a gusher, but Arjuna showed what he was made of, coming back with a left that knocked three of Hemingway's teeth through his lip. They then proceeded to beat the shit not only out of each other but out of the matronly teacher who tried to break them up.

When the teacher stopped crying and the pair of them stopped bleeding they returned to the lunch table, shook hands and traded sandwiches—affording Arjuna his first taste of Wonderbread and beef, and Hemingway his first eight-grained bread, avocado and sprouts. Thus was formed an awesome alliance that remains unbroken to this day.

We sat on the hay bales while the stump burned, the teenagers streamed from barn to barn and the parents flashlighted for fornicators. "Stupid party!" said Arjuna. "Ugly pigs!" snorted Hemingway, nodding toward two of his sisters. Then the pair of them hockered in the flames.

I asked where Rama was. Arjuna said, "Home. He's sick."

"Oh-oh. What's wrong?"

"Chicken pops," he said grimly. "He's gotta take sweat baths an' enemas. Momma makes him."

"Bummer," I said.

"What's *enemas*?" asked Hemingway.

"That's when they shoot water up your butthole," said Arjuna.

"*Naw!*"

"Sure it is," Arjuna insisted. "Huh, Gus."

I nodded.

"Gosh!" said Hemingway. "Poor Rama!"

"Better'n gettin' your nuts cut off like Betty," Arjuna observed.

"But Betty was a steer," said Hemingway.

"That's so," said Arjuna.

"Leastwise he ain't at this stupid party," Hemingway pointed out.

Arjuna and I nodded and we all hockered in the fire.

After a time, Hemingway asked, "You got any invisible friends, Gus?"

Half-drunk though I was, the question startled me. "Wha-what do you mean?"

Arjuna said, "You know, friends people can't see except you . . ."

"Yeah," Hemingway cut in. "Me an' Arjuna both got these invisible friends . . ."

"Yeah," Arjuna said. "An' they do stuff for us."

"Yeah," Hemingway added. "They're always there when ya really need 'em."

I was flabbergasted. It seemed the search for a spirit-helper wasn't so rare a thing . . . but wait a minute. "What sort of, uh, invisible friends're you guys talkin' about?"

"Mine's Googler," said Hemingway, his face grimly serious.

"Mine's Mangler," said Arjuna, just as solemn.

"Hnnh?" I said.

"Googler and Mangler," said Hemingway. "That's their names."

"I see," I said, and began to get the feeling that we were dealing with something a little less rarefied than sacred powers and spirits. "So, uh, what sort of stuff do these guys do for you?"

"Oh, like Mangler squashes green peas against the dining-room wall 'cause he knows I don't like 'em," Arjuna began. "And he flushes cauliflower down the toilet."

I nodded, struggling to straighten my face. "How 'bout Goggler, Hemingway?"

"*Googler!*" they corrected.

"Sorry."

"He unrolls the toilet paper onto the bathroom floor. . . ."

I snorted, but covered my lapse by hocking in the fire. "What else?"

"Well," said Hemingway, "Googler knows I hate zucchini. I hate its *guts*! So once he let Charles the Third eat Mom's squarsh patch, but Mom said *I* did it and gave me a whippin'! She don't believe in Googler. She's a Atheist!"

"What's a Atheist?" Arjuna asked.

"Somebody that don't believe in nothin' like Googler an' Mangler," Hemingway said.

"Oh," said Arjuna, and he and I hockered in the flames.

"Googler's green and purple, and he's skinny, and real tall," Hemingway said.

"Mangler's spotted—orange and brown. He's fat, with long teeth," said Arjuna.

"I see," I said.

"Mangler busts windows sometimes, or makes me hit Rama," said Arjuna. "And once he used some of Dad's candles t'make some rainbow floor wax for the kitchen."

"I see," I said.

"Googler carved up Marlene's and Charlene's Barbie dolls when they wouldn't let me watch the World Series," said Hemingway. "And when Kernie pushed me down in the mud, Googler stole his football and burned it in the woodstove."

"I see," I said.

"And once," Arjuna added, "Googler helped me—I mean helped *Mangler*—start a slash fire and airplanes had to come bomb it."

"Yeah," said Hemingway. "They did that. We tried to stop 'em."

"Yeah, we tried," Arjuna nodded.

"I see," I said, and we all hockered in the fire.

After I went home that night Googler and Mangler had apparently gotten busy; at least I later learned that one of the entries in the Pie-Eating Contest had consisted of fresh manure covered with Cool Whip. The hypercompetitive Bernie, pumped up and primed to out-eat all comers, devoured eight or ten mouthfuls before he recognized the flavor he was dealing with. He then blew breakfast, lunch, and dinner all over the table, the contestants and the barn. The contest's winner ate just one slice of genuine pie . . . no one else could stomach any. Arjuna, Hemingway and Rama gorged on the surplus for the next week and a half.

As for Bernie, he was in misery till somebody suggested phoning Maggie Eaton; at this idea he groaned so pitifully that Ernie Senior stepped in with his personal cure-all—a fifth of Old Crow. Questionable medicine, but a rare honor and a generous dose. Somehow it seemed to restore Bernie's spirits.

Meanwhile, Emma caught Arjuna and Hemingway guzzling a couple of Ernie Senior's Burgies out in the wood-rick. When accused of thievery—under cover of the cow-pie commotion—they adamantly denied it, claiming the beers were delivered to them by green and purple and orange and brown creatures who Atheists could not perceive. For Googler's deeds Hemingway was whipped with a balloon stick; for

Mangler's, Arjuna was given an hour-long lecture from Steve on the repercussions of bad karma and overly yang behavior. They afterward agreed that Hemingway got off far easier. For my part, I was impressed by the importance of choosiness in picking invisible friends, and a little relieved that my Friend remained so elusive.

The walk home was cold, and knowing I'd left no fire or light to return to made it colder. The moon was nearly full but a high fog obscured it so that its light illumined nothing, only turned things pallid. The wine had worn off, a headache in its place. A raw wind arose, rattling the skeleton trees. The jack-o-lanterns had kicked-in faces. I felt so lonely as I turned down into the blackness of the cedar grove that I'd have welcomed ghost or banshee, Googler or Mangler, anyone or anything but the cold, silent, empty cabin. But rounding the last bend in the driveway I froze:

there was smoke spiralling from the chimney; there was the soft light of lanterns glowing in every window; there was a Volkswagen bus parked beside my pickup. I circled to the cabin's side, peeked in a window and staggered back, disbelieving. Sitting on the hearthstones before a flickering fire was the hook, line and sinker of my dreams. Keeping to the shadows, I shook my head, drew a deep breath and looked again: she was really there! It was Eddy it was Eddy it was Eddy, alone in my cabin, waiting, for me.

7

Trick or Treat

Socrates: Will the art of the fisherman or of the rhapsode be better
able to judge whether these lines are rightly expressed?
Ion: Clearly, Socrates, the art of the fisherman.

—*Plato*

SHE WORE FADED blue jeans and an indigo flannel shirt, and her feet were
bare in brown sandals. An aureole shone round her fire-lit hair, and her
face was pale, apprehensive, and far more beautiful than I'd been able to
remember or dream it. I rushed around to the door, then stopped, took a
breath, and made my most dignified entry. . . .

She rose, looked me up and down—and not till she grinned did I
remember the old hobo coat and trousers I was wearing. All I could think
to do was hold up my frowsy coat pocket like a Halloween bag and say
"Trick or Treat." The sound of my voice amazed me: I *sounded* like a
trick-or-treater, about three years old—terrified as the door swings open,
half-choked as strange eyes take in mask and disguise, hopeful but
doubtful as he waits to see what he'll be given. . . . And into the brown
paper bag of my heart Eddy slipped a smile.

Stunned, I looked away—but the fire had turned so fiery, the wood
of the walls so luminous, the very air so fragrant and strange that I
thought I'd walked into *her* cabin, and blushed, thinking I'd better leave.

She wasn't watching, thank God. She was pulling things from a
handbag on the hearth. She turned, held up a newspaper, and I recognized the Dutchman's Twinkie column. She said, "Antoine Chapeau, I
presume?"

I nodded.

She said, "*I'm* the trick-or-treater. You owe me a fish and a pole."

I nodded again, threw off my hobo coat, jumped onto the couch,
swung up into the rafters and lowered down the fourteen-foot hazel, the
twin I'd made, the bamboo pole and the belly reel; then I jumped down

on the couch, bounced high and landed at her feet. She held an orange squirt-gun and Dutch's column in my face; I read *Bring a loaded pistol*. . . . She said, "I followed your advice to the letter."

I nodded, then dashed into the kitchen and down to the cellar, returning with the two Siletz steelhead, wrapped in foil and hickory smoked. She kept the gun on me. And she looked nervous. She said, "One fish, one pole—that's all you owe me. What's this other stuff?"

Trying for a tone like the manager's at the Benjamin Franklin, I said, "Interest on your investment. Thank you for banking at Tamanawis National—we're the trout-tongued people."

Eddy didn't smile. She looked me in the eye and asked, "What made you think I'd ever come for them?"

I exploded with laughter—but stopped when I heard how hysterical it sounded. "*Everything*," I croaked, "everything on earth made me think you'd *never, ever* come for them!" My head felt strange. I flopped down on the hearth. Next I knew, she was sitting beside me with a half-filled glass and a bottle of my wine.

"You all right?" she asked.

"I think so."

"You look kind of white."

"Yeah, well my dad's Indian—Winnebago. But Ma, she's pretty pale."

Eddy smiled. "I'm a Hesychast Wishram bhakti WASP myself."

I nodded, though "Wishram" was the only word I knew, unless "wasp" referred to her waist—but I kept my thoughts away from her waist, knowing it could turn my brain to mush. "Wishram," I said. "Isn't that the tribe that fished Celilo Falls?"

"One of 'em."

"Ever see 'em? The Falls, I mean."

"When I was four. . . ." she sighed. "Just before they drowned. And that night Elvis Presley sang 'Nuthin' But a Hound Dog' on Ed Sullivan. Worst day of my life!" She sipped a little wine, then passed the glass. "Felt jumpy busting in here so I helped myself. Hope you don't mind."

I looked up at Rodney. "She hopes I don't mind!"

Eddy looked up too. "Who're you talking to?"

"My flyrod. Rodney, Eddy. Eddy, Rodney."

"Charmed, I'm sure," she said, then she nodded toward the split-bamboo pole. "Does that one have a name?"

I said, "It's yours. You name it."

She frowned. "I don't see why you, why it ought to be mine."

"Call it a token of my depreciation," I said.

No reaction . . . I said, "It's an apology is all—because I scared you on the Siletz. The belly reel goes with it."

She glanced at the belly reel, but she'd gotten skittery—I didn't know why. She put the pole down, sat on the very edge of the rocker, fiddled with her squirt gun, then asked, "So how come two fish? I only caught one."

I tried to emanate calm as my head filled with amazingly discalming pictures of what I'd seen on the Siletz. I said, "Well, after you ran off I caught your pole, and the fish was still on it—that's one. And you had another already—that's two."

She gave me a quick, searching look, then turned to the fire. "There's something I should tell you about that day. . . ." (I waited.) "Pass the wine, please." I passed the glass. She drained it, then said, "I never ran."

"Huh?"

"I never ran away. I was barefoot; I'd been camped just upstream for three days; I wanted my pole and fish back; so I just hid in the woods." She paused, letting these resounding facts resound. "You left, and I heard a truck or car drive away, so I went looking for my pole. But it took me forever to find it, and just when I was wading out to grab it I heard somebody crashing down the canyon, so . . ."

"So *what?*"

"So I snuck up through the brush and spied."

"On *me?*"

She nodded. "God you were a mess!"

Now I nodded. "Sounds like me all right." I groped on the mantel for cigarettes, offered her one, almost burnt her nose lighting it, got to thinking how her nose gave me the same feeling a baby cottontail rabbit's nose gave me, got to thinking simultaneously about her spying—what I must have looked like, and acted like, and said; then I lit the filter of my cigarette and went on smoking it a while just as Bernie, at about that moment, was continuing to eat the cow-pie pie; then I broke off the filter, relit the torn end, slumped in the other rocker, turned crimson and managed to mutter, "So. What sort of mess?"

Eddy winced. "The sort that's covered with blood and mud and cuts and scratches. The sort that shivers and sweats and sighs and talks to himself, curses himself, groans to himself. The sort that says. . . ." she looked away and mumbled, "the sort that says 'Eddy, Eddy, Eddy' over and over and over."

"You were close enough to hear *that?*"

"You haven't heard the half of it," she said.

"Pass the wine. . . ."

She passed it. "Then you poked along the riverbank saying stuff like 'Gog O Gog I gotta find sumthin!' But all you found was my first steelhead. Then you climbed up the alder where I hooked it."

"You hooked it in that alder?" I exclaimed—proud of myself for remembering to play dumb.

She shot me a look. "Yes. And isn't it a coincidence that you climbed the same tree and looked all around in it."

"Oh, I was just looking for your pole out on the river," I lied.

She smiled sideways. "Whatever. Anyhow you finally settled down up there and started mumbling and sighing and punching yourself in the head...." she staved off a grin. "And when you finally stood up and jumped in the river I thought you were trying to kill yourself ... then I saw you could swim. Sort of." Now she laughed outright. "I saw you were after my pole, so I ducked and followed, and when you finally caught it the steelhead was about gone, and so were you, and you and it and the pole together looked like a lampoon cover for a *Field and Stream*, and I started feeling sorry, and started toward you, but—"

"But *what?*"

Eddy fingered her squirt gun, watched me like a hawk and said, "But I stepped on a bag of oranges."

I gulped. She said, "Sound familiar?"

"Hnnh? Huh? What? Whaddya mean?"

She shook her head. "You're a terrible actor, Gust."

"*Actor?* Whu, whrnhh, what huh?"

She laughed. "Do I have to spell it out?"

"Spell? Out what hnnh? Whoon-er, huh?"

She laughed harder.

"What's funny? Speel who? Whaddya? oranges? I don't, hnnh?"

Her laughter stopped. Abruptly. She said, "Listen: the oranges were fresh; they weren't mine; I hadn't seen a soul in three days—*except you*. But you were *upstream* from my alder when you came crashing along and charmed me with phrases like 'Flutblut?' and 'AWrg! Yore Rock Hown!', and those oranges were *downstream*. And it doesn't take Peter Bloody Wimsey or Philip Friggin Marlowe to figure out that you started out where your oranges were, or that you acted like you acted because you'd been *spying* on me for I don't know how long while I, while ... *you know!*"

She had me cold. I didn't know what to say. There was nothing *to* say—but she was waiting.... I gave up: I opened my heart and my mouth and let fly, come what may. "OK. All right, I saw you. And I'm sorry. I'm sorry but.... But goddammit I'm just *not sorry!* That's the trouble!" I jumped up and started pacing. "I mean, what's wrong with it? Hell, it wasn't my fault or my blasted bag of oranges' fault that we were walking along minding our business when all of a sudden there's this girl up in a tree, and, and she's *fishing*! You don't know me, Eddy. I mean you can't know about me and fishing—what it's been to me, how long and hard I've done it, how I've tried to understand it, penetrate it I mean, I mean, shit I can't explain it, but if you knew how many fishermen I've seen on how many rivers fishing how many lamebrained or boring or seen-one-seen-'em-all ways and then to see you up there fishing like that! Hell, if you'd been a hag or a whore or a zitty kid up in that alder fishing like that I'd have fallen for you! I'd have fallen for a one-eyed toad-faced frump in a Ronald McDonald outfit if she could fish like that! Because, I don't know, that huge nut-tree pole squirrels and birds used to sit on, and the insane way you handled it, and the Here-goes-nuthin' way you threw it, and the way you dove and swam . . . it showed you had a way of looking at things—not just at fishing but at the whole world—and it's a way of looking that's how I've been trying to look too, and all my life I only met one old Indian and one little kid and one scholar and his dog and one old convert that looked at things anywhere near that way and it was love at first sight with them too—that's how I am about that. So dammit, how can I help it if out in the middle of nowhere I stumble into someone who looks at things that way and is about my age and is a girl and is, well, *beautiful*, hell I'll say it, and maybe it's bad manners, but stop and think how *you* might feel if *I* was that beautiful and you stumbled into me! Maybe you wouldn't have talked no better'n I did! I mean the last thing a person does when they're seeing the best thing they ever saw is stop looking or scare it away or tell it to cover itself up! I mean when you're stunned you're stunned. You can't think what's right or polite. You watch. You're helpless. And, and I know I don't make sense and I'm sorry all I ever do is scare you and, but I just, I just had to try and tell you how it was for me before you go off and, and disappear again or something . . . ." I flopped down on the hearth, stared at my shoes and waited for the sound of her walking away forever. For a long time it was silent. Then, sure enough, she walked away. Then there was a thud . . .

it was the orange squirt-gun landing in the trash. And there stood Eddy, *grinning!* She said, "Who said anything about disappearing? I have to tell about *me* spying on *you!*" Utterly awash, I listened.

"You know," she began, taking up her rocker and wine, "when you look like me you get a lot of attention from a kind of guy I think it's safe to call 'a Jerk.' But I never met the Jerk yet who, if he saw he was scaring me, would walk in a river, swim across, wade through devil's club, climb a tree and start spouting stuff like 'Let me tell you, scholar, God never made a better berry than Angling!' I liked that, Gust. I didn't know what you were, but I knew you weren't a Jerk. I figured you busted out of some Bug House, or robbed some bank, or maybe killed somebody—but I thought you were a pretty nice deranged murderer-thief!" She laughed. "The next few days I kept thinking about you, and realized I might even be a little sweet on you—which was embarrassing, in light of your profession. But I thought I'd never see you again, so it did matter. . . .

"But a few weeks later I happened by my old man's warehouses— they're on the waterfront in Portland—and I happened to look down at this crummy creek that runs into the Willamette there, and this guy was sitting in the garbage with a board between his knees, so I pulled out my birdoculars—and it's ol' Gust, dressed like a meter reader, busy pulling threads out of a slimy drowned coat! I thought, 'Whew! *Really* buggy!' But then you stuck a hook in the board, tied a fly with the thread, carved a boat, stowed the fly on board, lowered the boat downstream and bang! you caught a trout!" She passed me the jug, clinked her glass against it and said, "Here's to a fancy piece of fishin'!"

We drank, then she went on: "I started wondering why you'd picked on a poor slum-dwelling trout like that one, but you stuck it in a milk carton, ran to the river, set it free, and sat for a bit. Then you started making weird gyrations in the air like you were some druid or shaman or something. And now I was curious. *Real* curious.

"So curious I drove to the Tamanawis the next weekend to see what I could see. And by a pool on an amazingly ugly dairy near here I met this little kid, called himself Hemingway, who without me saying boo launched off on some epic about this giant steelhead he'd caught thanks to a sage named Gus who was the greatest fisherman in the world and he'd knife anybody who said otherwise. He pointed to the deepest darkest part of the pool and told how this Gus of his dove in, wrassled the fish out with his bare hands, spent seven minutes down, one breath, came up grinning . . ."

"Bull!" I laughed.

"Sure," said Eddy. "But I could see in his eyes what little Hemingway thought of you, and his eyes made me more curious yet." She glanced at me. I felt like I had a tail and it was wagging like crazy and I couldn't make it stop. "Speaking of *bull*," she said, "a couple weeks later a fisherman friend of mine stopped by with a sports page and read me the Legend of Antoine Chapeau, and we were laughing our heads off—till he got to the last part, the message, and I realized it was you." She paused for more wine. "I read it about eight thousand times. I wanted to come, but, well, those oranges. . . .

"What I did instead was start fishing the Tamanawis, thinking maybe I'd bump into you and could pretend it was an accident. One trip I stopped by this candle-maker's house and bought some of his stuff, and the guy—Steve his name was—saw my fishing gear when he followed me outside, yelled 'Wait!,' ran back in, came back out, shoved a tiny little fly in my face and kept it there till I finally said, 'Looks like a flea.' He said 'You flashed heavy on it, didn't you!' Then he said this friend of his had what he called a tackle shop up the road, but what it really was was a gallery of piscine artwork—'anadromous masterpieces' he called them—and I'd flash heavy on a lot of them and maybe on the friend too, who wasn't yanged out even though his diet was. And before he even got close to saying it, I knew what name was coming . . . Gus this, Gus that, I was starting to feel *surrounded!* And to top it off, that same day I saw this guy across the river with a split-cane pole and a belly basket and a big fish on, so I pulled out my trusty birdoculars, and it was *you!*"

I laughed. "I *knew* I'd seen that bus before!"

She nodded. "Well. By this time I was thinking about you an awful lot, thinking how I'd kind of hoped I'd meet somebody like this Gust person, thinking how if I never got brave I might miss my chance to meet somebody like that for a long time, thinking maybe the oranges were an accident, or not even yours—and so what if they *weren't* an accident and *were* yours . . . so I decided to trick or treat. And tonight I drove clear from Portland and took a hell of a long time because every few miles I'd change my mind and turn around and change my mind and turn around again. But when I got here there were kicked-in jack-o-lanterns all the way down the driveway, and it was dark, and the cabin was black, and at long last I made up my mind once and for all: *NO WAY!* and I turned around so fast I killed the engine, pumped it so hard I flooded it, turned it over so fast so many times the battery croaked. And that did it. When my machine died at your door I figured we were doomed to meet. So in I came—it was unlocked—and lit lights, needed wine, waited and waited, and finally you came, dressed like a goon, and gave me this stuff that was the right sort of stuff, and said those things that were the right sort of things, and you seemed, *seem* like somebody I, um, we might, well, I think we . . ."

I took the glass from her hand and kissed her.

Then she took the glass from my hand and kissed me. I said, "Then what happened?" And she kissed me again. More than once. And vice versa. For a long, long time.

In the morning we slept—me on the couch, Eddy in the loft. At noon we milked Charles the Second, then Eddy fed peanuts to the chipmunks while I made breakfast: goat-milk custard, oranges and tea. The tea was oversteeped, the oranges dry, the custard unmentionable— and it was by far the best breakfast I ever had, there on the bluff overlooking the river where kingfishers fished, wrens flitted, ouzels dipped and salmon rolled. In the afternoon we went walking along the Taman- awis, and Eddy said the name of every bird, shrub, tree, flower and mushroom we saw. In the evening I showed her how to use the cane pole and belly basket. By dusk she wielded it more skillfully and far more gracefully than I ever will. That night we sat by the fire again, and I told her about my brother and dreefees and the mouse that sang, and taught her to whistle its song; and she told me about a grandfather she'd loved, how he'd lived and died, and about two friends—an old professor who lived in a mice-and-bat-filled attic (Eddy lived in her downstairs), and a fiddle-maker (named Thomas!) who carved cedar dugout canoes, and who showed her how to make the hazel poles. Then we told some secrets, and the best was Eddy's: the squirt-gun was orange because of the oranges, was full of lemon juice, and had I misbehaved she'd have shot me in the eyes! Then we talked about animals and rivers and mountains we knew while her eyes shone like a lake in a vision or dream, and we went walking in the middle of the night, and when the sky grayed and light- ened we took it for a second moonrise, and when we realized it was sunrise we were astonished. Then Eddy said, "Let's say grace and fall to break- fast." Which we did.

On the second day we slept till sundown—she in the loft (which she'd taken to calling "my house"), me on the couch (which she called "your house"). But when the last auburn light of day came sifting in through the cedars she came and woke me, and kissed me, and placed an orange in my hand. I looked at it, then at her—and saw that she was naked. She whispered, "Come with me to my house." And we went together to the loft, and scarcely spoke, and didn't sleep till daylight.

8

The Line of Light

Like brass inlay in ebony
a single leaf off one of sixty alders
pulls downriver,
as by six rowers rowed from death,

glides a handspan deep in black water,
the spectral pink and pearl and green
sheen of scales and wings from the timely
dead dragonflies dissolved in the eddies.

And the leaf pulls, down the black canal
dug by somber thought between walls of basalt
feathered and furred by herbs and mosses
—dark or holy as if it were

the ship of the silence
swimming the night sky to daybreak,
carrying grateful light in its closed eyes.

—Alice Likowski

LATE THE THIRD DAY we went to the river. The sun looked wintry, but was still warm. Eddy was barefoot, blue-jeaned, wearing an old gray cotton pullover she'd found in my closet. I kept gaping at that pullover: I'd fished in it for years, wiped blood and slime on it, sweated in it, smelled in it—and Eddy wore it now like Ocean wore her cloud daughters. . . . But I was no bloody Sun. Pullovers aside, I was miserable. I was carrying the split-cane pole and belly reel; I was stifling in waders, winter coat and fishing vest; and I was sick at heart. When we reached the river I leaned the pole against a boulder and would have taken off the coat, but Eddy put her arms around me, stood on my boots to keep her feet warm, assaulted my glum face with kisses and thanked and thanked me for cooperating with her plan.

This "plan" was the problem. It had sprung into existence an hour before, in the loft, when she told me she had to return to Portland, *alone*, by nightfall. I said nothing, but evidently it changed my appearance when my heart slithered out my mouth, rolled off the bed and landed with a squishy splat on the floor. She hugged me, said she was sorry, said not to worry, said to be happy, said Wait! Listen! she had this plan! So I listened. Part of the plan—the crucial part—was her promise to come back the very next evening. The next-best part was that when she did come back she could probably stay a solid week—"to fish the chinook run" (she winked), "at least that's what my father is going to hear." Then came the last part of the plan—the curve Mohammed the Prophet warned about: for the next two hours (after which she had to leave) I must do everything she asked me to do, provided it was "within reason, and within your power." Of course this sounded *outrageously* suspicious, but I agreed to it for two reasons: the first was that I was prepared to do anything, however chivalric, illegal or inane, to ensure the first two parts of the plan; the second was that as she proposed it she was straddling my belly, and she was naked as the sky. Who was I to argue?

The plan commenced: she had me put on warm fishing clothes, waders, winter coat and fishing vest; she asked for the shower, a towel, shampoo (she settled for Ivory soap) and the old cotton pullover; she had me fill my pockets with bread, fruit, cheese and nuts; she had me fetch fresh salmon roe from the cellar; she had me help take her things to the bus, then help her jump-start it. She dried her hair in the sun while the battery charged, shut off the engine, took my hand and said, "Now for the fun part." And she led me down to the river,

which brings us back to my glum face, to Eddy's bare feet on my boot tops, to Eddy's bare Eddy in my pullover, and to bare sunlight in Eddy's Ivory-soap-tousled hair. She turned to a river still green from the week's rain. Now and then a salmon sounded. She squinted at the sun and the horizon. She said, "The sooner I leave the sooner I'm back. Let's get on with it."

"On with what?"

She nodded toward the river. "The fun part."

I thought the hug was the fun part, but didn't argue. She said, "What's the lightest leader you've got?"

"Three-pound."

"Tie on a three-pound leader. Use a blood-knot. Tie on a #4 hook and bait it. Give me the pole." She grinned. "God this is fun!"

I didn't agree, but did as she said, baiting the hook with fresh red roe, tying the rainbow lamb's wool round her waist, handing her the pole. She stepped down to the fishiest part of H2O's drift, took a deep breath and a long look at the lay of the water, then laid out an arcing cast that would have carried itself into the alders overhanging the far shore, but she braked it at the last instant and the bait fell with almost no splash into a deep slot.

"Would it damage the Plan if I asked what you're doing, Eddy?"

"I'm fishing," she said. And she was. Was she ever. She stood on a driftwood log, her toes sunk in new green moss; the red sun bathed her and her back was arced in the same sloping curve as the curve of the line sweeping down the current. I no longer recognized my old lifelong pastime: Eddy transformed it into a kind of sacred dance. And it was inconceivable to me that there could be a fish within range of her hook—be it baited or bare—that would refuse to sacrifice itself for the sake of that dance.

But there was one thing I didn't understand. I said, "There are chinooks in this drift now, Eddy, and not much else."

"I know."

"Some of them weigh fifty pounds."

"I know."

"But you're using three-pound leader."

"I know."

She stripped in her line after the first cast tailed out. I said, "Even if it was possible to hook a chinook without breaking that leader, you couldn't land it if you played it all night."

"I know."

"But you said you had to leave by dark."

"I do," she said. "But you don't, Gust. You have to carry out the Plan!" Looking pointedly at my warm clothes, food-filled pockets and waders, she smiled the trick-or-treat smile . . .

. . . and a bright salmon boiled in the slot.

She shot me another grin, then sent out another arcing cast: the bait landed perhaps forty feet upstream from where the salmon had shown. And this time Eddy stood on tiptoe, her body taut as a drawn bow, her eyes alight with water-shattered sun. My native intelligence didn't just whisper: it shouted; it sang. It said not only that the strike was inevitable, but that the fish, the river, the trees, rocks, light and sky—all of it was made, in accordance with Immutable Laws, for beings such as Eddy, and for moments such as this.

And the line stopped drifting. The rod tip twitched. She lowered the tip almost to the water, letting the fish take, then she swept it back with a quick but gentle motion: the pole plunged downward. The sacred dance began.

She let line fly from the basket, applying no pressure. She whispered, "Chinook!" And when the massive silver shape rose thrashing to the surface she cackled like an old mad sage. The salmon moved upstream slowly, inexorably; Eddy gave line freely, applying so little pressure that the pole was hardly bent. Soon after the first sounding the chinook appeared to calm, moving as though it sensed no threat. It swam to the center of the drift and held behind a boulder, immovable as the boulder itself. Eddy turned. "Come here, Gus."

I had to obey.

"Untie the belly reel and put it on—quick! If the fish wants line, give it. Don't let it go slack, but don't *fight* the fish: just keep track of it. It's working!" She cackled again. "Here . . . take the pole!"

I took it. She tied the lamb's wool around my waist. Then she kissed me. "I have to go now . . . dreefee. I'll be back tomorrow, sunset. My last wish is this: *play the chinook!*" She turned and darted away toward the cabin.

If the salmon had wanted an easy getaway, then was its chance. I watched every stone her bare feet chose, watched her every stride, watched till her faded jeans and cotton pullover and yellow hair vanished in the cedars and a lump the size of an orange rose in my throat. But the fish held: it seemed to have forgotten that it was hooked. So. There I stood by the Tamanawis, alone, at sunset, wearing a belly reel, holding a split-cane pole, linked to a leviathan by an almost invisible and strategically negligible leader, with an order: *play the chinook!* It was impossible. But it was Eddy's wish—so I tried.

For some time the salmon stayed behind the boulder. I held rod and line lightly, waiting, feeling the slow tail-strokes of a massive fish. Having seen its bright sides I knew it was fresh from the ocean. And it was thick as a tree, and stronger than all the white water from here to its mountain spawning bed. With ten-pound test and a full day ahead I might have had some chance: I had three-pound, and the sun stood on the sea. But Eddy didn't say "Catch it." She said, "Play it!" She meant it to be a game. She knew I'd never land it—but to try not to lose it . . . well, it was something to do while she was away. What would I have done in the cabin but pule in the wine glass, pining for her return? And what would it be like to play a fish as long as it could be played, knowing from the start that I'd never catch it? Maybe I was just moonstruck, but I was beginning to like the idea. "All right fish," I said, "All right Gus. Take it slow. No tension in the head, or in the hands, or in the line."

I looked at my hands in the last of the light, saw the red groundwater flowing under the pale skin, thought of Nick and his pierced palm, thought of the tiny flies I'd tied, thought of great or implausible things that human hands had accomplished—and the old inner glimmerings that sent me up the River Road began once again. When the chinook began to move, I was ready.

It didn't wait to test me: it rounded the boulder on the far side and the nylon line raked the rock, but I jumped up on a log, stood on tiptoe, sent the rod-tip toward the sky—and the sharper angle freed the line. The fish moved out, surging up through $H2O$'s drift with calm, sure tail strokes. I eased my grip, slowed my breath, let the line run smoothly out between left thumb and forefinger. And as I set out after the salmon I realized what had begun: the pain of the hook forgotten, it had resumed its anadromous migration. It was journeying freely toward its spawning grounds, and because it sensed no tension in the too-light line, I, a landsman, could mark its course and follow!

It moved quickly, right up the center of the current. In the slow water at the tail of the next riffle I had to jog to keep close, but in the pool above it rested, giving me a chance to scramble over logs and catch up. The sun was gone now, but a gray light in the east promised the moonrise. The moon would be full—which meant the salmon would all be travel-ling—and there was a thin cover of cirrus to reflect its light, making the night almost day-bright, but blanketing it against the cutting cold of the night I'd spent on the way to the source. The chinook picked up its pace again. I payed out line and followed. Because of the concentration it took to maintain the tensionless tension I forgot my feet, but—as often happens when fishermen follow fish—they picked their own way over the logs and rocks, unerring. The river wasn't high, and this was to my advantage: there was a wide stony shoulder to walk, clear of the stream-side brush. The fish thrust steadily up through a long array of glides and easy rapids, and I soon lost track of time. I was bent on keeping the line taut but tensionless: how long, how far, how smoothly we travelled—all this was up to the fish.

When the salmon sidled toward my side of the river I had to crouch to keep from being seen. Sometimes it swam in shoals not two rod-lengths away. It entered such a shoal just as the moonbeams sank into the water and I saw it perfectly—a pulsing, silvery shape the size of a dog, hovering in an element as clear as air. The sight of it so fascinated me that I stumbled, the line tensed, the hook stung the salmon's mouth—and the shallows exploded! The chinook plunged into the mainstream with strokes like the strides of a running elk. Any hidden notions I'd had of capturing it were destroyed: the power in its thrusts was awesome. I scrambled upstream as fast as I could, but the fish surged so far ahead that the reel nearly emptied, and then the current's pull put tension in the line, driving the hook deeper. The chinook began to bulldog. I knew then that if tooth touched leader, the game was up. I gathered the lost line, caught up with the salmon, erased all the tension. The bulldogging stopped: the leader held. Eddy must have hooked it perfectly, at the very edge of the jaw.

After a long wait the fish resumed its migration at the early, regal pace. Watching the line cut the shimmering river, I followed.

The chinook moved up the Tamanawis with the ease of a cloud shadow gliding up a valley. After many pools it slid in behind another rock and held. I waited. The moon rose higher. When the fish didn't move I found a rock myself, and sat. I zipped my coat, ate cheese and an apple, even smoked a pipe. It seemed the chinook waited for me. Perhaps we were making friends. Some night bird approached down the river corridor, gliding for long, silent spaces, then thrusting its wings just once, then gliding some more: it was swimming breaststroke through the air. When it neared me it wheeled into the trees with a hooing cry and I recognized a great horned owl. As if the cry were a sign, the salmon moved out.

As time and water passed I got better at the game. The moon brightened my rocky path, and it seemed that the deeper the fish and I journeyed into the night the less cautious I had to be. Only in the shallow rapids was there frenzy to the chinook's pace; in riffle, pool, eddy and glide it proceeded with stately calm. Perhaps its wound was numb now; perhaps its ancient instincts told it that night meant safety no matter what dark shapes might follow beyond the fringe of the water; or perhaps it was aware of me all along and simply grew used to me. Whatever the reason, I walked more and more boldly, no longer crouching, no longer tiptoeing over the stones. And much more often than not the salmon seemed to choose my side of the river—as if it preferred my company. I couldn't get used to this: I know the fish could see me plainly, yet it swam at its unaltering pace along a close, parallel path. In places I had to wade to stay clear of overhanging brush or log jams, but in time even my splashing didn't cause the chinook to shy. I really think the fish grew curious, wondering who on earth was walking beside it through the night.

As my walking and wading and attending to the line became less conscious, more free and easy, I found I could free my mind. My thoughts of Eddy were constant as the sound of the river, but beneath or beside them I found myself remembering Titus, talking about the ancient Taoists—and of an "Equilibrium" of which they spoke. He said this

Equilibrium derived from a kind of inner balance: it transmitted itself from the soul to the mind, and from the mind to the body, and when a man possessed of it put his hand to an art or craft he was capable of unheard-of feats. The masters of Zen archery, the Sufi poets, the Taoist landscape painters, the early Celtic mariners—these people had this Equilibrium. The Fianna of pre-Christian Ireland, the master painters of Persian miniatures, the architects of the great mosques and gothic cathedrals—they possessed it as well. And just as I'd wondered whether Thomas Bigeater might have possessed it Titus said that in China there had been simple fishermen who, because of this Equilibrium, could catch enormous fish using cane-poles and a *single strand* of silk. "A line breaks," Titus said, "at a stress point. But if the fisherman experiences no stress, and if he transmits this experience through his hands to his pole, to his line, to his hook, then there will be no stress point, therefore no point at which the strand can break." By virtue of this principle, he said, these fishermen could hook the biggest fish that swam and still coax them at last into their waiting hands. . . .

I tried to invoke the peace I'd felt during the long days of rain watching, to find again that empty place inside me; I sensed that if I could constantly know such a peace, if I could be filled with such an emptiness, then I might come to possess this Equilibrium. . . .

Then I burst out laughing. The emptiness was gone—utterly gone. . . .

Because Eddy had come: she'd come and filled it, and overflowed it, and there was no better name for what shone there now than *love. Eddy had come!* and as I walked with the salmon that love overwhelmed me, and I laughed like a drunk in the night. I thought, *Why shouldn't love be my Equilibrium?* Why shouldn't love be the forceless force running from heart to hand, down the line to the hook, from the hook through the wound and into the fish? Couldn't love create that sacred balance? Wouldn't love dissolve all stress? And from my depths came a wavelike rush of certainty: love *could* sustain the frailest of lines! As long as I loved I would not lose this salmon. It didn't matter how big or strong it was: with love alone coursing down the line it would have no desire to escape!

As the moon climbed the sky so the fish and I climbed the river, without struggle, almost without effort. I'd already sensed that the chinook had come to trust me, and soon after I saw that so, it seemed, did the animals and birds. A second owl, breaststroking down the corridor like the first, did not wheel away but coasted over in silence, its bewildering eyes glaring as it passed over my rod-tip. In an eddying backwash a pair of raccoons hunted crawdads: they mounted a rock as I strolled past, and bossed me in soft, clicking bandito voices—but when I held out the last of the goat cheese they let me come near and place it on the rock between them. The first deer I saw were yearlings, so I took their lack of caution to be inexperience—but later a four-point blacktail buck let me near enough to roll him an apple, watched while I passed, then bent his neck to eat it. Still later a beaver paddled by and neither slapped its tail nor plunged under. And when I crossed a gravel bar where seven mergansers slept they untucked heads from wings at the sound of my feet, but neither swam nor flew as my line passed right over them. And with each of these encounters the love deepened, and the certainty grew. It had always been my way to approach the river like a wanded magician out to work deception. But this night, thanks to Eddy, thanks to love, I came as a blind man led by a seeing-eye salmon—and it showed me a world I'd believed was destroyed, a world where a man could still walk unfeared among the animals and birds he calls "wild."

Moved and shamed by the animals' trust, feeling hour after hour the faithful pulse of the salmon's tail beating like the river's silver heart, I felt the fisherman in me being unmade. The angler/fish, hunter/quarry paradigm began melting away like blood in water. There could be no question, with so light a line, of ever bringing this great fish to bay. There could be no betrayal, no treachery, no struggle and death. There was only a chinook on its primordial journey, and an undone fisherman following, being led deeper into the night.

The salmon's pace remained steady and untiring. My fatigue grew, my thoughts slowed, my feet would sometimes stumble. But my hands kept pulsing the heart's secret down the line, through the water, to the fish.

As I looked out of myself, unthinking, the night grew more and more extraordinary, yet more and more familiar: I felt as though I were returning to some forgotten, ancient home. The river shimmered and glowed and shattered the moon, flowing from east to west like the horizontal bar of a cross; the line, too, shone pale in the light, reaching vertically from sky to water. The cirrus cover thinned away into a high mist, and a huge and pale spherical rainbow encompassed and journeyed with the moon. The moist sky with its few faint stars seemed to flow like a boundless river, and the Tamanawis with its glittering bands of moonshine seemed like a ribbon of Milky-Wayed sky. I felt overturned and overwhelmed, and walked in a slow hush, awed by all I'd seen and was seeing, yet I sensed that still greater secrets were impending.

Now and then in the deeper pools other salmon would roll close to mine. In a glassy glide above one such pool I saw that my fish had drawn companions—an escort of scurrying jacks, darting crisscross in its wake. I knew then that my guide was a female, laden with eggs; and I knew that if by some miracle I should coax her into my grasp, I could never harm her. She swam on and on, seeming even statelier now compared to the veering, nervous jacks. In one violent rapid I know the line dragged and she felt the sting of the hook. But after so long an association it seemed not to disturb her: she swam on with the calm, sure strokes of one who knows she carries the hope of her people. She swam fearlessly, though she swam toward her death.

In a wide, leaf-strewn eddy my fish again drew near me and I looked for the trailing jacks: I was thinking I watched her shadow when the dark patch suddenly eased ahead—it was another big chinook. When they continued to swim in tandem I realized she'd found her mate. The buck, too, grew used to my presence, though he was not so tolerant of splashing; I tried to keep more to the shore. But often they would come close to me, letting me watch them journey together, breathing the wind woven into the water as I breathed the ether entwined in the air. Animals and night birds called out to one another, marking our passage. The haloed moon crossed the sky. The salmon led me up the river while men were sleeping. And the newly bestirred love coursed through me as steadily and easily as the light line cut through the water.

Far, far later, in the hour before dawn, the two salmon came to rest behind a fallen tree in waist-deep water. The moon and rainbow slipped toward the sea. I knew that the night journey was ending: the two chinooks would stay here till first light, then move on to the next deep pool to wait out the day. My companion hovered by her mate with such tranquility: I wanted our parting to be as tranquil.

I began to wade in toward her. Both of them saw me, yet made no move. Inch by inch I crept toward them, hardly stirring the water, feeling my legs had turned to water, making no sound. When I was exactly a rod-length away I laid my pole down on the river and took the line in my hands. I waded on until the hooked salmon hovered at my knees. I was too tired for dumb amazement, but her tameness and the throb of her hovering stirred me like music heard in sleep. Moving nothing but my fingers, I drew in the line. When it came taut my fish tensed, but stayed where she was. I waited for the pink and blue bands of the moon's rainbow to sink past the tip of the tallest fir, then again I drew in line: I pulled it toward me in increments, praying that she wouldn't fear. Still she stayed. Then slowly, so slowly, I leaned down toward her;

my fingers touched the water: she saw them crease the river surface, but still she held. I bent lower—trying to enter the river with the imperceptible motion of sinking moons or suns. I kept my hands together as I inched in the line; the water numbed them, yet more than ever they pulsed with strange certainty, pulsed in obedience to secret law. My arms sank silently; my sleeves filled with water; I felt the blood-knot; I began to inch in the invisible leader. The buck grew skittish and moved away, circled, brushed against my salmon, circled again: but only she had felt the hook and watched the line all through the night. She stayed.

I drew in line till only inches separated my hand from her. I held the line with my right hand, but with my left I reached still lower. Now my hair touched the water, my beard, my face. I drew a long breath and bent still lower. . . .

My face entered the river; I felt my ears fill; the water poured in at the neck of my coat and ran freezing down my chest. I opened my eyes: she was blurred to me now, but still my salmon hadn't moved. I slipped my numbed left hand down. I touched her moonlit silver side—

and still she held, unmoving. I rested my cold hand upon her gleaming side. She suffered my touch, and stayed.

My breath ran out. I had to draw away. Water poured from me to the river, and still my salmon stayed. So at last, with the slightest tug, I let the line be broken at the blood knot. Bearing the hook, trailing the wisp of unseen leader, the chinook eased slowly away.

I wiped the water from my face. I lifted the pole off the face of the water. I walked toward the River Road and home.

I found myself on a rise about seven miles upstream from my cabin. The road was empty. I walked a long way, watching the moon expand and redden and sink. For a while as I walked I tried to think about what had happened, but I was too tired, too wet and cold.

The sky began to grow light in the east behind me. I just walked and watched. Mist clung to the river as sunlight crept over the Coast Range. The road was white with frost: it shone like a strip of moon surface in the early light, running from east to west like the horizontal bar of a cross. The entire valley hovered, still, before me. Somewhere a raven called. . . .

And then I felt it—a sharp pain in the heart, like a hook being set. I whirled around: sunlight struck me full in the face. My eyes closed.

And then I saw it—the vertical bar—a line so subtle it must be made of nothing nameable. And it ran from my heart of earth and blood, through my head, to the sky; ran like a beam of watery light; ran from the changing, flowing forms of the world to a realm that light alone could enter. But my pain grew sharper: mad with joy, I sank to my knees on the white road,

and I felt the hand, resting like sunlight on my head. And I knew that the line of light led not to a realm but to a Being, and that the light and the hook were his, and that they were made of love alone. My heart was pierced. I began to weep. I felt the Ancient One drawing me toward him, coaxing me out of this autumn landscape, beckoning me on toward undying joy.

The hand was lifted. The nameless presence faded, and the light around me blended with the sunlight I knew. But in my heart the wound stayed, and the good hurt. I rose from the road, brushed off my knees, wiped my eyes and drew breath. Then I walked—though I knew that from this point on the road, and from this point in my soul, there was no escape, and nowhere to go.

Book Five

At the End of the Line

Rains pour down without water,
and the rivers are streams of light.
One love it is
that pervades the world;
few there are who know it fully.

—*Kabir*

God lies in wait for us with nothing so much as love, and love is like a fisherman's hook: without it he could never catch a fish, but once the hook is taken the fisherman is sure of the fish. Even though the fish twists hither and yon, still the fisherman is sure of him. So, too, I speak of love: he who is caught by it is held by the strongest of bonds, and yet the stress is pleasant; he who takes this sweet burden upon himself gets further, and comes nearer to what he aims at, than he would by means of any harsh ordinance ever devised by man. Moreover, he can sweetly bear all that happens to him; all that God inflicts he can take cheerfully. Nothing makes you God's own, or God yours, as much as this sweet bond. When one has found this way, he looks for no other. To hang on this hook is to be so completely captured that feet and hands, and mouth and eyes, the heart, and all a man is and has become God's own. . . . Whatever he does, who is caught by this hook, love does it, and love alone. . . .

—*Meister Eckhart*

Wherever He drags me
I go
with no say in the matter.

—*Rumi*

Last Chapter

THERE'S NOT MUCH more to tell. It was of the line of light and of the touch of the hand of love that I wanted to speak. Now I've spoken, or tried. Maybe now old Izaak Walton's shade and book and controversy will let me be. Or maybe they won't. I don't much care now; I'm not so particular as I used to be. Taking the good with the bad, I'm just living happily ever after. That is, I'm being hung by the heart until dead. Dreefee dead. Who could ask for more?

Eddy came back at sunset, just like she promised. I did my best to tell her what had happened through the night and at dawn, but I was exhausted and excited and my best wasn't very good. Yet when I finished she sat still for a moment, considering. Then she said, "I love you." Can you imagine? She'd never said anything like *that* to me before! And I hadn't even done anything. The God in the Light did it: all I did was dangle at the end of the line. But that's what she said. She said she'd stay the week, too—but she didn't: she stayed the month, stayed three months, stayed six months. Then one day in May we drove into Portland, nabbed Titus and Descartes at their flat, kidnapped Bill Bob out of fifth-grade PE, drove up to a podunk county courthouse in central Washington and had ourselves an old-time Justice-of-the-Peace-style wedding. Bill Bob was best man. Titus gave a speech on the Chivalric Code and the Figure of Beatrice and Mystical Union and Avataric Consorts and Majnun and Leila and so on and so forth till Eddy whispered that we should have made Titus best man and let Bill Bob do the speech. Meanwhile, Descartes just sat in a chair, witnessing—but he sat in the swivelling office chair behind the Justice of the Peace's desk, and when he began to rock it the chair began creaking, and when the Justice heard it he turned to the dog in mid-ceremony and barked, "Hey boy! Git *down!*" . . . Descartes stopped rocking; he furrowed his formidable brow; he turned his sky-eyes upon the Justice and kept them upon the Justice, and he sang. It was a silent song, sung with the eyes alone: it was a song of power, and of fangs, of sudden leaps and rending flesh, of spurting blood and horrible pain. The Justice heard the song, turned red, turned white, turned blue, cleared his throat, straightened his tie and completely mangled the dearly-beloved-we-are-gathered speech he'd been suavely making for thirty years. The song added some much-needed solemnity to the solemnities. (The best man was in gym clothes, slurping a grape pop while we said "I do."). Afterward Descartes hopped down, wagged his tail, licked us both and according to Titus growled, "Gus and Eddy Orviston by God and that's it!" It was touching to see him at a near loss for words.

We dumped our pals off in Portland and returned to the Tamanawis. What "honeymoon" we had we had at home: there was the cedar grove, the river, the fire and wine and loft. . . . What the hell did Niagara Falls or Waikiki Beach have to offer us? We just strung a rope across the driveway with a board on it and painted on the board,

JUST MARRIED.   GET LOST.

And the rope stayed strung there for two weeks. I know it doesn't make for a spicy story to censor things this way, but hells bells, we still live here: the neighbors will be reading this, and our parents and friends. What can I say? It was a nice two weeks. Get lost.

We took the rope down on the evening of May 21st, a Friday, because May 22nd was all sorts of things: it was opening day of trout season on the coastal streams; it was a year from the day I'd signed the lease on the cabin; it was my twenty-first birthday, which meant that I was now a *man*—because in America a man is defined not as a person who can vote or think or be drafted or carry guns or preach or pray, but as somebody who can get drunk legally (a definition I like!). But most especially, May 22nd was the day I met Julie, which made it the most amazing day of my life. I didn't say *important*: the most important day was the night I travelled with the chinook. And I didn't say *enjoyable*: the most enjoyable day was the sixty-some-hour one with Eddy, starting Halloween. But it *was* the most *amazing*. And it began as everything in my life has begun—

with a fishing trip. Eddy and me and Rodney and Rodneyetta (Eddy's eight-foot flyrod), hoofing it up the Tamanawis, ascending the same swirling stairway I'd climbed with the seeing-eye salmon, but this time stopping to catch native cutthroat. Neither of us had fished since mid-March when the last few steelhead were in: it was good to be taken by the old magic. There's just nothing like the feel of a trout dancing through the river, making the pole pulse like a heart in your hands. It does to the hands what the sight of your sweetie does to your body, what dreams of eternity do to your heart, what milk chocolate does to your mouth. . . . And yet we killed two trout. It's strange to kill your dance partners, but that's what we did. We did it because the world is strange—because this is a world where no matter who you are or where you live or what you eat or whether you choose or don't choose to understand and be grateful, it is sacrifice—sweet, bleeding sacrifice—that sustains you. So we killed two trout, but knew no sacrificial prayers, and so simply knelt by the river, commended them on how well they'd fought, whispered, "Swim, little soul. Go be a bird, or a singing mouse, or a whale," then broke their bodies to sustain our own.

As we hiked back down to the cabin we passed a fisherman out on H2O's drift—a highbrow lady, her tweedy back turned as she made spectacular casts to the slot on the far shore—the slot where Eddy had hooked the chinook. Evidently women liked that piece of water. Away down in Ma's pool was another fisherman, an old plunker—a straw hat down over his nose; a pipe clenched in his jaw; two-thirds asleep; an adherent of the Crawdad Benson School of Fishing. Then up by the cordwood Chipmunkdominium we stumbled onto Bill Bob.

He was building something—we couldn't tell what, but he'd obviously been at it since early morning. He had a small chainsaw, hammer and nails, a level, a drill, bolts and wrenches, and out of a pile of scrap lumber and molding and cardboard tubes he was building a labyrinth of ramps, tunnels, trestles and over-and-under-passes that looked like a Reader's Digest Condensed Version of the Los Angeles Freeway System. He also had his two radios plugged in and turned up so loud that he wasn't aware of us till Eddy pulled the plugs. He jumped, then grinned, then gave us hugs—especially Eddy—and she asked what he was making. He said it was something for the chipmunks and me on my birthday. She asked what it was called. He said, "A Ratrace."

"Oh great," I said.

"Don't be sourcastic," said Bill Bob.

"A Ratrace. Just what the chipmunks and me always wanted."

"Don't worry. There won't be no rats in it."

"Oh swell," I said.

"What's it do?" asked Eddy.

"You fill it up with peanuts, then you stand back and watch and the chipmunks come out and run all around on it. It lets 'em sort of find out what it's gonna be like when they get to be people."

I snorted. "You've been talking to that blasted Titus."

"I have not!"

"Then where'd you get the idea chipmunks were going to be people? Or that they ought to find out what it's like to be people?"

"Descartes."

"Hmph. And who did Descartes's talking for him?"

"Titus. But *so?*"

"So even if Titus can speak Descartes's mind, Descartes ain't no chipmunk."

"So?"

"So how does he know chipmunks want to know about people?"

"How do you know they don't?"

"I don't," I admitted.

"I know ya don't," said Bill Bob. "But Descartes did. He told me so."

"You mean Titus told you so."

"I mean Descartes." Bill Bob glared at me. "You're just jealous. Don't be jealous, Gus. Don't worry, I'll ask you and not Titus or Descartes if I ever wanna know what it's like to be a *shitepoke!*"

"What's that?" Eddy asked.

"A compliment," I said.

"A scraggly ol' cowlick-headed goony-lookin' long-legged fish-stabbin' heron," said Bill Bob. "Now go on, Shitepoke. Go beak some bullheads or somethin'. I got work to do."

I shrugged and started for the back door—

and there, in the sun, in a tiny wicker chair slept the smallest human being I'd ever seen—a girl, not two months old. Barely one month old. Eddy gasped. Bill Bob giggled. I gaped, "Who in the hell is *that!*"

"Shhhhh," said Bill Bob. "That's Julie."

Julie? Who was Julie? Or *whose?* I hadn't known a pregnant woman since Ma ten years back. I whirled on Bill Bob, a lurid suspicion lurching into my mind. . . . No. Impossible! He didn't even have any peach fuzz on him. But where did she come from?

I joined Eddy, who'd rushed up and knelt by the baby. Bill Bob slipped between us and put his arms around us. Julie was so small and her face so fat and innocent and her arms so full of folds and her hair so blond—what there was of it—that it took me a while to see that she looked familiar. *Uncannily* familiar. The face was not pretty by any stretch of the imagination, but it was wonderful: looked like the world's smallest, sweetest old man. But which old man? This took time to sink in—not because it wasn't obvious, but because it was so implausible. At last, however, it sank:

"Oh my God! Bill Bob! She looks *just like H2O!*"

He laughed. Pointedly.

"Holy shit! This is our baby sister!"

"Yep," said Bill Bob.

"Mind your manners, Gus," said Eddy. "She's come a long way to meet you."

But I couldn't mind anything but Julie. "Judas Priest! Look at her! Like an H2O that got shrunk in the wash!"

Eddy and Bill Bob laughed and hugged each other and me, but I was like a lump of mud. I was flummoxed. The baby's existence made no sense. She was obviously not adopted—poor thing. But what was Ma, forty? And what was H2O, ninety? *Julie*. Named after Juliana Berners, no doubt—the mother of modern flyfishing. . . .

Bill Bob turned off his radios. He was watching my face. "What's the matter, Gus?"

"I don't know. Nuthin'."

"Come on," he said, smiling and grabbing my arm. "Come on down here and see what Julie can do." We leaned down close to our sister's face. He whispered, "Hear? Hear her? Hear how good she can make the air whistle in an' out her nose, *all by herself?*"

I listened: sure enough, in went the cool cedar-scented air through an H2O-shaped nose the size of my fingernail, then out it came again all warm and moist and Julie-scented, and she did it all by herself. I began to feel the old place in my heart. I began to blink and swallow. "Where's Ma?" I croaked. "Where's H2O?" I hadn't seen them for so long—not since the day I'd climbed Sisisicu. The day I'd thought Ma was getting dumpy—hells bells, she'd been pregnant! God, I wanted to see them! They probably thought I hated them. . . . I hadn't let them meet Eddy, hadn't written, hadn't called,

but what was Bill Bob doing?

He began pulling me along to the bluff overlooking the river and pointing down to H2O's drift: there was the woman Eddy and I had passed. She wore chest-waders and English tweeds—like a female H2O-doppelgänger—and while we watched she sent out a ninety-foot cast so wonderfully controlled that her fly dropped like manna beneath an overhanging log; then a trout slashed the fly and she struck hard. But not till the Comanche warwhoop splattered our ears did I let out a whoop myself: Ma! I scrambled down toward her, Bill Bob right behind me, Eddy following with Julie—but a weird notion so quickly froze me in my tracks that Bill Bob ran into my back: I looked upstream. There sat the plunker by Ma's pool with his bib overalls and cob pipe, terrorizing a can of worms. And when he saw me turn his way he doffed his straw hat and waved it Hopalong Cassidy–style—exposing the bald pate of Henning Hale-Orviston. I didn't know which way to turn then: I wanted to hug both of them so bad I ended up just standing where I was, waiting for them to join us. While we waited, Bill Bob talked:

"Your friend started comin' t'see us last fall. . . ."

"Which friend?"

"Ma calls him 'Perfesser Pockets.'"

"*Titus* comes to see you?"

"Sure. Him and Ma and H2O are pals. All of us are, Descartes too."

"But—what do you talk about? I mean, Titus and H2O? Titus and *Ma?*"

"Well, we have High Teas, with dogs allowed. And the first thing Titus ever told 'em was . . ." (he fell into a pretty fair Titus impersonation, except his voice was two octaves higher) "'Henning, Carolina, I thought you ought to know that in Arabic the word "ma" means *water*. So you see, Ma, H2O, without knowing it Gus has given you both the same name.'"

"What'd they make of that?" I asked.

"They started calling each other Ma and H2O and told Titus and me to do the same if we wanted, and now everybody calls 'em that, even the High Churchers. But that ain't what changed 'em. They been diffent ever since that night you burned Nijinsky. That's when they started goin' fishin' together an' each learnin' how the other fished, an' that's when I started goin' too 'cause it started bein' fun. An' along in there is when they made Julie I guess. An' that was when H2O got a bike an' started goin' ridin' with me."

"*H2O* goes ridin' with you?"

Bill Bob nodded. I pictured him with his flags and cards and orange-juice tubes and radios, and H2O in his tweeds, huffling along behind. It was too much. I started blinking and swallowing all over again.

"He does lots of stuff with me now," said Bill Bob. "An' he wanted t'start doin' stuff with you too 'cept Ma decided they should surprise ya. That's why I said we was playin' musical chairs, remember that time, 'cause Ma was fly-tyin' an' H2O was makin' a plunkin' pole an' it was a secret we was keepin' so I lied t'fool ya."

I shook my head. "It sure worked."

"An' sometimes me an' Descartes just go t'the park t'pee and stuff 'cause Titus brings Ma an' H2O crap to read an' they help H2O on his new book. An' don't tell Titus, but only H2O reads the crap, then he tells Ma about it so they can both gas away at Titus."

"What's Titus's 'crap' about?" Eddy asked.

"Oh, fishin' an' souls an' that, I dunno. An' Julie. One book was by the lady Julie's named after."

"Juliana Berners, right?" I said.

"Juliana Burners wrong," said Bill Bob. "Who's she s'posed t'be? Some arsonist or somethin'?"

"No, Flamebrain. She was an old-time flyfisherman. But who *is* Julie named after?"

"Lady Julian of Norwich."

"Who's she?"

"Some kinda ol' English lady Titus wanted H2O t'know 'bout 'cause she talked to God an' people like that."

"Oh."

"Know what he said?"

"Who?"

"God, Dummy. To Lady Julian."

"Oh. No."

"Want me to tell ya?"

"Yeah. You tell me."

"He told her, 'I *may* make all things well: and I *can* make all things well: and I *shall* make all things well and I *will* make all things well: and *thou shalt see thyself* that all manner of things shall be well. . . .'"

I looked at Eddy, and she looked at me: we felt the hook twist. Bill Bob puffed up his chest. "I rememorized it," he said, "'cause of Julie."

Ma reached us first. (She'd released the trout after landing it!) She came striding up the bank in her H2O outfit, threw her arms around Eddy and said, "Daughter!" Eddy smiled and said, "Ma." And I couldn't hold back any longer. . . . Ma took one look at my face and screeched, "Cripes O. Riley! It's *Glum Gus!*" But she laughed and hugged me. Then she asked, "What ya think of yer sister, boy?," and I tried to say but started to sob, and H2O came up and saw me and his face started to quiver—and all at once I was flooded with the memory of riding on his back across fast, deep streams when I was small, how I'd cling to his neck and watch the current crash against his staff and legs, how never once did he fall. And I threw myself on him, and again clung to his neck— and we lost it completely and hugged and sobbed till Ma was utterly disgusted.

"Shitaree, Eddy," she said. "Looks like we married us a couple o' saltwater drinkin' fountains. Anybody thirsty?" And she stepped up to H2O and licked his face.

People often don't know what they're talking about, but when they talk about love they *really* don't know what they're talking about. The one sure thing you can say about love is that there isn't much you can say about it. Not that you shouldn't try. You can make analogies; love is *like* lots of things. One thing it's like is a trout stream: try to capture a trout stream with a dam and you get a lake; try to catch it in a bucket and you get a bucket of water; try to stick some under a microscope and you get a close-up look at some writhing amorphous microcooties. A trout stream is only a trout stream when it's flowing between its own two banks, at its own pace, in its own sweet way.

Love is also like poison oak. You can't explain poison-oak itch to somebody who's never had it. And you can't explain love to somebody who's never had poison oak . . . ha! just kidding. What I started to say is that love really *is* like poison oak: it's highly contagious. Scratch it, it gets worse. Touch other people with it, they catch it too. What love is *not* like is your average fish; if love was a fish it would be suicidal: it *wants* to get caught.

I don't know where I caught it first. I suspect maybe I had it all my life but didn't know it—maybe because of all that cool trout-water purling over it, lulling it, numbing it, hypnotizing me into not feeling it. I suspect maybe everybody is covered with it, but most everybody doesn't know it for one reason or another. And I suspect that anybody who thinks they don't have it and thinks they don't want it had better be damned careful, because it can get you anytime, anyplace, anyhow, and you don't even know you have it till you find yourself scratching, and the more you scratch the more it itches, and the more it itches the more you like it till you're so infested with the stuff that you sit around writing crap like this when you could be out fishing! It's scary, that love! It can make you dangerous to yourself. It can change you. It can make you do strange things. Take the thing it made me do to my draft card.

The December before Eddy and I got married I got a draft card, practically for Christmas. It came in an envelope with a letter from the Government and I'd never gotten a letter from the Government before so I looked it over pretty carefully. It was sort of a self-conscious-looking letter; I could see it thought it was very important and it wanted me to think so too; and I might have thought so if it hadn't been for Eddy and the chinook and the touch of a hand that really *was* important. Still, the letter was interesting. The Government said I had to carry the draft card around with me all the time, because it was the law; the Government didn't say which type of law it was, like whether it was a higher law or a lower law, but it told me the number and sections and letters of the law it was, and there were quite a few: it was one of those 45-Sec. rGff 1289bdbdbd-$XK-type of laws. Necromantic stuff. Governmental Number Magic. It might have intimidated me, but you find a hell of a lot of that type of thing in the fishing-tackle industry, and in the fishing-tackle industry you learn to ignore all the numbers and letters and hyphens and you ask simple questions—questions like, "I see it's a 45-Sec. rGff rod and a $XK reel and a 1289bdbdbd line, but what I want to know is, how will it handle? does it please the hand and eye? does it give any tinklings or inklings to the old native intelligence when you pick it up and swish it around a bit?" And if it does these things, then maybe I buy it, or try to build one like it.

So that's the sort of thing I tried to do while I looked over the card the Government wanted me to carry. The card wasn't heavy or anything; it posed no problem from a physical point of view; I could easily keep it in my pocket—although it would almost certainly get wet. I read the card: it said my name; it said my age and address; it said the same thing as the letter about me having to carry it; it said I was classified "1-H"; it said other things I can't remember. But I remember I was standing by the mailbox, and there were clouds scudding over—awesome winter storm clouds, billowing by in slow motion—and the trees whispered among themselves about those clouds; I remember there were steelhead in the river and animals in the woods, and now and then a bird veering through the sky; and there was Eddy in the cabin, and our people scattered down the valley, she and they all going about their goings-abouts; and there was a Garden Twin hidden in my shadow, and my shadow was hidden by the clouds; and there was a line I couldn't see running from my heart up through my head, away into the Realm where the Being of Light awaited me, awaited us all . . .

and then there was this draft card. It was beginning to look pretty unimportant. I wasn't sure I wanted to be told my name or my address or my birthday or the fact that I was considered "1-H", over and over and over. I didn't even know what 1-H meant. It sounded like a compliment, being the first number; it sounded better than being 23-H or 135-H or something like that. But if it was a compliment, what then? I didn't know. I took it in and showed it to Eddy.

Eddy didn't like the card or the letter. She didn't like them at all. She said they meant I was eligible to be drafted by the Armed Forces and that I'd waited too long to enroll at any school and apply for a student deferment; she said that if I *was* drafted I would probably end up in Vietnam. She looked pretty upset. I tried to cheer her up; I told her I wouldn't have gone to any school anyhow, unless it was to teach about fishing—but she got excited and told me I didn't know what I was saying and did I realize what was going on in Vietnam and what I might have to do if I went there? I said No, I didn't realize. Then I got the Atlas and opened it up to the map of the world. Eddy sat down by me and we looked at Vietnam over there and at Oregon over here and it hit me that whatever else Vietnam was, it was a hell of a long way away; and I said so. Eddy called me her fool and hugged me and almost cried. I asked how long I'd have to stay if I had to go. She said the better part of two years. Then I asked if she would go if she were me. She said No. I said, "Well, we're one flesh, aren't we?" She said Yes. I said, "And it's not a law that makes us one flesh: it's a sacred vow, right?" She said Right. I said, "Well, in Titus's books, when laws tell people to break sacred vows, the people don't do it. I guess I won't do it either." And I got an empty wine bottle, put the draft card and letter in it, corked it, took it down and threw it into the middle of the Tamanawis. I never saw it again. I don't know what happened to it. Maybe it crashed on a rock and sank. Maybe it drifted out to sea. Maybe it drifted clear to Vietnam, I don't know. It was up to the river, not me.

A few weeks later I got another letter from the Government. This one said there was going to be a lottery; it said that this lottery would decide whether or not I would be drafted, and if not me, then who; it said that this would be done by putting everybody's birthday into a kind of vat or barrel or something, then they would shake the vat around, then somebody named General Louis B. Hershey would reach into the vat and pull out everybody's birthdays one by one, and the order in which General Louis B. Hershey pulled them out was the order in which the people whose birthdays they were would be drafted and sent to Vietnam or wherever. This was the letter that proved to me that not everyone who worked in the Government was entirely sane. It was an incredible arrangement. It must have taken a number of not-very-sane people quite a while to work it all out. But I wasn't sure why the Government was telling me all this since they'd decided on it without even asking me about it; I wasn't sure why they sent me letters in the first place; I didn't know anything about Vietnam, or why some of us should go there, or who we should kill when we got there, or why we should kill them. I guessed maybe it was my right as a taxpayer to get to go there and kill some people, but since I didn't know which people to kill or why, I figured I'd just as soon stay home and let the ones who knew go. I figured the whole thing was none of my business. In fact, I figured it was so absolutely none of my business that I went for another wine bottle. . . .

Then I started worrying. Who knew how many letters the Government might see fit to send me? They might keep it up for years. I couldn't just sail them all off in wine bottles. In the first place, I might run out of bottles. In the second place, the bottles might wash into rocks and break and people might cut their feet on them; stupid little fish might eat the shards; seagulls might choke on the corks. Or maybe the bottles wouldn't break: maybe whales would swallow them whole, thinking they were little green Jonahs, and maybe they'd break inside the whales and hurt them; or maybe seals would play with them and cut their mouths; or maybe pelicans would mistake them for fish; or maybe Japanese or Scandinavian or Russian or Peruvian commercial fishermen would catch the bottles in their nets and be confused and depressed by the messages in them because they couldn't read or speak English and maybe neither could anyone else on the whole boat. Who knows? I didn't. I burned the letter instead.

I got one more letter from the Government. It said, in a very roundabout way, that General Louis B. Hershey had picked my born-date—May 22—three-hundred-and-first out of three hundred and sixty-five. I showed it to Eddy and she was happy because it meant I wouldn't be going to jail or Vietnam or anywhere else I didn't want to go. But it didn't make *me* happy. It pissed me off. Think of it! I could have gone to *jail*, just like that, just for having a birthday, just for opening my lousy mail!

But I didn't go to jail. Why? Because General Louis B. Hershey had a line of light running from his heart away into the Realm of Light, and the Fisherman who waited at the end of the line worked that line like a puppet string so that General Louis B. Hershey pulled the birthdays out of the vat in an order that was meant to be. And it was meant to be that some people whose birthdays were pulled from the vat were led by their lines of light to jail, and others were led to Canada, and others to Vietnam, and others stayed where they were, like me. What a strange world! Sometimes I wish it was more like a line of thousand-pound-test monofilament than a line of light and love. Sometimes I wish the line of light was a bloody steel cable. Because when the line is so fine and the equilibrium in the Fisher's hand so great, it's awfully easy for the trash fish of the human race to think and act as if the line of love weren't there, and to do stupid and nonsensical and terrible things to other people like put their birthdays in a vat and pick some of them to go kill other people. When things like that go on I can't help wishing He'd yank hard on the line—give some jerks some jerks. But that's all in my head. In my heart I know the Man-fisher knows best: river-armed and ocean-handed, He tends his lines with infinite patience, gracious to those who love Him, a mirage to those who don't.

In the end it all rides on how you look at things. And how you look at things depends on how His line leads you to look. Lately I've been led to try and look at things as much as I can like a man named Hu:

There was an old Taoist who lived in a village in ancient China, named Master Hu. Hu loved God and God loved Hu, and whatever God did was fine with Hu, and whatever Hu did was fine with God. They were friends. They were such good friends that they kidded around. Hu would do stuff to God like call him "The Great Clod." That's how he kidded. That was fine with God. God would turn around and do stuff to Hu like give him warts on his face, wens on his head, arthritis in his hands, a hunch in his back, canker sores in his mouth and gout in his feet. That's how He kidded. That God. What a kidder! But it was fine with Hu.

Master Hu grew lumpy as a toad; he grew crooked as cherry wood; he became a human pretzel. "You Clod!" he'd shout at God, laughing. That was fine with God. He'd send Hu a right leg ten inches shorter than the left to show He was listening. And Hu would laugh some more and walk around in little circles, showing off his short leg, saying to the villagers, "Haha! See how the Great Clod listens! How lumpy and crookedy and ugly He is making me! He makes me laugh and laugh! That's what a Friend is for!" And the people of the village would look at him and wag their heads: sure enough, old Hu looked like an owl's nest; he looked like a swamp; he looked like something the dog rolled in. And he winked at his people and looked up at God and shouted, "Hey Clod! What next?" And splot! Out popped a fresh wart.

The people wagged their heads till their tongues wagged too. They said, "Poor Master Hu has gone crazy." And maybe he had. Maybe God sent down craziness along with the warts and wens and hunch and gout. What did Hu care? It was fine with him. He loved God and God loved Hu, and Hu was the crookedest, ugliest, happiest old man in all the empire till the day he whispered,

Hey Clod! What now?

and God took his line in hand and drew him right into Himself. That was fine with Hu. That's what a Friend is for.

acknowledgements
and dedications

Without my editor, doctor, druid and dreefee, Alice—who is both the best eddy-fisherman and more like an eddy herself than anyone else I know—*The River Why* wood be speld somthing like this hear, punctuated;like:this,here = .,and would at times perchance exhibit a not unperverse and not unmaddening which is to say not unstupid verbosity not unlike this here.

Without Boyd's preschool appearance, Craig's haircut, Helen's old red-taped glasses, Geordie's sound-effects, Doug's Garden Angels, Alp's rare pre-sleep soliloquies and the amazingly suburban spirituality of my friends in the Bay Area, there would be no Bill Bob.

"Without the many lovely streams of Northern California there would be no Tamanawis River." —Antoine Chapeau

Sisisicu is dedicated to Fairview Creek (now defunct), to the diseased body of Johnson Creek, and to the two little boys who tried to save baby steelhead from detergent dumped in time of drought by sticking them in cottage cheese cartons and bicycling them all the way down to the Willamette while the Game Commission man stood quoting his textbooks.

Titus is dedicated to the Classicist J. Bluesandwich, to the Islamic Doctor Ernst, and to our mutual fishing hero, The Coom.

Gus's gray rock is respectfully reserved for Kevin.

Kids throughout are thanks to Jo, Megan, Lucy, Huma, Wanderin' Gus, Dusty, Loren, Lise, Sophie, Eruch, Seanji, Bodhi, Owen, Evan and Doonie.

All the fish that don't get killed, especially Sigrid, are for Jane the Jain. The singing mouse is for Steve: it's going to take some miraculous singing to get virginity back into the woods! 'The Carp' is for Japhey, who will, we trust, employ his bulldozerian passion to raze condos and subdivisions in the New Age, not to fill estuaries in the Old.

All bourbon is dedicated to Andrew Lytle, all nymphs to Henry, and young 'Hemingway' to Keith. Use or abuse of the word 'man' is dedicated to Ed, R.D., and the dwarf polar bear is for Ursula. Descartes is for my only disciple, Hafiz Pancake, who hasn't yet learned that there's nothing but half-chewed scraps and a bad smell to be gained at *my* feet.

Thanks to Curt for the tip which became the Shat Creek Twinkie, and to Lovena's goat, Kitty, for Charles the Second. Thanks to Jim for rescuing Whitey, and to Gale Quail for the bootiful tale. Thanks to Mart for innumerable fine mutant phrases, particularly Ma's. Xeroxorial thanks to Chuckie the Ferret, tennisorial thanks to J.C. 'William' Faulkner, pecuniary thanks to Stan and piggyback thanks to E. Dean.

Thanks to Dr. Charles R. Schwenk of the University of Illinois School of Business for Googler and Mangler—who made me print his full name here in hopes of teaching his students that there is more to business than business.

The Tillamook who sits still is, like it or not, for Bernard. Nick is for Casey.

For help and hope in all colors, shapes and sizes, thanks to Donna J., Judy, Dr. Hart, Katie, Lois, Spot, Renee, Chithra and Gil, Mary Lou, the Rangers Cordero, Duck and Marnie, de De Rhams, Bonnie, Shireen and Jay, G. 'Evelyn Wood' Harding, Lynwood, Danny, and others here mentioned for other reasons, or here unmentioned because the braincell that should have remembered them is either dead or stuck on the bottom of the stack.

First and Last, thanks to the Keeper of the Silence, who touched wild water seldom, but wrought great works when he did.

about the author

David James Duncan is a lifelong Oregon resident who learned to read and fish in 1957. He lives with his family in Neskowin, Oregon.